COMPUTATIONAL METHODS FOR THE STUDY OF DYNAMIC ECONOMIES

Computational Methods for the Study of Dynamic Economies

Edited by

RAMON MARIMON
ANDREW SCOTT

This book has been printed digitally and produced in a standard specification in order to ensure its continuing availability

OXFORD
UNIVERSITY PRESS

Great Clarendon Street, Oxford OX2 6DP

Oxford University Press is a department of the University of Oxford. It furthers the University's objective of excellence in research, scholarship, and education by publishing world-wide in

Oxford New York

Auckland Bangkok Buenos Aires Cape Town Chennai Dar es Salaam Delhi Hong Kong Istanbul Karachi Kolkata Kuala Lumpur Madrid Melbourne Mexico City Mumbai Nairobi São Paulo Shanghai Taipei Tokyo Toronto

Published in the United States by Oxford University Press Inc., New York

Reprinted 2004

ISBN 0-19-924827-3

Antony Rowe Ltd., Eastbourne

PREFACE

Thomas J. Sargent

In September 1996 the European University Institute convened the 7th Summer School of the European Economic Association on computational methods for dynamic macroeconomics. Fifty-six graduate students from Europe and 11 faculty from Europe and America gathered for 14 days of lectures and student seminars at the Badia in Fiesole. This book assembles papers whose first drafts served as the lecture notes for the conference. The conference aimed to disseminate ideas about how to compute solutions of dynamic economic models and how to apply them. Faculty and students took turns talking and listening. Algorithms were discussed and computer programs supplied. Teachers gave two lectures a day. The remainder of each day was filled with student presentations of their work. More work was done informally over lunch and coffee tables. The papers in this volume capture some of what we, the teachers, told the students. Unfortunately they cannot reflect the energy, interest, and promise that the students showed us in their questions and their presentations of their accomplishments and their plans. The conference and this volume are about ways to circumvent or confront the 'curse of dimensionality' associated with the functional equations that solve dynamic equilibrium models. Though they are designed to find rational expectations equilibria, before they have converged, computational algorithms resemble learning algorithms. Successive iterates of the algorithm are approximations that adapt to information about approximation errors. Several of the teachers at the conference (Uhlig, Marcet, McGrattan, Marimon, and I) have used what we know about computational algorithms to think about adaptive models of bounded rationality. Marimon lectured on some of this work at the conference, and other lecturers touched on it. The same tools that support computation of rational expectations models will be relied upon to venture beyond rational expectations, when we choose to do so. An air of enthusiasm about computational dynamic economics came to the conference from the beautiful setting overlooking Florence, the presence and pleasant interruptions of the youngest conference participant Zoe McCandler in her stroller, and the commitment of our students.

ACKNOWLEDGEMENTS

We would like to acknowledge those who have helped us in putting together this book; especially Marcia Gastaldo, for doing a superb editing job and keeping track of everything as she always does so well, and Pieter Omtzigt, for submitting all the chapters to the "student test" and for preparing the final index. We would like to thank Andrew Schuller who has been a very supportive publisher.

The *7th Summer School* was sponsored by the European Economic Association and the European University Institute. Several other people were involved in its organization: Angel Ubide, who was the first to insist that we should have a book out of it; Gonzalo Fernández de Córdoba, who helped on the computational side; and Barbara Bonke, who acted as secretary. The presence of Carolyn and Zoe in Florence, and of Giorgia, Laura and newly-born Pau in nearby Elba, also helped to make these days memorable. Ramon wishes to thank them, and all the participants in the School, for their contribution in the conception of this project. Andrew would like to express his gratitude to Lorraine, Helena, and Louis for their uncompromising support.

CONTENTS

LIST OF CONTRIBUTORS

Craig Burnside is an economist at the World Bank, and previously was an assistant professor at the University of Pittsburgh and at Queen's University. He obtained his Ph.D. at Northwestern University. His main areas of research include business cycle theory, finance and time series methods for applied macroeconomics.
E-mail address: `aburnside@worldbank.org`

Graham Candler is currently an associate professor of aerospace engineering and mechanics at the University of Minnesota and a consultant for the Institute for Defense Analyses. Candler received his B.Eng. in mechanical engineering from McGill University and M.S. and Ph.D. degrees in aeronautics and astronautics from Stanford University. His current areas of research include computational fluid dynamics of reacting flows, high-temperature gas dynamics, re-entry and hypersonic aerodynamics, and the numerical simulation of turbulent reacting flows.
E mail address: `candler@aem.umn.edu`
WWW address: `http://aem.umn.edu`

Javier Díaz-Giménez received his Ph.D. from the University of Minnesota, and he teaches economics at the Universidad Carlos III de Madrid (Spain). His main research interests are in the field of quantitative macroeconomics, and more specifically in business cycle theory, monetary theory and distribution.
E-mail address: `kueli@eco.uc3m.es`

Emilio Domínguez received his Ph.D. in economics from Universidad Computense in 1995. He is currently an assistant professor of economics at Universidad Pública de Navarra. His research interests are the term structure of interest rates, and solution methods for nonlinear rational expectations models.

Ayşe İmrohoroğlu received her Ph.D. from the University of Minnesota and is currently on the faculty of the Marshall School of Business at the University of Southern California. Her research is in the fields of macroeconomics and monetary economics. She is currently working on the economics of public pensions.

Selahattin İmrohoroğlu received his Ph.D. from the University of Minnesota and is currently on the faculty of the Marshall School of Business at the University of Southern California, and an associate editor of the *Journal of Economic Dynamics and Control*. His recent research concerns the macroeconomic and intergenerational effects of social security reform.
E-mail address: `simrohoroglu@marshall.usc.edu`
WWW address: `http://www-rcf.usc.edu/~simrohor/`

Douglas H. Joines received his Ph.D. from the University of Chicago and is currently on the faculty of the Marshall School of Business at the University of Southern California. His research is in the fields of macroeconomics, monetary economics, and public finance,

and his recent work has dealt with the macroeconomic effects of public pension systems and tax-based saving incentives.
E-mail address: djoines@sba.usc.edu
WWW address:
www.marshall.usc.edu/main/faculty/facultymembers/JoinesD.html

Guido Lorenzoni born in Rome in 1971, received his *laurea* from the University of Rome I, his master's from Universitat Pompeu Fabra, Barcelona, and he is currently a Ph.D. student at MIT. His interests include macroeconomics and contract theory.

Albert Marcet, born in Terrassa in 1960, received his *llicenciatura* from Universitat Autonoma de Barcelona in 1982, and his Ph.D. from the University of Minnesota in 1987. He has been a professor at Carnegie Mellon University (Pittsburgh) and Universitat Pompeu Fabra (Barcelona), and he has been a visiting professor at the Centro de Estudios Monetarios y Financieros (Madrid), Universitat Autonoma de Barcelona, Institut d'Analisi Economica, Federal Reserve Bank of Minneapolis and London Business School. His interests include models of learning, time series econometrics and macroeconomic dynamics.
E-mail address: marcet@upf.es

Ramon Marimon received his Ph.D. from Northwestern University in 1984. He is currently a professor of economics at the European University Institute, on leave from Universitat Pompeu Fabra (Barcelona), and previously was an assistant and an associate professor at the University of Minnesota. He is a research fellow of the Centre de Recerca en Economia Internacional, the National Bureau of Economic Research, and the Centre for Economic Policy Research. His research covers monetary theory, labour, contract theory, political economy, learning and experimental economics. He is an editor of the *Review of Economic Dynamics*.
E-mail address: marimon@datacomm.iue.it
WWW address: http://www.iue.it/Personal/Marimon/Welcome.html

Ellen McGrattan is currently a senior economist at the Federal Reserve Bank of Minneapolis, an adjunct research professor at the University of Minnesota, and a research economist at the National Bureau of Economic Research. She received a B.S. in economics and mathematics from Boston College and a Ph.D. from Stanford University. Most of her work concerns estimating the effects of fiscal and monetary policy on aggregate economic activity.
E-mail address: erm@ellen.mpls.frb.fed.us
WWW address: http://research.mpls.frb.fed.us

Alfonso Novales received his Ph.D. in economics from the University of Minnesota in 1983. He was assistant professor of economics at the State University of New York at Stonybrook and currently is a professor of economics at Departamento de Economía Cuantitativa, Universidad Complutense de Madrid (Spain). Research interests include macroeconomics; optimal monetary and fiscal policy design and financial econometrics; the term structure of interest rates; estimation and testing of alternative theories of the term structure of interest rates.
E-mail address: eccua09@sis.ucm.es

Javier J. Pérez is an assistant professor of economics at Departamento de Economía Cuantitativa, Universidad Complutense de Madrid (Spain). His current research project is optimal monetary policy design under alternative fiscal rules. Other research interests include monetary economics, business cycle theory, monetary and fiscal policy coordination.

E-mail address: javierj_perez@ccee.ucm.es

José-Víctor Ríos-Rull studied economics and sociology in Madrid as an undergraduate. He obtained his Ph.D. in economics in Minnesota in 1990. He has taught in Carnegie Mellon University and has worked in the Research Department of the Federal Reserve Bank of Minneapolis for several years. He is currently a professor of economics at the University of Pennsylvania and has active academic contacts with his Spanish colleagues.
E-mail address: vr0j@anaga.sas.upenn.edu
WWW address: http://www.ssc.upenn.edu/~vr0j/index.html

Jesús Ruiz received his Ph.D. in economics from Universidad Complutense in 1997. He is an assistant professor of economics at Universidad Europea de Madrid. His research interests include dynamic macroeconomics, fiscal policy in stochastic general equilibrium models.

Thomas J. Sargent is a professor of economics at Stanford University and a senior fellow of the Hoover Institution. He researches and teaches monetary economics and monetary history, macroeconomic theory and macroeconometrics.
E-mail address: sargent@riffle.stanford.edu
WWW address: http://riffle.stanford.edu/

Andrew Scott is an associate professor at the Department of Economics, London Business School and a fellow of the Centre for Economic Policy Research and All Souls College, Oxford. He received his Masters from the London School of Economics and his doctorate from Oxford University. He has taught at Oxford and Harvard University and is an academic consultant to the Bank of England. His research focuses on business cycles and monetary and fiscal policy.
E-mail address: ascott@lbs.ac.uk

Harald Uhlig, born in Bonn in 1961, received his Ph.D. in economics from the University of Minnesota in 1990 under the supervision of Christopher A. Sims. From 1990 to 1994, he was an assistant professor at Princeton University. Since 1994, he has been a research professor of macroeconomics at Tilburg University. He has publications in *Econometrica* and several other journals. He is an editor of the *European Economic Review* and is on the editorial board of the *Review of Economic Studies*.
E-mail address: uhlig@kub.nl
WWW address: http://cwis.kub.nl/~few5/center/staff/uhlig/

François R. Velde is an economist at the Federal Reserve Bank of Chicago. He received his doctorate from Stanford University in 1992 and taught at Johns Hopkins University from 1992 to 1997.
E-mail address: fvelde@frbchi.org

1

INTRODUCTION: FROM PIPELINE ECONOMICS TO COMPUTATIONAL ECONOMICS

Ramon Marimon and Andrew Scott[1]

Few single pieces of work have generated as much research in economics as A.W. Phillips's (1958) *Economica* paper "The relationship between unemployment and the rate of change on money wages in the United Kingdom, 1861–1957". But if one day you happen to get lost in the labyrinthine corridors of the London School of Economics you may come across another of his lasting contributions to economics. It is not a written piece of work but a curious piece of apparatus assembled one summer in Phillips's garage from various bits of piping and valves: a *physical economic model* designed to teach students the complexities of macroeconomics. The pipeline structure of the model was used to emphasize the circular flow of income in the economy while fluids of different colours were used to illustrate the interaction of different variables. In addition, the effect of stabilization policies was simulated by the use of different valves which altered the magnitude and direction of flows. No doubt, an original piece of work into which Phillips tried to put his best engineering skills to study and present the economy as a system, not very different from systems studied in engineering schools of the time.

With the benefit of forty years of increasing economic sophistication it is easy to look back in fond amusement or with a dismissive manner to Phillips's "plumbernomics". However, what is it that leads us to disregard Phillips's machine while still pondering the relevance of his curve? It certainly cannot be his attempt to study the economy as a system (albeit of pipes) that has an equilibrium, nor the fact that he felt he could not explain the economy at work by just using the blackboard (on which, by the way, he could easily explain his curve!). If anything, we have strengthened our belief that even relatively simple questions in economics are better addressed by studying their implications in a general equilibrium context and that an economy in equilibrium may present very interesting and possibly empirically relevant dynamics (e.g. growth and business cycles). Furthermore, we have become more ambitious in the questions that we want to address, and pencil and paper have become even more obsolete than when Phillips was teaching.

Two developments account for the obsolescence of Phillips's machine. Firstly, macroeconomics now bases itself on the optimizing decision of individual agents who have to form expectations about an uncertain future. This has involved changes in the way we teach economics, perform research and answer policy-orientated questions. For example,

[1]Correspondence addresses: Ramon Marimon, Department of Economics, European University Institute, Badia Fiesolana, 50016 San Domenico di Fiesole (Fi), Italy; Andrew Scott, Department of Economics, London Business School, Sussex Place, Regent's Park, London NW1 4SA.

there is an emphasis on using Euler equations and dynamic programming to analyse the dynamic properties of our economies. None of these features is incorporated in the ensemble of pipes, valves and fluids that constitute Phillips's machine. The second major change is not specific to economics and is the huge increase in computational power that is now cheaply available. The computer has become part of our set of tools and can be used not only for editing, e-mailing and navigating but also for solving and studying model economies. This use of computers has already been rapidly taken up in other disciplines. For instance, Phillips's machine would also be a mild source of amusement for contemporary engineers and physicists. Rather than resort to working the summer in the garage soldering pipes together and connecting valves they would instead build a computer model/algorithm to replace the pipes and use keyboard input instead of valves to construct the model. Putting it differently, if Phillips were to take up economics today with a contemporary engineering background he would not have spent the summer months plumbing and messing about with fluids but rather messing about with codes.

The reason why engineers, physicists and architects, among others, use computational methods so extensively is that they offer an extremely low-cost means of analysing the behaviour of objects without resorting to building actual-size versions or conducting expensive laboratory experiments. Given the difficulties, costs and limitations of experimental economics, the potential benefits of computational economics are substantial.

However, just as Phillips required certain skills before he could build his model, so the use of the computer in economics requires a certain craftsmanship to be learned. The purpose of this book is to provide an introductory knowledge to computational techniques so as to enable the reader to construct and solve virtual economic models. The book is orientated towards economists who already have the equivalent of a first year of graduate studies or to any advanced undergraduates or researchers with a solid mathematical background. It has been written in the belief that these techniques will increasingly become an essential part of the toolkit used in economic research. While we assume some prior economic and mathematical knowledge, we do not assume any competence with actually writing computer codes. However, reading a book on computational techniques without actually using the computer is as foolish as reading a cook-book without ever entering the kitchen. For that reason many of the authors have available on the World Wide Web computer algorithms with which to solve the problems in this book and other additional examples.[2] Many of these are written in easy-to-learn programs such as MATLAB and the use of these programs should be seen as an essential part of understanding the material in this book.

1.1 About the structure of economic models

The emphasis of this book is on how to use computational techniques to solve dynamic stochastic nonlinear economic models. However, one thing that is of paramount importance is that these techniques cannot deliver interesting results if used with insufficient thought (e.g. economic theory, understanding of the computer algorithm, etc.). As other scientists well know, even with the most powerful computers at hand, one often has to

[2]Each chapter provides information as to whether programs are available and their address. A Web door that provides access to all this information is
`http://www.iue.it/Personal/Marimon/Welcome.html`.

go back to the basic questions. We economists may usefully share some techniques and methodologies with, for example, engineers but we should understand – and solve – our own specific problems. Ironically, this was forcefully made apparent through research related to Phillips's work. As shown by the work of Phelps, Lucas, Sargent and others in the late 1960s and early 1970s, it is important to account properly for agents' expectations regarding future inflation when using the Phillips curve. Such emphasis, which has been at the core of the rational expectations revolution, showed a crucial drawback of the Phillips machine, a drawback that sets economists apart from natural scientists and engineers: fluid mechanics can hardly capture the fact that expectations over future events may affect today's outcomes. Naturally this distinctive structure of economics poses specific difficulties and requires a proper development of computational techniques. Such development is a central theme of this book.

More formally, at the core of most dynamic (and *dynamic* is by now a redundant modifier) economic models, we encounter an equation of the form

$$x_t = E_t\left[x_{t+1}y_{t+1}\right] \tag{1.1}$$

where E_t denotes the conditional expectation (conditional on information up to period t), and $\{x_t\}$ and $\{y_t\}$ are two stochastic processes which must simultaneously satisfy other equilibrium restrictions.

Perhaps the most classical example displaying a type (1.1) equation is the *Lucas asset pricing* model. A consumer who wants to maximize the expected present discounted value of utility from consumption ($E_0 \sum_{t=0}^{\infty} \beta^t u(c_t)$) decides how much to consume or save in period t, by equating – at the margin – the cost of saving today with the benefit of consuming tomorrow, using assets that give a stochastic return of R_{t+1}. In this case equation (1.1) becomes

$$u'(c_t) = \beta E_t\left[u'(c_{t+1})R_{t+1}\right] \tag{1.2}$$

If there is a unique asset with a stochastic dividend process $\{d_t\}$ and, in period t, an asset price p_t, then $R_{t+1} = (p_{t+1} + d_{t+1})/p_t$. Adding the further assumption that dividends are the only source of income, the consumer's budget constraint is

$$c_t + p_t s_{t+1} = s_t(d_t + p_t) \tag{1.3}$$

where s_t denotes the share holdings of the consumer at the beginning of period t. If, in addition, one assumes (as Lucas originally did) that there is a representative consumer, endowed with $s_0 = 1$, then market equilibrium requires that

$$s_t = 1 \quad \text{and} \quad c_t = d_t \tag{1.4}$$

Under these assumptions there is little to be gained from applying computational techniques to this model. Nevertheless this paradigmatic model is useful in displaying the main ingredient of many dynamic economic models that we are interested in studying.[3]

This example illustrates two general aspects to the problem of finding solutions to dynamic economic models. One is that the stochastic processes $\{x_t\}$ and $\{y_t\}$ must be

[3] See, for example, Stokey *et al.* (1989) and Chapter 5, by C. Burnside, for a numerical analysis.

equilibrium solutions. That is, in the asset pricing model, equations (1.2), (1.3) and (1.4) must be satisfied. In general, we can express this as a fixed-point problem in the form

$$F(\{x_t\}, \{y_t\}) = 0 \tag{1.5}$$

where F is a functional form defined in an appropriate space (we are purposefully being loose in this introduction). The second is that equilibrium solutions must satisfy any conditional expectations relations, such as (1.1).

In a sense, both these aspects of finding solutions are conceptually simple. They amount to finding a zero of some functional form and solving some integrals (or, in another sense, they are as difficult as the concepts of a fixed point and of conditional expectations can be). In fact, there are many numerical methods for finding zeros of a function (Newton's method is the most classical one and, in its own way, Phillips's machine was another one) or for solving integrals. We will present – and build on – some of them in this book.

Considerable impulse to computational methods in economics has been given by exploiting the *recursive structure* of many dynamic economic models: that is, the ability to reduce the search for solutions to those where decisions (allocations) and prices are functions of a small number of state variables. In a *recursive competitive equilibrium*, the fixed-point problem (1.5) reduces to

$$F(\{x(\theta_t)\}, \{y(\theta_t)\}) = 0 \tag{1.6}$$

where $\{\theta_t\}$ denotes the evolution of the state variables (vectors). Although this is a lower-dimensional problem than (1.5), it may not be trivial and, in fact, a large part of this book deals with this problem.

A further advantage of a recursive competitive equilibrium is that agents' decisions can be obtained as the policy solutions to standard *dynamic programming* problems. For example, in the above Lucas asset pricing model, if the dividend process $\{d_t\}$ is a stationary Markov process (and the only source of uncertainty), then $\theta_t \equiv (s_t, d_t)$ and the consumer's problem reduces to:

$$v(s_t, d_t) = \max \{u(s_t d_t + p(d_t)(s_t - s_{t+1})) + \beta E_t v(s_{t+1}, d_{t+1})\} \tag{1.7}$$

Then the computational problem can be reduced to either finding an optimal policy $s_{t+1} = f(\theta)$ or finding the value function $v(\theta)$.[4] A simpler, but again, non-trivial problem.

An alternative to exploiting directly the structure of a dynamic programming problem is to use computational methods which instead study the Euler equation (1.1) (e.g. (1.2) in the asset model). However, as is well known, in order to guarantee that solutions to a sequence of intertemporal equations – of type (1.1) – result in an optimal solution a *transversality* (or terminal, or stability) condition must be satisfied; guaranteeing, for example, that consumers satisfy their present value budget constraints. That is, methods that study Euler equations will have to deal with such a transversality issue. Notice that an Euler equation approach can take advantage of the fact that the policy function also

[4]In terms of our general notation the Lucas asset pricing model defines $x(\theta_t) = p(d_t)u'(s_t d_t + p(d_t)(s_t - f(s_t, d_t)))$ and $y(\theta_t) = (p(d_t) + d_t)$.

satisfies the Euler equation. For example, in the asset pricing model, one may want to look for a solution to

$$u'(g(s_t, d_t)) - \beta E_t \left[u'(g(f(s_t, d_t), d_{t+1})) \frac{p(d_{t+1}) + d_{t+1}}{p(d_t)} \right] = 0$$

where $g(s_t, d_t) = s_t d_t + p(d_t)(s_t - f(s_t, d_t))$. That is, with this formulation, we are back to the problems of finding zeros of functional forms and solving integrals!

Although the asset pricing model has most of the ingredients present in many dynamic economic models, being a "representative agent" greatly simplifies the fixed-point problem (1.6). In particular, in equilibrium individual policies and economy-wide laws of motion are simultaneously identified (as equations (1.4) require). Such a construction is not as restrictive as it may seem. When the necessary conditions apply, it follows from the second welfare theorem that solutions to "planners' problems" implement competitive equilibrium allocations. That is, in classical economies "the planner" can be called to act as a "representative agent" and solving the corresponding Bellman equation (1.7) is equivalent to solving the full recursive competitive equilibria with transfer payments (see, for example, Cooley and Prescott, 1995). Nevertheless, many interesting problems escape the classical restrictions of the welfare theorems (i.e. problems with distortionary taxes, etc.). In these cases, an Euler equation based approach may be more suitable (or, alternatively, one can solve multiple dynamic programming problems and the corresponding fixed-point problem).

1.2 About the use of computational techniques

Lucas (1978) outlines his asset pricing model and shows some of its properties without resorting to computational techniques. The corresponding theory was firmly established before computational solutions were attempted. In other words, there are models that can be solved analytically under certain simplifying assumptions. The pedagogical advantages of analytic solutions are obvious and the transparency of economic intuition that these models provide makes them crucial for communicating advances in research. In these cases what computational methods provide is clear: numerical solutions to more sophisticated versions of the model which, for example, may enable us to assess the empirical relevance of the theory. For instance, there are numerous models which under certain assumptions can be used to show that changes in monetary policy can have real effects. The intuition behind these models is clear and their results are informative but by using computational techniques it is possible to go further and assess the magnitude of these non-neutralities.

However, computational techniques are not just about quantifying the qualitative results of theoretical models. In many problems we have no alternative but to rely on the computer for any solution. For such problems existing economic theory only provides the building blocks (e.g. how rational consumers behave), and one must generate the corresponding virtual economies to understand the complete implications of the theory, the corresponding equilibrium trade-offs, etc. In these cases numerical solutions may not lead to the mere calibration of analytic results but instead actually suggest analytical theorems to researchers.

More specifically, suppose we want to address a question, such as how a tax reform (or a social security reform) affects the growth of an economy, the budget of the government and the wealth of different groups of the population. Such questions have been addressed by and to economists for as long as the profession has existed. What distinguishes scientific answers from journalistic responses is our ability to address them properly. Given the current knowledge of economic theory, a proper answer requires solving the corresponding dynamic stochastic equilibrium model. This, in turn, requires solving a type (1.5) problem, and – simultaneously – the corresponding sequence of type (1.1) equations, etc.

As with the Phillips machine, the methods presented in this book are useful tools for teaching purposes too. General equilibrium results are often far from straightforward and frequently complex to grasp. By enabling students to solve model economies and see how the model properties alter when underlying parameters and market structure change, computational techniques offer a useful intermediate step to macroeconomic theorizing in general equilibrium.

1.3 About this book

There is by now an extensive literature studying dynamic macroeconomic models, showing, for example, how they can be framed in a recursive structure. See, for example, Stokey *et al.* (1989), Sargent (1987a), Cooley (1995) and Sargent and Ljungqvist (1998).[5] This book builds on this literature and, we hope, broadens its scope. There is also a recent literature on how to solve stochastic dynamic equilibrium models. Unfortunately, this knowledge is fairly dispersed in specialized articles and, therefore, for the interested researcher, an introduction to computational methods for the study of dynamic economies has been needed. This is the aim of this book: to provide a toolkit, a menu of existing methods, to help researchers who know how to formulate an economic model but need computational techniques to obtain quantitative solutions. It is also a toolkit that should help to develop economic theory: that is, to solve models for which existing economic theory only provides a very fragmented understanding.

Computational economics is an emerging field of research. This book provides a fairly broad introduction to the topic.[6] But even if broad, we have had to constrain our scope. In particular, we do not cover static computable general equilibrium models; dynamic linear models (although such a discussion is implicit in Part I); models with learning; or models with strategic (contractual or game-theoretical) interactions. Similarly, we do not present computational techniques based on artificial intelligence methods. Furthermore, the methods and economic applications presented in this book often raise interesting questions, having to do with the underlying mathematical or statistical structure of the models, or with further computational implementations. Again, we have chosen to be very brief in explorations of this type.

As we have said, most computational methods for solving dynamic economic models take advantage of the recursive structure of these models. Some of them take advantage

[5] Furthermore, Marcet and Marimon (1992, 1998) have shown how many economic problems that do not have a recursive structure can be modified so as to attain one.

[6] Judd (1998) offers a complementary exposition of some of the methods presented here (see also Amman *et al.*, 1996). Other expositions, however, must be found in specialized articles (see, in particular, the special issue on solving nonlinear rational expectations models in Vol. 8 of the *Journal of Business and Economic Statistics,* 1990; and Christiano and Fisher, 1998). See also the *Journal of Computational Economics.*

of another very useful feature: many economic models – at least locally around their steady states – may be studied by using linear approximations (or, if needed, log-linear approximations). That is, some models have a *linear quadratic* structure and, therefore, linear methods can be used to study them; or, by extensively using *Taylor approximations*, one can at least locally reduce the problem to a linear one. To be able to use *linear algebra*, with its powerful theorems and numerical techniques, is certainly a great help in developing computational methods.

The methods presented in Part I use, in different forms, linear approximations. Chapter 2, by Javier Díaz-Giménez, provides a brief introduction to dynamic programming and the method of using *linear quadratic approximations* to the return function. As Díaz shows, using this approach and the certainty equivalence principle, solving for the value function is a relatively easy task. That is, for example, once $u(\cdot)$ is replaced by a linear approximation, then $v(\cdot)$ in (1.7) can be attained using linear algebra. In Chapter 2 we see the first instance of a recurrent example throughout the book: the standard one-sector stochastic (Brock and Mirman) growth model.[7]

Chapter 3, by Harald Uhlig, provides an extensive treatment (with a very user-friendly set of MATLAB programs) of methods that use log-linear approximations. These methods, based on their linear counterparts, have been extensively used in the macroeconomic literature, starting from the work of McCallum (1983) on *undetermined coefficients*,[8] Blanchard and Kahn (1980) and King *et al.* (1987). Uhlig integrates and compares these methods. He extensively exploits two basic facts. First, once variables have been log-linearized – around a steady state – the corresponding equation (1.1) is linear. Second, if the recursive policy functions are also linear the resulting system is of *linear stochastic difference equations* and one can obtain the recursive linear law of motion as a solution to a (matrix) quadratic equation. Furthermore, Uhlig shows how, with no need to generate the corresponding time series, one can analyse the solutions with impulse-response analysis and study its second-order properties. Examples of this approach are presented in an appendix: in particular, Hansen's (1985) real business cycle model and a model where equilibria may be indetermined.

The methods studied by Uhlig are based on Euler equation and while allowing for a wide range of applications they must take into account *transversality* or *stability* restrictions. One method in the "Uhlig class" that fully exploits the stability properties is that proposed by Sims.[9] Alfonso Novales, with Emilio Domínguez, Javier Pérez and Jesús Ruiz, presents this method in Chapter 4. As they discuss, there are two other specific features of Sims's approach. One is the treatment of conditional expectations as variables, the other the fact that linearizations (or log-linearizations) are kept to a minimum, in some applications may allow for better approximations. Enabling easier comparison across these various techniques, they also discuss Hansen's model.

In summary, one can derive a clear conclusion from Part I: if linear (or log-linear) approximations are good approximations to the underlying nonlinear model, then the methods presented here offer a very convenient toolkit. Unfortunately, in some economic

[7] Hansen and Sargent (1999) and Sargent and Ljungqvist (1998) provide additional treatments of *linear quadratic methods*.

[8] See also McCallum (1998).

[9] See, for example, Sims (1999).

models such approximations may result in important distortions. The methods presented in Part II help to solve these nonlinear models (of course, they can also be used to solve the models presented in Part I). However, without the extensive help of *linear algebra,* finding zeros of a functional form and solving integrals becomes a more delicate matter.

Chapter 5, by Craig Burnside, can be seen as a chapter on carefully "solving integrals". As in the process of approximating an integral with sums over finer and finer grids, the *discrete state-space* method proceeds by finding solutions to discretized approximations of the original problem. Burnside studies first the Euler equation problem, using a Lucas asset pricing model as his canonical example. As Prescott and Mehra have shown, the asset pricing model – with one agent and one asset – has a relatively easy solution if the dividend process is a Markov chain because then solving (1.2) reduces to solving a finite system of equations (which, for example, can be solved if preferences are isoelastic). Burnside also shows how the method can be applied to find the value function in the context of the Brock–Mirman growth model. As in the process of approximating an integral with sums, the secret to a good discrete approximation to a continuous (state-space) problem lies in the choice of the grids and the weight that is attached to different grid points. *Quadrature methods* provide a rule to make these choices and are explained in this chapter.

If Chapter 5 is about solving integrals, Chapter 6, by Ellen McGrattan, can be seen as a chapter on "finding a zero of a functional form". An integral is approximated by sums; a nonlinear function, say x, that solves $F(x) = 0$, is approximated by polynomials. With sums we have to make the right choice of grid and of weights attached to grid points; with polynomials we have to make the right choice of polynomials. The method of *weighted residuals* uses as its "polynomials" linear combinations of relatively simple polynomials, and uses as criteria of "good fit" the weighted residuals (from the desired zero). The *finite-element* method further elaborates on that by splitting the problem into smaller problems or elements – not that different from the splitting that lies behind the approximation of an integral by sums. McGrattan shows how these methods apply, for example, to the stochastic growth model in an Euler equation based approach.

Once we concentrate on the problem of computing conditional expectations, as in solving (1.1) in an Euler equation based approach, we may as well approximate the conditional expectation "functions" with polynomials. This is the *parameterized expectations approach* (PEA), rediscovered in economics by Albert Marcet, who, with Guido Lorenzoni, discusses the method in Chapter 7, guiding the reader through a good number of examples and potential pitfalls.[10] The theme of "solving integrals and finding zeros" reappears. As a method for "finding zeros", PEA is very closely related to the methods discussed by McGrattan in Chapter 6. However, since the integral (of the approximated conditional expectation) is taken over realized paths (in a Monte Carlo fashion), how weights are attached (a recurrent issue in Chapters 5 and 6) is entirely endogenous. In other words, the fit must necessarily be better in often visited states. This makes a lot of sense in evaluating an economic model; however, one must be cautious if computing transitional dynamics. Nevertheless, as Christiano and Fisher (1998) have shown,

[10]Recall that in Sims's method (Chapter 4) conditional expectations are treated as *random variables*. With PEA (Chapter 7), instead, they are treated as *random functions*. An earlier version of PEA is due to Wright and Williams (1984).

modified versions of PEA tend to out perform other algorithms – say, in the context of a stochastic growth model with binding constraints.

All the methods presented in Chapters 2–7 solve dynamic *discrete-time* stochastic models. However, *continuous-time* models are often used (e.g. in models of economic growth) since in their simpler forms one can obtain closed-form solutions (a rarer event in discrete time); but then one would like to be able to compute them more generally. Chapter 8, by Graham V. Candler, shows how to solve continuous-time stochastic dynamic programming problems. Now, the specific approximation problem is that of approximating continuous time with discrete time (the only time that the computer understands). Candler shows how the methods of *finite differences* perform these approximations, using again the (continuous-time) stochastic growth model as an example.

As we have previously mentioned, the emphasis throughout this book is on implementing computational techniques rather than focusing on macroeconomic issues. But we also want to show how one can close the gap between the basic computational methods (with their few canonical examples) and more developed models, which are fit to address a wider range of economic questions. This is the purpose of the last part of the book. In particular, Part III shows how one can develop models ready to address issues which are at the core of current macroeconomic research.

Chapter 9, by Thomas J. Sargent and François R. Velde, is a contribution to the theory of optimal fiscal policy based on linear quadratic methods similar to those presented in Part I. It is a good example of how development of economic theory and computational economics can go hand-in-hand. In particular, a standard problem in designing fiscal policies in stochastic economies is how to compute the present value of the government's surplus. Sargent and Velde show how this can be done by solving a version of equation (1.1) and then derive the corresponding optimal tax and debt policies (they also provide the corresponding MATLAB programs).

Another core topic of current research (and of policy debate) is the evaluation of social security systems and their possible reforms. In Chapter 10, Ayşe İmrohoroğlu, Selahattin İmrohoroğlu and Douglas H. Joines show how one can compute models of social security in economies where agents have uncertain life-spans and earnings profiles.[11] In particular, they show how to solve stationary equilibria and (within a linear quadratic formulation) how to solve transitional equilibria, such as the transition following a reform of the system.

Models of social security are part of the more general class of models with *heterogeneous agents,* where every single agent is solving problems of the form of (1.2). The final chapter, Chapter 11 by José-Víctor Ríos-Rull, discusses this more general class of models (see also Cooley, 1995; Huggett, 1993). These heterogeneous agent models are particularly complex because, in contrast to *representative agent* models, individual recursive policies (e.g. derived from versions of (1.7)) and economy-wide laws of motion differ. In particular, the state space may be fairly large (e.g. the distribution of agents may become part of "the state") and, correspondingly, the equilibrium problem (1.6) far from trivial. Ríos-Rull closes the chapter (and thus the book) by discussing models of *politico-economic equilibrium,* no doubt at the forefront of current macroeconomic research.

[11] See also Rust and Phelan (1997).

1.4 Pre-history

This book has its origins in a building where, as in the London School of Economics, one is also likely to get lost: the Badia Fiesolana in San Domenico di Fiesole, an old monastery, now the site of the European University Institute. There took place in September of 1996 the 7th Summer School of the European Economic Association on "Computational Methods for the Study of Dynamic Economies", organized by Ramon Marimon. The success of the school far exceeded the expectations of the organizers – in particular, of the EEA! First, an excess of demand resulted in many graduate students being unable to attend; second, those attending showed an eagerness to learn and work not normally associated with summer schools (in fact, several subsequently used the methods of the school in their Ph.D. thesis work[12]). To develop further some of the lectures presented, supplementing them with additional topics, and to collect all the work in an integrated volume, was the most logical consequence. As with Phillips and his pipelines, the completion of our work has taken a little longer than we first intended. As also with the Phillips machine, we expect that future well-trained economists will smile when they see how we studied economic systems, not very different from engineering systems, at the end of the twentieth century.

[12] And, in some cases, in further developing computational methods. See, for example, Javier Pérez (Chapter 4), Guido Lorenzoni (Chapter 7) and Paul Klein (1998).

Part I

Almost linear methods

2

LINEAR QUADRATIC APPROXIMATIONS: AN INTRODUCTION

Javier Díaz-Giménez[1]

2.1 Introduction

The main purpose of applied economic analysis is to evaluate the welfare consequences of economic policy (see Lucas, 1987, Chapter 2). To achieve this ambitious goal, the first step is to construct computable model economies that can be used as laboratories to simulate the effects of economic policies. To capture the main features of the economic decision problems solved by people in the real world, the decision problems solved by the households that live in the model economies must be dynamic and stochastic.

Unfortunately, there are no closed-form solutions for the dynamic decision problems that arise once the functional forms for preferences and for the aggregate technology of the model economies are calibrated to mimic key features of the aggregate behaviour of real economies. One way to get around this difficulty is to use numerical methods to compute approximated solutions to those calibrated decision problems.

The linear quadratic (LQ) approximation is one of these methods. It is an approximation because it computes the solution to a quadratic expansion of the utility function about the steady state or the stable growth path of the model economies. The main purposes of this chapter are to review the theoretical basis for the LQ approximation and to illustrate its use with a detailed example.

The LQ approximation can be used to compute the solutions to many extensions of the neoclassical growth model. Some examples of this literature are the following: Brock and Mirman (1972), Kydland and Prescott (1982; 1988), Kydland (1984), Hansen (1985), Prescott (1986), Cho and Rogerson (1988), Christiano (1988), Greenwood *et al.* (1988), Hansen and Sargent (1988), and King *et al.* (1988).

Very little of the material included in this chapter is original. Most of what is here can be found in Sargent (1987a), Stokey *et al.* (1989) and Hansen and Prescott (1995). Essentially this chapter contains a summarized review of dynamic programming as it applies to the calibrated neoclassical growth model, and a description of the LQ approximation to social planner problems. A detailed algorithm that can be used to solve this class of problems is also provided. The algorithm is illustrated with a simple example. The example has been programmed using MATLAB but it can also be easily implemented in any computer language that can handle matrix algebra such as GAUSS, FORTRAN 90 or C.

[1]The comments of Andrés M. Alonso, Florin Bidian, Jorge Durán, Pieter Omtzigt, Luis Puch and Andrew Scott are gratefully acknowledged. Jorge Durán also provided the MATLAB code. Address correspondence about this chapter to: Javier Díaz-Giménez, Departamento de Economía, Universidad Carlos III de Madrid, Calle Madrid 126, 28903 Getafe, Spain.

The rest of this chapter is organized as follows: Section 2.2 describes the standard neoclassical growth model. Section 2.3 describes a social planner problem that can be used to solve the model. Section 2.4 contains a recursive formulation of the planner's problem. Section 2.5 describes the LQ approximation to this problem. Section 2.6 offers some concluding comments and, finally, Section 2.7 contains a MATLAB program that illustrates the computational methods described in this chapter.

2.2 The basic neoclassical growth model

In this section we describe the basic neoclassical growth model in terms of population, endowments, preferences, and technology.

2.2.1 *Population*

We assume that the model economy is inhabited by a large number of identical households who live for ever.

2.2.2 *Endowments*

We assume that the model economy households are endowed with one unit of productive time that they can allocate to work in the market or to other uses. We also assume that the model economy households are endowed with $k_0 > 0$ units of productive capital which depreciates geometrically at a constant rate $0 < \delta < 1$, and which they may augment through investment, i.

2.2.3 *Preferences*

We assume that households in this economy order their stochastic processes on consumption and leisure according to

$$E \sum_{t=0}^{\infty} \beta^t U(c_t) \tag{2.1}$$

where E denotes the expectation operator, $0 < \beta < 1$ is the time discount factor, the function U is generally assumed to be twice continuously differentiable, strictly increasing and strictly concave, and c_t denotes period t consumption. This description of household preferences implies that households do not value leisure. Hence, we are abstracting from the choice between labour and leisure. This assumption is customarily made in many exercises in growth theory (see Cooley and Prescott, 1995). We adopt it here because it reduces the household decision problem to choosing between consumption and savings, and therefore it simplifies the notation. The methods described in this chapter can be easily extended to solve model economies that include more than one decision variable, such as those that model the choice between labour and leisure, which is an essential feature in the study of business cycles.

2.2.4 *Technology*

We assume that in the model economy there is a freely accessible technology that makes it feasible to transform capital, k, into output, y, and that output can be costlessly transformed into either consumption or investment.[2] We make this assumption for simplicity. If we are to take it literally, we can think of an agricultural economy where the harvest of barley can be costlessly split between barley used for seeding (investment) and barley used for the costless production of beer (consumption).

We assume that the production technology can be described by the following neoclassical production function:

$$c_t + i_t = y_t = F(k_t, z_t) \tag{2.2}$$

where the production function, F, is generally assumed to be twice continuously differentiable, strictly increasing and strictly concave in k.[3]

Given our assumptions on capital depreciation, the law of motion of the capital stock is the following:

$$k_{t+1} = (1-\delta)k_t + i_t \tag{2.3}$$

Finally, the variable z represents a technology shock. This shock is observed at the beginning of the period and it is assumed to follow a first-order linear Markov process that can be described by

$$z_{t+1} = L(z_t) + \varepsilon_{t+1} \tag{2.4}$$

where the function L is assumed to be linear and where the random variables ε_j are assumed to be independently and identically distributed with zero mean and finite variance.

2.3 A social planner problem

One way to formalize the model economy described above is to use an appropriate specialization of the language of Arrow and Debreu (see Debreu, 1959) and to define a competitive equilibrium for this economy. Essentially this entails: defining the competitive decision problems faced by the households and firms in the economy; and finding the stochastic processes for (y_t, c_t, i_t, k_t), and the corresponding vector of prices such that, when taking the price vector as given, the processes on quantities solve both the households' and the firms' decision problems, and that the prices are such that the processes on (y_t, c_t, i_t) clear the goods market every period.

In general, finding the competitive equilibrium of this class of model economies is a difficult computational problem. Fortunately, for many of these model economies – essentially those that both assume complete markets and exclude externalities and distortionary taxes – we can prove that some version of the second welfare theorem applies. This implies that the competitive equilibrium allocations that solve the model economies

[2]Note that this assumption implies that in equilibrium the prices of consumption and investment must be identical.

[3]The standard neoclassical production function is $F(k_t, n_t, z_t)$, where n_t denotes the labour input. The function F is generally assumed to be twice continuously differentiable and strictly concave in both arguments and to display constant returns to scale. In our simplified version of the problem households do not value leisure. Hence, part of their optimal plan is to allocate their entire endowment of productive time to the market. Therefore $n_t^* = 1$ and $F(k_t, n_t, z_t)$ becomes $F(k_t, 1, z_t) = F(k_t, z_t)$.

are identical to the Pareto optimal allocations that would be chosen by a benevolent social planner whose objective was to maximize the welfare of the representative household. This welfare theorem is useful because social planner problems are generally easier to solve than competitive equilibrium problems, since they do not include prices, and therefore their dimension is smaller.[4]

A version of the problem solved by a benevolent social planner of the model economy described in the previous section is the following:

$$\max_{\{c_t, i_t\}_{t=0}^{\infty}} E \sum_{t=0}^{\infty} \beta^t u(c_t) \tag{2.5}$$

subject to constraints (2.2), (2.3) and (2.4) and with $k_0 > 0$ and $z_0 > 0$ given.

Now that we have a low-dimension characterization of the problem that solves the model economy described in Section 2.2, our next task is to solve it. But first let us simplify the notation. Let $f(k, z) = F(k, z) + (1 - \delta)k$. Then we can substitute constraints (2.2) and (2.3) into expression (2.5) to obtain

$$\max_{\{k_{t+1}\}_{t=0}^{\infty}} E \sum_{t=0}^{\infty} \beta^t U(f(k_t, z_t) - k_{t+1}) \tag{2.6}$$

subject to expression (2.4) and with $k_0 > 0$ and $z_0 > 0$ given.

The first-order conditions of this problem can be summarized by the following Euler equations that must hold for every $t = 0, 1, 2, \ldots$:

$$U'\left[f(k_t, z_t) - k_{t+1}\right] = \beta E\left\{U'\left[f(k_{t+1}, z_{t+1}) - k_{t+2}\right] f'(k_{t+1}, z_{t+1})\right\} \tag{2.7}$$

This is a second-order stochastic difference equation and in most cases it is hard to solve because closed-form solutions cannot be found. One way to get around this problem is to use numerical methods to obtain approximate numerical solutions. Since numerical methods typically are computationally intensive, an efficient way to implement these methods is to use a computer. Since, as it stands, the problem described in expression (2.5) is not suitable for solving using a computer, our next step is to find an alternative formulation of the social planner's problem.

2.4 A recursive formulation of the social planner's problem

Suppose that the problem described in expression (2.5) had been solved for every possible value of k_0 and z_0. Then we could define a function V such that $V(k_0, z_0)$ would give us the value of the maximized objective function when the initial conditions are (k_0, z_0). Thus defined, V gives us the value for the household, measured in utils, of following its optimal plan. For obvious reasons we call this function a value function. If V is such avalue function, and if the initial conditions of the planner's problem are given by the

[4]The methods described in this chapter have been specifically designed to be applied to social planner problems. For a description of the computational methods that can be used to solve non-optimal economies, see Danthine and Donaldson (1995).

pair (k_0, z_0), then the definition of V is the following:

$$V(k_0, z_0) \equiv \max_{\{k_{t+1}\}_{t=0}^{\infty}} E \sum_{t=0}^{\infty} \beta^t U\left[f(k_t, z_t) - k_{t+1}\right] \tag{2.8}$$

subject to expression (2.4).

Our next task is to transform expression (2.8) in order to unveil its recursive structure. Moving the first term and β out of the summation sign we obtain:

$$\begin{aligned} V(k_0, z_0) &\equiv \max_{\{k_{t+1}\}_{t=0}^{\infty}} \left\{ U\left[f(k_0, z_0) - k_1\right] + E \sum_{t=1}^{\infty} \beta^t U\left[f(k_t, z_t) - k_{t+1}\right] \right\} \\ &= \max_{\{k_{t+1}\}_{t=0}^{\infty}} \left\{ U\left[f(k_0, z_0) - k_1\right] + \beta E \sum_{t=0}^{\infty} \beta^t U\left[f(k_{t+1}, z_{t+1}) - k_{t+2}\right] \right\} \end{aligned} \tag{2.9}$$

Note that the second term of expression (2.9) is β times the value, as defined in expression (2.8), of the optimal plan when the initial conditions are given by the pair (k_1, z_1). Formally, then, we can rewrite expression (2.9) as follows:

$$V(k_0, z_0) = \max_{k_1} \{U\left[f(k_0, z_0) - k_1\right] + \beta E[V(k_1, z_1)|z_0]\} \tag{2.10}$$

subject to expression (2.4).

This formulation of the planner's problem highlights its recursive structure. In every period t, the planner faces the same decision: choosing the following period capital stock, k_{t+1}, that maximizes the current return plus the discounted value of the optimal plan from period $t+1$ onwards. Since this problem repeats itself every period the time subscripts become irrelevant, and we can transform expression (2.10) into

$$V(k, z) = \max_{k'} \left\{U\left[f(k, z) - k'\right] + \beta E[V(k', z')|z]\right\}. \tag{2.11}$$

subject to expression (2.4).[5]

Expression (2.11) is a version of Bellman's equation, named after Richard Bellman (1957). Since V is unknown, expression (2.11) is a functional equation. A consequence of the recursive structure of problem (2.11) is that its optimal solutions are self-enforcing. This means that as time advances the planner has no incentive to deviate from the original optimal plans. This property is known as Bellman's principle of optimality and the decision rules that satisfy this property are said to be time-consistent.[6]

[5]Henceforth we adopt the dynamic programming convention by which primes denote the forwarded values of variables.

[6]Some examples of policies that are not time-consistent have been described by Kydland and Prescott (1977) and by Calvo (1978). They mostly arise when agents are assumed to play differential games (e.g. the responses of some policy-makers to the taking of hostages. For instance, a policy that calls for negotiations today once the hostages have been taken and that promises never to negotiate again in the future is not time-consistent).

In general not every maximization problem can be mapped into a recursive problem. A characterization, perhaps not minimal, of problems that can be thus mapped is the following: the return function, U, has to be time separable in the contemporaneous state and control variables;[7] and the objective function and the constraints have to be such that current decisions affect current and future returns but not past returns.[8]

If we knew the function V, we could use expression (2.11) to define a function g such that for every value of the current capital stock, k, and the current technology shock, z, the function $k' = g(k, z)$ would give us the value of the capital stock one period ahead that attains the maximum of expression (2.11), and, where they are equivalent, of expression (2.5). Since g gives us the optimal capital accumulation decision we call it the optimal decision rule. Unfortunately we do not know V – in fact, we are not even sure of its existence – and therefore we cannot compute g. Bellman (1957) developed the methods of dynamic programming that prove the existence of V, characterize its properties, and allow us to compute it. A formal description of these methods and their application to economics is beyond the scope of this chapter and can be found in Sargent (1987a) and Stokey *et al.* (1989), among others.

Heuristically, one of these methods is the following: since we do not know V, we start out by choosing any differentiable and concave function as our initial candidate. Then we use Bellman's equation to compute the associated decision rule and the iterated value function and we proceed repeatedly until the sequence of functions thus defined converges. In algorithmic language this method amounts to the following:

- *Step* 1. Guess a differentiable and concave candidate value function, $V_n(k, z)$.
- *Step* 2. Use Bellman's equation to compute $k' = g_n(k, z)$ and $V_{n+1}(k, z) = T[V_n(k, z)]$, where $T[V_n(k, z)] = \max_{k'} \{U[f(k, z) - k'] + \beta E[V_n(k', z')|z]\}$, subject to expression (2.4).
- *Step* 3. If $V_{n+1} = V_n$, we are done. Otherwise, update V_n and go to step 1.

This algorithm returns a sequence of functions defined recursively as follows: $V_1 = T(V_0), V_2 = T(V_1), \ldots, V_{n+1} = T(V_n)$. It attempts to compute the limit of the sequence, $V^* = \lim_{n\to\infty} V_n$.[9]

Before we discuss the existence of this limit function, V^*, it is important to understand that if did exist, V^* would be the optimal value function that we are looking for. Suppose, by way of contradiction, that $V_{n+1} \neq V_n$; that is, that we have not found a fixed point of mapping T. Could V_n be the optimal value function? The answer to this question should be "no", and the intuitive reason for this answer can be found in Bellman's principle of optimality. If V changes, then the optimal decision rule will also change and the optimal decisions will not be self-enforcing. In fact, a necessary and sufficient condition

[7] In dynamic programming jargon the state variables are the variables that summarize the position of the system before the current period decisions are made, and the control variables are those decisions. The possible choices for state and control variables need not be unique, and they can incorporate some redundancies. In our example, the state variables are k_t and z_t, and the control variable is k_{t+1}. In Section 2.5 we change the control variable to i_t.

[8] A formal analysis of the equivalence between the maximization and the recursive problems can be found in Sections 4.1 and 9.1 of Stokey *et al.* (1989).

[9] Note that finding the limit of the sequence is equivalent to finding a fixed point of the operator T, $V^* = T(V^*)$.

for decisions to be self-enforcing is that the value function does not change. Then, and only then, the optimization problem will be always the same, the optimal decisions will also be the same, the households have no incentive to deviate from their original plans, and the solutions to the optimization problems will be self-enforcing.

The formal proof of the existence of an optimal value function, V^*, is beyond the scope of this chapter and can be found in the literature referred to above. Informally the proof shows that Bellman's operator, T, is a contraction in the appropriate metric space, and then it uses the contraction mapping theorem to establish that a unique fixed point, $V^* = T(V^*)$, exists, and that it can be attained recursively using Bellman's operator starting from any differentiable and concave function, V_0. In the next section we exploit this result to compute the LQ approximation to dynamic programs.

Exercise 2.1 Consider the deterministic version of the standard neoclassical growth model where $U(c_t) = \log c_t$ and $f(k_t) = k_t^\alpha$. Define Bellman's operator, T, associated to the social planner's problem for this economy. Assume that $V_0(k) = 0$, and compute $V_1(k) = T[V_0(k)]$, $V_2(k) = T[V_1(k)]$, and the associated decision rules, $g_0(k)$, $g_1(k)$ and $g_2(k)$.
Solution: Bellman's operator, T, for this problem can be defined as

$$V_{n+1} = T(V_n) = \max_{k'}\{\log(k_t^\alpha - k_{t+1}) + \beta V_n(k')\}$$

The first three terms in the sequence of functions are:

$$V_0(k) = 0, \qquad V_1(k) = \alpha \log k,$$

$$V_2(k) = (\alpha + \alpha^2\beta)\log k + (1 + \alpha\beta)\log[\alpha\beta/(1 + \alpha\beta)]$$

The associated decision rules are:

$$g_0(k) = 0, \qquad g_1(k) = [\alpha\beta/(1 + \alpha\beta)]k^\alpha,$$

$$g_2(k) = [(\alpha + \alpha^2\beta)/(1 + \alpha + \alpha^2\beta)]k^\alpha$$

2.5 A linear quadratic approximation

As Exercise 2.1 illustrates, a problem with using Bellman's operator recursively to compute the limit in the sequence of value functions is that this method is algebraically very demanding. An important exception to this rule is the case of quadratic return functions. In the following pages we show that if the return function is quadratic in the state and control variables, and if the constraints are linear in the states, forwarded states and control variables, then the optimal value function is quadratic in the state variables. Moreover, in this case Bellman's operator maps quadratic functions into quadratic functions. Therefore, in the case of linear quadratic problems, if our initial guess is a quadratic function, then Bellman's operator returns another quadratic function, and therefore every function in the recursive sequence is quadratic.

Unfortunately quadratic return functions are not very useful in macroeconomics since they are not supported by the stylized facts that describe the aggregate time series of most real economies. Instead, evidence from real economies suggests that we should consider CES (constant elasticity of substitution) utility functions. One way to get around this problem is to use Taylor's expansion to approximate the CES functions that we are interested in with a quadratic function. This procedure and the proposition described in the previous paragraph are the gist of the LQ approximation.[10]

The LQ approximation is a reasonable approximation when the following conditions are met: the deterministic versions of the model economies converge to stable steady states, or to stable growth paths;[11] and the local dynamics about the steady state of the real economy in which we are interested is well approximated by a linear law of motion. The reason for this last condition is that, as we have already mentioned, the optimal decision rules obtained using the LQ approximation are linear and, therefore, this method should not be used when there is evidence of nonlinearities in the real economy data. The real business cycle literature is full of examples where the LQ approximation has been successfully used. Some specific examples of economies that can be solved using this method are those described in the papers listed in Section 2.1.

2.5.1 *A general solution algorithm*

We now generalize the problem described in expression (2.11) to the case of multiple state and control variables. A general notation for this extended class of problems is the following:

$$V(z, s) = \max_{d} \left\{ r(z, s, d) + \beta E \left[V(z', s') \mid z \right] \right\} \tag{2.12}$$

such that

$$s' = A(z, s, d) \tag{2.13}$$

$$z' = L(z) + \varepsilon' \tag{2.14}$$

where z is now a vector of n_z exogenous state variables, s is a vector of n_s endogenous state variables, d is a vector of n_d control variables, ε is a vector of n_ε random variables with zero mean and finite variance, r is the return function, and the functions A and L are linear.[12]

It is important to note that the LQ approximation can only be used in those problems that can be mapped into a structure similar to that described in expressions (2.12)–(2.14). Therefore every nonlinear constraint in the original problem must be first substituted into the original return function. This restriction limits the class of problems that can be solved using the LQ approximation to those that at most have as many nonlinear constraints as there are arguments in the utility function.

[10] Note that when we use Taylor's expansion the original function and the approximated function take the same value typically at only one point (the point about which the original function is being "expanded"). In most cases, therefore, Taylor's expansion is a good approximation only in a small neighbourhood of that point.

[11] Note that these steady states or stable growth paths are the points about which the original return functions are expanded.

[12] Note that henceforth, for reasons that will become clear later, the precise ordering of variables z, s and d is crucially important. The exogenous state variables, z, must come first, the endogenous state variables, s, must come next, and the decision variables, d, must come last.

Exercise 2.2 Consider a stochastic version of the standard neoclassical growth model where $U(c_t) = \log c_t$, $F(k_t, z_t) = e^{z_t} k_t^{\alpha}$, $z_{t+1} = \rho z_t + \varepsilon_{t+1}$, $\varepsilon_t \sim N(0, \sigma_\varepsilon^2)$, $0 < \alpha < 1$, $0 < \rho < 1$.

(a) Write the Bellman equation associated with the planner problem.

(b) Substitute the nonlinear constraints into the utility function and identify the vector of exogenous states, z, the vector of endogenous states, s, the vector of controls, d, the return function, r, and the linear functions A and L that map the example that we have discussed in the previous section into the generalized notation described above.

Solution: The Bellman equation associated with the planner's problem is

$$V(k, z) = \max_{c, k'} \{\log c + \beta E[V(k', z')|z]\}$$

such that

$$c + i = e^z k^\alpha$$
$$\acute{k}' = (1 - \delta)k + i$$
$$z' = \rho z + \varepsilon'$$

After substituting the nonlinear constraint into the utility function the Bellman equation becomes

$$V(k, z) = \max_i \left\{\log(e^z k^\alpha - i) + \beta E[V(k', z')|z]\right\}$$

such that

$$k' = (1 - \delta)k + i$$
$$z' = \rho + \varepsilon'$$

where $z = z$, $s = k$, $d = i$, $r(z, k, i) = \log(e^z k^\alpha - i$, $A(z, k, i) = (1 - \delta)k + i$ and $L(z) = \rho z$.

A solution algorithm for solving dynamic programs of the class described in expressions (2.12)–(2.14) is the following:

- *Step* 1. Choose a point about which to expand the return function. In most cases this point is the steady state of the deterministic version of the model economy, $(\bar{z}, \bar{s}, \bar{d})$, that we obtain when we substitute the random variables with their unconditional means.[13]
- *Step* 2. Construct a quadratic approximation of $r(z, s, d)$ about $(\bar{z}, \bar{s}, \bar{d})$.
- *Step* 3. Compute the optimal value function $V^*(z, s)$ by successive iterations on Bellman's operator $V_{n+1}(z, s) = T[V_n(z, s)] = \max_d \left\{r(z, s, d) + \beta E[V(z', s')|z]\right\}$ subject to expressions (2.13) and (2.14).

In the subsections that follow we discuss these steps in greater detail.

[13]Henceforth a bar over a variable denotes the steady-state value of that variable.

2.5.2 *Step* 1: *Computing the steady state*

To compute the steady states of the model economies, we first substitute the shocks with their unconditional means and obtain the first-order conditions of the resulting deterministic versions of social planner problems. Then we impose the appropriate steady-state conditions. Finally we calculate the steady-state values for both the endogenous and the exogenous state variables and for the control variables, $(\bar{z}, \bar{s}, \bar{d})$. In the case of model economies that converge to stable growth paths we first transform the problem so that its solution is stationary over time.[14] Exercise 2.3 illustrates this procedure.

Exercise 2.3 Consider the stochastic version of the standard neoclassical growth model described in Exercise 2.2 and compute the steady state of the deterministic version of this economy as a function of parameters $(\alpha, \beta, \delta, \rho, \sigma_\varepsilon^2)$.

Solution: To compute the steady state, it is easier to consider the maximization problem, which in this case is the following:

$$\max_{\{c_{-t}, k_{t+1}\}} E \sum_{t=0}^{\infty} \beta^t \log c_t$$

such that

$$\begin{aligned} c_t + i_t &= e_t^z k_t^\alpha \\ k_{t+1} &= (1-\delta)k_t + i_t \\ z_{t+1} &= \rho z_t + \varepsilon_{t+1} \end{aligned}$$

Substituting the shocks by their unconditional means and dropping the expectations operator, this problem becomes:

$$\max_{c_t, k_{t+1}} \sum_{t=0}^{\infty} \beta^t \log c_t$$

such that

$$\begin{aligned} c_t + i_t &= k_t^\alpha \\ k_{t+1} &= (1-\delta)k_t + i_t \end{aligned}$$

Computing the first-order conditions for this problem and substituting out the Lagrange multipliers, we obtain the following Euler equation:

$$c_{t+1} = \beta c_t[\alpha k_{t+1}^\alpha - 1 + (1-\delta)]$$

Imposing the steady-state condition, $c_t = c_{t+1} = \bar{c}$, this expression becomes:

$$1 = \beta[\alpha \bar{k}^\alpha - 1 + (1-\delta)]$$

Finally, after solving for $\bar{k}$, we obtain the steady state, $(\bar{z}, \bar{k}, \bar{i})$, given by:

$$\bar{z} = 0, \quad \bar{k} = [\alpha\beta/(1-\beta+\beta\delta)]^{[1/(1-\alpha)]}, \quad \bar{i} = \delta\bar{k}$$

[14] For an example where this transformation is carried out explicitly, see Hansen and Prescott (1995).

2.5.3 *Step 2: Constructing the quadratic approximation*

The next step is to approximate the return function, $r(z, s, d)$, about the model economy's steady state, $(\bar{z}, \bar{s}, \bar{d})$. In the remainder of this chapter we switch to matrix notation for its conciseness and because it is particularly suitable for implementation using a computer. In matrix notation, the second-order Taylor approximation of function r is:[15]

$$r(z, s, d) \simeq \bar{R} + (W - \bar{W})^T \bar{J} + \tfrac{1}{2}(W - \bar{W})^T \bar{H}(W - \bar{W}) \tag{2.15}$$

where the number $\bar{R}$ is the function r evaluated at the model economy's steady state, $\bar{R} = r(\bar{z}, \bar{s}, \bar{d})$, the column vector W is the vector of ordered state and control variables, $W = [z \quad s \quad d]^T$, the column vector $\bar{W}$ is the vector W evaluated at the steady state, $\bar{W} = [\bar{z} \quad \bar{s} \quad \bar{d}]^T$, the column vector $\bar{J}$ is the Jacobian evaluated at the steady state, $\bar{J} = [\bar{J}_z \quad \bar{J}_s \quad \bar{J}_d]^T$, and the matrix $\bar{H}$ is the Hessian evaluated at the steady state,

$$\bar{H} = \begin{bmatrix} \bar{H}_{zz} & \bar{H}_{zs} & \bar{H}_{zd} \\ \bar{H}_{sz} & \bar{H}_{ss} & \bar{H}_{sd} \\ \bar{H}_{dz} & \bar{H}_{ds} & \bar{H}_{dd} \end{bmatrix}$$

Multiplying out expression (2.15), and grouping the independent terms, the linear terms and the quadratic terms, we obtain

$$r(z, s, d) \simeq \left(\bar{R} - \bar{W}^T \bar{J} + \tfrac{1}{2}\bar{W}^T \bar{H}\bar{W}\right) + W^T(\bar{J} - \bar{H}\bar{W}) + \tfrac{1}{2}W^T \bar{H} W \tag{2.16}$$

Since expression (2.16) is a quadratic form, we can rewrite it as:

$$r(z, s, d) \simeq \begin{bmatrix} 1 & W^T \end{bmatrix} \begin{bmatrix} Q_{11} & Q_{12}^T \\ Q_{12} & Q_{22} \end{bmatrix} \begin{bmatrix} 1 \\ W \end{bmatrix} \tag{2.17}$$

where $Q_{11} = \bar{R} - \bar{W}^T \bar{J} + \frac{1}{2}\bar{W}^T \bar{H}\bar{W}$, $Q_{12} = \frac{1}{2}(\bar{J} - \bar{H}\bar{W})$, and $Q_{22} = \frac{1}{2}\bar{H}$ and where the role played by the 1s is to select the constant term of the quadratic expression. As we illustrate in Section 2.7, this partitioning of matrix Q simplifies the inputting of the data.

In a more compact notation, expression (2.17) becomes

$$r(z, s, d) \simeq \begin{bmatrix} 1 & W^T \end{bmatrix} Q \begin{bmatrix} 1 \\ W \end{bmatrix} \tag{2.18}$$

where matrix Q is a square symmetric matrix of dimension $1 + n_z + n_s + n_d$.

Exercise 2.4 Consider the model economy described in Exercise 2.2. Obtain a quadratic expansion of the return function about the model economy's steady state. Write out the expansion in matrix notation.

Solution: See Section 2.7.

[15]Henceforth the superscript, T, indicates the transpose of a matrix.

2.5.4 *Step 3: Computing the optimal value function*

The next step is to compute the optimal value function V^* by repeated iterations on Bellman's operator, $V_{n+1}(z, s) = T[V_n(z, s)]$. Using matrix notation, the definition of Bellman's operator is the following:

$$V_{n+1}(z, s) = T[V_n(z, s)] = \max_d \left\{ \begin{bmatrix} 1 & W^T \end{bmatrix} Q \begin{bmatrix} 1 \\ W \end{bmatrix} + \beta E\left[V_n(z', s') \mid z \right] \right\} \tag{2.19}$$

subject to constraints (2.13) and (2.14).

The initial guess for the value function, V_n, can be any quadratic and concave function $V_n(s, z) = F^T P_n F$, where the ordered column vector $F = [1 \quad z \quad s]^T$, and where P_n is any symmetric and negative semi-definite matrix of dimension $1 + n_z + n_s$.[16]

Substituting this expression for V_n into expression (2.19), we obtain:

$$V_{n+1}(z, s) = \max_d \left\{ \begin{bmatrix} 1 & W^T \end{bmatrix} Q \begin{bmatrix} 1 \\ W \end{bmatrix} + \beta E\left[(F')^T P_n F' \mid z \right] \right\} \tag{2.20}$$

subject to constraints (2.13) and (2.14).

Next we must compute the vector of decision rules, d_n, associated with V_n, and the next element in the sequence of value functions, V_{n+1}. To do this we start out by taking care of the expectation operator, E.

In general, operating with expectations is hard, but in the case of LQ problems the certainty equivalence principle simplifies matters considerably. LQ problems have the following two features: the covariance matrix of the vector of random variables, Σ, only shows up in the independent terms of the optimal value functions, V^*; and the optimal decision rules, d^*, are independent of this matrix.[17] These two features of linear quadratic problems are known as the certainty equivalence principle.[18]

Returning to our problem, the certainty equivalence principle allows us to assume, without loss of generality, that $\Sigma = 0$. Therefore we can drop the expectations operator by simply replacing the vector of random variables, ε, by its unconditional mean, $\mu(\varepsilon) = 0$. Once we carry out this substitution, expression (2.20) and constraints (2.13) and (2.14) become

$$V_{n+1}(z, s) = \max_d \left\{ \begin{bmatrix} 1 & W^T \end{bmatrix} Q \begin{bmatrix} 1 \\ W \end{bmatrix} + \beta (F')^T P_n F' \right\} \tag{2.21}$$

subject to $s' = A(z, s, d)$ and $z' = L(z)$.

[16] Any square matrix of the appropriate dimension made up of small negative numbers in the diagonal and zeros elsewhere satisfies these two conditions.

[17] More specifically, it can be shown that $V^*(z, s) = F^T P^* F + a$, where P^* is a symmetric and negative semi-definite matrix and $a = [\beta/(1-\beta)]\text{tr} P^* \Sigma$ (tr denotes the trace of a matrix), and that $d^* = (J^*)^T F$, where J^* is a vector of constants which is independent of Σ.

[18] Note that the certainty equivalence principle only holds when the objective function is quadratic and the constraints are linear. It does not characterize stochastic control problems in general.

The next step is to transform expression (2.21) into a quadratic form in $[1 \;\; W^T]$. To do this we use constraints $s' = A(z, s, d)$ and $z' = L(z)$ to substitute the forwarded values of the states out of expression (2.21). Specifically, we have to find a rectangular matrix B of dimension $(1+n_z+n_s)\times(1+n_z+n_s+n_d)$ that satisfies $F' = B[1 \;\; W^T]^T$. In some cases this transformation might require some ingenuity.[19]

Exercise 2.5 Find B for the model economy described in Exercise 2.2.

Solution:

$$B = \begin{bmatrix} 1 & 0 & 0 & 0 \\ 0 & \rho & 0 & 0 \\ 0 & 0 & 1-\delta & 1 \end{bmatrix}$$

Once we have found the matrix B, we substitute $F' = B[1 \;\; W^T]^T$ into expression (2.21) to obtain

$$V_{n+1}(z,s) = \max_d \left\{ [1 \;\; W^T]\, Q \begin{bmatrix} 1 \\ W \end{bmatrix} + \beta\, [1 \;\; W^T]\, B^T P_n B \begin{bmatrix} 1 \\ W \end{bmatrix} \right\} \tag{2.22}$$

Note that henceforth we no longer need to consider any constraints because we have substituted them into the utility function.

Using the distributive law of matrix sums and products, expression (2.22) becomes

$$V_{n+1}(z,s) = \max_d \left\{ [1 \;\; W^T]\, [Q + \beta B^T P_n B] \begin{bmatrix} 1 \\ W \end{bmatrix} \right\} \tag{2.23}$$

where matrix $[Q + \beta B^T P_n B]$ is a square, symmetric and negative semi-definite matrix and, therefore, the expression inside the braces is indeed quadratic in z, s and d.

The next step is to differentiate expression (2.23) to obtain the vector of decision rules, $d_n(z, s)$.[20] To simplify the algebra involved in differentiating expression (2.23), let $M_n = B^T P_n B$, and partition Q and M_n so as to separate the state variables from the control variables.[21] Specifically, let

$$Q = \begin{bmatrix} Q_{FF} & Q_{Fd}^T \\ Q_{Fd} & Q_{dd} \end{bmatrix} \quad \text{and} \quad M = \begin{bmatrix} M_{FF} & M_{Fd}^T \\ M_{Fd} & M_{dd} \end{bmatrix}$$

where Q_{FF} and M_{FF} are symmetric matrices of dimension $1 + n_z + n_s$, Q_{dd} and M_{dd} are symmetric matrices of dimension n_d, and Q_{Fd} and M_{Fd} are rectangular matrices of dimension $n_d \times (1 + n_z + n_s)$.[22]

[19] Note that to perform this transformation the constraints $s' = A(z, s, d)$ and $z' = L(z)$ must be linear in (z, s, d).

[20] Note that since expression (2.23) is quadratic in (z, s, d) the first-order conditions are linear in (z, s).

[21] Note that M_n changes with every iteration, n. To avoid cluttering the notation when we partition matrix M_n, we drop the subscript n. On the other hand, Q remains invariant throughout the iterations.

[22] Note that this partition of Q is completely unrelated to the partition that we have used in expression (2.17). Once again, the reason for these partitions is to simplify the calculations.

Substituting the partitioned matrices into expression (2.23), we obtain[23]

$$V_{n+1}(z,s) = \max_d \left\{ [F^T \; d^T] \begin{bmatrix} Q_{FF} + \beta M_{FF} & Q_{Fd}^T + \beta M_{Fd}^T \\ Q_{Fd} + \beta M_{Fd} & Q_{dd} + \beta M_{dd} \end{bmatrix} \begin{bmatrix} F \\ d \end{bmatrix} \right\} \tag{2.24}$$

Expression (2.24) is a quadratic form in $[F^T \; d^T]$, and hence it is equivalent to

$$V_{n+1}(z,s) = \max_d \Big\{ F^T[Q_{FF} + \beta M_{FF}]F + 2d^T[Q_{Fd} + \beta M_{Fd}]F + d^T[Q_{dd} + \beta M_{dd}]d \Big\} \tag{2.25}$$

Differentiating expression (2.25) with respect to d^T and equating to zero, we obtain the following first-order conditions:

$$2[Q_{Fd} + \beta M_{Fd}]F + 2[Q_{dd} + \beta M_{dd}]d = 0 \tag{2.26}$$

from which we can readily compute the vector of linear decision rules, $d_n(z,s)$, associated with the value function $V_n(z,s)$, to be[24]

$$d_n(z,s) = -(Q_{dd} + \beta M_{dd})^{-1}(Q_{Fd} + \beta M_{Fd})F = J_n^T F \tag{2.27}$$

where J_n is the vector of the coefficients of the decision rules associated with the value function, $V_n(z,s)$. Specifically,

$$J_n^T = -(Q_{dd} + \beta M_{dd})^{-1}(Q_{Fd} + \beta M_{Fd}) \tag{2.28}$$

Substituting expression (2.27) into (2.25), we can drop the maximization operator and we obtain

$$V_{n+1}(z,s) = F^T\big[Q_{FF} + \beta M_{FF} - (Q_{Fd} + \beta M_{Fd})^T(Q_{dd} + \beta M_{dd})^{-1}(Q_{Fd} + \beta M_{Fd})\big]F \tag{2.29}$$

which is, indeed, the quadratic expression that we are looking for, $V_{n+1} = F^T P_{n+1} F$. In this expression P_{n+1} is the symmetric matrix that we use to define the iterated value function $V_{n+1}(z,s)$. Specifically,

$$P_{n+1} = Q_{FF} + \beta M_{FF} - (Q_{Fd} + \beta M_{Fd})^T(Q_{dd} + \beta M_{dd})^{-1}(Q_{Fd} + \beta M_{Fd}) \tag{2.30}$$

The last step in this iterative procedure is to compare P_n and P_{n+1}. If it turns out that $P_n = P_{n+1} = P^*$, then it immediately follows that $V_n = V_{n+1} = V^*$ and we have found the optimal value function. If, on the other hand, $P_n \neq P_{n+1}$, then we update P_n and we iterate once again until convergence.[25]

[23]Note that $[1 \; W^T] = [1 \; z \; s \; d] = [F^T \; d]$.

[24]Note that the concavity of V_n guarantees that the first-order necessary conditions described in expression (2.26) are also sufficient.

[25]In the case of linear quadratic programs, the contraction mapping theorem guarantees that $\lim_{n\to\infty} P_n = P^*$, which of course is equivalent to $\lim_{n\to\infty} V_n = V^*$.

Exercise 2.6 Let $\alpha = 0.33$, $\beta = 0.96$, $\delta = 0.1$ and $\rho = 0.95$ and compute the optimal value function, V^*, and the associated optimal decision rule, d^*, for the LQ approximation to the social planner's problem of the model economy described in Exercise 2.2.

Solution: See Section 2.7.

2.6 Conclusion

In this chapter we have described an LQ approximation to social planner problems. Our method is based on the following two basic results of dynamic programming: that in LQ problems Bellman's operator maps quadratic functions into quadratic functions; and that the contraction mapping theorem guarantees the convergence of the sequence of value functions obtained using Bellman's operator recursively. We have used algorithmic language and matrix notation to simplify the implementation of this method using a computer. As we have already mentioned, the LQ approximation has been successfully used in many exercises in real business cycle theory. Since the proof of the pudding is in the eating, to consolidate the reader's understanding of the subject, we provide the one last exercise taken from literature.

Exercise 2.7 Consider the basic Kydland and Prescott divisible labour calibrated model economy described in Hansen (1985).

(a) Use the LQ approximation to compute the optimal value function and the optimal decision rules associated with the social planner problem of that economy.

(b) Use the decision rules to reproduce the results reported in the third and fourth columns of Hansen's Table 1.

Solution: Sorry, this time you are on your own.

2.7 Appendix: A MATLAB program to illustrate the LQ method

```
% This program computes the value function and the optimal
% decision rules of the linear-quadratic approximation to
% the problem described in Exercise 2.6.
% Author: Jorge Duran
% e-mail: xurxo@eco.uc3m.es
% This message is for the loop below.
disp(' The program is iterating on Bellman's equation.
Please wait...')

% Step 0: Input the parameter values
a = 0.33; % alpha
b = 0.96; % beta
p = 0.95; % rho
d = 0.10; % delta
e = exp(1); % Number e (transcendent but necessary)
% Step 1: Compute the steady state
K = ((a*b)/(1-b*(1-d)))^(1/(1-a));
X = d*K;
Z = 0;
```

```
% Step 2: Construct the quadratic expansion of the utility
% function
% Step 2.1: Evaluate all the first and second order
% derivatives of the utility function at the steady state:
R = log(e^Z*K^a - X);
Jz = (e^Z*K^a) / (e^Z*K^a - X);
Jk = (e^Z*a*K^(a-1)) / (e^Z*K^a - X);
Jx = (-1) / (e^Z*K^a - X);
Hzz = (((e^Z*K^a) * (e^Z*K^a - X)) - (e^Z*K^a)^2) / ((e^Z*K^a
- X)^2);
Hkk = (((e^Z*a*(a-1)*K^(a-2))*(e^Z*K^a - X)) - ...
(e^Z*a*K^(a-1))^2 )/((e^Z* K^a - X)^2);
Hxx = (-1)/((e^Z*K^a - X)^2);
Hzk = (((e^Z*a*K^(a-1))*(e^Z*K^a - X)) - (e^Z*K^a*e^Z*a*K^
(a-1)))/...((e^Z*K^a - X)^2);
Hzx = (e^Z*K^a) / ((e^Z*K^a - X)^2);
Hkx = (e^Z*a*K^(a-1))/((e^Z*K^a - X)^2);
% Step 2.2: Define the Jacobian vector and the Hessian
% matrix evaluated
% at the steady state
DJ = [Jz Jk Jx ]';
D2H = [Hzz Hzk Hzx
Hzk Hkk Hkx
Hzx Hkx Hxx];
% Step 2.3: Define matrix Q
W = [Z K X]';
Q11 = R - W'*DJ + 0.5*W'*D2H*W;
Q12 = 0.5*(DJ-D2H*W);
Q22 = 0.5*D2H;
Q=[ Q11 Q12'
Q12 Q22];
% Step 3: Compute the optimal value function.
% Step 3.1: Partition matrix Q to separate the state and
% control variables
Qff = Q(1:3,1:3);
Qfd = Q(4,1:3);
Qdd = Q(4,4);
% Step 3.2: Input matrix B
B = [ 1 0 0 0
0 p 0 0
0 0 1-d 1];
% Step 3.3: Input matrix P0
```

```
P = [-0.1 0 0
0 -0.1 0
0 0 -0.1 ];
% Step 3.4: Initialize auxiliary matrix A
A=ones(3);
% Step 3.5: Iterate on Bellman's equation until convergence
% while (norm(A-P)/norm(A))>0.0000001
A = P;
M=B'*P*B;
Mff = M(1:3,1:3);
Mfd = M(4,1:3);
Mdd = M(4,4);
P=Qff + (b*Mff) - (Qfd'+(b*Mfd)')*inv(Qdd +(b*Mdd))
*(Qfd+(b*Mfd));
end
% Step 4: Output the results
disp(' ')
disp(' The linear policy for investment is d*=J'F, where
vector J is:')
J=-(inv(Qdd+(b*Mdd))*(Qfd+(b*Mfd)))';
J
disp(' ')
disp(' The optimal value function is V*=F'PF, where matrix P
is:')
P
% END OF MATLAB FILE
```

The output of this program should be the following:

```
J =
  0.4983
0.8607
-0.0411
P =
-0.4025 8.0839 0.7369
8.0839 1.0029 -0.1915
0.7369 -0.1915 -0.0819
```

3

A TOOLKIT FOR ANALYSING NONLINEAR DYNAMIC STOCHASTIC MODELS EASILY

Harald Uhlig[1]

3.1 Introduction

Researchers often wish to analyse nonlinear dynamic discrete-time stochastic models. This chapter provides a toolkit for solving such models easily, building on log-linearizing the necessary equations characterizing the equilibrium and solving for the recursive equilibrium law of motion with the method of undetermined coefficients.[2]

This chapter contains nothing substantially new. Instead, the point of it is to simplify and unify existing methods in order to make them accessible to a large audience of researchers, who may always have been interested in analysing, say, real business cycle models on their own, but hesitated to make the step of learning the numerical tools involved. This chapter reduces the pain from taking that step. The methods here can be used to analyse most of the models studied in the literature. We discuss how to log-linearize the nonlinear equations without the need for explicit differentiation and how to use the method of undetermined coefficients for models with a vector of endogenous state variables. The methods explained here follow directly from McCallum (1983), King *et al.* (1987) and Campbell (1994), among others.[3] We provide a general solution built on solving matrix quadratic equations (see also Binder and Pesaran, 1995), and provide frequency-domain techniques, building on results in King and Rebelo (1993), to calculate the second-order moments of the model in its Hodrick–Prescott filtered version without resorting to simulations. Since the method is an Euler equation based

[1] I am grateful to Michael Binder, Toni Braun, Paul Klein, Jan Magnus, Ramon Marimon, Ellen McGrattan, Víctor Ríos-Rull and Yexiao Xu for helpful comments. I am grateful to Andrew Atkeson for pointing out to me a significant improvement. An earlier version of this chapter was completed while visiting the Institute for Empirical Macroeconomics at the Federal Reserve Bank of Minneapolis: I am grateful for the Institute's hospitality. Any views expressed here are those of the author and not necessarily those of the Federal Reserve Bank of Minneapolis or the Federal Reserve System. This is an updated version of Discussion Paper 101 at the Institute for Empirical Macroeconomics and of CentER DP 9597. Further work was done while visiting the Institute for International Economic Studies in Stockholm: thanks are due to colleagues there, in particular Paul Klein.

[2] Note that the nonlinear model is thus replaced by a linearized approximate model. "Essential" nonlinearities like chaotic systems are unlikely to be handled well by the methods in this paper.

[3] Campbell even touts the approach followed in his paper as "analytical", but note that in his cases as well as in ours, one needs to linearize equations and solve quadratic equations. Campbell presumably attaches the attribute "analytical" to this numerical procedure, since it is rather straightforward indeed and carrying it out by hand is actually feasible in many cases. Otherwise, every numerical calculation anywhere could be called "analytical", since it could in principle be carried out and analysed by hand – it would just take a very long time.

approach rather than an approach based on solving a social planner problem, solving models with externalities or distortionary taxation does not pose additional problems. Since the (nonlinear) Euler equations usually need to be calculated in any case in order to find the steady state, applying the method described in this paper requires little in terms of additional manipulation by hand, given some preprogrammed routines to carry out the matrix calculations of Section 3.4. MATLAB programs to carry out these calculations, given the log-linearized system, are available on my home page[4] and are also discussed in Section 3.9. The method in this chapter therefore allows nonlinear dynamic stochastic models to be solved easily.

Numerical solution methods for solving nonlinear stochastic dynamic models have been studied extensively in the literature; see in particular Kydland and Prescott (1982), the comparison by Taylor and Uhlig (1990) and the methods proposed by various authors in the same issue, Judd (1991), Hansen and Prescott (1995) and Danthine and Donaldson (1995). The literature on solving linear quadratic dynamic stochastic models or linear stochastic difference equations is even larger. The key paper here is Blanchard and Kahn (1980). Furthermore, there are the textbook treatments in Sargent (1987b, Chapters IX and XI), as well as Muth (1961), McGrattan (1994) or Hansen *et al.* (1994), to name a random few. Subject to applicability, all the methods relying on a log-linear approximation to the steady state have in common that they will find the same recursive equilibrium law of motion as the method described in this chapter, since the linear space approximating a nonlinear differentiable function is unique and "immune" to differentiable transformations of the parameter space. But while McGrattan (1994) and Hansen *et al.* (1994) focus on solving models via maximizing a quadratic objective function, and while Blanchard and Kahn (1980) solve linear systems by searching for the stable manifold in the entire system of necessary equations describing the equilibrium relationships, this chapter by contrast, solves directly for the desired recursive equilibrium law of motion. This approach is quite natural. The stability condition is imposed at the point where a certain matrix quadratic equation is solved. It is shown how this matrix quadratic equation can be reduced to a standard eigenvalue problem of another matrix with twice as many dimensions.

Three related contributions are McCallum (1983), which is the key reference for the method of undetermined coefficients, Ceria and Ríos-Rull (1992) and Binder and Pesaran (1996). These contributions also derive the recursive equilibrium law of motion. McCallum (1983) reduces the coefficient-finding problem to a problem solvable with the methods in Blanchard and Kahn (1980), whereas Ceria and Ríos-Rull (1992) reduce the problem to one of solving a matrix quadratic equation as do we, but do not reduce the matrix quadratic equation problem to a standard eigenvalue problem. Binder and Pesaran (1995), finally, may be most closely related in that they reduce the matrix quadratic equation characterizing the solution to an eigenvalue problem as we do. These three contributions, however, for the most part do not distinguish between endogenous variables which have to be part of the state vector, and other endogenous variables. Thus applying these models in somewhat larger systems can result in unnecessarily large and computationally demanding eigenvalue problems in which "bubble solutions" have to be removed in a

[4]`http://cwis.kub.nl/~few5/center/STAFF/uhlig/toolkit.dir/toolkit.htm` is the address of the Web site for the programs.

painstaking fashion, or being forced to reduce the system beforehand to make it fit their description.[5] Furthermore, recent related contributions include Christiano and Valdivia (1994), King and Watson (1995; 1997), Sims (1999) and Klein (1998).

But all these technical differences to the existing literature are not in any way essential. It shall be stressed again that the main purpose and merit of this chapter is to make solving nonlinear dynamic stochastic models easy. In fact, this paper describes the entire method as a "cook-book recipe", which should be of great practical use to Ph.D. students and researchers alike. Since the focus here is entirely on the computational aspect of studying these models, some issues are entirely left aside. In particular, the issue of existence or multiplicity of equilibria as well as the reasons for concentrating on stable solutions are not discussed. The methods in this chapter should therefore not be applied blindly, but only in light of, say, McCallum (1983), Stokey *et al.* (1989) and the related literature.

The outline of the paper will be evident from the description of the general procedure in the next section.

3.2 The general procedure

The general procedure for solving and analysing nonlinear dynamic stochastic models consists of the following steps.

1. Find the necessary equations characterizing the equilibrium, i.e. constraints, first-order conditions, etc.; see Section 3.8.1.
2. Pick parameters and find the steady state(s); see Section 3.8.1.
3. Log-linearize the necessary equations characterizing the equilibrium of the system to make the equations approximately linear in the log-deviations from the steady state; see Sections 3.3 and 3.8.1.
4. Solve for the recursive equilibrium law of motion via the method of undetermined coefficients, employing the formulae of Section 3.4.
5. Analyse the solution via impulse-response analysis and second-order-properties, possibly taking account of, say, the Hodrick–Prescott filter. This can be done without having to simulate the model; see Section 3.6.

The next section skips directly to step 3 of the procedure outlined above and describes how to log-linearize nonlinear equations without explicit differentiation. Section 3.8.1 studies Hansen's (1985) benchmark real business cycle model as a prototype example, in which calculation of the Euler equations, the steady state and the log-linearization is carried out to see how this method works. Once a linearized system has been obtained, the methods in Section 3.4 provide the desired recursive equilibrium law of motion.

3.3 Log-linearization and model formulation

Log-linearizing the necessary equations characterizing the equilibrium is a well-known technique. In the context of real business cycle models, log-linearization has been proposed in particular by King *et al.* (1987) and Campbell (1994). Log-linearization also

[5] Furthermore, McCallum (1983) uses eigenvalue methods also to solve some other equations in his method, which are solved here by a simple linear equation solution techniques; compare his solution to equation (A.6) in his paper to equation (3.26).

appears frequently in text books such as Obstfeld and Rogoff (1996, pp. 503–505). Nonetheless, the technique often seems to create more headaches than it should. It may be useful for the purposes of this chapter to review how it is done. Section 3.8.1 simplifies the approach of Campbell (1994). Readers who are familiar enough with log-linearization or have their model already in linear form are advised to skip directly to Section 3.4.

The principle is to use a Taylor approximation around the steady state to replace all equations by approximations, which are linear functions in the log-deviations of the variables. Of course, for larger models, it may be convenient to obtain the linearized versions from the original nonlinear equations by numerical differentiation: there is nothing wrong with that, and doing so can speed things up in routine work. But the linearization step itself is not a cumbersome one, as we shall see.

Formally, let X_t be the vector of variables, $\bar{X}$ their steady state and

$$x_t = \log X_t - \log \bar{X}$$

the vector of log-deviations. The vector $100x_t$ tells us by what percentage the variables differ from their steady-state levels in period t. The necessary equations characterizing the equilibrium can be written as

$$1 = f(x_t, x_{t-1}) \tag{3.1}$$

$$1 = E_t[g(x_{t+1}, x_t)] \tag{3.2}$$

where $f(0,0) = 1$ and $g(0,0) = 1$, i.e. the left-hand side of (3.1) and (3.2). Taking first-order approximations around $(x_t, x_{t-1}) = (0,0)$ yields[6]

$$0 \approx f_1 \cdot x_t + f_2 \cdot x_{t-1}$$

$$0 \approx E_t\left[g_1 \cdot x_{t+1} + g_2 \cdot x_t\right]$$

One obtains a linear system in x_t and x_{t-1} in the deterministic equations and x_{t+1} and x_t in the expectational equations. This linear system can be solved with the method of undetermined coefficients, described in Section 3.4.

In the large majority of cases, there is no need to differentiate the functions f and g formally. Instead, the log-linearized system can usually be obtained as follows. Multiply

[6]An alternative to approximate (3.2) rewrites it as

$$0 = \log\left\{E_t\left[\exp\left(\tilde{g}(x_{t+1}, x_t)\right)\right]\right\}$$

where $\tilde{g} = \log g$. Assuming x_t and x_{t+1} to be (approximately) conditionally jointly normally distributed with an (approximately) constant conditional variance-covariance matrix, and assuming that

$$\log g(0,0) \approx \tfrac{1}{2}\mathrm{Var}_t\left[\tilde{g}_1 \cdot x_{t+1} + \tilde{g}_2 \cdot x_t\right] \tag{3.3}$$

independent of t (rather than $\log g(0,0) = 0$) yields

$$0 \approx \log E_t\left[\exp\left(\tilde{g}(0,0) + \tilde{g}_1 \cdot x_{t+1} + \tilde{g}_2 \cdot x_t\right)\right]$$

$$\approx E_t\left[\tilde{g}_1 \cdot x_{t+1} + \tilde{g}_2 \cdot x_t\right]$$

using $E[e^X] = e^{E[X]+\mathrm{Var}[X]/2}$ for normally distributed variables. The two ways of approximating (3.2) differ essentially only in their choice for $g(0,0)$, since $g_1 = \tilde{g}_1$ if $g(0,0) = 1$.

out everything before log-linearizing. Replace a variable X_t with $X_t = \bar{X}e^{x_t}$, where x_t is a real number close to zero. Likewise, let y_t be a real number close to zero. Take logarithms, where both sides of an equation only involve products, or use the following three building blocks, where a is some constant:

$$e^{x_t + a y_t} \approx 1 + x_t + a y_t$$
$$x_t y_t \approx 0$$
$$E_t\left[a e^{x_{t+1}}\right] \approx E_t\left[a x_{t+1}\right] \text{ up to a constant}$$

For example, these building blocks yield

$$e^{x_t} \approx 1 + x_t$$
$$a X_t \approx a \bar{X} x_t \text{ up to a constant}$$
$$(X_t + a) Y_t \approx \bar{X}\bar{Y} x_t + (\bar{X} + a)\bar{Y} y_t \text{ up to a constant}$$

Constants drop out of each equation in the end, since they satisfy steady-state relationships, but they are important in intermediate steps: compare, for example, the two equations above.

Rather than describing the general principles further, it is fruitful to consider a specific example instead. Take Hansen's (1985) benchmark real business cycle model and log-linearize it in the manner described above. Details are described in Section 3.8.1. One obtains

$$-c_t = \lambda_t \tag{3.4}$$
$$n_t = y_t + \lambda_t \tag{3.5}$$
$$\bar{R} r_t = \rho \frac{\bar{Y}}{\bar{K}} (y_t - k_{t-1}) \tag{3.6}$$
$$y_t = z_t + \rho k_{t-1} + (1 - \rho) n_t \tag{3.7}$$
$$\bar{C} c_t + \bar{K} k_t = \bar{Y} y_t + (1 - \delta) \bar{K} k_{t-1} \tag{3.8}$$
$$\lambda_t = E_t[\lambda_{t+1} + r_{t+1}] \tag{3.9}$$
$$z_t = \psi z_{t-1} + \epsilon_t \tag{3.10}$$

Here, c_t denotes the log-deviation of consumption, while $\bar{C}$ denotes the steady-state value of consumption, etc. Those familiar with Hansen's model will readily recognize equation (3.4) to be the first-order condition with respect to consumption C_t (λ_t is the log-linearized Lagrange multiplier on the resource constraint), equation (3.5) to be the first-order condition with respect to labour, equation (3.6) to be the equation defining the return on capital, equation (3.7) to be the log-linearized version of the Cobb–Douglas production function, equation (3.8) to be the resource constraint, equation (3.9) to be the Lucas asset pricing equation, and equation (3.10) to show the evolution of the exogenous total factor productivity. Depending on taste, one obtains a different set of equations which are, however, all equivalent if the calculations are done correctly. For example, one may decide to eliminate λ_t by substituting $-c_t$ right away in all equations.

Note that we use the *dating convention* k_{t-1} for capital created in period $t-1$ and used in production in period t: in general, we shall date all variables with respect to the date at which they are *known*. This contrasts with the notational practice in parts of the literature, but there obviously is no substantial difference: it is just important to keep this in mind when applying the method.

Note that all equations only contain variables dated $t, t-1$ or, possibly, expectations as of time t of variables dated $t+1$. This is the form we need to proceed further. For some models, this may require introducing "dummy" variables to capture further lags of variables or expectations of variables further into the future. So instead of, for example,

$$x_t = E_t[y_{t+2}]$$

write

$$x_t = E_t\left[y_{t+1}^{(1)}\right]$$
$$y_t^{(1)} = E_t[y_{t+1}]$$

and instead of

$$y_t = x_{t-2} + z_t$$

write

$$y_t = x_{t-1}^{(1)} + z_t \tag{3.11}$$
$$x_t^{(1)} = x_{t-1} \tag{3.12}$$

Strictly speaking, the last equation violates our dating convention, but never mind.

Once a linear or linearized system such as (3.4)–(3.10) is obtained, one can proceed to solve for its dynamics.

3.4 Solving recursive stochastic linear systems with the method of undetermined coefficients

This section describes how to find the solution to the recursive equilibrium law of motion in general, using the method of undetermined coefficients. MATLAB programs performing the calculations in this section are available on my home page. The idea is to write all variables as linear functions (the "recursive equilibrium law of motion") of a vector of endogenous variables x_{t-1} and exogenous variables z_t, which are given at date t – that is, which cannot be changed at date t. These variables are often called state variables or predetermined variables. In the real business cycle example of Section 3.8.1, these are at least k_{t-1} and z_t, since they are clearly unchangeable as of date t and, furthermore, show up in the linearized equations system. In principle, any endogenous variable dated $t-1$ or earlier could be considered a state variable. Thus, in Section 3.4.1, we use brute force and simply declare all endogenous variables to be state variables, whereas in Section 3.4.2 we try to be a bit more sensitive and exploit more of the available structure. The latter is typically done in practice; see, for example, Campbell (1994). Both subsections will characterize the solution with a matrix quadratic equation; see also Ceria and Ríos-Rull (1992) and Binder and Pesaran (1995). Section 3.4.3 shows how to solve that equation. For models with just one endogenous state variable, such as the real business cycle model of Section 3.8.1 when analysed with the more structured approach in Section 3.4.2, the matrix quadratic equation is simply a quadratic equation in a real number: for an explicit example and its high-school algebra solution, see Section 3.8.3. This case is contained as a special case of the general solution in Section 3.4.3. In Section 3.5 we discuss our solution method, and compare it in particular to the Blanchard and Kahn (1980) approach.

3.4.1 *With brute force...*

To begin, one may simply use all variables without distinction as a vector of endogenous state variables[7] x_{t-1} of size $m \times 1$ or as a vector of exogenous stochastic processes z_t of size $k \times 1$. It is assumed that the log-linearized equilibrium relationships can be written as

$$0 = E_t[Fx_{t+1} + Gx_t + Hx_{t-1} + Lz_{t+1} + Mz_t] \tag{3.13}$$

$$z_{t+1} = Nz_t + \epsilon_{t+1}, \qquad E_t[\epsilon_{t+1}] = 0 \tag{3.14}$$

where F, G, H, L and M are matrices collecting the coefficients. It is assumed that N has only stable eigenvalues. The real business cycle example (3.4)–(3.10) above can be easily written in this form. For example, the resource constraint (3.8) would be

$$0 = E_t[\bar{C}c_t + \bar{K}k_t - \bar{Y}y_t - (1-\delta)\bar{K}k_{t-1}]$$

since c_t, k_t, k_{t-1} and y_t are already known at date t and hence nothing changes when one takes their expectations given all information up to date t. Note that $F = L = 0$ for this equation. Of course, there are other equations in the real business cycle model, and one of them involves non-zero entries for F and L.

What one is looking for is the recursive equilibrium law of motion

$$x_t = Px_{t-1} + Qz_t \tag{3.15}$$

that is, matrices P and Q such that the equilibrium described by these rules is stable. The solution is characterized in the following theorem; see also Binder and Pesaran (1995). The characterization involves a matrix quadratic equation; see equation (3.16). Section 3.4.3 discusses how it can be solved. For the purpose of that section, let m be the length of the vector x_t, and let $l = n = 0$.

Theorem 3.1 *If there is a recursive equilibrium law of motion solving equations* (3.13), *and* (3.14), *then the following must be true.*

[7] To make this work really general, one should actually not only include all the variables dated $t-1$ but also all the variables dated $t-2$ as part of the state vector x_{t-1}. Even more is required if the equations already contain further lags of endogenous variables, see also footnote 8. Usually, however, this is unnecessary.

1. *P satisfies the (matrix) quadratic equation*

$$0 = FP^2 + GP + H \tag{3.16}$$

The equilibrium described by the recursive equilibrium law of motion (3.15) *and* (3.14) *is stable if and only if all eigenvalues of P are less than unity in absolute value.*

2. *Given P, let V denote the matrix*

$$V = N' \otimes F + I_k \otimes (FP + G)$$

Then,

$$VQ = -\mathrm{vec}(LN + M) \tag{3.17}$$

where vec(·) *denotes columnwise vectorization.*

Obviously, if the matrix V in this theorem is invertible, then multiplication of equation (3.17) by V^{-1} yields the unique solution for Q.

Proof Plugging the recursive equilibrium law of motion (3.15) into equation (3.13) twice and using (3.14) to calculate the expectations yields

$$\begin{aligned} 0 = {} & ((FP + G)P + H)x_{t-1} \\ & + ((FQ + L)N + (FP + G)Q + M)z_t \end{aligned} \tag{3.18}$$

The coefficient matrices of x_{t-1} and z_t need to be zero. Equating the coefficient of x_{t-1} to zero yields equation (3.16) for P. Taking the columnwise vectorization of the coefficient matrices of z_t in this equation and collecting terms in vec(Q) yields the equation (3.17) for Q. □

3.4.2 ... *or with sensitivity*

We now exploit more of the structure in the linearized model. Analysing the equations of the real business cycle example of Section 3.8.1, one sees that the only endogenous variable dated $t-1$ which shows up in any of the equations is capital, k_{t-1}. It is thus a reasonable guess to treat k_{t-1} as the only endogenous state variable together with the exogenous state variable z_t. This principle is general: in the vast majority of cases, this is how one can identify the vector of state variables.[8] In practice, one often sees researchers exploiting some of the equilibrium equations to get rid of some variables, and have only a few variables remaining. For the real business cycle example of Section 3.8.1, it is actually possible to reduce everything to a single equation for the endogenous variables, containing only k_{t+1}, k_t, and k_{t-1}. Often, one sees reductions to a system involving two equations in two endogenous variables such as λ_t and k_{t-1} (see e.g. Campbell, 1994; and

[8]There are exceptions. Variables chosen at a date earlier than $t-1$ may need to be included: this can be treated as in equations (3.11), (3.12). One may also need to add additional variables like e.g. c_{t-1} or k_{t-2} as state variables, even though they don't show up in the equations with these dates, when the model exhibits sun spot dynamics. This can be done in the same manner, but one needs to be careful with interpreting the results. Appendix 3.8 and in particular 3.8.8 elaborates on this in more careful detail.

Section 3.8.2 below), presumably because this allows thinking in terms of a state-space diagram (see e.g. Blanchard and Fisher, 1989, Chapter 2). However, there is no reason to bother with "eliminating" variables by hand, using some of the equations: since this is all just simple linear algebra applied to a system of equations, it is far easier to leave all the equations in, and leave it to the formulae to sort it all out. That is what is done below.

We thus make the following assumptions.[9] There is an endogenous state vector x_t, of size $m \times 1$, a list of other endogenous variables ("jump variables") y_t, of size $n \times 1$, and a list of exogenous stochastic processes z_t, of size $k \times 1$. The equilibrium relationships between these variables are

$$0 = Ax_t + Bx_{t-1} + Cy_t + Dz_t \tag{3.19}$$

$$0 = E_t[Fx_{t+1} + Gx_t + Hx_{t-1} + Jy_{t+1} + Ky_t + Lz_{t+1} + Mz_t] \tag{3.20}$$

$$z_{t+1} = Nz_t + \epsilon_{t+1}; \quad E_t[\epsilon_{t+1}] = 0 \tag{3.21}$$

where it is assumed that C is of size $l \times n$, $l \geq n$ and[10] of rank n, that F is of size $(m + n - l) \times n$, and that N has only stable eigenvalues. Note that one could have written all equations (3.19) in the form of equation (3.20) with the corresponding entries in the matrices F, J and L set to zero. Essentially, that is what is done in Section 3.4.1. Instead, the point here is somehow to exploit the structure inherent in equations of the form (3.19), which do not involve taking expectations.

What one is looking for is the recursive equilibrium law of motion

$$x_t = Px_{t-1} + Qz_t \tag{3.22}$$

$$y_t = Rx_{t-1} + Sz_t \tag{3.23}$$

that is, matrices P, Q, R, and S such that the equilibrium described by these rules is stable. The solution is characterized in the next theorem. To calculate the solution, one needs to solve a matrix quadratic equation: how this is done is explained in Section 3.4.3.

The important special case $l = n$ is treated in Corrollary 3.3. The special case $l = n = 0$ was the topic of Section 3.4.1.

Theorem 3.2 *If there is a recursive equilibrium law of motion solving equations* (3.19), (3.20), *and* (3.21), *then the coefficient matrices can be found as follows. Let C^+ be the pseudo-inverse*[11] *of C. Let C^0 be an $(l - n) \times l$ matrix whose rows form a basis for the null space*[12] *of C'.*

[9] Note that the notation differs from the notation in Section 3.3.

[10] The case $l < n$ can be treated as well: the easiest approach is simply to "redeclare" some other endogenous variables to be state variables instead – that is, to raise m and thus lower n – until $l = n$.

[11] The pseudo-inverse of the matrix C is the $n \times l$ matrix C^+ satisfying $C^+CC^+ = C^+$ and $CC^+C = C$. Since it is assumed that rank$(C) \geq n$, one obtains $C^+ = (C'C)^{-1}C'$; see Strang (1980, p. 138). The MATLAB command to compute the pseudo-inverse is pinv(C).

[12] C^0 can be found via the singular value decomposition of C'; see Strang (1980, p. 142). The MATLAB command for computing C^0 is (null(C'))$'$.

1. *P satisfies the (matrix) quadratic equations*

$$0 = C^0 AP + C^0 B \tag{3.24}$$

$$0 = (F - JC^+ A)P^2 - (JC^+ B - G + KC^+ A)P - KC^+ B + H \tag{3.25}$$

The equilibrium described by the recursive equilibrium law of motion (3.22), (3.23) *and by* (3.21) *is stable if and only if all eigenvalues of P are less than unity in absolute value.*

2. *R is given by*

$$R = -C^+(AP + B)$$

3. *Given P and R, let V be the matrix*

$$V = \begin{bmatrix} I_k \otimes A, & I_k \otimes C \\ N' \otimes F + I_k \otimes (FP + JR + G) & N' \otimes J + I_k \otimes K \end{bmatrix}$$

where I_k is the identity matrix of size $k \times k$. Then

$$V \begin{bmatrix} \text{vec}(Q) \\ \text{vec}(S) \end{bmatrix} = - \begin{bmatrix} \text{vec}(D) \\ \text{vec}(LN + M) \end{bmatrix} \tag{3.26}$$

where vec($\cdot$) *denotes columnwise vectorization.*

Obviously, if V in this theorem is invertible, then multiplication of equation (3.26) with V^{-1} yields the unique solution for Q.

Proof Plug the recursive equilibrium law of motion into equation (3.19). This yields

$$(AP + CR + B)x_{t-1} + (AQ + CS + D)z_t = 0 \tag{3.27}$$

which has to hold for arbitrary x_{t-1} and z_t. Thus, the coefficient matrices on x_{t-1} and z_t in (3.27) are zero. Plugging the recursive equilibrium law of motion into equation (3.20) twice and using (3.21) yields

$$\begin{aligned} 0 =& ((FP + JR + G)P + KR + H)x_{t-1} \\ &+ ((FQ + JS + L)N + (FP + JR + G)Q + KS + M)z_t \end{aligned} \tag{3.28}$$

Again, the coefficient matrices on x_{t-1} and z_t need to be zero. Taking the columnwise vectorization of the coefficient matrices of z_t in equations (3.27) and (3.28) and collecting terms in vec(Q) and vec(S) yields the formula for Q and S. To find P and thus R, rewrite the coefficient matrix on x_{t-1} in equation (3.27) as

$$\begin{aligned} R &= -C^+(AP + B) \\ 0 &= C^0 AP + C^0 \end{aligned} \tag{3.29}$$

noting that the matrix $[(C^+)', (C^0)']$ is non-singular and that $C^0 C = 0$; see Strang (1980, p. 88). Use (3.29) to replace R in the coefficient matrix on x_{t-1} in (3.28), yielding (3.25). Note finally that the stability of the equilibrium is determined by the stability of P, since N has stable roots by assumption. □

Corollary 3.3 *Suppose that $l = n$, that is, that there are as many expectational equations as there are endogenous state variables. If there is a recursive equilibrium law of motion solving equations* (3.19), (3.20), *and* (3.21), *then their coefficient matrices can be found as follows.*

1. *P satisfies the (matrix) quadratic equation*

$$(F - JC^{-1}A)P^2 - (JC^{-1}B - G + KC^{-1}A)P - KC^{-1}B + H = 0 \quad (3.30)$$

   The equilibrium described by the recursive equilibrium law of motion (3.22), (3.23) *and by* (3.21) *is stable if and only if all eigenvalues of P are less than unity in absolute value.*

2. *R is given by*

$$R = -C^{-1}(AP + B)$$

3. *Q satisfies*

$$\begin{aligned}(N' \otimes (F - JC^{-1}A) + I_k \otimes (JR + FP + G - KC^{-1}A))\text{vec}(Q) \quad (3.31)\\ = \text{vec}((JC^{-1}D - L)N + KC^{-1}D - M)\end{aligned}$$

   where I_k is the identity matrix of size $k \times k$, provided the matrix which needs to be inverted in this formula is indeed invertible.

4. *S is given by*

$$S = -C^{-1}(AQ + D)$$

Proof This corollary can be obtained directly by inspecting the formulae of Theorem 3.2 above for the special case $l = n$. In particular, C^+ is just the inverse of C. Alternatively, a direct proof can be obtained directly by following the same proof strategy as above. □

The formulae in these theorems become even simpler if $m = 1$ or $k = 1$. If $m = 1$, there is just one endogenous state variable and the matrix quadratic equation above becomes a quadratic equation in the real number P, which can be solved using high-school algebra: this is the case for the real business cycle model and thus the case which Campbell (1994) analyses. If $k = 1$, there is just one exogenous state variable, in which case the Kronecker product $\otimes$ in the formulae above becomes multiplication, and in which case $\text{vec}(Q) = Q$ and $\text{vec}(S) = S$, since Q and S are already vectors rather than matrices.

3.4.3 *Solving the matrix quadratic equation*

To solve the matrix quadratic equations (3.16) or (3.24), (3.25) for P, write them as

$$\Psi P^2 - \Gamma P - \Theta = 0 \quad (3.32)$$

For equations (3.24) and (3.25), define

$$\Psi = \begin{bmatrix} 0_{l-n,m} \\ F - JC^+A \end{bmatrix}$$
$$\Gamma = \begin{bmatrix} C^0 A \\ JC^+B - G + KC^+A \end{bmatrix}$$
$$\Theta = \begin{bmatrix} C^0 B \\ KC^+B - H \end{bmatrix}$$

where $0_{l-n,m}$ is an $(l-n) \times m$ matrix with only zero entries. In the special case $l = n$, the formulae for Ψ, Γ and Θ become slightly simpler:

$$\Psi = F - JC^{-1}A$$
$$\Gamma = JC^{-1}B - G + KC^{-1}A$$
$$\Theta = KC^{-1}B - H$$

For equation (3.16), simply use $\Psi = F$, $\Gamma = -G$ and $\Theta = -H$.

Equation (3.32) can now be solved in two ways. In Theorem 3.4, we will solve it by turning it into a generalized eigenvalue and eigenvector problem,[13] for which most mathematical packages have preprogrammed routines.[14] In Theorem 3.5, we will solve it, using the QZ method.

Recall that a generalized eigenvalue λ and eigenvector s of a matrix Ξ with respect to a matrix Δ are defined to satisfy

$$\lambda \Delta s = \Xi s \tag{3.33}$$

A standard eigenvalue problem is obtained if Δ is the identity matrix. More generally, the generalized eigenvector problem can be reduced to a standard one, if Δ is invertible, by calculating standard eigenvalues and eigenvectors for $\Delta^{-1}\Xi$ instead.

Theorem 3.4 *To solve the quadratic matrix equation*

$$\Psi P^2 - \Gamma P - \Theta = 0, \tag{3.34}$$

for the $m \times m$ matrix P, given $m \times m$ matrices Γ and Θ, define the $2m \times 2m$ matrices Ξ and Δ by

$$\Xi = \begin{bmatrix} \Gamma & \Theta \\ I_m & 0_{m,m} \end{bmatrix}$$

[13] An earlier version of this chapter proposed to study an altered version of these equations by postmultiplying equation (3.24) with P. This altered equation, together with (3.25), can then often be reduced to a standard rather than a generalized eigenvalue problem, but has the drawback of introducing spurious zero roots. The version presented here does not involve this alteration, and thus does not introduce spurious zero roots. This update is due to Andy Atkeson (1997), and I am very grateful to him for pointing it out to me. Any errors here are mine, of course.

[14] The MATLAB command for finding the generalized eigenvalues and eigenvectors is eig(Ξ,Δ).

and

$$\Delta = \begin{bmatrix} \Psi & 0_{m,m} \\ 0_{m,m} & I_m \end{bmatrix}$$

where I_m is the identity matrix of size m, and where $0_{m,m}$ is the $m \times m$ matrix with only zero entries.

1. *If s is a generalized eigenvector and λ the corresponding generalized eigenvalue of Ξ with respect to Δ, then s can be written as $s' = [\lambda x', x']$ for some $x \in \mathbb{R}^m$.*
2. *If there are m generalized eigenvalues $\lambda, \ldots, \lambda_m$ together with generalized eigenvectors $s_1, \ldots, s_m$ of Ξ with respect to Δ, written as $s_i' = [\lambda_i x_i', x_i']$ for some $x_i \in \mathbb{R}^m$, and if $(x_1, \ldots, x_m)$ is linearly independent, then*
$$P = \Omega\Lambda\Omega^{-1}$$
is a solution to the matrix quadratic equation (3.34), where $\Omega = [x_1, \ldots, x_m]$ and $\Lambda = \text{diag}(\lambda, \ldots, \lambda_m)$. The solution P is stable if $|\lambda_i| < 1$ for all $i = 1, \ldots, m$. Conversely, any diagonalizable solution P to (3.34) can be written in this way.
3. *If $m = 1$, then the solutions P to equation (3.34) are given by*
$$P_{1,2} = \frac{1}{2\Psi}(\Gamma \pm \sqrt{\Gamma^2 + 4\Psi\Theta})$$
if $\Psi \neq 0$, and by
$$P = -\frac{\Theta}{\Gamma}$$
if $\Psi = 0$ and $\Gamma \neq 0$.

Proof First, examine the last *m* rows of equation (3.33) to see that any eigenvector *s* for some eigenvalue λ of the matrix Ξ with respect to Δ can indeed be written as

$$s = \begin{bmatrix} \lambda x \\ x \end{bmatrix}$$

for some $x \in \mathbb{R}^m$ because of the special form of Ξ and Δ. Examining the first *m* rows of equation (3.33) then shows that

$$\lambda^2\Psi x - \lambda\Gamma x - \Theta x = 0 \tag{3.35}$$

It follows that

$$\Psi\Omega\Lambda^2 - \Gamma\Omega\Lambda - \Theta\Omega = 0$$

and hence

$$\Psi P^2 - \Gamma P - \Theta = 0$$

as claimed, after multiplying with Ω^{-1} from the right.

Reversing the steps shows that any diagonalizable solution P to (3.34) can be written in this way. □

One further generalization step can be made by using the QZ decomposition instead of a (generalized) diagonalization; see, in particular, Sims (1999). In particular, the QZ decomposition can deal with repeated eigenvalues easily, and is thus the preferred method. The next theorem shows how it works, but before stating it, we need an additional piece of notation. For any $2m \times 2m$ matrix X, say, write its partition as

$$X = \begin{bmatrix} X_{11} & X_{12} \\ X_{21} & X_{22} \end{bmatrix}$$

where X_{ij} denotes a submatrix of size $m \times m$. Likewise, any vector $v \in \mathbb{R}^{2m}$ shall be partitioned in this way.

Theorem 3.5 *To solve the quadratic matrix equation*

$$\Psi P^2 - \Gamma P - \Theta = 0 \tag{3.36}$$

for the $m \times m$ matrix P, given $m \times m$ matrices Γ and Θ, define the $2m \times 2m$ matrices Ξ and Δ by

$$\Xi = \begin{bmatrix} \Gamma & \Theta \\ I_m & 0_{m,m} \end{bmatrix}$$

and

$$\Delta = \begin{bmatrix} \Psi & 0_{m,m} \\ 0_{m,m} & I_m \end{bmatrix}$$

where I_m is the identity matrix of size m, and where $0_{m,m}$ is the $m \times m$ matrix with only zero entries.

Find the QZ decomposition (or generalized Schur decomposition) of Δ and Ξ, that is, find unitary[15] *matrices*[16] *Y and Z as well as upper triangular matrices Σ and Φ such that*[17]

$$Y'\Sigma Z = \Delta$$
$$Y'\Phi Z = \Xi$$

Assume that Z_{21} and Y_{21} are invertible.

1. *The matrix*

$$P = -Z_{21}^{-1} Z_{22}$$

solves the matrix quadratic equation (3.36).

[15]The matrix Y is unitary if and only if $Y'Y = I_{2m}$, where Y' denotes the complex conjugate transpose of Y.

[16]Matrix Y is usually denoted by Q, but we have used that symbol for another matrix already.

[17]Such a QZ decomposition always exists, although it may not be unique.

2. *Let ϕ_{ij} be the (i, j)th element of Φ and, likewise, let σ_{ij} be the (i, j)th element of Σ. Suppose that the QZ decomposition has been chosen so that the ratios $|\phi_{ii}/\sigma_{ii}|$ of the diagonal elements are in ascending order.*[18] *Furthermore, assume that $|\phi_{mm}/\sigma_{mm}| < 1$. Then, P is stable in the sense that $P^n x \to 0$ as $n \to \infty$ for any $x \in \mathbb{R}^m$.*

Proof We first show the first claim, that P indeed solves the matrix quadratic equation (3.36). We need to show that

$$\left(\Psi P^2 - \Gamma P - \Theta\right) x = 0$$

for any vector $x \in \mathbb{R}^m$. Equivalently, define $v(x) \in \mathbb{R}^{2m}$ via

$$v(x) = \begin{bmatrix} Px \\ x \end{bmatrix}$$

We need to show that

$$\Delta v(Px) = \Xi P x \tag{3.37}$$

or

$$\begin{bmatrix} \Psi P^2 x \\ Px \end{bmatrix} = \begin{bmatrix} \Gamma P x + \Theta x \\ Px \end{bmatrix} \tag{3.38}$$

for any $x \in \mathbb{R}^m$. Equation (3.38) shows that the claim (3.37) is already trivially true for the last m rows.

Define $w(x) = Zv(x)$ and note that

$$w(x) = \begin{bmatrix} Z_{11} P x + Z_{12} x \\ 0_{m,1} \end{bmatrix}$$

Equation (3.37) can therefore be written as

$$\begin{bmatrix} Y_{11} \Sigma_{11} \left(Z_{11} P^2 x + Z_{12} P x\right) \\ Y_{21} \Sigma_{11} \left(Z_{11} P^2 x + Z_{12} P x\right) \end{bmatrix} = \begin{bmatrix} Y_{11} \Phi_{11} \left(Z_{11} P x + Z_{12} x\right) \\ Y_{21} \Phi_{11} \left(Z_{11} P x + Z_{12} x\right) \end{bmatrix} \tag{3.39}$$

which needs to be shown. Comparing the last m rows of equations (3.38) and (3.39) and using the invertibility of Y_{21}, we see that

$$\Sigma_{11} \left(Z_{11} P^2 x + Z_{12} P x\right) = \Phi_{11} \left(Z_{11} P x + Z_{12} x\right)$$

Substituting this into the first m rows of (3.39) and comparing it to equation (3.38), we

[18] This can always be achieved, starting from a given QZ decomposition, by "swapping" axes in appropriate pairs. The MATLAB command to compute one QZ decomposition for A and B is qz(A, B). An algorithm for MATLAB for performing the swapping has been written by C. Sims to accompany his paper, Sims (1996). The reader is referred to these programs or to the literature on linear algebra for further discussion.

finally see that

$$\begin{aligned}\Psi P^2 x &= Y_{11}\Sigma_{11}\left(Z_{11}P^2 x + Z_{12}Px\right)\\ &= Y_{11}\Sigma_{11}\left(Z_{11}Px + Z_{12}x\right)\\ &= \Gamma Px + \Theta x\end{aligned}$$

as claimed.

We now show the second claim about stability. For any $x \in \mathbb{R}^m$ as above, let

$$v(x) = \begin{bmatrix} Px \\ x \end{bmatrix}$$

and

$$w(x) = Zv(x) = \begin{bmatrix} Z_{11}Px + Z_{12}x \\ 0_{m,1} \end{bmatrix}$$

Fix $x \in \mathbb{R}^m$. Note that $P^n x \longrightarrow 0$ if and only if $v(P^n x) \longrightarrow 0$, which is true if and only if $w(P^n x) \longrightarrow 0$. Let $n \geq 1$. Note that $\Delta v(P^n x) = \Xi v(P^{n-1}x)$ or, equivalently, $\Sigma w(P^n x) = \Phi w(P^n - 1x)$. Write out the latter expression explicitly. Keep in mind that $(w(P^{n-1}x))_2 = (w(P^n x))_2 = 0$. The first m rows deliver

$$(w(P^n x))_1 = \Sigma_{11}^{-1}\Phi_{11}(w(P^{n-1}x))_1$$

where Σ_{11} must be invertible and where $\left(\Sigma_{11}^{-1}\Phi_{11}\right)^n \longrightarrow 0$ due to our assumption about the diagonal elements. Hence,

$$(w(P^n x))_1 \longrightarrow 0 \quad \text{as } n \longrightarrow \infty$$

completing the proof. □

3.5 Discussion

Theorems 3.4 links the approach used here to Blanchard and Kahn (1980), which is the key reference for solving linear difference equations. A more detailed discussion, in particular with respect to the differences between saddle-point stable models *vis-à-vis* models with indeterminacies can be found in Section 3.8.

Consider solving the second-order difference equation

$$\Psi x_{t+1} - \Gamma x_t - \Theta x_{t-1} = 0 \tag{3.40}$$

The approach in Blanchard and Kahn (1980) amounts to finding the stable roots of Ξ by instead analysing the dynamics of the "stacked" system $s_t' = [x_t', x_{t-1}']$,

$$\Delta s_{t+1} = \Xi s_t$$

that is, by reducing (3.40) to a first-order difference equation. The approach here solves for the matrix P in the recursive equilibrium law of motion $x_{t+1} = Px_t$. Theorem 3.4 above states that both approaches amount to the same problem. The advantage of the method here is that it is easily applied to the entire system (3.19)–(3.21), reducing it eventually to (3.40), while finding the stable roots in the entire system given by these equations and at the same time taking care of the expectation operators, using the Blanchard and Kahn (1980) procedure is often perceived as complicated. Fundamentally, there is no difference.

To apply Theorem 3.4, one needs to select m out of $2m$ possible eigenvalues. Note that P has only non-zero eigenvalues if the state space was chosen to be of minimal size: attention can be restricted to the roots $|\lambda_i| > 0$ in that case. In general, there may be quite a bit of choice left. In practice, however, there will often be exactly m stable eigenvalues remaining so that the stable solution is unique.[19] For a one-dimensional vector of endogenous state variables, this condition is called saddle-point stability. The literature on solving linear rational expectations equilibria typically assumes this condition to hold or shows it to hold in social planning problems under reasonable conditions; see Blanchard and Kahn (1980), Kollintzas (1985) and Hansen *et al.* (1994). If there are fewer stable eigenvalues than endogenous state variables, the equilibrium might be inherently unstable. The method above then still permits calculation of an equilibrium which satisfies the nonlinear equilibrium conditions at least locally. In particular, in models involving more than one agent or sector or country, one may find as many unit roots as there are more agents (sectors, countries) than one since shocks may affect the relative wealth (capital) of any two agents (sectors, countries) and thus may result in permanent changes in their consumption paths (or capital stocks): in these cases, the method above allowing for unit roots still gives useful results, which obviously should then be used with some care. These unit roots typically already show up as an undetermined steady state: any of the possible steady states can then serve as a starting point for the dynamic calculation, keeping in mind that a simulation based on the dynamics calculated here will eventually wander away too far to be numerically useful. If there are more stable eigenvalues than endogenous state variables, enlarging the number of endogenous state variables by including further lagged values might help. Nonetheless, the presence of an excess of stable roots may then point to the existence of sunspots or endogenous fluctuations; see, example Farmer and Guo (1994). These matters are discussed in greater detail in Section 3.8.

If not all eigenvalues of Ξ are distinct, P in turn might have repeated eigenvalues. Since the eigenspace for a repeated eigenvalue is (usually) multi-dimensional, there will be infinitely many choices for the eigenvectors and hence infinitely many choices for P in that case. Note, for example, that for any given λ and any three real numbers a, b, c satisfying $a^2 + bc = \lambda^2$, all matrices

$$P = \begin{bmatrix} a & b \\ c & -a \end{bmatrix}$$

[19] Another approach to select a unique solution is given in McCallum (1983), who suggests using those roots that can be obtained continuously from the zero roots of the equation $\Psi P^2 - \Gamma P - \alpha\Theta$ for $\alpha = 0$, as α changes from 0 to 1. However, not only is following these roots as functions of α computationally very demanding, it is also the case that uniqueness is lost once two or more such paths cross each other. If these paths do not cross in a particular application, and if additionally all roots for all α are positive real numbers, say, then the McCallum proposal simply amounts to using the roots of minimal value. The MATLAB programs supplied by the author use the roots of minimal absolute value, subject to eliminating spurious zero roots, and try to use complex roots in conjugate pairs, as described below.

solve

$$P^2 - \begin{bmatrix} \lambda^2 & 0 \\ 0 & \lambda^2 \end{bmatrix} = 0$$

These cases are rare in practice, since Ξ is diagonalizable with distinct eigenvalues generically in the coefficients of the system (3.19)–(3.21). In any case, the QZ method can deal with them without difficulty; see Theorem 3.5.

More disconcerting is the possibility that some of the roots may be complex rather than real. Consider, for example, $\Psi = I_2$, $\Gamma = -I_2$ and

$$\Theta = \begin{bmatrix} 0.23 & 0.64 \\ -0.64 & 0.23 \end{bmatrix}$$

Using the theorem above, one obtains exactly two stable roots, which happen to be complex, $\lambda_{1,2} = 0.3 \pm 0.4\mathrm{i} = 0.5e^{\pm\alpha\mathrm{i}}$, where $\alpha \approx 0.9273$. Their associated eigenvectors are complex, too. Calculating P results in a matrix with only real entries, however, given by

$$P = \begin{bmatrix} 0.3 & 0.4 \\ -0.4 & 0.3 \end{bmatrix} = 0.5 \begin{bmatrix} \cos\alpha & \sin\alpha \\ -\sin\alpha & \cos\alpha \end{bmatrix}$$

Since Ξ is a real-valued matrix, complex eigenvalues only arise in complex conjugate pairs. When using both roots of a complex conjugate pair to calculate Λ and thus P, the resulting solution should be a real-valued matrix. In order to do this, one may have to enlarge the state space of endogenous state variables to be at least two-dimensional; see again Farmer and Guo (1994) for an example. The complex roots then give rise to endogenous damped cycles of frequency α. Again, see Section 3.8 (in particular, Section 3.8.8) for further discussion.

3.6 Interpreting the results

The results obtained, that is, the recursive equilibrium law of motion

$$\begin{aligned} x_t &= Px_{t-1} + Qz_t \\ y_t &= Rx_{t-1} + Sz_t \\ z_t &= Nz_{t-1} + \epsilon_t \end{aligned}$$

can be used to examine model implications. Since x_t, y_t and z_t are log-deviations, the entries in P, Q, R, S and N can be understood as elasticities and interpreted accordingly; see, for example, Campbell (1994).

Impulse responses to a particular shock ϵ_1 can be calculated by setting $x_0 = 0$, $y_0 = 0$ and $z_0 = 0$, as well as $\epsilon_t = 0$ for $t \geq 2$, and recursively calculating z_t and then x_t and y_t, given x_{t-1}, y_{t-1}, z_{t-1} and ϵ_t for $t = 1, \ldots, T$ with the recursive equilibrium law of motion and the law of motion for z_t.

To find the second moment properties of the model such as variances and autocorrelations of certain variables, as well as the small-sample properties of their estimators, simulation methods are often used. Before calculating these moments, the Hodrick–Prescott filter is typically applied. This section demonstrates a frequency-domain technique to obtain these moments (albeit without the small-sample properties of their estimators) without the need for any simulations.[20] Obviously, the methods here do not deliver properties of the small-sample distribution, which may be necessary for testing.

The matrix-valued spectral density for $[x_t', z_t']'$ is given by

$$f(\omega) = \frac{1}{2\pi} \begin{bmatrix} (I_m - Pe^{-i\omega})^{-1} Q \\ I_k \end{bmatrix} (I_k - Ne^{-i\omega})^{-1} \Sigma \\ \times (I_k - N' e^{i\omega})^{-1} \left[Q'(I_m - P' e^{i\omega})^{-1}, I_k \right]$$

where I_k and I_m are the identity matrices of dimension k and m; see formula (10.4.43) in Hamilton (1994). Two ways to calculate the matrix-valued spectral density for the entire vector of variables $s_t = [x_t', y_t', z_t']'$ are

$$g(\omega) = \begin{bmatrix} I_m & 0_{m,k} \\ Re^{-i\omega} & S \\ 0_{k,m} & I_k \end{bmatrix} f(\omega) \begin{bmatrix} I_m & R' e^{i\omega} & 0_{m,k} \\ 0_{k,m} & S' & I_k \end{bmatrix} = W f(\omega) W'$$

where

$$W = \begin{bmatrix} I_m & 0_{m,k} \\ RP^+ & S - RP^+ Q \\ 0_{k,m} & I_k \end{bmatrix}$$

where P^+ is the pseudo-inverse of P and where the last equality exploits $s_t = W[x_t', z_t']'$, replacing x_{t-1} with $P^+ x_t - P^+ Q z_t$ in the recursive equilibrium law of motion for y_t. The Hodrick–Prescott filter aims to remove a smooth trend τ_t from some given data s_t by solving

$$\min_{\tau_t} \sum_{t=1}^{T} \left((s_t - \tau_t)^2 + \lambda \left((\tau_{t+1} - \tau_t) - (\tau_t - \tau_{t-1}) \right)^2 \right)$$

The solution is a linear lag polynomial $r_t = s_t - \tau_t = h(L) s_t$ which has the transfer function

$$\tilde{h}(\omega) = \frac{4\lambda (1 - \cos(\omega))^2}{1 + 4\lambda (1 - \cos(\omega))^2}$$

(see, King and Rebelo, 1993). Thus, the matrix spectral density of the Hodrick–Prescott filtered vector is simply

$$g_{\mathrm{HP}}(\omega) = \tilde{h}^2(\omega) g(\omega)$$

[20] Some of these methods were originally contained in an early version of Uhlig and Xu (1996), but were eventually deleted from that paper.

from which one can obtain the autocorrelations of r_t in the time domain via an inverse Fourier transformation,

$$\int_{-\pi}^{\pi} g_{\text{HP}}(\omega) e^{\mathrm{i}\omega k} d\omega = E[r_t r'_{t-k}]$$

see formula (10.4.4) in Hamilton (1994). Inverse Fourier transformations are part of many numerical packages.

3.7 Conclusions

We have provided a toolkit to analyse nonlinear dynamic stochastic models easily. The main contribution of this chapter is to simplify and unify existing approaches, showing how to log-linearize the necessary equations characterizing the equilibrium without explicit differentiation, to provide a general solution to a linearized system using the method of undetermined coefficients, allowing in particular for a vector of endogenous states, and to provide simulation-free frequency-domain based method to calculate the model implications in its Hodrick–Prescott filtered version. These methods are easy to use if a numerical package such as MATLAB is available. This chapter should therefore be useful for anybody interested in analysing nonlinear stochastic dynamic models.

3.8 Appendix: Undetermined Coefficients versus Blanchard–Kahn: two examples

The purpose of this appendix is to go through the log-linearization exercise for one model in detail, to solve the model "by hand" and to relate the method of undetermined coefficients to the Blanchard–Kahn approach for the case of saddle-point stability and for the case of indeterminacy.

3.8.1 *Hansen's real business cycle model: saddle-point stability*

The following model is the benchmark real business cycle model due to Hansen (1985) and explained there in detail. Here, the mathematical description shall suffice. The main point of this example, as far as we are concerned, is to explain how to perform the first three steps of the general procedure.

The social planner solves the problem of the representative agent

$$\max E \sum_{t=1}^{\infty} \beta^t \left(\log C_t - AN_t\right)$$

such that

$$\begin{aligned} C_t + K_t &= Y_t + (1-\delta)K_{t-1} \qquad (3.41)\\ Y_t &= Z_t K_{t-1}^{\rho} N_t^{1-\rho} \\ \log Z_t &= (1-\psi)\log \bar{Z} + \psi \log Z_{t-1} + \epsilon_t \end{aligned}$$

where the ϵ_t are independently and identically normally distributed with zero mean and variance σ^2, C_t is consumption, N_t is labour, I_t is investment, Y_t is production, K_t is capital, Z_t is the total factor productivity, and A, β, δ, ρ, $\bar{Z}$, ψ and σ^2 are parameters.

Collapse the first two equations into one, and let Λ_t be its Lagrange multiplier. The first-order conditions are

$$\frac{1}{C_t} = \Lambda_t$$

$$A = \Lambda_t (1 - \rho) \frac{Y_t}{N_t}$$

$$\Lambda_t = \beta E_t \left[\Lambda_{t+1} R_{t+1} \right] \tag{3.42}$$

where

$$R_t = \rho \frac{Y_t}{K_{t-1}} + 1 - \delta \tag{3.43}$$

Note that we wrote the Lagrange multiplier as Λ_t rather than λ_t for the sake of consistency with our notational convention to use lower-case letters for log-deviations. Equation (3.42) is the Lucas (1978) asset pricing equation which typically arises in these models.

In contrast to some of the real business cycle literature and to avoid confusion in the application of the method in Section 3.4, it is very useful to stick to the following *dating convention.* A new date starts with the arrival of new information. If a variable is chosen and/or (eventually) known at date t, it will be indexed with t. Use only variables dated t and $t - 1$ in deterministic equations and variables dated $t + 1$, t and $t - 1$ in equations involving expectations $E_t[\cdot]$.

The steady state for the real business cycle model above is obtained by dropping the time subscripts and stochastic shocks in the equations above, characterizing the equilibrium. Formally, this amounts to finding steady-state values such that $f(0, 0) = 1$ and $g(0, 0) = 1$ in the notation of Section 3.3.[21] For example, equations (3.42) and (3.43) result in

$$1 = \beta \bar{R}$$

$$\bar{R} = \rho \frac{\bar{Y}}{\bar{K}} + 1 - \delta$$

where bars over variables denote steady-state values. One needs to decide what one wants to solve for. If one fixes β and δ, these two equations will imply values for $\bar{R}$ and $\bar{Y}/\bar{K}$. Conversely, one can fix $\bar{R}$ and $\bar{Y}/\bar{K}$ and then these two equations yield values for β and δ. The latter procedure maps observable characteristics of the economy into "deep parameters", and is the essence of calibration; see Kydland and Prescott (1991).

Introduce lower-case letters to denote log-deviations: write

$$C_t = \bar{C} e^{c_t}$$

[21] Alternatively, find the steady state so that (3.3) is satisfied. This is, however, rarely done.

for example. The resource constraint (3.41) then reads

$$\bar{C}e^{c_t} + \bar{K}e^{k_t} = \bar{Y}e^{y_t} + (1-\delta)\bar{K}e^{k_{t-1}}$$

This can be written approximately as

$$\bar{C}(1+c_t) + \bar{K}(1+k_t) = \bar{Y}(1+y_t) + (1-\delta)\bar{K}(1+k_{t-1})$$

Since $\bar{C} + \delta\bar{K} = \bar{Y}$ due to the definition of the steady state, the constant terms drop out[22] and one obtains

$$\bar{C}c_t + \bar{K}k_t = \bar{Y}y_t + (1-\delta)\bar{K}k_{t-1} \tag{3.44}$$

The resource constraint is now stated in terms of percentage deviations: the steady-state levels in this equation rescale the percentage deviations to make them comparable. Note that no explicit differentiation is required to obtain the log-linearized version of the resource constraint: log-linearization is obtained just by using the building blocks described in section 3.3.

Similarly log-linearizating the other equations, one obtains:

#	Equation	Log-linearized version
(i)	$\frac{1}{C_t} = \Lambda_t$	$-c_t = \lambda_t$
(ii)	$A = \Lambda_t(1-\rho)\frac{Y_t}{N_t}$	$n_t = y_t + \lambda_t$
(iii)	$R_t = \rho\frac{Y_t}{K_{t-1}} + 1 - \delta$	$\bar{R}r_t = \rho\frac{\bar{Y}}{\bar{K}}(y_t - k_{t-1})$
(iv)	$Y_t = \bar{Z}e^{z_t}K_{t-1}^{\rho}N_t^{1-\rho}$	$y_t = z_t + \rho k_{t-1} + (1-\rho)n_t$
(v)	$C_t + K_t = Y_t + (1-\delta)K_{t-1}$	$\bar{C}c_t + \bar{K}k_t = \bar{Y}y_t + (1-\delta)\bar{K}k_{t-1}$
(vi)	$\Lambda_t = \beta E_t[\Lambda_{t+1}R_{t+1}]$	$\lambda_t = E_t[\lambda_{t+1} + r_{t+1}]$
(vii)	$\log Z_t = (1-\psi)\log\bar{Z} + \psi\log Z_{t-1} + E_t$	$Z_t = \psi Z_{t-1} + E_t$

The equations are written so that only variables dated t, $t-1$ and expectation at date t of variables dated $t+1$ appear. To find the state variables, one needs to find all (linear combinations of) variables dated $t-1$ in these equations: the endogenous state variable is capital, k_{t-1}, whereas the exogenous state variable is the technology parameter, z_{t-1}. Note that there are as many expectational equations as there are endogenous state variables.

3.8.2 *Simplify*

The coefficients of the equations above need to be collected in the appropriate matrices to restate these equations in the form required for Section 3.4: this is a straightforward

[22] Another way to see that constants can in the end be dropped is to note that the steady state is characterized by $c_t = k_t = y_t = k_{t-1} = 0$. If one replaces all log-deviations with zero, only the constant terms remain, and that equation can be subtracted from the equation for general c_t, k_t, y_t and k_{t-1} above.

exercise. Here, however, we plan to proceed to solve the model "by hand". Aside from a bit of algebra, this turns out to be reasonably easy to do.

Formally, equations (i)–(iv) in their log-linearized form can be solved for c_t, n_t, y_t, r_t in terms of k_t, λ_t and z_t at leads and lags by matrix inversion: the solution can then be used to substitute out these variables in equations (v) and (vi). Doing it by hand proceeds as follows. Replace n_t in (iv) with (ii):

$$y_t = \frac{1}{\rho} z_t + k_{t-1} + \frac{1-\rho}{\rho} \lambda_t$$

Now, eliminate c_t, n_t, y_t, r_t in (v) and (vi). Using the abbreviations

$$\alpha_1 = \frac{\bar{Y}}{\bar{K}} + (1-\delta)$$

$$\alpha_2 = \frac{\bar{C}}{\bar{K}} + \frac{1-\rho}{\rho} \frac{\bar{Y}}{\bar{K}}$$

$$\alpha_3 = \frac{\bar{Y}}{\rho \bar{K}}$$

$$\alpha_4 = 0$$

$$\alpha_5 = 1 + (1-\rho) \frac{\bar{Y}}{\bar{R}\bar{K}}$$

$$\alpha_6 = \frac{\bar{Y}}{\bar{R}\bar{K}}$$

we obtain

$$0 = -k_t + \alpha_1 k_{t-1} + \alpha_2 \lambda_t + \alpha_3 z_t \tag{3.45}$$

$$0 = E_t[-\lambda_t + \alpha_4 k_t + \alpha_5 \lambda_{t+1} + \alpha_6 z_{t+1}] \tag{3.46}$$

(We keep α_4 for later use. Obviously, we could drop it here.)

3.8.3 *Method* 1: *Undetermined coefficients*

Postulate that

$$k_t = \eta_{KK} k_{t-1} + \eta_{Kz} z_t \tag{3.47}$$

$$\lambda_t = \eta_{\lambda K} k_{t-1} + \eta_{\lambda z} z_t \tag{3.48}$$

Note that $\eta_{\lambda K}$ etc. can be interpreted as elasticities: if $k_{t-1} = 0.01$, that is, if K_{t-1} deviates from its steady state by 1 per cent, and $z_t = 0$, then $\lambda_t = 0.01 * \eta_{\lambda K}$, that is, Λ_t

deviates from its steady state by $\eta_{\lambda K}$ per cent. In terms of the notation in Section 3.4:

$$\eta_{\lambda K} = R$$
$$\eta_{\lambda z} = S$$
$$\eta_{KK} = P$$
$$\eta_{Kz} = Q$$

Plug the postulated relationships into equations (3.45) once and (3.46) "twice" and exploit $E_t[z_{t+1}] = \psi z_t$, so that only k_{t-1} and z_t remain:

$$\begin{aligned} 0 &= (-\eta_{KK} + \alpha_1 + \alpha_2\eta_{\lambda K})\, k_{t-1} \\ &\quad + (-\eta_{Kz} + \alpha_2\eta_{\lambda z} + \alpha_3)\, z_t \\ 0 &= (-\eta_{\lambda K} + \alpha_4\eta_{KK} + \alpha_5\eta_{\lambda K}\eta_{KK})\, k_{t-1} \\ &\quad + (-\eta_{\lambda z} + \alpha_4\eta_{Kz} + \alpha_5\eta_{\lambda K}\eta_{Kz} + (\alpha_5\eta_{\lambda z} + \alpha_6)\,\psi)\, z_t \end{aligned}$$

Compare coefficients.

1. On k_{t-1}:

$$\begin{aligned} 0 &= -\eta_{KK} + \alpha_1 + \alpha_2\eta_{\lambda K} \\ 0 &= -\eta_{\lambda K} + \alpha_4\eta_{KK} + \alpha_5\eta_{\lambda K}\eta_{KK} \end{aligned}$$

Solve the first equation for $\eta_{\lambda K}$ and substitute out in the second. One gets the *characteristic quadratic equation*

$$0 = \eta_{KK}^2 - \left(\alpha_1 - \frac{\alpha_2}{\alpha_5}\alpha_4 + \frac{1}{\alpha_5}\right)\eta_{KK} + \frac{\alpha_1}{\alpha_5} \tag{3.49}$$

solvable with the usual formula:

$$\eta_{KK} = \frac{1}{2}\left(\left(\alpha_1 - \frac{\alpha_2}{\alpha_5}\alpha_4 + \frac{1}{\alpha_5}\right) \pm \sqrt{\left(\alpha_1 - \frac{\alpha_2}{\alpha_5}\alpha_4 + \frac{1}{\alpha_5}\right)^2 - 4\frac{\alpha_1}{\alpha_5}}\right) \tag{3.50}$$

Note finally that

$$\eta_{KK,1}\eta_{KK,2} = \frac{\alpha_1}{\alpha_5} = \bar{R} = \frac{1}{\beta}$$

to see that at most one root is stable. Use that one. Calculate $\eta_{\lambda K}$.

2. On z_t:

$$\begin{aligned} 0 &= -\eta_{Kz} + \alpha_2\eta_{\lambda z} + \alpha_3 \\ 0 &= -\eta_{\lambda z} + \alpha_4\eta_{Kz} + \alpha_5\eta_{\lambda K}\eta_{Kz} + (\alpha_5\eta_{\lambda z} + \alpha_6)\,\psi \end{aligned}$$

Given that we already know $\eta_{\lambda K}$, these two equations are two linear equations in $\eta_{\lambda z}$ and η_{Kz}, which can be solved easily:

$$\begin{aligned} \eta_{\lambda_z} &= \frac{\alpha_4\alpha_3 + \alpha_5\eta_{\lambda K}\alpha_3 + \alpha_6\psi}{1 - \alpha_4\alpha_2 - \alpha_5\eta_{\lambda K}\alpha_2 - \alpha_5\psi} \\ \eta_{Kz} &= \alpha_2\eta_{\lambda z} + \alpha_3 \end{aligned}$$

3.8.4 *Method* 2: *Blanchard–Kahn*

This section is inspired by Blanchard and Kahn (1980) as well as the work by Roger Farmer and his colleagues, in particular Farmer (1993). Let ϕ_t be the prediction error in equation (3.46),

$$0 = \phi_{t+1} - (-\lambda_t + \alpha_5 \lambda_{t+1} + \alpha_4 k_t + \alpha_6 z_{t+1}) \tag{3.51}$$

Write this equation together with equation (3.45) and the equation for z_t as a three-variable first-order difference equation,

$$X \begin{bmatrix} k_t \\ \lambda_{t+1} \\ z_{t+1} \end{bmatrix} = Y \begin{bmatrix} k_{t-1} \\ \lambda_t \\ z_t \end{bmatrix} + Z \begin{bmatrix} \epsilon_{t+1} \\ \phi_{t+1} \end{bmatrix} \tag{3.52}$$

where[23]

$$X = \begin{bmatrix} \alpha_4 & \alpha_5 & \alpha_6 \\ 1 & 0 & 0 \\ 0 & 0 & 1 \end{bmatrix}, \qquad Y = \begin{bmatrix} 0 & 1 & 0 \\ \alpha_1 & \alpha_2 & \alpha_3 \\ 0 & 0 & \psi \end{bmatrix}, \qquad Z = \begin{bmatrix} 0 & 1 \\ 0 & 0 \\ 1 & 0 \end{bmatrix} \tag{3.53}$$

Multiply by X^{-1} and diagonalize the matrix $X^{-1}Y$:

$$X^{-1}Y = Q^{-1}\Omega Q$$

where Ω is diagonal,[24] containing the eigenvalues $\omega_1, \omega_2, \omega_3$. To be a little more explicit, note that

$$X^{-1} = \begin{bmatrix} 0 & 1 & 0 \\ 1/\alpha_5 & -\alpha_4/\alpha_5 & -\alpha_6/\alpha_5 \\ 0 & 0 & 1 \end{bmatrix} \tag{3.54}$$

$$X^{-1}Y = \begin{bmatrix} \alpha_1 & \alpha_2 & \alpha_3 \\ -\alpha_1\alpha_4/\alpha_5 & (1-\alpha_2\alpha_4)/\alpha_5 & (-\alpha_3\alpha_4 - \psi\alpha_6)/\alpha_5 \\ 0 & 0 & \psi \end{bmatrix}$$

$$X^{-1}Z = \begin{bmatrix} 0 & 0 \\ -\alpha_6/\alpha_5 & 1/\alpha_5 \\ 1 & 0 \end{bmatrix}$$

In particular, the characteristic equation for the eigenvalues is given by

$$p(\omega) = \left((\alpha_1 - \omega)\left(\frac{1-\alpha_2\alpha_4}{\alpha_5} - \omega \right) + \frac{\alpha_1\alpha_2\alpha_4}{\alpha_5} \right)(\psi - \omega)$$

[23] The notation here differs from the notation in Theorem 3.5.

[24] In general, X may not be invertible, in which case it is better to try to solve a generalized eigenvalue problem. Furthermore, it may be the case that Ω is not diagonalizable. One can then use the QZ method instead; see recent papers by Sims (1999), King and Watson (1995, 1997) and Klein (1998).

Comparing the expression in the first bracket to equation (3.49), we see that one can pick ω_1 to be the explosive root in (3.50), ω_2 to be the stable root in (3.50) and $\omega_3 = \psi$. Let

$$x_t = Q \begin{bmatrix} k_{t-1} \\ \lambda_t \\ z_t \end{bmatrix}, \qquad \zeta_{t+1} = QX^{-1} \begin{bmatrix} \epsilon_{t+1} \\ \phi_{t+1} \end{bmatrix}$$

so that the first-order matrix difference equation can be written in "decoupled" form as

$$\begin{bmatrix} x_{1,t+1} \\ x_{2,t+1} \\ x_{3,t+1} \end{bmatrix} = \begin{bmatrix} \omega_1 & 0 & 0 \\ 0 & \omega_2 & 0 \\ 0 & 0 & \omega_3 \end{bmatrix} \begin{bmatrix} x_{1,t} \\ x_{2,t} \\ x_{3,t} \end{bmatrix} + \begin{bmatrix} \zeta_{1,t+1} \\ \zeta_{2,t+1} \\ \zeta_{3,t+1} \end{bmatrix} \tag{3.55}$$

(To compare this to Farmer, note that he usually calculates ω_i^{-1} as roots λ_i. There is no substantive difference.) What can we learn from this?

1. The first of these three equations can be iterated forward to give

$$\begin{aligned} x_{1,t} &= \omega_1^{-1} x_{1,t+1} - \omega_1^{-1} \zeta_{1,t+1} \\ &= \omega_1^{-2} x_{1,t+2} - \omega_1^{-2} \zeta_{1,t+2} - \omega_1^{-1} \zeta_{1,t+1} \\ &= \dots \\ &= -\sum_{j=1}^{\infty} \omega_1^{-j} \zeta_{1,t+j} \end{aligned}$$

   Taking conditional expectations with respect to t on both sides, we see that

$$x_{1,t} \equiv 0$$

   This thus imposes one linear restriction on the vector $[k_{t-1}, \lambda_t, z_t]'$,

$$0 = Q_{11} k_{t-1} + Q_{12} \lambda_t + Q_{13} z_t$$

   It turns out that this linear restriction can be written as

$$\lambda_t = \eta_{\lambda K} k_{t-1} + \eta_{\lambda z} z_t$$

   with the same coefficients $\eta_{\lambda K}$ and $\eta_{\lambda z}$ as calculated in Section 3.8.3.
2. Furthermore, we obtain

$$\zeta_{1,t+1} = x_{1,t+1} - \omega_1 x_{1,t} \equiv 0$$

   which imposes a linear relationship between the forecast error ϕ_{t+1} and the productivity innovation ϵ_{t+1},

$$0 = (QX^{-1})_{11} \epsilon_{t+1} + (QX^{-1})_{12} \phi_{t+1}$$

   This too turns out to be a restatement of what we have already found in Section 3.8.3: with the decision rules there, one can calculate

$$\begin{aligned} \phi_{t+1} &= (-\lambda_t + \alpha_4 k_t + \alpha_5 \lambda_{t+1} + \alpha_6 z_{t+1}) \\ &\quad - E_t[-\lambda_t + \alpha_4 k_t + \alpha_5 \lambda_{t+1} + \alpha_6 z_{t+1}] \\ &= (\alpha_5 \eta_{\lambda z} + \alpha_6)\, \epsilon_{t+1} \end{aligned}$$

3. Equipped with this knowledge, replace ϕ_{t+1}, λ_t and λ_{t+1} in the second equation in (3.55). Additionally taking conditional expectations with respect to t,[25] this equation in (3.55) now turns out to be rewritable as

$$k_t = \eta_{KK} k_{t-1} + \eta_{Kz} z_t$$

with the coefficients calculated in Section 3.8.3.

4. Finally, the third equation in (3.55) is the original equation

$$z_{t+1} = \psi z_t + \epsilon_{t+1}$$

We see that we re-created the solution found in Section 3.8.3.

3.8.5 *Farmer's model: Indeterminacy*

In Farmer's (1993) model, there are decreasing returns at the firm level but increasing returns in the aggregate: the aggregate production function is given by

$$Y_t = Z_t K_{t-1}^{\mu} N_t^{\nu}$$

whereas the factors capital and labour receive the shares $\tilde{\mu}$ and $\tilde{\nu}$. In addition, the instantaneous utility function is given by

$$\log C_t - A \frac{N_t^{1+\chi}}{1+\chi}$$

with $\chi \geq 0$. Finally, there is a time trend in log-productivity growth, which introduces a factor γ in some equations. The model in Section 3.8.1 is the special case

$$\rho = \mu = 1 - \nu = \tilde{\mu} = 1 - \tilde{\nu}, \qquad \chi = 0, \qquad \gamma = 1$$

and hence,

$$\frac{1+\chi}{1+\chi-\nu} = \frac{1}{\rho}$$

Collecting the equations for Farmer's model, one obtains the following:

#	Equation	Log-linearized
(i)	$\frac{1}{C_t} = \Lambda_t$	$-c_t = \lambda_t$
(ii)	$AN_t^{\chi} = \Lambda_t \tilde{\nu} \frac{Y_t}{N_t}$	$(1+\chi) n_t = y_t + \lambda_t$
(iii)	$R_t = \tilde{\mu} \frac{Y_t}{K_{t-1}} + 1 - \delta$	$\bar{R} r_t = \tilde{\mu} \frac{\bar{Y}}{\bar{K}} (y_t - k_{t-1})$
(iv)	$Y_t = \bar{Z} e^{z_t} K_{t-1}^{\mu} N_t^{\nu}$	$y_t = z_t + \mu k_{t-1} + \nu n_t$
(v)	$C_t + \gamma K_t = Y_t + (1-\delta) K_{t-1}$	$\bar{C} c_t + \gamma \bar{K} k_t = \bar{Y}\, y_t + (1-\delta) \bar{K} k_{t-1}$
(vi)	$\Lambda_t = \frac{\beta}{\gamma} E_t[\Lambda_{t+1} R_{t+1}]$	$\lambda_t = E_t[\lambda_{t+1} + r_{t+1}]$
(vii)	$\log Z_t = (1-\psi) \log \bar{Z} + \psi \log Z_{t-1} + E_t$	$Z_t = \psi Z_{t-1} + E_t$

[25]Note that k_t is chosen at date t, and thus it cannot depend on information dated $t+1$ or later. Regardless of the timing convention for the subscript of k_t, this has to be true. For this reason, the notation k_t rather than k_{t+1} for the capital stock chosen at date t may be preferable.

As before, use (ii) to replace n_t in (iv), yielding

$$y_t = \frac{1+\chi}{1+\chi-\nu} z_t + \frac{\mu(1+\chi)}{1+\chi-\nu} k_{t-1} + \frac{\nu}{1+\chi-\nu} \lambda_t$$

and as before, reduce the remaining equations to the two-equation system (3.45) and (3.46), where now

$$\alpha_1 = \frac{\mu(1+\chi)}{1+\chi-\nu} \frac{\bar{Y}}{\gamma\bar{K}} + \frac{1-\delta}{\gamma}$$

$$\alpha_2 = \frac{\bar{C}}{\gamma\bar{K}} + \frac{\nu}{1+\chi-\nu} \frac{\bar{Y}}{\gamma\bar{K}}$$

$$\alpha_3 = \frac{1+\chi}{1+\chi-\nu} \frac{\bar{Y}}{\gamma\bar{K}}$$

$$\alpha_4 = \left(\frac{\mu(1+\chi)}{1+\chi-\nu} - 1 \right) \frac{\tilde{\mu}\bar{Y}}{\bar{R}\bar{K}}$$

$$\alpha_5 = 1 + \frac{\tilde{\mu}\nu}{1+\chi-\nu} \frac{\bar{Y}}{\bar{R}\bar{K}}$$

$$\alpha_6 = \frac{\tilde{\mu}(1+\chi)}{1+\chi-\nu} \frac{\bar{Y}}{\bar{R}\bar{K}}$$

3.8.6 *Undetermined coefficients: A first try*

One could try to solve this model with the method of undetermined coefficients just as in Section 3.8.3. So, let us postulate the law of motion (3.48), (3.47) and see what we get. As before, we get the characteristic equation (3.49) with the two solutions given by equation (3.50). Since Hansen's model is contained as a special case, we may again get one stable and one unstable root and then we can proceed to the complete solution as above in Section 3.8.3. However, there is now no longer a guarantee that at most one root is stable. In fact, the whole point of Farmer's investigation is to provide a model in which both roots are stable. So, what should one do? Should one just pick one of the two roots in some arbitrary manner? Or does one need to start from another law of motion? We will come back to answer these questions in Section 3.8.8.

3.8.7 *Blanchard–Kahn*

It may be helpful to take a look first at what the Blanchard–Kahn method delivers. As before, introduce ϕ with equation (3.51), and write equations (3.45) and (3.46) as equation (3.52) with the matrices as in (3.53). We proceed in the same manner and get to equation (3.55). If exactly one of the roots ω_i is greater than unity, we can proceed as before. But the interesting case is now that in which $|\omega_i| < 1$.[26] In that case, we must

[26] In fact, some roots may even be complex-valued. This can impose some restrictions: obviously, we want the economic variables to be real-valued. The principle is that a real-valued characteristic polynomial will always give rise to pairs of *conjugate* complex roots, if it gives rise to complex roots at all. It is then important that either both roots of such a pair are carried along in the calculations or both are eliminated. This usually assures that all economic variables remain real-valued.

iterate all three equations "backwards". A simpler way to state this is that equation (3.52) is already the correct forward dynamics of the model,

$$\begin{bmatrix} k_t \\ \lambda_{t+1} \\ z_{t+1} \end{bmatrix} = X^{-1}Y \begin{bmatrix} k_{t-1} \\ \lambda_t \\ z_t \end{bmatrix} + X^{-1}Z \begin{bmatrix} \epsilon_{t+1} \\ \phi_{t+1} \end{bmatrix} \tag{3.56}$$

provided ϕ_{t+1} is such that k_t does *not* depend on information dated $t + 1$ or beyond. Put differently, ϕ_{t+1} must be such that

$$0 = (X^{-1}Z)_{11}\epsilon_{t+1} + (X^{-1}Z)_{12}\phi_{t+1} \tag{3.57}$$

Check equation (3.54): since $(X^{-1}Z)_{11} = (X^{-1}Z)_{12} = 0$, equation (3.57) imposes *no* restrictions on ϕ_{t+1}. In particular, we see the following:

1. There is now a second, "artificial" state variable λ_t. Obviously, while λ_t has always been in the information set when choosing λ_{t+1}, that information was "irrelevant" before in Hansen's model: the only dynamic linkage between periods came from capital k_t and from productivity z_t. Put differently: sometimes the state variables may not be what you think they should be!
2. There is no longer some linear restriction on the relationship between ϵ_{t+1} and ϕ_{t+1}. Thus, ϕ_{t+1} can be "anything" (as long as it satisfies $E_t[\phi_{t+1}] = 0$). In economic terms, ϕ_{t+1} introduces *sunspots*, *self-fulfilling prophecies* or *animal spirits*. In particular, agents may "co-ordinate" on the random variable ϵ_{t+1}, $\phi_{t+1} = \tau\epsilon_{t+1}$ for some coefficient τ: any value for τ is legitimate! This creates an *endogenous* sunspot.

3.8.8 *Undetermined coefficients: A second try*

With an eye on the Blanchard–Kahn approach, we see that we need as many state variables as there are stable roots. One interesting special case is the solution in which λ_{t+1} is *predetermined*, that is, already known[27] at date t. That case can now be solved with the method of undetermined coefficients by postulating the law of motion,

$$\begin{aligned} \lambda_{t+1} &= \eta_{\lambda K}k_{t-1} + \eta_{\lambda\lambda}\lambda_t + \eta_{\lambda z}z_t \\ k_t &= \eta_{KK}k_{t-1} + \eta_{K\lambda}\lambda_t + \eta_{Kz}z_t \end{aligned}$$

Note what happened compared to equations (3.48) and (3.47):

1. There is a second state variable, which we simply pick[28] to be λ.
2. The decision rule is now for λ_{t+1} rather than λ_t, since λ_{t+1} is now postulated to be predetermined.

[27] Blanchard and Kahn introduced the term "predetermined". Thus, both λ_{t+1} and k_t are now predetermined. This terminology can be useful but can also be confusing. A better way may be to think of some variables to be known at date t and others at date $t+1$ etc., and to use the subscripts in a manner consistent with that. Unfortunately, it can be the case that a linear combinations of some variables is already known at date t, whereas the variables individually are only known at date $t + 1$.

[28] In general, some variables may turn out to be unsuitable candidates as additional state variables.

The solution for the undetermined coefficients is simple: compare the equations above with equation (3.56) to see that the coefficients are given directly by the appropriate coefficients in $X^{-1}Y$. Also note that we implicitly picked ϕ_{t+1} to satisfy

$$0 = (X^{-1}Z)_{21}\epsilon_{t+1} + (X^{-1}Z)_{22}\phi_{t+1}$$

or, with equation (3.54),

$$\phi_{t+1} = \alpha_6 \epsilon_{t+1}$$

To introduce sunspots into the solution as well, one can proceed as follows. Distinguish between λ_{t+1}, known at date $t+1$, and $\lambda_t^e = E_t[\lambda_{t+1}]$. In addition to the two equations (3.45) and (3.46), we now have a third equation

$$\lambda_t^e = E_t[\lambda_{t+1}] \tag{3.58}$$

Introduce a "sunspot" random variable θ_{t+1} with $E_t[\theta_{t+1}] = 0$. Regard λ_t^e as the additional state variable and postulate

$$\begin{aligned}
\lambda_t^e &= \eta_{\lambda^e K} k_{t-1} + \eta_{\lambda^e \lambda^e} \lambda_{t-1}^e + \eta_{\lambda^e z} z_t + \eta_{\lambda^e \theta} \theta_t \\
k_t &= \eta_{KK} k_{t-1} + \eta_{K\lambda^e} \lambda_{t-1}^e + \eta_{Kz} z_t + \eta_{K\theta} \theta_t \\
\lambda_t &= \eta_{\lambda K} k_{t-1} + \eta_{K\lambda^e} \lambda_{t-1}^e + \eta_{\lambda z} z_t + \eta_{\lambda\theta} \theta_t
\end{aligned}$$

and solve by the method of undetermined coefficients. Note that this is legitimate whether we have one or two stable roots from (3.50): so we shall proceed with both in mind. Since θ_t is not a fundamental shock, the scale of its coefficients will be undetermined. Thus, normalize by setting $\eta_{\lambda\theta} = 1$. That way,

$$\theta_t = \lambda_t - \lambda_{t-1}^e$$

is the forecast error in λ_t. Comparison with equations (3.56) and (3.54) reveals that

$$\begin{aligned}
\theta_{t+1} &= (X^{-1}Z)_{21}\epsilon_{t+1} + (X^{-1}Z)_{22}\phi_{t+1} \\
&= \frac{-\alpha_6}{\alpha_5}\epsilon_{t+1} + \frac{1}{\alpha_5}\phi_{t+1}
\end{aligned}$$

Equation (3.58) turns out to deliver

$$\eta_{\lambda K} = 0, \qquad \eta_{\lambda\lambda^e} = 1, \qquad \eta_{\lambda z} = 0$$

To proceed further, distinguish between the saddle-point stable case and the case of two stable roots:

1. If there is one stable and one unstable root, it turns out that

   $$\eta_{\lambda^e\lambda^e} = \eta_{K\lambda^e} = 0$$

   In words, even though a second state variable was added, the method of undetermined coefficients eliminates it automatically. Furthermore, there will be tight relationship between θ_{t+1} and ϵ_{t+1}.

2. If there are two stable roots, $\eta_{\lambda^e\lambda^e}$ and $\eta_{K\lambda^e}$ are no longer zero. Furthermore, because $(X^{-1}Z)_{11} = (X^{-1}Z)_{12} = 0$, there no longer will be a tight relationship between θ_{t+1} and ϵ_{t+1}, indicating the admissibility of a sunspot.

So, with the rule that one needs (at least) as many state variables as there are stable roots, the method of undetermined coefficients can be used fairly simply for the case of two stable roots as well, if one is only interested in the solution in which λ_{t+1} is "predetermined" at date t. Introducing sunspots requires a little more work, and, at least for this simple model, the Blanchard–Kahn approach seems clearer and more straightforward. On the other hand, the method of undetermined coefficients seems more straightforward for the saddle-point stable case. So it is useful to know about both.

3.8.9 *Final remarks*

The method of undetermined coefficients is particularly useful if the economy is saddle-point stable. Sometimes, however, there are "too many" stable roots. The method of undetermined coefficients can still be used then. Sunspot solutions may arise.

3.9 Appendix: Description of the MATLAB programs

Here we will describe some MATLAB programs to carry out the calculations for Sections 3.4 and 3.6.

The easiest way to learn about these programs is to store all of them, start MATLAB from the directory where they are stored and type "readme". This will execute the **readme.m** file, providing some documentation.

As the time of writing, the newest version of the files is version 2. To see how version 2 files differ from the previous version, distributed until spring 1997, type "whatsnew" within MATLAB, which executes the file **whatsnew.m**, printing relevant messages as a result. To see quickly how these files work, start MATLAB and type "exampl0" to calculate through example 0, which is the stochastic neoclassical growth model, or type "exampl1" to calculate through example 1, which is Hansen's (1985) real business cycle model of Section 3.8.1, linearized slightly differently. There are more examples, enumerated as "examplNN", where NN stands for their number. To see what any particular example, say, **exampl1.m**, does, type "help exampl1" within MATLAB. Use the example files as templates for your own work. Alternatively, declare all required matrices and type "do_it" to do all calculations. All the **examplNN.m** files call **do_it.m** at the very end.

The files which perform all the calculations (i.e. all the files aside from the **examplNN.m** files, the **readme.m** file and the **whatsnew.m** file) are as follows:

do_it.m does it all, once all needed matrices are defined. This file calls all the other programs. Thus, examining this file will tell you in which sequence all the other calculations are performed.

enlarge.m allows you to manipulate letter sizes on plots and other properties of plots. Useful for producing slides or plots for publication.

impresp.m calculates and shows impulse responses to shocks (see Section 3.6).

mom_out.m produces output. To be called after **moments.m**.

moments.m calculates second moment properties (see Section 3.6).

options.m sets the options for all programs. It is called by **do_it.m** and needs to be called if one of the following routines is used in isolation.

sol_out.m produces output. To be called after **solve.m**.

solve.m solves for the recursive equilibrium law of motion with the theorems of Section 3.4.

All files are extensively documented. Type, say, "help impresp" in MATLAB to get more information on what the program **impresp.m** does. Note that these files set some additional variables, which you may have used before: thus, be careful not to use names appearing in the programs. If you have a question, please read this chapter and the documentation carefully. These files are provided as a free service, without technical support. However, if there are serious flaws or serious ways to improve on these programs, I would like to hear about them. Feel free to copy and modify these files, and use them at your own risk. There is absolutely no guarantee that they work as intended.

4

SOLVING NONLINEAR RATIONAL EXPECTATIONS MODELS BY EIGENVALUE–EIGENVECTOR DECOMPOSITIONS

Alfonso Novales, Emilio Domínguez, Javier J. Pérez, and Jesús Ruiz[1]

4.1 Introduction

We discuss in this chapter the main issues involved in practical applications of solution methods that have been proposed for rational expectations models, based on eigenvalue–eigenvector decompositions. Methods to solve linear stochastic difference equations under rationality of expectations go back to at least Blanchard and Kahn (1980) and have been studied by many authors ever since; for general surveys, see Whiteman (1983), the special issue of Vol. 8 of the *Journal of Business and Economic Statistics* (1990), Marcet (1993) or Danthine and Donaldson (1995). Our presentation relies heavily on Sims (1998), who has extended the existing practice in important directions that are discussed in this chapter. Although, strictly speaking, the methods apply exactly to systems of linear equations, the extension to computing an approximate solution to nonlinear rational expectations models is straightforward.

In this solution approach, each conditional expectation and the associated expectation error are treated as additional endogenous variables and an equation is added to the model, defining the expectation error. The numerical solution is in the form of a set of time series for all variables in the model economy, including all the conditional expectations and the associated expectations errors. In addition, as a by-product, an approximate characterization of the analytical dependence between expectations errors and structural shocks is obtained. Since it produces time series for the expectations errors, it allows for the possibility of multiple tests of the rationality hypothesis in the form of: lack of serial correlation in one-step-ahead expectations errors; a specific moving average structure for expectations errors of a given function at different horizons; and orthogonality between errors of expectations made at time t and variables in the information set available at that time, in the form of the accuracy test in den Haan and Marcet (1994). Numerical solutions to rational expectations errors are hardly ever tested along these directions. Precisely because so much emphasis has been given to rationality as the benchmark when dealing with uncertainty in economic environments where agents solve optimization problems, it is quite surprising that so little attention has been paid to testing for the nature of the computed solution.

[1]Correspondence addresses: Alfonso Novales, Universidad Complutense de Madrid, Departamento de Economía Cuantitativa, Campus de Somosaguas, 28223 Madrid, Spain; Emilio Domínguez, Universidad Pública de Navarra, Departamento de Economía, Campus de Arrosadía, 31006 Pamplona (Navarra), Spain; Javier J. Pérez, Universidad Complutense de Madrid, Departamento de Economía Cuantitativa, Campus de Somosaguas, 28223 Madrid, Spain; Jesús Ruiz, Universidad Europea de Madrid, Departamento de Fundamentos del Análisis Económico, Madrid, Spain.

Since the solution method applies to any given set of (possibly nonlinear) stochastic difference equations, the method is not restricted to dealing with the planning problems we concentrate on in this chapter. It can equally well handle situations in which distortionary taxation, externalities, indivisibilities, public goods, etc., lead to decentralized allocation of resources which are inefficient. For applications of a very different nature, see Sims (1994; 1998).

Economic models usually place bounds on the rates of growth of specific variables or linear combinations of variables. Well-known cases are standard planner's problems, in which state variables and their shadow prices cannot grow too fast in order for transversality conditions to hold and objective functions to be bounded. Methods based on eigenvalue–eigenvector decompositions rest on the use of stability conditions guaranteeing that the resulting solution satisfies the upper bounds on growth rates implied by underlying economic theory. In the simple applications we discuss, the stability conditions are obtained by imposing orthogonality between each eigenvector associated with an unstable eigenvalue in the decomposition of the linear system and the vector of variables in it. However, in more complex models, stability conditions will adopt a different form (for a more general version of stability conditions, see Sims, 1998). The *stability conditions* link decisions to state variables and exogenous shocks. They can sometimes be written to represent some decision variables as functions of states and exogenous variables. Together with other relations in the system, they characterize how optimal decisions are made and can therefore be interpreted as *decision rules*. In some other cases, they will represent relationships between prices and states and exogenous variables, having therefore the interpretation of *pricing rules*.

Different solution methods for nonlinear models differ in: the way they characterize the stable solution manifold; the computation of the expectations in the model, the amount of information they provide on them; and the amount of nonlinearity that they preserve when computing the numerical solution. In our case, the application of the eigenvalue–eigenvector decomposition method to nonlinear models requires constructing a linear approximation to the model around the steady state, from which to derive the stability conditions. They are then added to the original nonlinear model to compute a numerical solution. Even though the actual nonlinear structure of the model is used to produce the numerical solution, the set of stability conditions is obtained from a linear approximation, which introduces some numerical error. The approximation error that is introduced by the specific computational details of a particular solution approach will always end up being absorbed by the expectations errors, which is why testing for rationality should be considered a crucial component of a reported numerical solution.

The details we provide should be enough to allow the application of the solution method to simple environments. As more interesting and complex models begin to be considered, rather more technical considerations are bound to arise. These more technical aspects emerge because stochastic nonlinear quadratic dynamic control problems under the assumption of rationality are hard to solve: rationality of expectations imposes very tight restrictions, which can either lead to non-existence of solutions, or to a difficult process of computation of the solutions, if they exist. In addition, the existence of state variables that accumulate over time will generally tend to produce unstable paths, which would violate the transversality conditions of the problem or the more general restrictions on growth rates that may exist. That motivates the consideration of stability conditions in this approach as a crucial part of solving a model. The need to guarantee stability is also present in deterministic problems, as we review in Section 4.2, but it becomes more complex in stochastic models. Solution methods will increasingly have to be able to accommodate these issues.

In Section 4.2 we review how a numerical solution can be derived for the standard deterministic Cass–Koopmans–Brock–Mirman economy, pointing out the relevance of stability conditions. In Section 4.3 we summarize the general structure used to solve linear rational expectations models and its extension to nonlinear models. In Section 4.4 we apply the solution method to Hansen's (1985) model of indivisible labour, which is also used as an illustration in other chapters of this book. Comparisons with other solution approaches are discussed in Section 4.5. In Section 4.6 we show how the eigenvalue–eigenvector decomposition can help to separately identify variables of a similar nature, as is the case when physical capital and inventories are inputs in an aggregate production technology. Section 4.7 shows how the solution method can be adapted to deal with endogenous growth models. The chapter closes with a summary.

4.2 Stability conditions and the initial choice of control variables in deterministic growth models

This section is a reminder to the reader that: (i) stability conditions are also needed in standard deterministic models to guarantee that transversality conditions will hold; and (ii) as is the case in stochastic applications, the stability conditions in deterministic models are given by the left eigenvectors corresponding to the unstable eigenvalues of the linear approximation to the model economy.

Let us consider the deterministic version of the standard Cass–Koopmans–Brock–Mirman planner's problem in an economy with decreasing returns to scale in physical capital and labour, but constant returns in the aggregate. In this economy, the only sustainable steady state is with zero growth for all per-capita variables. It is well known that the model has a *saddle-point* structure, so that in the consumption–capital stock plane there is a single trajectory taking the economy towards its steady state. Given an initial stock of capital k_0, an initial choice of consumption other than that corresponding to k_0 on the stable manifold will lead the economy to diverge from its steady state. Furthermore, optimality requires staying on the stable manifold for ever, so stability and optimality are in this simple model two sides of the same coin.

The model is usually formulated in continuous time, in which the specific issues dealing with time series generation do not arise. Let us suppose a constant relative risk aversion utility of consumption for the representative agent $U(c_t) = (c_t^{1-\sigma} - 1)/(1-\sigma)$, $\sigma > 0$. Labour is supplied inelastically, since leisure is not an argument in the utility function. Physical capital is subject to a depreciation rate of δ. Population growth could be easily incorporated into the model. The planner's problem in the Cass–Koopmans–Brock–Mirman economy is characterized by the intertemporal first-order condition that links the marginal rate of substitution of consumption over time to the marginal product of capital, the law of motion of the capital stock, and the transversality condition:

$$\frac{c_t^{\sigma}}{c_{t-1}^{\sigma}} = \beta\left(f'(k_{t-1}) + (1-\delta)\right) \tag{4.1}$$

$$k_t = (1-\delta)k_{t-1} + f(k_{t-1}) - c_t \tag{4.2}$$

$$\lim_{\tau\to\infty} \beta^{t+\tau} c_{t+\tau}^{-\sigma} k_{t+\tau} = 0$$

Equations (4.1) and (4.2) can be approximated around steady-state values of consumption and capital, c_{ss} and k_{ss}:

$$\begin{pmatrix} k_t - k_{ss} \\ c_t - c_{ss} \end{pmatrix} = \begin{pmatrix} a_{11} & a_{12} \\ a_{21} & a_{22} \end{pmatrix} \begin{pmatrix} k_{t-1} - k_{ss} \\ c_{t-1} - c_{ss} \end{pmatrix} \tag{4.3}$$

Using the standard decomposition of the A matrix of coefficients in the linear system (4.3), $A = \Gamma\Lambda\Gamma^{-1}$, (where Λ has the eigenvalues of A along the diagonal and zeros elsewhere, Γ has as columns the right-eigenvectors of A, and Γ^{-1} has as rows the left-eigenvectors of A), we can represent the dynamics of the solution from starting values k_0, c_0 as:[2]

$$\begin{aligned}\begin{pmatrix} k_t - k_{ss} \\ c_t - c_{ss} \end{pmatrix} &= \begin{pmatrix} x_1 & y_1 \\ x_2 & y_2 \end{pmatrix} \begin{pmatrix} \lambda_1 & 0 \\ 0 & \lambda_2 \end{pmatrix} \begin{pmatrix} u_1 & v_1 \\ u_2 & v_2 \end{pmatrix} \begin{pmatrix} k_{t-1} - k_{ss} \\ c_{t-1} - c_{ss} \end{pmatrix} \\ &= \begin{pmatrix} x_1 & y_1 \\ x_2 & y_2 \end{pmatrix} \begin{pmatrix} \lambda_1^t & 0 \\ 0 & \lambda_2^t \end{pmatrix} \begin{pmatrix} u_1 & v_1 \\ u_2 & v_2 \end{pmatrix} \begin{pmatrix} k_0 - k_{ss} \\ c_0 - c_{ss} \end{pmatrix} \end{aligned} \tag{4.4}$$

That the model has a saddle-point structure is reflected in the fact that one of the eigenvalues, λ_1, say, is greater than 1 in absolute value, while λ_2 is less[3] than 1.

The matrix product in the previous expression is:

$$\begin{pmatrix} k_t - k_{ss} \\ c_t - c_{ss} \end{pmatrix} = \begin{pmatrix} x_1\lambda_1^t(u_1(k_0 - k_{ss}) + v_1(c_0 - c_{ss})) \\ + y_1\lambda_2^t(u_2(k_0 - k_{ss}) + v_2(c_0 - c_{ss})) \\ x_2\lambda_1^t(u_1(k_0 - k_{ss}) + v_1(c_0 - c_{ss})) \\ + y_2\lambda_2^t(u_2(k_0 - k_{ss}) + v_2(c_0 - c_{ss})) \end{pmatrix}$$

and the transversality condition on the capital stock will hold only if the coefficient on the unstable eigenvalue, λ_1, is set equal to zero. But x_1 depends on the values of the

[2] The right eigenvectors are $(x_1, x_2) = (1, (\lambda_1 - a_{11})/a_{12})$ and $(y_1, y_2) = (1, (\lambda_2 - a_{11})/a_{12})$, and the inverse matrix is:

$$\begin{pmatrix} u_1 & v_1 \\ u_2 & v_2 \end{pmatrix} = \begin{pmatrix} x_1 & y_1 \\ x_2 & y_2 \end{pmatrix}^{-1} = \frac{1}{x_1y_2 - x_2y_1}\begin{pmatrix} y_2 & -y_1 \\ -x_2 & x_1 \end{pmatrix}$$

[3] As we will see later on, the critical rate of growth below which the solution is stable is model-specific. The requirement for a well-defined solution to exist is that the objective function remains bounded, which will require upper bounds on its variable arguments. These bounds will depend on the functional form of the objective function. Sometimes transversality conditions take care of that. In other cases, transversality conditions may be needed for feasibility or optimality even when the objective function is bounded, so that extra upper bounds on growth rates will then need to be added, to guarantee that transversality conditions hold.

structural parameters, and cannot be chosen to be zero. So, it is the bracketed term accompanying λ_1^t which will be zero. *This condition is the same for the capital stock and consumption equations*: $u_1(k_0 - k_{ss}) + v_1(c_0 - c_{ss}) = 0$, so that stability requires that initial consumption be chosen by:

$$c_0 - c_{ss} = -(k_0 - k_{ss})\frac{u_1}{v_1} = (k_0 - k_{ss})\frac{y_2}{y_1} = (k_0 - k_{ss})\frac{\lambda_2 - a_{11}}{a_{12}}$$

which implies that, from then on,

$$\begin{aligned} k_t - k_{ss} &= y_1\lambda_2^t(u_2(k_0 - k_{ss}) + v_2(c_0 - c_{ss})) \\ c_t - c_{ss} &= y_2\lambda_2^t(u_2(k_0 - k_{ss}) + v_2(c_0 - c_{ss})) = \frac{y_2}{y_1}(k_t - k_{ss}) \\ &= \frac{\lambda_2 - a_{11}}{a_{12}}(k_t - k_{ss}) \end{aligned}$$

so that *the same condition between the deviations from steady state of the capital stock and consumption will hold at each point in time as at time* 0. This is the approximate linear representation of the stable manifold for this problem. Precisely because the condition will actually hold for every t, the model can be solved using this condition and just one of the first-order conditions (4.1), (4.2). *The condition which is not used will hold each period.* The stability condition above can be written as the inner product $(y_2, -y_1)(k_0 - k_{ss}, c_0 - c_{ss})' = 0$, where $(y_2, -y_1)$, is the left eigenvector of A associated with the unstable root, λ_1.

Therefore, in deterministic models, the stability conditions can be seen as picking the *stable* initial values of the decision variables, as functions of the given initial values of the states. If we have fewer stability conditions than decision variables in the system,[4] we will just be able to solve the model as a function of a given (arbitrary) starting value for one (or more) decision variables. In that case, given a vector of state variables, a whole continuum of initial decisions will take us to the steady state, and the solution is *indeterminate*, in the sense of Benhabib and Perli (1994) and Xie (1994). On the other hand, the system does not have a solution when there are more independent stability conditions than control variables to be chosen. The stable subspace will then reduce to the steady state, if it exists, and the economy will be globally *unstable*, getting into divergent paths as soon as it experiences even minimum deviations from its steady state. Finally, the solution will be *unique* when the set of stability conditions can be used to represent all the control variables as functions of the state and exogenous variables, the system of equations having a unique solution.

The single stability condition we have described for the Cass–Koopmans–Brock–Mirman economy is very similar to the stability conditions we will compute in stochastic models in the following sections to guarantee that the conditional expectations version of the transversality conditions will hold.

[4] After using equations that involve only contemporaneous values of control variables to eliminate some control variables from the problem.

4.3 An overview of the solution strategy

Recently, Sims (1998) has generalized the work of Blanchard and Kahn (1980) in several directions, proposing a general discussion of the problem of solving stochastic linear rational expectations models:

$$\Gamma_0 y_t = \Gamma_1 y_{t-1} + C + \Psi z_t + \Pi \eta_t \tag{4.5}$$

where C is a vector of constants, y_t is the vector of variables determined in the model (other than expectations errors), z_t is a vector of innovations in exogenous variables, and η_t is a vector of rational expectations errors, satisfying $E_t(\eta_{t+1}) = 0$.

Models with more lags can be accommodated by adding as new variables first-order lags of already included variables, as is standard in dynamic representations. On the other hand, additional expectations variables can be introduced so that the resulting expectations errors are all one period ahead. Models with more lags, lagged expectations, or expectations of more distant future values can be accommodated by defining variables at intermediate steps, and enlarging the y vector.

The core of the procedure consists of defining each conditional expectation as a new variable and adding to the model the associated expectations error and the equation defining the error. Taking arbitrary initial conditions y_0 and using (4.5) to generate a set of time series for the variables in y_t, conditional on sample realizations for z_t, will generally lead to unstable paths, which will violate the transversality conditions unless stability conditions are added to the system. These conditions are defined by the eigenvectors associated with unstable eigenvalues of the matrices in (4.5), although the structure of the stability conditions is generally model-specific. When Γ_0 is invertible we compute the eigenvalues of $\Gamma_0^{-1}\Gamma_1$, while when Γ_0 is singular we need to compute the generalized eigenvalues of the pair (Γ_0, Γ_1).

The vector y_t includes the variables in the model with the more advanced subindices, as well as the conditional expectations in the model, which are redefined as new variables. All of them are determined in the system. They may be decision variables for an economic agent, such as consumption, the stock of capital, real balances, real debt, leisure or hours of work; or variables which are determined as a function of them, such as prices or interest rates. Also included in y_t are variables which are exogenous to the agents but follow laws of motion which have been added to the system, as may happen with some policy variables or exogenous random shocks. The vector z_t contains variables which are determined outside the system, like policy variables which we have not endogenized and do not show any serial correlation, or the innovations in policy variables or in the exogenous random shocks.[5] These can be either *demand shocks*, such as those affecting the individual's preferences or government expenditures, *supply shocks*, affecting the ability to produce commodities, or *errors in controlling* government policy variables. When they are not white noise, the exogenous shocks themselves are included in y_t. For instance, the standard autoregression for a productivity shock, $\log(\theta_t) = \rho\log(\theta_{t-1}) + \epsilon_t$, will lead to a component of y_t being $\log(\theta_t)$, while ϵ_t will

[5] Variables in z_t are independent: if two exogenous shocks are related, the linear approximation to their relationship will be added to the system; one of them will be in z_t while the other will be included in y_t.

be a component of z_t. The vector η_t contains the rational expectations errors, which will be solved for endogenously, together with the state and decision variables in the model.

The solution method can also be applied to obtain approximate solutions to a set of stochastic nonlinear difference equations, as in the applications we present in this chapter. To do so, we start by computing the linear approximation around the steady state of the set of nonlinear equations so that, without loss of generality, we can consider the vector of constants C to be zero.[6] After appropriately redefining variables, the matrices Γ_0 and Γ_1 in the linear approximation to a nonlinear model contain: the partial derivatives of each equation of the system with respect to each of the variables in y_t, evaluated at the steady state; and rows of ones and zeros, corresponding to intermediate variables which have been added to the system to make it a first-order autoregression in the presence of higher-order lags, or higher-order expectations. In this case, (4.5) will approximate the set of decision rules, budget constraints, policy rules and laws of motion for the exogenous variables, and all variables will be expressed as deviations from their steady-state values. The stability conditions are then obtained in this linear approximation, but the original, nonlinear model is used to generate the solution, in the form of a set of time series realizations for all the variables in the economy, including the expectations that appear in the original system and the associated expectations errors.

In this chapter we describe how to apply this method to relatively simple problems, and explain how to use it to simulate nonlinear rational expectations models emerging from optimizing behaviour on the part of economic agents. The reader interested in a complete discussion of the technical and practical aspects of the solution method for linear models should read Sims (1998), which gives detailed account of the arguments that apply to a more general class of problems than those we consider here. Sims's paper also contains a detailed explanation of a variety of unproved claims that we make in this chapter. Where possible, we employ the same notation as in his paper to facilitate references to it.

The methods used to characterize the stability conditions differ depending on whether or not Γ_0 in (4.5) is invertible. If a singular Γ_0 matrix is obtained, then a slightly more general procedure will be needed. We will examine both cases in the following sections.

4.4 Solving a standard stochastic growth model

We start by describing some practical details of the implementation of the solution method to Hansen's (1985; 1997) model with indivisible labour which is considered in other chapters of this volume (see, for instance, Chapter 3). In the linear approximation to this model the Γ_0 matrix is invertible. Numerical solutions to the more straightforward growth model with productivity shocks but no labour or leisure decisions, the other benchmark used in this volume, can easily be derived as a special case of the discussion in this section.

Given an initial value of the capital stock, k_0, let us assume that the representative household chooses sequences of consumption, employment and capital stock that solve

[6] In a later section we will also consider the case when the levels of the variables are not constant in steady state, as is the case in endogenous growth models.

the problem

$$\max_{\{k_t, c_t, N_t\}_{t=1}^{\infty}} E_0 \sum_{t=1}^{\infty} \beta^{t-1} \left[\frac{c_t^{1-\sigma} - 1}{1-\sigma} - A_N N_t \right] \tag{4.6}$$

subject to

$$-c_t - k_t + (1-\delta)k_{t-1} + \theta_t k_{t-1}^{\alpha} N_t^{1-\alpha} = 0$$
$$-\log(\theta_t) + \rho \log(\theta_{t-1}) + \epsilon_t = 0$$

given k_0, θ_0, where N_t denotes the number of hours devoted to the production of the consumption commodity, A_N measures the relative disutility of working hours and the innovation ϵ_t in the productivity process is assumed to be $N(0, \sigma_\epsilon)$. After forming the Lagrangian and eliminating the Lagrange multipliers, we obtain the equilibrium characterized by the set of equations:

$$c_t = \theta_t k_{t-1}^{\alpha} N_t^{1-\alpha} - k_t + (1-\delta)k_{t-1} \tag{4.7}$$
$$c_t^{-\sigma} = \beta E_t \left[c_{t+1}^{-\sigma} \left((1-\delta) + \alpha \theta_{t+1} k_t^{\alpha-1} N_{t+1}^{1-\alpha} \right) \right] \tag{4.8}$$
$$A_N = c_t^{-\sigma} \theta_t k_{t-1}^{\alpha} (1-\alpha) N_t^{-\alpha} \tag{4.9}$$

and

$$\log(\theta_t) = \rho \log(\theta_{t-1}) + \epsilon_t \tag{4.10}$$
$$\epsilon_t \sim N(0, \sigma_\epsilon^2)$$

plus the transversality condition $\lim_{\tau \to \infty} E_t \left[c_{t+\tau}^{-\sigma} k_{t+\tau} \beta^{\tau} \right] = 0$, and the initial conditions k_0, θ_0.

We now define a new variable W_t as equal to the conditional expectation in (4.8), and introduce the corresponding expectation error, η_t:

$$0 = -W_t + E_t \left[c_{t+1}^{-\sigma} \left((1-\delta) + \alpha \theta_{t+1} k_t^{\alpha-1} N_{t+1}^{1-\alpha} \right) \right] \tag{4.11}$$
$$0 = -c_t^{-\sigma} + \beta W_t \tag{4.12}$$
$$0 = -W_{t-1} + c_t^{-\sigma} \left[(1-\delta) + \alpha \theta_t k_{t-1}^{\alpha-1} N_t^{1-\alpha} \right] - \eta_t \tag{4.13}$$

where $E_t[\eta_{t+1}] = 0$.

Treating the conditional expectations in the model as additional variables is distinctive of this method. It comes together with also adding as new variables the associated expectations errors, which will be solved for endogenously together with the rest of the variables, including the expectation.

The conditions characterizing the steady state are:

$$c_{ss} = \theta_{ss} k_{ss}^{\alpha} N_{ss}^{1-\alpha} - k_{ss} + (1-\delta)k_{ss}$$
$$W_{ss} = c_{ss}^{-\sigma} \left((1-\delta) + \alpha \theta_{ss} k_{ss}^{\alpha-1} N_{ss}^{1-\alpha} \right)$$
$$A_N = c_{ss}^{-\sigma} \theta_{ss} k_{ss}^{\alpha} (1-\alpha) N_{ss}^{-\alpha}$$
$$0 = -c_{ss}^{-\sigma} + \beta W_{ss}$$

where the steady state for technology is $\theta_{ss} = 1$. Then we can solve for the steady state of all the variables of the economy:

$$\frac{k_{ss}}{N_{ss}} = \left[\frac{1}{\alpha}\left(\frac{1}{\beta} - 1 + \delta\right)\right]^{1/(\alpha-1)}$$
$$c_{ss} = \left(\frac{A_N}{1-\alpha}\right)^{\frac{-1}{\sigma}}\left(\frac{k_{ss}}{N_{ss}}\right)^{\alpha/\sigma}$$
$$k_{ss} = c_{ss}\left(\left(\frac{k_{ss}}{N_{ss}}\right)^{\alpha-1} - \delta\right)^{-1}$$
$$W_{ss} = \frac{1}{\beta}c_{ss}^{-\sigma}$$
$$N_{ss} = k_{ss}\left(\frac{k_{ss}}{N_{ss}}\right)^{-1}$$

The system to be linearized is that formed by the optimality conditions (4.7), (4.9), and (4.12), the definition of the expectation error (4.13), and the process for the exogenous shock (4.10). State variables are k_{t-1}, W_{t-1} and $\log(\theta_t)$, and decision variables are c_t, k_t and N_t. To linearize, we view each equation as a function $f(c_t, N_t, W_t, k_t, \log(\theta_t), \eta_t, \epsilon_t) = 0$ and then, defining the vector $y_t = (c_t - c_{ss}, N_t - N_{ss}, W_t - W_{ss}, k_t - k_{ss}, \log(\theta_t))'$, the vector η_t which contains the single expectation error denoted by the same letter, and the 1×1 vector z_t containing the single exogenous innovation ϵ_t, the first-order approximation around the steady state is:[7]

$$\left.\frac{\partial f}{\partial y_t}\right|_{ss} y_t + \left.\frac{\partial f}{\partial y_{t-1}}\right|_{ss} y_{t-1} + \left.\frac{\partial f}{\partial \eta_t}\right|_{ss} \eta_t + \left.\frac{\partial f}{\partial \epsilon_t}\right|_{ss} \epsilon_t = 0$$

where steady-state values of η_t and ϵ_t are equal to zero. Stacking these approximations, we can write the linearized system as:

$$\Gamma_0 y_t = \Gamma_1 y_{t-1} + \Psi z_t + \Pi \eta_t \qquad (4.14)$$

where

$$\Gamma_0 = \begin{pmatrix} 1 & -k_{ss}^{\alpha}(1-\alpha)N_{ss}^{-\alpha} & 0 & 1 & -k_{ss}^{\alpha}N_{ss}^{1-\alpha} \\ A_1 & c_{ss}^{-\sigma}k_{ss}^{\alpha}(1-\alpha)\alpha N_{ss}^{-\alpha-1} & 0 & 0 & -c_{ss}^{-\sigma}k_{ss}^{\alpha}(1-\alpha)N_{ss}^{-\alpha} \\ -\sigma c_{ss}^{-\sigma-1} & 0 & -\beta & 0 & 0 \\ A_2 & -c_{ss}^{-\sigma}\alpha k_{ss}^{\alpha-1}(1-\alpha)N_{ss}^{-\alpha} & 0 & 0 & -\alpha c_{ss}^{-\sigma}k_{ss}^{\alpha-1}N_{ss}^{1-\alpha} \\ 0 & 0 & 0 & 0 & 1 \end{pmatrix}$$

[7] Obtaining the derivatives of the function f for the approximation is not necessarily hard work since one can use numerical or analytical differenciation with MATLAB, for example.

in which

$$A_1 = \sigma c_{ss}^{-\sigma-1} k_{ss}^{\alpha}(1-\alpha)N_{ss}^{-\alpha}$$
$$A_2 = \sigma c_{ss}^{-\sigma-1}\left(\alpha k_{ss}^{\alpha-1}N_{ss}^{1-\alpha}+1-\delta\right)$$

$$\Gamma_1 = \begin{pmatrix} 0 & 0 & 0 & \alpha k_{ss}^{\alpha-1}N_{ss}^{1-\alpha}+1-\delta & 0 \\ 0 & 0 & 0 & c_{ss}^{-\sigma}\alpha k_{ss}^{\alpha-1}(1-\alpha)N_{ss}^{-\alpha} & 0 \\ 0 & 0 & 0 & 0 & 0 \\ 0 & 0 & -1 & \alpha(1-\alpha)c_{ss}^{-\sigma}k_{ss}^{\alpha-2}N_{ss}^{1-\alpha} & 0 \\ 0 & 0 & 0 & 0 & \rho \end{pmatrix}, \quad \Psi = \begin{pmatrix} 0 \\ 0 \\ 0 \\ 0 \\ 1 \end{pmatrix}, \quad \Pi = \begin{pmatrix} 0 \\ 0 \\ 0 \\ 1 \\ 0 \end{pmatrix}$$

4.4.1 *Characterizing the stability conditions*

The constant term in (4.14) is zero, since variables in y_t are expressed as deviations around their steady-state values. As already mentioned, for any sensible set of parameter values, Γ_0 is invertible in this model. Premultiplying by the inverse of Γ_0, we obtain a transformed system with an identity matrix of coefficients in y_t and, after appropriate redefinition of matrices ($\tilde{\Gamma}_1 = \Gamma_0^{-1}\Gamma_1$; $\tilde{\Psi} = \Gamma_0^{-1}\Psi$; $\tilde{\Pi} = \Gamma_0^{-1}\Pi$):

$$y_t = \Gamma_0^{-1}\Gamma_1 y_{t-1} + \Gamma_0^{-1}\Psi z_t + \Gamma_0^{-1}\Pi\eta_t = \tilde{\Gamma}_1 y_{t-1} + \tilde{\Psi}z_t + \tilde{\Pi}\eta_t \tag{4.15}$$

$\tilde{\Gamma}_1$ has Jordan decomposition $\tilde{\Gamma}_1 = P\Lambda P^{-1}$,[8] where P is the matrix of right eigenvectors of $\tilde{\Gamma}_1$, P^{-1} is the matrix of left eigenvectors, and Λ has the eigenvalues of $\tilde{\Gamma}_1$ in its diagonal, and zeros elsewhere.[9] Multiplying the system by P^{-1} and defining $w_t = P^{-1}y_t$, we obtain:

$$w_t = \Lambda w_{t-1} + P^{-1}\left(\tilde{\Psi}z_t + \tilde{\Pi}\eta_t\right) \tag{4.16}$$

which is a system in linear combinations of the variables in the original vector y_t. We will have a corresponding equation for each eigenvalue λ_j of $\tilde{\Gamma}_1$

$$w_{jt} = \lambda_{jj}w_{j,t-1} + P^{j\bullet}\left(\tilde{\Psi}z_t + \tilde{\Pi}\eta_t\right) \tag{4.17}$$

where $P^{j\bullet}$ denotes the jth row of P^{-1}.

Economic models usually impose upper bounds on the rate of growth of some functions. A special case is the standard planner's problems that we are considering in which the product of state variables and their shadow prices cannot grow at a rate faster than β^{-1} for the transversality conditions to hold. Even though it is not necessary, this condition is usually imposed through the requirement that both state variables and shadow prices grow at a rate less than $\beta^{-1/2}$. Further, the quadratic approximation to the objective functions in an optimization problem will be bounded only if its variable arguments grow at

[8] The MATLAB function for doing this is: eig(Γ_0, Γ_1).

[9] We confine ourselves to the simpler case when all the eigenvalues are different from each other. For cases with repeating eigenvalues, see Sims (1998).

a rate less than $\beta^{-1/2}$. More general restrictions can be approximated by an upper bound φ on the rate of growth of a linear combination ϕy_t of the variables in the model. Using the relationship between y_t and w_t, a condition of the form $\lim_{s\to\infty} E_t\left[\phi y_{t+s}\varphi^{-s}\right] = 0$ amounts to $\phi P \lim_{s\to\infty} E_t\left[w_{t+s}\varphi^{-s}\right] = (\phi P)\lim_{s\to\infty}\left(\Lambda^s w_t \varphi^{-s}\right) = 0$, where we have set to zero current expectations of future z_ts and η_ts. Therefore, each of the w_j variables corresponding to a $|\lambda_{jj}| > \varphi$ and to a ϕP product different from zero, must be equal to its steady-state value of zero for all t:

$$w_{jt} = P^{j\bullet} y_t = 0, \quad \forall t \tag{4.18}$$

producing a stability condition in the form of an orthogonality condition between an unstable left eigenvector of the matrix product $\tilde{\Gamma}_1 = \Gamma_0^{-1}\Gamma_1$ and the vector of variables y_t, in deviations around steady state.

The resulting condition will be a linear relationship between decision variables, current and past states and exogenous variables, which could be interpreted either as a *decision rule*, if it is used to write one decision variable as a function of the other variables, or as a *pricing function*, if it is used to represent a mapping from states and decisions to prices.

In the special case when ϕP turns out to be zero, the upper bound on the growth rate of ϕy_t does not impose any obvious constraint, and the precise form of the associated stability condition needs to be worked out specifically.

4.4.2 *Generating time series for a specific parameterization*

For parameter values $\sigma = 1.5, \delta = 0.025, \alpha = 0.36, \beta = 0.99, \rho = 0.95$, and an A_N value such that $N_{ss} = \frac{1}{3}$, we have the numerical estimates

$$\Gamma_0 = \begin{pmatrix} 1 & -2.3706 & 0 & 1 & -1.2347 \\ 4.4026 & 2.9103 & 0 & 0 & -2.6947 \\ -1.8572 & 0 & -0.99 & 0 & 0 \\ 1.8759 & -0.0766 & 0 & 0 & -0.0399 \\ 0 & 0 & 0 & 0 & 1 \end{pmatrix}$$

$$\Gamma_1 = \begin{pmatrix} 0 & 0 & 0 & 1.0101 & 0 \\ 0 & 0 & 0 & 0.0766 & 0 \\ 0 & 0 & 0 & 0 & 0 \\ 0 & 0 & -1 & -0.0020 & 0 \\ 0 & 0 & 0 & 0 & 0.95 \end{pmatrix}$$

and the matrix $\tilde{\Gamma}_1 = \Gamma_0^{-1}\Gamma_1$ has Jordan decomposition $\tilde{\Gamma}_1 = P\Lambda P^{-1}$ with

$$P = \begin{pmatrix} 1 & 0 & 0.0302 & 0.0317 & 0 \\ 0 & 1 & -0.0178 & -0.0158 & -0.0245 \\ 0 & 0 & -0.0566 & -0.0595 & 0 \\ 0 & 0 & 0.9978 & 0.9976 & -0.9997 \\ 0 & 0 & 0 & 0.0049 & 0 \end{pmatrix} \quad \Lambda = \begin{pmatrix} 0 & 0 & 0 & 0 & 0 \\ 0 & 0 & 0 & 0 & 0 \\ 0 & 0 & 0.9418 & 0 & 0 \\ 0 & 0 & 0 & 0.95 & 0 \\ 0 & 0 & 0 & 0 & 1.0725 \end{pmatrix}$$

and

$$P^{-1} = \begin{pmatrix} 1 & 0 & 0.5331 & 0 & 0 \\ 0 & 1 & -0.7464 & -0.0245 & -0.8417 \\ 0 & 0 & -17.6576 & 0 & -213.9769 \\ 0 & 0 & 0 & 0 & 203.6377 \\ 0 & 0 & -17.6237 & -1.0003 & -10.3588 \end{pmatrix}$$

where the eigenvalues have been ordered increasingly along the diagonal of Λ, and the right eigenvectors, the columns of P, have been ordered accordingly.

The stability condition is given by the last row of P^{-1}, which corresponds to the only eigenvalue above $0.99^{-1/2}$. We denote that row by $P^{5\bullet} = (0, 0, -17.6237, -1.0003, -10.3588)$, so the stability condition turns out to be:

$$w_{5t} = P^{5\bullet} y_t = 0 \ \forall t \ \Rightarrow W_t - W_{ss} + 0.0568(k_t - k_{ss}) + 0.5878 \log(\theta_t) = 0 \quad (4.19)$$

which happens not to involve consumption or labour.

A single stability condition is what should be expected from the point of view of the discussion of the deterministic model in Section 4.2, since, even though there are two control variables, consumption and labour, whose initial values need to be chosen, there is also a contemporaneous relationship (4.9) between them, so that we just need to figure out how to choose one of them to obtain a stable equilibrium. Furthermore, since there is a single expectations error in the model, a single stability condition is, in general, all that is needed to identify it.

The difference between this and the deterministic case is that the stability condition does not guarantee that the stochastic Euler equation (4.8) will hold in every period, since it incorporates the expectation error. The role of this equation, once it is written as (4.13), is precisely to provide us with the realization of the expectation error,[10] which shows that the stability condition can also be seen as imposing an exact relationship between the rational expectation error and the innovation in the productivity shock, as should be expected. Estimating the stability conditions allows us also to characterize numerically the relationships between expectations errors and innovations in structural processes, as we are about to see.

Stable solutions can be computed by adding the estimated stability condition (4.19) to the original nonlinear model to give an enlarged system that can be solved for all the endogenous variables in the model, plus the expectations errors. Conditional on k_0 and θ_1, (4.7), (4.9) and (4.12) form a system in c_1, k_1, N_1, and W_1 which can be used to write the three latter variables as functions of c_1. Plugging those expressions into the stability condition (4.19), we obtain c_1. The optimal value for labour, N_1, is then obtained from (4.9), while from the budget constraint (4.7) we obtain physical capital, and the realization of the conditional expectation W_1 is obtained from (4.12). Then, the expectation error, η_1, can be obtained from (4.13). The process can be repeated every period.

[10]The resulting expectations error is an approximation to the true expectations error, since it also incorporates the numerical error of the approximation to the stable manifold.

It is clear from (4.16) that, as we said, setting up w_{jt} to be zero each period when $|\lambda_{jj}| > \varphi$ and $\phi P \neq 0$ amounts to imposing an exact relationship between the vector of innovations in the structural shocks and the vector of expectations errors:

$$P^{j\bullet}\left(\tilde{\Psi}z_t + \tilde{\Pi}\eta_t\right) = 0 \quad \forall t \tag{4.20}$$

implying that expectations errors must fluctuate as functions of the structural innovations, in such a way as to prevent any deviation of (4.20) from its steady-state value of zero.

In this specific model, setting w_{jt} to zero each period in (4.17) implies

$$P^{5\bullet}\left(\tilde{\Psi}z_t + \tilde{\Pi}\eta_t\right) = 0 \ \forall t \quad \Rightarrow \quad -1.6163\epsilon_t + \eta_t = 0 \ \forall t \tag{4.21}$$

which is an exact relationship between the expectations error in the model and the innovation in the single structural shock. However, the expectations error we have computed from (4.13) depends in a nonlinear fashion on state and decision variables and, hence, on exogenous shocks. It will not satisfy (4.21) exactly, which is a different approximation to the true, nonlinear relationship between expectation error and the innovation in the structural shock in productivity.

Problems related to the *existence* of a solution will tend to arise when there are more linearly independent stability conditions than conditional expectations in the model. The set of expectations errors cannot possibly adjust, in this case, so as fully to offset the fluctuations in the exogenous processes, in such a way that (4.20) holds, and there will not be a well-defined relationship between expectations errors and structural innovations. If (4.20) cannot hold the stability conditions cannot all hold simultaneously. Hence, a stable solution will generally not exist. Unfortunately, an absolute result on existence cannot be produced out of a counting rule of unstable eigenvalues and expectations: it is conceivable that some stability conditions are redundant with the rest of the system in such a way that (4.20) can hold, even if the number of rows in $P^{j\bullet}$ exceeds the dimension of the vector η_t.

If there are as many stability conditions as expectations in the model, none of them being redundant with the rest of the system, a unique solution will generally exist. In the simple models we present in this chapter, as well as in some more complex applications we have developed, this has always been the case.[11] Then, stable solutions may be obtained by combining the stability conditions with the rest of the (nonlinear) model. That system will provide us with a set of time series for all the variables in the original system, plus the variables we have defined as expectations, and the expectations errors. If there are fewer stability conditions than expectations in the model, we will generally have *sunspot equilibria*, since we could arbitrarily fix some expectation, and still solve for the rest in such a way that all the equations in the model hold. In this case we will have a continuum of equilibria.

[11] In linear models, a rank condition for uniqueness can be found (see Sims, 1998) but it is not applicable to the nonlinear case. The condition has to do with the possibility that the model can be solved without having to condition on any endogenous expectation error.

4.5 Comparison to other solution methods

Since there is a broad variety of methods to solve nonlinear rational expectations models, it is important to understand their differences and similarities. In a specific situation, one method may be more accurate than another but also computationally more demanding, and the researcher should choose one or the other in terms of this trade-off. Given the characteristics of rational expectations models, differences among solution methods may fall into: (i) how much of the nonlinearity in the original model is preserved; (ii) how they deal with expectations (whether they are treated as an essential part of the model and numerical values are obtained for them endogenously, as part of the solution); and (iii) the way they handle the associated expectations errors and, in particular, whether numerical values can be easily obtained for them. Precision in computing these errors should be considered as an important component of a solution, since rational expectations models impose a quite tight structure on their probability distribution.

These characteristics are not independent of each other: departing from the original nonlinearity will make computation easier, but the functional form approximation error will be mostly captured by the expectations errors, which are generally computed residually if at all, once the solution has been obtained for the rest of the variables. This numerical error will tend to show up as deviations from rationality, in the form of autocorrelated expectations errors, or as correlations between them and variables in the information set available to the agents when they made their decisions. That is why conducting thorough tests of rationality is so important.

Regarding *nonlinearity*, in the method based on the *eigenvalue–eigenvector decomposition* of the linear approximation to the standard stochastic nonlinear growth model in Section 4.4, a single linear stability condition, with the variables either in levels or in logs,[12] was added to the model. That is the degree of artificial linearity introduced in the solution since, other than that, the full structure of the original nonlinear model is used to generate the numerical solution. As a result, a nonlinear system of equations has to be solved each period to compute the solution.

Relative to this approach, the method of *undetermined coefficients* proposed by Uhlig (Chapter 3, this volume) suggests taking a log-linear approximation to the set formed by the optimality conditions, the budget constraint, and the autoregressive process for the productivity shock. State and decision variables are then supposed to be linear functions of the initial states, $\tilde{k}_{t-1}, \tilde{\theta}_t$, where tilde now denotes log-deviations from steady state:

$$\begin{pmatrix} \tilde{k}_t \\ \tilde{c}_t \\ \tilde{N}_t \end{pmatrix} = \begin{pmatrix} \nu_{kk} & \nu_{kz} \\ \nu_{ck} & \nu_{cz} \\ \nu_{Nk} & \nu_{Nz} \end{pmatrix} \begin{pmatrix} \tilde{k}_{t-1} \\ \tilde{\theta}_t \end{pmatrix} = \begin{pmatrix} 0.9418 & 0.1382 \\ 0.3930 & 0.3989 \\ -0.6376 & 1.1155 \end{pmatrix} \begin{pmatrix} \tilde{k}_{t-1} \\ \tilde{\theta}_t \end{pmatrix} \tag{4.22}$$

and the ν_{ij} parameters are obtained by plugging this linear representation into the set of optimality conditions, to identify the *undetermined coefficients*. For the parameter values in the previous section, numerical values of the undetermined coefficients are as shown above. Consistent with the log-linearization proposed in that method as a starting step,

[12]Even though we obtain linear approximations around steady state, log-linear approximations could alternatively be used.

approximations to the conditional expectations of nonlinear functions can be obtained using the representation above. Expectations errors could then be computed which will incorporate some numerical error, derived from the linear approximation.

Another popular solution approach (see Díaz-Giménez, Chapter 2, this volume) which is useful for solving stochastic dynamic optimization problems, consists of building a *linear quadratic approximation* to the original model and applying the techniques of *dynamic programming*. The goal is to derive the value function, generally after eliminating some decision and state variables from the objective function by repeated substitutions of the available optimality conditions and constraints in their deterministic form. Then the linear solution to the problem of maximizing the resulting value function for the linear-quadratic approximation is obtained. In the analysis of Hansen's model, the budget constraint can be used to eliminate consumption from the objective function, and a linear-quadratic approximation to the return function $r(\log(\theta_t), k_{t-1}, k_t, N_t)$ can be obtained, showing that the solution to this model is in the form of a set of two decision rules, for physical capital and labour, as linear functions of the beginning-of-period capital stock and the productivity shock, the two state variables. For the parameter values used in the previous section, they are:

$$\begin{aligned} k_t &= 0.7368 + 1.7499\log(\theta_t) + 0.9418k_{t-1} \\ N_t &= 0.5459 + 0.3718\log(\theta_t) - 0.0168k_{t-1} \end{aligned} \tag{4.23}$$

Once we have the optimal values of labour and the capital stock for time t, we obtain output from the production function, and consumption from the budget constraint. Relative to the two previous methods, we are in this case adding two linear relationships to the original model when computing the numerical solution, while the method of undetermined coefficients imposes linear dependence of the logs of all current state and decision variables on the logs of the state variables.

The method of *parameterized expectations* of den Haan and Marcet (1990) and Marcet and Lorenzoni (Chapter 7, this volume) computes time series for the conditional expectations using a proposed polynomial function. This function must be estimated, to minimize the size of the average error between each conditional expectation and the value of the nonlinear function of state and decision variables which is being forecasted. It fully preserves the nonlinearity in the original model, so that if the polynomial expectation function can be precisely estimated and the implied set of time series is stable, this is a convincing solution approach.

Summarizing, different solution methods preserve a different amount of the nonlinearity in the original model. The more nonlinearity is preserved, the more accurate the obtained solution will be, although at the cost of having to solve each period a nonlinear system of equations to obtain the realization of the period t vector of variables, which is computationally demanding. The alternative of using some degree of linear approximation to the model to get around this difficulty will produce expectations errors with some deviations from rationality.

Regarding the treatment of *conditional expectations*, since it is not based on any linear approximation, the method of parameterizing expectations might provide the more accurate realization for the conditional expectations in the model. However, reaching convergence in the algorithm that estimates the expectation function might take some effort: even when the algorithm works, thousands of artificial data values are needed for convergence. As in any other method, the trade-off between computational simplicity and accuracy is quite evident but, in principle, parameterizing expectations may be the method better suited to producing acceptable expectations errors, so long as a careful search for a good specification of the polynomial function used to represent expectations is conducted.

On this issue, we have seen in the previous section how methods based on eigenvalue–eigenvector decompositions produce realizations for the conditional expectations and the associated errors at the same time as for any other variable in the model, while preserving most of the nonlinearity in the model. In this sense, deviations from rationality due to numerical approximation errors should be generally expected not to be substantial. We have also seen how the solution method provides additional evidence in terms of the relationship between rational expectations errors and the innovations in the structural shocks, which is an interesting characteristic of the model. With other solution methods, including the parameterized expectations approach, this type of relationship can be estimated through linear projections, although there is no guarantee that such a projection will be a well-specified model. For instance, one might find evidence of expectation errors responding not only to contemporaneous but also to past endogenous innovations as well, which would obviously be a contradiction of rationality.

Finally, dealing with conditional expectations under rationality raises additional issues under which solution methods will have to be increasingly scrutinized in the future. One of them is how to impose the restrictions among expectations of a given function at different horizons, which are standard in theoretical rational expectations models. Another issue is how to impose in the solution strategy the restrictions that theoretical models sometimes impose among expectations under rationality, as is the case in the model in the next section. Not all the solution methods are similarly equipped to deal with these questions and we should expect to see increasing discussion on specific subjects like these, concerning the modelling of expectations under rationality.

Having discussed the implementation of the solution method in a simple baseline real growth model and having established some comparisons with alternative solution strategies, we now proceed to discuss its implementation in a more general set-up.

4.6 Solving some identification issues: capital stock and inventories in the production function

Singular Γ_0 matrices are a frequent occurrence. Sometimes, singularity can be avoided by solving for some variables as functions of others and reducing system size, but that is not always feasible. A typical cause of singularity is that a subset of r variables appear in just q equations, $r > q$, so that it is then impossible to solve for all of them and reflecting the fact that identification of those variables is weak.

An interesting case in which this situation arises is Kydland and Prescott (1982), where physical capital, k_t, and inventories, i_t, play a very similar role: both accumulate and both are production inputs. In that paper, the technology shock, which is the only source of randomness in the economy, is assumed to have a complex stochastic structure that allows for separate identification of fixed investment and inventory investment. The redundancy between physical capital and inventories shows up in that their contemporaneous values appear just in the budget constraint. We will see that, as a consequence, Γ_0 will be singular, producing an eigenvalue equal to infinity, and the associated eigenvector will allow for solving one variable apart from the other.

Let us consider the production technology

$$F_t(\theta_t, k_{t-1}, i_{t-1}) = \theta_t \left[(1-\psi)k_{t-1}^{-\nu} + \psi i_{t-1}^{-\nu}\right]^{-\alpha/\nu} \tag{4.24}$$

where θ_t is an exogenous technology shock, as in previous sections. The marginal products of k_{t-1} and i_{t-1} are, at time t,

$$F_t^k = \alpha(1-\psi)k_{t-1}^{-\nu-1}\theta_t \left[(1-\psi)k_{t-1}^{-\nu} + \psi i_{t-1}^{-\nu}\right]^{(-\alpha/\nu)-1} \tag{4.25}$$

$$F_t^i = \alpha\psi i_{t-1}^{-\nu-1}\theta_t \left[(1-\psi)k_{t-1}^{-\nu} + \psi i_{t-1}^{-\nu}\right]^{\frac{-\alpha}{\nu}-1} \tag{4.26}$$

Maintaining the assumption of a continuum of identical consumers, each endowed with a utility function with constant relative risk aversion, $U(c_t) = (c_t^{1-\sigma} - 1)/(1-\sigma)$, $\sigma > 0$, the optimality conditions are:

$$c_t + k_t - (1-\delta)k_{t-1} + i_t - i_{t-1} - F(\theta_t, k_{t-1}, i_{t-1}) = 0 \tag{4.27}$$

$$c_t^{-\sigma} - \beta E_t\left[(1-\delta+F_{t+1}^k)c_{t+1}^{-\sigma}\right] = 0 \tag{4.28}$$

$$c_t^{-\sigma} - \beta E_t\left[(1+F_{t+1}^i)c_{t+1}^{-\sigma}\right] = 0 \tag{4.29}$$

$$\log(\theta_t) - \rho\log(\theta_{t-1}) - \epsilon_t = 0 \tag{4.30}$$

where the ϵ_t are independently and identically normally distributed with zero mean and variance σ_ϵ^2, and we have assumed that physical capital depreciates at a rate δ, $0 < \delta < 1$. Since they involve the realization of the productivity shock at time $t+1$, θ_{t+1}, the marginal products F_{t+1}^k, F_{t+1}^i are random variables when period t decisions, k_t and i_t, are made.

Additionally, two stability conditions must hold:

$$\lim_{\tau\to\infty} E_t\left[c_{t+\tau}^{-\sigma}k_{t+\tau}\beta^{-\tau}\right] = 0$$

$$\lim_{\tau\to\infty} E_t\left[c_{t+\tau}^{-\sigma}i_{t+\tau}\beta^{-\tau}\right] = 0$$

Conditions (4.28) and (4.29) imply that the two conditional expectations of the cross-products of each marginal productivity by the marginal utility of future consumption are equal to each other at every point in time. However, it is convenient to maintain both of them in the model, and define new variables W_{k_t}, W_{i_t} equal to each expectation,

$$W_{k_t} = E_t\left[(1-\delta+F_{t+1}^k)c_{t+1}^{-\sigma}\right] \tag{4.31}$$

$$W_{i_t} = E_t\left[(1+F_{t+1}^i)c_{t+1}^{-\sigma}\right] \tag{4.32}$$

as well as the associated one-step-ahead, serially uncorrelated, rational expectations errors η_t^k and η_t^i:

$$(1 - \delta + F_t^k)c_t^{-\sigma} - W_{k_{t-1}} - \eta_t^k = 0 \tag{4.33}$$

$$(1 + F_t^i)c_t^{-\sigma} - W_{i_{t-1}} - \eta_t^i = 0 \tag{4.34}$$

With this, equations (4.28) and (4.29) become:

$$c_t^{-\sigma} - \beta W_{k_t} = 0 \tag{4.35}$$

$$c_t^{-\sigma} - \beta W_{i_t} = 0 \tag{4.36}$$

The conditions characterizing steady state are:

$$\begin{aligned}
W_{k_{ss}} &= \left(1 - \delta + F_{ss}^k\right) c_{ss}^{-\sigma} \\
W_{k_{ss}} &= W_{i_{ss}} = \frac{1}{\beta} c_{ss}^{-\sigma} \\
W_{i_{ss}} &= \left(1 + F_{ss}^i\right) c_{ss}^{-\sigma} \\
c_{ss} &= F(\theta_{ss}, k_{ss}, i_{ss}) - \delta k_{ss} \\
F_{ss}^k &= \alpha(1 - \psi) k_{ss}^{-\nu-1} \theta_{ss} F(\theta_{ss}, k_{ss}, i_{ss})^{-1} \\
F_{ss}^i &= \alpha \psi i_{ss}^{-\nu-1} \theta_{ss} F(\theta_{ss}, k_{ss}, i_{ss})^{-1} \\
\theta_{ss} &= 1
\end{aligned}$$

from which we obtain the dependence of steady-state values from structural parameters:

$$\begin{aligned}
F_{ss}^k &= \frac{1}{\beta} - (1 - \delta) \\
F_{ss}^i &= \frac{1}{\beta} - 1 \\
\frac{k_{ss}}{i_{ss}} &= \left[\frac{\psi}{1 - \psi} \frac{1 - \beta(1 - \delta)}{1 - \beta}\right]^{-1/\nu+1} \\
i_{ss} &= \left[F_{ss}^i \frac{1}{\alpha\psi} \left[(1 - \psi)\left(\frac{k_{ss}}{i_{ss}}\right)^{-\nu} + \psi\right]^{-\alpha/\nu}\right]^{-1/1+\alpha+\nu} \\
k_{ss} &= \left(\frac{k_{ss}}{i_{ss}}\right) i_{ss} \\
F(\theta_{ss}, k_{ss}, i_{ss}) &= \theta_{ss} \left[(1 - \psi)\left(\frac{k_{ss}}{i_{ss}}\right)^{-\nu} + \psi\right]^{-\alpha/\nu} i_{ss}^{\alpha} \\
c_{ss} &= -\delta k_{ss} + F(\theta_{ss}, k_{ss}, i_{ss})
\end{aligned}$$

We can now compute the linear approximation to the system (4.27), (4.35), (4.36), (4.33), (4.34), and (4.30) around steady state:

$$\Gamma_0 y_t = \Gamma_1 y_{t-1} + \Psi z_t + \Pi \eta_t \tag{4.37}$$

where the vectors y_t, z_t, η_t are:

$$\begin{aligned} y_t &= \left[c_t - c_{ss},\ k_t - k_{ss},\ i_t - i_{ss},\ W_{k_t} - W_{k_{ss}},\ W_{i_t} - W_{i_{ss}},\ \log(\theta_t)\right]' \\ z_t &= \epsilon_t \\ \eta_t &= (\eta_t^k, \eta_t^i)' \end{aligned} \tag{4.38}$$

The matrices in the linear approximation are:

$$\Gamma_0 = \begin{pmatrix} 1 & 1 & 1 & 0 & 0 & a_2^{-\alpha/\nu} k_{ss}^{\alpha} \\ -\sigma c_{ss}^{-\sigma-1} & 0 & 0 & -\beta & 0 & 0 \\ -\sigma c_{ss}^{-\sigma-1} & 0 & 0 & 0 & -\beta & 0 \\ B_1 & 0 & 0 & 0 & 0 & \alpha(1-\psi) a_2^{-(\alpha+\nu)/\nu} k_{ss}^{\alpha-1} c_{ss}^{-\sigma} \\ B_2 & 0 & 0 & 0 & 0 & \alpha\psi a_2^{-(\alpha+\nu)/\nu} a_1^{-\nu-1} k_{ss}^{\alpha-1} c_{ss}^{-\sigma} \\ 0 & 0 & 0 & 0 & 0 & 1 \end{pmatrix}$$

$$\Gamma_1 = \begin{pmatrix} 0 & C_1 & C_2 & 0 & 0 & 0 \\ 0 & 0 & 0 & 0 & 0 & 0 \\ 0 & 0 & 0 & 0 & 0 & 0 \\ 0 & -F_{ss}^{kk} c_{ss}^{-\sigma} & -F_{ss}^{ki} c_{ss}^{-\sigma} & 1 & 0 & 0 \\ 0 & -F_{ss}^{ik} c_{ss}^{-\sigma} & -F_{ss}^{ii} c_{ss}^{-\sigma} & 0 & 1 & 0 \\ 0 & 0 & 0 & 0 & 0 & \rho \end{pmatrix}$$

$$\Psi = \begin{pmatrix} 0 \\ 0 \\ 0 \\ 0 \\ 0 \\ 1 \end{pmatrix}, \qquad \Pi = \begin{pmatrix} 0 & 0 \\ 0 & 0 \\ 0 & 0 \\ 1 & 0 \\ 0 & 1 \\ 0 & 0 \end{pmatrix}$$

where

$$\begin{aligned} B_1 &= -\sigma c_{ss}^{-\sigma-1}\left(1 - \delta + \alpha(1-\psi) a_2^{-(\alpha+\nu)/\nu} k_{ss}^{\alpha-1}\right) \\ B_2 &= -\sigma c_{ss}^{-\sigma-1}\left(1 + \alpha\psi a_2^{-(\alpha+\nu)/\nu} a_1^{-\nu-1} k_{ss}^{\alpha-1}\right) \\ C_1 &= (1-\delta) - \alpha(1-\psi) a_2^{-(\alpha+\nu)/\nu} k_{ss}^{\alpha-1} \\ C_2 &= 1 + \alpha\psi a_2^{-(\alpha+\nu)/\nu} a_1^{-\psi-1} k_{ss}^{\alpha-1} \end{aligned}$$

and

$$a_1 = \frac{\psi}{1-\psi}\frac{1-\beta(1-\delta)}{1-\beta}$$
$$a_2 = (1-\psi) + \psi a_1^{-\nu}$$
$$a_3 = \alpha(1-\psi)a_2^{-(\alpha+\nu)/\nu}$$
$$F_{ss}^{kk} = \left[(\alpha+\nu)(1-\psi)\frac{1}{a_2} - \nu - 1\right]\alpha(1-\psi)a_2^{-(\alpha+\nu)/\nu}a_1^{-\nu-2}k_{ss}^{\alpha-2}$$
$$F_{ss}^{ii} = \left[(\alpha+\nu)\psi\frac{1}{a_2}a_1^{-\nu} - \nu - 1\right]\alpha\psi a_2^{-(\alpha+\nu)/\nu}a_1^{-\nu-2}k_{ss}^{\alpha-2}$$
$$F_{ss}^{ik} = \alpha(1-\psi)(\alpha+\nu)\psi a_2^{-(\alpha+\nu)/\nu}a_1^{-\nu-1}k_{ss}^{\alpha-2} = F_{ss}^{ki}$$

4.6.1 *Characterizing stability conditions*

Each row of Γ_0 in (4.37) contains the partial derivatives of each equation in the system with respect to the components of the vector y_t. Since k_t and i_t just appear in (4.27), only the first element in the second and third columns of Γ_0 is non-zero. As a consequence, Γ_0 is singular and it is necessary to compute a QZ decomposition[13] to obtain generalized eigenvalues: for any pair of square matrices like (Γ_0, Γ_1), there exist orthonormal matrices Q, Z ($QQ' = ZZ' = I$) and upper triangular matrices Λ and Ω such that[14]

$$\Gamma_0 = Q'\Lambda Z', \qquad \Gamma_1 = Q'\Omega Z'$$

Furthermore, Q and Z can be chosen so that all possible zeros of Λ occur in the lower right corner and such that the remaining ratios $(\omega_{ii}/\lambda_{ii})$ of diagonal elements in Ω and Λ are non-decreasing in absolute value as we move down the diagonal. These ratios are the *generalized eigenvalues* of the pair (Γ_0, Γ_1).

Premultiplying the system by Q and replacing $Z'y_t$ with w_t, we obtain:

$$\Lambda w_t = \Omega w_{t-1} + Q(\Psi z_t + \Pi\eta_t) \tag{4.39}$$

If we partition the set of generalized eigenvalues into those below and above the upper bound which is used as stability criterion (it could be $\beta^{-1/2}$), and order them decreasingly along the diagonal of Λ, we will have

$$\begin{pmatrix}\Lambda_{11} & \Lambda_{12}\\ 0 & \Lambda_{22}\end{pmatrix}\begin{pmatrix}w_{1t}\\ w_{2t}\end{pmatrix} = \begin{pmatrix}\Omega_{11} & \Omega_{12}\\ 0 & \Omega_{22}\end{pmatrix}\begin{pmatrix}w_{1,t-1}\\ w_{2,t-1}\end{pmatrix} + \begin{pmatrix}Q_{1\bullet}\\ Q_{2\bullet}\end{pmatrix}(\Psi z_t + \Pi\eta_t) \tag{4.40}$$

where the second block of equations corresponds to the *unstable* eigenvalues. Some diagonal elements in Λ_{22}, but not in Λ_{11}, may be zero.

[13] The MATLAB command to perform a QZ decomposition is qz(Γ_0, Γ_1). The resulting matrices can be reorganized using the qzdiv.m program in C.Sims' web page.

[14] Q, Z, Λ and Ω could be complex, in which case the matrix transposition has to be changed to transposition and complex conjugation. On the other hand, upper triangularity of Λ and Ω has to do with the possibility of repeated eigenvalues. When all eigenvalues are different from each other, both matrices are diagonal.

A zero element in the diagonal of Λ implies some lack of identification in the system, and an infinite generalized eigenvalue will arise. If Ω does not have a zero in the same position, the associated eigenvector will generally allow us to solve the identification problem, as we will see below. Γ_0 is then singular, but all the equations in the system are in this case linearly independent. If Ω has a zero in the same position, then there is an equation which is linear combination of the others so that, even though the system has as many equations as variables it is, in fact, incomplete.

In (4.40), let us denote the vector

$$x_t = Q\,(\Psi z_t + \Pi\eta_t) = \begin{pmatrix} Q_{1\bullet}\,(\Psi z_t + \Pi\eta_t) \\ Q_{2\bullet}\,(\Psi z_t + \Pi\eta_t) \end{pmatrix} = \begin{pmatrix} x_{1t} \\ x_{2t} \end{pmatrix}$$

Since the lower block of (4.40) corresponds to *unstable* eigenvalues, it must be solved towards the future, which makes w_{2t} depend on the whole future path of x_{2t}. Sims (1998) shows how the discounted sum of future values of linear combinations in x_{2t} that defines w_{2t} must be equal to its conditional expectation, which yields as many stability conditions as there are variables in w_{2t}. Imposing those conditions, we again obtain a set of relationships between the vector of rational expectations errors and the vector of innovations in the exogenous stochastic processes, similar to (4.20).

In the applications we discuss here, the vector x_t contains linear combinations of the innovations in the stochastic processes for the structural shocks and the expectations errors. Structural shocks themselves are included in the vector y_t, and it is just their innovations which are in x_t. Hence, $E_t(x_{2t+s}) = 0$ for all $s > 0$, and the stability conditions we have just described become

$$w_{2t} = Z'_{2\bullet} y_t = 0 \quad \forall t \tag{4.41}$$

where $Z'_{2\bullet}$ is the appropriate submatrix of Z. This set of conditions, substituted in (4.40), amounts to having the following relationships between rational expectations errors and structural innovations:[15]

$$Q_{2\bullet}\,(\Psi z_t + \Pi\eta_t) = 0 \quad \Rightarrow \quad Q_{2\bullet}\Psi z_t = -Q_{2\bullet}\Pi\eta_t \tag{4.42}$$

For reasonable parameterizations, there are two generalized eigenvalues in (4.39) with absolute size greater than $\beta^{-1/2}$. One of them is common to the version of the model without inventories (not analysed in this chapter) so that it is associated with a standard stability condition, of the kind we saw in Hansen's model in Section 4.4. The other eigenvalue is equal to infinity.

The partition described in (4.40) leads in this model to an unstable block

$$\begin{pmatrix} a_{11} & a_{12} \\ 0 & 0 \end{pmatrix} \begin{pmatrix} z'_{5\bullet} y_t \\ z'_{6\bullet} y_t \end{pmatrix} = \begin{pmatrix} b_{11} & b_{12} \\ 0 & b_{22} \end{pmatrix} \begin{pmatrix} z'_{5\bullet} y_{t-1} \\ z'_{6\bullet} y_{t-1} \end{pmatrix} + \begin{pmatrix} q_{5\bullet} \\ q_{6\bullet} \end{pmatrix} (\Psi z_t + \Pi\eta_t) \tag{4.43}$$

[15]However, we will impose (4.41), but not (4.42) when solving, since we will actually use the original, nonlinear model to compute an equilibrium realization, which will satisfy (4.42) only as an approximation. If we used the linear approximation (4.37) to the model to compute the solution, (4.42) would hold exactly.

where $z'_{5\bullet}$, $z'_{6\bullet}$, $q_{5\bullet}$, $q_{6\bullet}$ denote the fifth and sixth rows of Z' and Q, that is, $z'_{5\bullet}$ and $z'_{6\bullet}$ form the submatrix $Z'_{2\bullet}$ in (4.41), while $q_{5\bullet}$, $q_{6\bullet}$ form $Q_{2\bullet}$ in (4.42). The zero in the lower end of the diagonal in the first matrix shows the existence of a generalized eigenvalue equal to infinity, due to the weak identification of k_t and i_t. The other generalized eigenvalue is equal to b_{11}/a_{11}.

Written at time t, the last equation states $b_{22}z'_{6\bullet}y_t = -q_{6\bullet}(\Psi z_{t+1} + \Pi\eta_{t+1})$. Taking expectations and noticing the lack of autocorrelation in ϵ_t, as well as in the two one-step-ahead forecast errors in η_t, this equation leads to $z'_{6\bullet}y_t = 0$, which is a linear restriction among contemporaneous values of the conditional expectations and decision and state variables. Substituting in the previous equation, we obtain:

$$a_{11}z'_{5\bullet}y_t = b_{11}z'_{5\bullet}y_{t-1} + q_{5\bullet}(\Psi z_t + \Pi\eta_t) \tag{4.44}$$

which is an explosive autoregression in $z'_{5\bullet}y_t$, since the generalized eigenvalue, $b_{11}/a_{11} > \beta^{-1/2}$, and the resulting trajectories for the variables in y_t will not satisfy the transversality conditions. Furthermore, the triangular structure of the system will transmit the explosiveness of (4.44) to the rest of the equations of the system. These explosive trajectories can be eliminated only if we impose $z'_{5\bullet}y_t = 0$. Together with the budget constraint and the remaining equations in the system, these two conditions will provide us with the period t values of decision variables, state variables and conditional expectations, c_t, k_t, i_t, W_{k_t}, and W_{i_t}.

4.6.2 *Identifying capital stock and inventories separately*

With the parameterization $\sigma = 1.5, \alpha = 0.36, \beta = 0.99, \delta = 0.025, \rho = 0.95, \nu = 4.0, \psi = 2.8 \times 10^{-6}$ (the two last parameters as in Kydland and Prescott, 1982), steady-state values are $c_{ss} = 2.7261, k_{ss} = 36.2067, i_{ss} = 3.6009, W_{k_{ss}} = 0.2244, W_{i_{ss}} = 0.2244, \theta_{ss} = 1$, and the numerical estimates of the Γ_0, Γ_1 matrices become

$$\Gamma_0 = \begin{pmatrix} 1.0000 & 1.0000 & 1.0000 & 0 & 0 & -3.6313 \\ -0.1222 & 0 & 0 & -0.9900 & 0 & 0 \\ -0.1222 & 0 & 0 & 0 & -0.9900 & 0 \\ -0.1235 & 0 & 0 & 0 & 0 & 0.0078 \\ -0.1235 & 0 & 0 & 0 & 0 & 0.0022 \\ 0 & 0 & 0 & 0 & 0 & 1.0000 \end{pmatrix}$$

$$\Gamma_1 = \begin{pmatrix} 0 & 1.0101 & 1.0101 & 0 & 0 & 0 \\ 0 & 0 & 0 & 0 & 0 & 0 \\ 0 & 0 & 0 & 0 & 0 & 0 \\ 0 & 0.0002 & -0.0003 & 1.0000 & 0 & 0 \\ 0 & -0.0003 & 0.0030 & 0 & 1.0000 & 0 \\ 0 & 0 & 0 & 0 & 0 & 0.9500 \end{pmatrix}$$

while Λ, Ω, ordered so that generalized eigenvalues increase in absolute size as we move down the diagonal of Λ are

$$\Lambda = \begin{pmatrix} 1.0297 & 0.0002 & -1.3716 & -3.5179 & 0.3177 & -0.0112 \\ 0 & 0.0023 & 0.1487 & 0.2742 & -0.6340 & 0.7892 \\ 0 & 0 & -0.3106 & -0.7072 & 0.5853 & 0.3701 \\ 0 & 0 & 0 & -0.9945 & 0.0835 & -0.0478 \\ 0 & 0 & 0 & 0 & 0.6118 & 0.4668 \\ 0 & 0 & 0 & 0 & 0 & 0 \end{pmatrix}$$

$$\Omega = \begin{pmatrix} 0 & 0 & -1.3887 & 0.0219 & 0.1540 & 0.0020 \\ 0 & 0 & 0.1431 & -0.0023 & -0.0159 & -0.0002 \\ 0 & 0 & -0.3027 & -0.1069 & -0.7527 & 0.0004 \\ 0 & 0 & 0 & -0.9447 & 0.0744 & 0.0004 \\ 0 & 0 & 0 & 0 & 0.6342 & 0 \\ 0 & 0 & 0 & 0 & 0 & 1.0000 \end{pmatrix}$$

with a generalized eigenvalue equal to infinity. The finite eigenvalues are 1.0366, 0.9500, 0.9745, and there are two eigenvalues equal to zero. The Q, Z matrices of the QZ decomposition are

$$Q = \begin{pmatrix} 0.9711 & -0.1187 & -0.1187 & -0.1199 & -0.1199 & 0 \\ -0.1001 & 0.1410 & -0.9848 & 0.0124 & 0.0124 & 0 \\ 0.2166 & 0.6112 & 0.0790 & 0.5354 & 0.5354 & 0 \\ -0.0004 & -0.0722 & -0.0093 & 0.0391 & 0.0446 & -0.9956 \\ -0.0039 & 0.7663 & 0.0990 & -0.4442 & -0.4437 & -0.0939 \\ 0.0000 & 0.0000 & 0.0000 & -0.7071 & 0.7071 & 0.0039 \end{pmatrix}$$

$$Z = \begin{pmatrix} 1.0000 & 0 & 0 & 0 & 0 & 0 \\ 0 & 0.7071 & -0.7071 & 0.0009 & -0.0061 & -0.0003 \\ 0 & -0.7071 & -0.7071 & 0.0012 & -0.0081 & \\ 0 & -0.0003 & 0.0061 & -0.0968 & -0.7004 & -0.7071 \\ 0 & 0.0023 & 0.0082 & -0.1020 & -0.6997 & 0.7071 \\ 0 & 0 & 0 & 0.9901 & -0.1406 & 0.0037 \end{pmatrix}$$

Since there are two generalized eigenvalues above $\beta^{-1/2}$, there are also two stability conditions needed for transversality conditions to hold, given by the two last columns of Z (two last rows of Z'):

$$0.0061\tilde{k}_t + 0.0081\tilde{i}_t + 0.7004\tilde{W}_{k_t} + 0.6997\tilde{W}_{i_t} + 0.1406\log(\theta_t) = 0 \qquad (4.45)$$

$$0.0003\tilde{k}_t - 0.0023\tilde{i}_t - 0.0037\log(\theta_t) = 0 \qquad (4.46)$$

where the first relationship happens not to involve consumption and the expectations $\tilde{W}_{k_t}$ and $\tilde{W}_{i_t}$ have dropped out of the second, since they are equal to each other. The second equation allows us to identify k_t and i_t separately from each other. These two stability conditions, obtained from the unstable eigenvalues, impose a relationship between the structural innovation and the expectation errors, as in (4.42), $\eta_t = -(Q_{2\bullet}\Pi)^{-1}Q_{2\bullet}\Psi z_t$, which, under our parameterization, becomes:

$$\eta_t^k = -0.1029\epsilon_t, \qquad \eta_t^i = -0.1085\epsilon_t$$

which very clearly illustrates that the two expectations errors are an exact function of each other.

The actual mechanism to generate the set of time series that solve the model from initial values k_0, i_0, is as follows. First, a sample realization for the productivity shock θ_t is generated using (4.30). Then, initial values for W_{k_0}, W_{i_0}, c_0 come from (4.35), (4.36), and (4.45). Then, using the value of θ_1, equations (4.35), (4.36), (4.45), (4.46), and (4.27) form a complete system in $W_{k_1}, W_{i_1}, c_1, k_1, i_1$. This procedure can be iterated for each period. Having time series for all the variables, we can compute the expectations errors from (4.33) and (4.34) and run rationality tests on them, if desired.

A solution to the linear system (4.37) exists only if representation (4.42) is feasible, that is, if the space spanned by the columns of $Q_{2\bullet}\Psi$ is included in the space spanned by the columns of $Q_{2\bullet}\Pi$. This condition becomes necessary and sufficient for the simpler cases in which $E_t(z_{t+1}) = 0$. In the specific model in this section, $Q_{2\bullet}\Psi$ is a 2×1 vector, while $Q_{2\bullet}\Pi$ is a full-rank 2×2 matrix, so that the condition is clearly satisfied. As an alternative, Sims (1998) suggests testing the condition for existence of a solution by regressing the columns of $Q_{2\bullet}\Psi$ on the columns of $Q_{2\bullet}\Pi$, to see if the resulting residuals are all equal to zero. In our example, the residual sum of squares turned out to be of order 10^{-34}, showing that the solution, in fact, exists.

4.6.3 *Special case: Zero depreciation rate*

With zero depreciation on physical capital, there is no difference between the accumulation processes followed by the two inputs, and the equality of conditional expectations in (4.28) and (4.29) becomes:

$$E_t\left[F_{t+1}^i c_{t+1}^{-\sigma}\right] = E_t\left[F_{t+1}^k c_{t+1}^{-\sigma}\right] \tag{4.47}$$

On the other hand, the marginal rate of transformation between physical capital, k_t, and inventories, i_t, which is in principle a random variable at time t, is

$$RMT_{t+1}^{i,k} = \frac{F_{t+1}^i}{F_{t+1}^k} = \frac{\psi}{1-\psi}\left(\frac{i_t}{k_t}\right)^{-\nu-1} \tag{4.48}$$

which belongs to the information set available at time t. This feature of the model implies an exact relationship between two expectations:

$$E_t\left[F_{t+1}^i c_{t+1}^{-\sigma}\right] = E_t\left[RMT_{t+1}^{i,k} F_{t+1}^k c_{t+1}^{-\sigma}\right] = RMT_{t+1}^{i,k} E_t\left[F_{t+1}^k c_{t+1}^{-\sigma}\right] \tag{4.49}$$

so that, in the special case of zero depreciation, (4.47) and (4.49) imply:

$$RMT_{t+1}^{i,k} = 1 \quad \text{or} \quad k_t = \left(\frac{1-\psi}{\psi}\right)^{1/(1+\nu)} i_t \tag{4.50}$$

This particular form for the optimality condition eliminates the lack of identification between the optimal amounts of the two production inputs in the special case of zero depreciation. The infinite eigenvalue disappears and, with it, the stability condition (4.46) that we used to identify physical capital separately from inventories, which is no longer needed. That condition corresponds to the case of non-zero depreciation, which explains why the productivity shock appears in it. If we use $\delta = 0$ but ignore (4.50), the eigenvalue equal to infinity again arises, and the associated stability condition analogous to (4.46) becomes $k_t = 12.8989\, i_t$, which is exactly equal to (4.50). Therefore, using stability conditions associated with infinite eigenvalues, we can solve identification issues that only in special cases (here with zero depreciation) can also be solved analytically.

4.7 Solving endogenous growth models

Numerical solution methods must be applied with great care to endogenous growth models, since we need to distinguish between the lack of stability that can and should be eliminated through conditions like those in the previous sections, and the lack of stationarity which is intrinsic to these models, even in steady state. In our particular approach, it looks as if the stability conditions could not possibly be obtained in endogenous growth models. Since they are derived from an approximation around the steady state, and the steady-state levels of the variables change over time, it would seem necessary to compute the linear approximation for each single period, which would be clearly hopeless.

Luckily, the method described in the previous sections can, in fact, be easily adapted to solve endogenous growth models. As an illustration, we will consider a planner's problem in an economy with aggregate constant returns to scale in physical and human capital, as in Uzawa (1965). Once the optimality conditions (including resources and technological constraints, as well as laws of motion for exogenous variables) have been obtained, we proceed as follows:

1. We transform the set of optimality conditions into ratios of the relevant variables, and compute the steady-state values for the ratios, which will be uniquely defined.
2. We obtain the appropriate stability conditions for this transformed system. The stability conditions depend upon the approximation around the steady state for the model in terms of ratios, which does not change over time. Hence, the conditions do not need to be revalued each period. We save these stability conditions.
3. We again rewrite the optimality conditions to make growth explicit for all those variables that experience non-zero growth in steady state, by multiplying and dividing each observation by the corresponding power of its growth rate.
4. We use the optimality conditions from step 3 together with the stability conditions from step 2, initial conditions for the state variables and sample realizations for the

exogenous shocks, to generate time series for the variables in the economy in levels, excluding the deterministic growth components. These can be obtained separately.

Summarizing, the set of time series that solve the model are generated from the version of the model in levels in which deterministic growth has been made explicit. *That way, we can decide whether the potential instability of the ultimately obtained time series for the original variables is purely due to their deterministic growth rate, or reflects a more fundamental instability of the solution, which might be unacceptable*. The procedure we have just outlined guarantees that the non-stationarity of the solution can be fully represented by a single unit root, as should be the case in any endogenous growth model, due to the presence of a unit eigenvalue in the coefficient matrix of its linear approximation.

We consider an economy with two sectors. In the first, output is produced from physical and human capital. In the second, human capital is produced from itself, without the need for physical capital. The unit of time which is available each period is split between both production activities. Output is obtained from a Cobb–Douglas technology in physical capital, k_t, and effective working hours, $u_t h_t$, the product of hours devoted to production, u_t, by human capital, h_t. In the second sector, human capital is accumulated through a linear technology, as a function of the amount of time devoted to this sector, $1 - u_t$. There are random productivity shocks θ_t, ξ_t in both sectors, following first-order autoregressive structures. Physical and human capital depreciate at constant rates δ_k and δ_h each period. The representative consumer has a constant relative risk aversion utility function in just one argument, consumption, and discounts utility over time at a rate β, where $0 < \beta < 1$. Population grows at a rate n, and the planner maximizes aggregate utility

$$\max_{\{\hat{c}_t, u_t, \hat{k}_t, \hat{h}_t\}_{t=1}^{\infty}} \quad E_0 \sum_{t=1}^{\infty} (\beta n)^{t-1} \left[\frac{\hat{c}_t^{1-\sigma} - 1}{1-\sigma} \right]$$

subject to

$$n\hat{k}_t = A\hat{k}_{t-1}^{\alpha}(u_t \hat{h}_{t-1})^{1-\alpha}\theta_t + (1-\delta_k)\hat{k}_{t-1} - \hat{c}_t \tag{4.51}$$

$$\hat{h}_t = B(1-u_t)\hat{h}_{t-1}\xi_t + (1-\delta_h)\hat{h}_{t-1} \tag{4.52}$$

$$\log(\theta_t) = \phi_\theta \log(\theta_{t-1}) + \epsilon_t^\theta, \quad \epsilon_t^\theta \sim N(0, \sigma_\theta^2) \tag{4.53}$$

$$\log(\xi_t) = \phi_\xi \log(\xi_{t-1}) + \epsilon_t^\xi, \quad \epsilon_t^\xi \sim N(0, \sigma_\xi^2) \tag{4.54}$$

given $\hat{k}_0, \hat{h}_0, \theta_0, \xi_0$

$$u_t \in (0, 1) \tag{4.55}$$

$$\hat{c}_t, \hat{k}_t, \hat{h}_t \geq 0$$

where variables with ^ exhibit non-zero steady-state growth, and we have the optimality conditions:

$$0 = -1 + E_t\left[\beta\left(\frac{\hat{c}_{t+1}}{\hat{c}_t}\right)^{-\sigma}\left(\alpha A\left(\frac{\hat{k}_t}{\hat{h}_t}\right)^{\alpha-1} u_{t+1}^{1-\alpha}\theta_{t+1} + 1 - \delta_k\right)\right] \tag{4.56}$$

$$0 = -\left(\frac{\hat{k}_{t-1}}{\hat{h}_{t-1}}\right)^{\alpha} u_t^{-\alpha}\frac{\theta_t}{\xi_t} + E_t\left[\beta n\left(\frac{\hat{c}_{t+1}}{\hat{c}_t}\right)^{-\sigma}\left(\frac{\hat{k}_t}{\hat{h}_t}\right)^{\alpha} u_{t+1}^{-\alpha}\frac{\theta_{t+1}}{\xi_{t+1}}\left(B\xi_{t+1} + 1 - \delta_h\right)\right] \tag{4.57}$$

together with (4.51) to (4.55).

Endogenous growth shows in the fact that this system can be solved for the steady-state levels of the variables with zero steady-state growth but only for ratios of variables with non-zero steady-state growth. All ratios are referred in this case to human capital. Their steady-state values can be obtained, but not those of the individual variables with steady-state growth. On the other hand, we can also compute the steady-state growth rate which is common, in this economy, to all variables with non-zero growth. Precisely because we can compute this growth rate, we cannot possibly solve for the steady-state values of all variables, since we have the same number of equations as we would have in an exogenous growth model.

Denoting by ϖ_t^{ch} and ϖ_t^{kh} the ratios $\hat{c}_t/\hat{h}_{t-1}$ and $\hat{k}_t/\hat{h}_t$, defining each expectation as a new variable, and introducing the associated expectations errors, we have the system:

$$0 = -n\varpi_t^{kh}\left(B(1-u_t)\xi_t + 1 - \delta_h\right) + A\left(\varpi_{t-1}^{kh}\right)^{\alpha} u_t^{1-\alpha}\theta_t + (1-\delta_h)\varpi_{t-1}^{kh} - \varpi_t^{ch} \tag{4.58}$$

$$0 = -\left(\varpi_t^{ch}\right)^{-\sigma} + \beta W_t^1 \tag{4.59}$$

$$0 = -W_{t-1}^1 + \left[\left(\varpi_t^{ch}\right)^{-\sigma} \times \left(B(1-u_{t-1})\xi_{t-1} + 1 - \delta_h\right)^{-\sigma} \times \left(\alpha A\left(\varpi_{t-1}^{kh}\right)^{\alpha-1} u_t^{1-\alpha}\theta_t + 1 - \delta_k\right)\right] - \eta_t^1 \tag{4.60}$$

$$0 = -\left(\varpi_{t-1}^{kh}\right)^{\alpha} u_t^{-\alpha}\frac{\theta_t}{\xi_t} + \beta n W_t^2 \tag{4.61}$$

$$0 = -W_{t-1}^2 + \left[\left(\frac{\varpi_t^{ch}}{\varpi_{t-1}^{ch}}\right)^{-\sigma} \times \left(B(1-u_t)\xi_{t-1} + 1 - \delta_h\right)^{-\sigma} \times \left(\left(\varpi_{t-1}^{kh}\right)^{\alpha} u_{t-1}^{-\alpha}\frac{\theta_t}{\xi_t}\right)\left(B\xi_t + 1 - \delta_h\right)\right] - \eta_t^2 \tag{4.62}$$

together with the stochastic processes (4.53) and (4.54). Thus we have a system of seven equations in nine variables $(\varpi_t^{ch}, \varpi_t^{kh}, u_t, \theta_t, \xi_t, W_t^1, W_t^2, \eta_t^1, \eta_t^2)$, but the associated generalized eigenvalue problem produces two unstable eigenvalues.[16]

With parameter values $\sigma = 1.5, \beta = 0.99, A = 1, \alpha = 0.36, B = 0.0201, 1 - \delta_k = 0.975, 1 - \delta_h = 0.992, n = 1.0035, \phi_\theta = 0.95, \phi_\xi = 0.95$, we obtain as stability conditions

$$-1.4126\left(\frac{c_t}{h_{t-1}} - \varpi_{ss}^{ch}\right) - 0.0806\left(\frac{k_t}{h_t} - \varpi_{ss}^{kh}\right) + 0.0205\tilde{u}_t - 1.6923\tilde{W}_t^1 + 0.2811\tilde{W}_t^2 - 0.8823\log(\theta_t) = 0 \tag{4.63}$$

$$-5.2034\left(\frac{c_t}{h_{t-1}} - \varpi_{ss}^{ch}\right) + 0.0493\left(\frac{k_t}{h_t} - \varpi_{ss}^{kh}\right) - 0.1193\tilde{u}_t + 0.4284\tilde{W}_t^1 + 1.0355\tilde{W}_t^2 + 0.3801\log(\theta_t) = 0 \tag{4.64}$$

which amount to the following relationships between expectation errors and structural innovations:

$$\eta_t^1 = 0.5924\epsilon_t^\theta - 0.1938\epsilon_t^\xi$$
$$\eta_t^2 = 0.1490\epsilon_t^\theta + 0.4184\epsilon_t^\xi$$

Once we have the two stability conditions, we turn to the original model, to rewrite it in a slightly different way. The steady-state rate of growth in this model is $\gamma = (\hat{c}_{t+1})/(\hat{c}_t) = [\beta n\,(B + 1 - \delta_h)]^{1/\sigma}$. We now rewrite the optimality conditions (4.51), (4.52), (4.56), and (4.57) making explicit this growth rate $\left(x_t = \hat{x}_t\gamma^{-t}\right.$, with $\left.x_t = (c_t, k_t, h_t)\right)$:

$$0 = -c_t^{-\sigma} + E_t\left[\beta\gamma^{-\sigma}c_{t+1}^{-\sigma}\left(\alpha A\left(\frac{k_t}{h_t}\right)^{\alpha-1}u_{t+1}^{1-\alpha}\theta_{t+1} + 1 - \delta_k\right)\right] \tag{4.65}$$

$$0 = -\left(\frac{k_{t-1}}{h_{t-1}}\right)^\alpha u_t^{-\alpha}\frac{\theta_t}{\xi_t} + E_t\left[\beta n\gamma^{-\sigma}\left(\frac{c_{t+1}}{c_t}\right)^{-\sigma}\left(\frac{k_t}{h_t}\right)^\alpha \times u_{t+1}^{-\alpha}\frac{\theta_{t+1}}{\xi_{t+1}}(B\xi_{t+1} + 1 - \delta_h)\right] \tag{4.66}$$

$$0 = -n\gamma k_t + Ak_{t-1}^\alpha(u_t h_{t-1})^{1-\alpha}\theta_t + (1 - \delta_k)k_{t-1} - c_t \tag{4.67}$$

$$0 = -\gamma h_t + B(1 - u_t)h_{t-1}\xi_t + (1 - \delta_h)h_{t-1} \tag{4.68}$$

It is not hard to show that the two conditional expectations in (4.65) and (4.66) are precisely W_t^1 and W_t^2 in (4.59) and (4.61). Therefore, their associated errors are the same η_t^1 and η_t^2 as in (4.60) and (4.62).

Together with the stochastic processes for the exogenous shocks, the definitions of the expectations errors (4.60) and (4.62), and the stability conditions from the model in

[16] The transformation into ratios eliminates the unit eigenvalue that arises in all endogenous growth models as a consequence of the steady state being a one-dimensional manifold.

ratios[17] (4.63), (4.64), this system has ten equations in as many variables ($c_t, k_t, h_t, u_t, \theta_t, \xi_t, W_t^1, W_t^2, \eta_t^1, \eta_t^2$). Furthermore, the system has a structure that allows for a solution to the original, endogenous growth model in the levels of the variables, to be obtained, starting from a sample realization for the structural innovations, along the following lines. The global constraint of resources (4.67), the law of accumulation of human capital (4.68), the expectations equations (4.59) and (4.61), and the two stability conditions (4.63) and (4.64) form a nonlinear system in $k_1, h_1, c_1, u_1, W_1^1$ and W_1^2, as functions of k_0, h_0, θ_1 and ξ_1. By repeated substitutions, the stability conditions can be transformed into a system of two nonlinear equations in c_1, u_1 as functions of state variables and exogenous shocks. Then, we would obtain h_1 and k_1 from (4.67) and (4.68), and W_1^1 and W_1^2 from (4.59) and (4.61), and the same procedure would be implemented to obtain optimal values for subsequent periods. Once we have produced time series for these variables, realizations for the expectations errors would be obtained from (4.60) and (4.62), and we could proceed to test for rationality, if desired.

The transformation of the model in ratios to human capital is time-invariant in steady state, because in this model all variables that grow in steady state experience the same growth rate. Hence, their ratio stays constant. However, even if the rates of growth were different, an appropriately defined ratio would still be constant in steady state, and the same procedure as we have described above would lead to a stable solution.

Endogenous growth models can also be solved by parameterizing expectations or following Uhlig's approach, among other possible methods. They differ from our approach in the way they recover time series for the levels of the variables that experience non-zero steady-state growth. Most methods would compute time series for ratios like $\hat{c}_t/\hat{h}_{t-1}$ or $\hat{k}_t/\hat{h}_t$ so that, to obtain time series for c_t, h_t and k_t, one would have to proceed as follows:

1. Use the law of motion of physical capital, $\hat{h}_t = B(1-u_t)\xi_t\hat{h}_{t-1} + (1-\delta_h)\hat{h}_{t-1}$, and normalize variables to make growth explicit, $\hat{h}_t = h_t\gamma^t$, to give:

$$\frac{h_t}{h_{t-1}} = [B(1-u_t)\xi_t + (1-\delta_h)]\,\frac{1}{\gamma} \tag{4.69}$$

2. Then, given an initial condition h_0 for human capital, we would compute

$$h_t = \left[\Pi_{s=1}^t\left(\frac{B(1-u_s)\xi_s + (1-\delta_h)}{\gamma}\right)\right]h_0, \quad t = 1, 2, \ldots, T \tag{4.70}$$

3. Once we have the h_t path, we obtain time series for physical capital and consumption from

$$k_t = \varpi_t^{kh}h_t = \left(\frac{k_t}{h_t}\right)h_t, \quad t = 1, 2, \ldots, T$$

$$c_t = \varpi_t^{ch}h_{t-1} = \left(\frac{c_t}{h_{t-1}}\right)h_{t-1}, \quad t = 1, 2, \ldots, T$$

[17] Note that the ratios of consumption and physical capital to human capital are the same with and without the deterministic trend, which is why we can also use for the detrended variables the previously calculated stability conditions.

However, the numerical precision error involved in generating the u_t time series, which in a single period may be arbitrarily small, will become sizeable when it is compounded over time as in (4.69). As a result, there will be some increasing error in the h_t series for long horizons, which will translate through (4.70) into errors for some other endogenous variables. In our experience, these errors are not negligeable: for instance, in the situation known as the *exogenous growth* case in Caballé and Santos (1993) (with the exogenous shock fixed at their expected value of one), the numerical errors are large enough for the resulting time series not to return to the same steady-state point where the economy was before undergoing an instantaneous shock, even though it is known theoretically that the economy should converge to that same initial state.

In contrast, the approach we have proposed computes the values for the variables in the economy each time t by solving a nonlinear system of equations. As a result, precision errors do not accumulate over time, and remain small every single period. After experiencing an instantaneous perturbation, the resulting time series converge to exactly the same steady-state point where the economy was before the shock.

Mendoza (1991) and Correia *et al.* (1995) propose stochastic, general equilibrium models of small and open economies in which some endogenous variables are integrated of order 1, $I(1)$, although with some cointegrating relationships among them. In that situation, whenever the model can be written in terms of the ratios of those variables with unit roots in such a way that the ratios are stationary, we will generally be able to find approximate stability conditions around a time-invariant steady-state. Using those stability conditions together with the optimality conditions as described in this section should allow us to obtain more accurate solutions for the integrated variables.

In particular, to be able to solve the model using the alternative approach of accumulating growth from an initial condition as in (4.69), it is necessary that ratios to state variables can be found that are stationary. This will not be possible if the only $I(1)$ variables are decision variables, as is the case in Correia *et al.* (1995), where consumption, foreign debt, the balance of trade and the level of net foreign asset holdings are $I(1)$, the first two being cointegrated, while the stock of physical capital, the only state variable, is stationary. These authors worry about the numerical accuracy of their solution (see their footnote 3), computed through a linear approximation as in King *et al.* (1988), which amounts to linearizing the Euler equations and solving numerically the resulting system of stochastic difference equations.

4.8 Conclusions

We have summarized in this chapter some of the practical details involved in the implementation of a solution strategy to produce stable solutions to rational expectations models, which is based on eigenvalue–eigenvector decompositions. We have taken as a base recent work by Sims (1998), who has produced a quite general discussion of the characterization of stable manifolds in linear models. He has extended the initial proposal of Blanchard and Kahn (1980) to accommodate a number of interesting generalizations. Even though the method is exact for linear models, it can also be applied to nonlinear models, starting from a linear approximation to the model around steady state, and we have discussed applications to some standard business cycle economies.

A distinctive feature of the method is the consideration of each conditional expectation, as well as the associated expectations error, as additional variables in the model. The addition of stability conditions, derived from the eigenvalue–eigenvector decomposition of the coefficient matrices in the linear system of stochastic difference equations, allows a numerical solution to be generated, in the form of a set of time series for all the relevant variables, including the conditional expectations and the rational expectations errors.

The approach is similar in spirit to any other method based on linear quadratic approximation, even though it fully exploits the nonlinear structure of the original model to produce a numerical solution. The stability conditions can be written as relationships between conditional expectations of (generally) nonlinear functions of future state and decision variables, and state variables known at the time the expectations were made. These functions could be compared to those emerging from the parameterized expectations method of den Haan and Marcet (1990) and Marcet and Lorenzoni (Chapter 7, this volume), which does not explicitly consider stability conditions. On the other hand, the method based on the eigenvalue–eigenvector decomposition is quite close to the undetermined coefficients method proposed by Uhlig (Chapter 3, this volume), which it would resemble even more closely if we started from a log-linear rather than from a linear approximation. A more developed set of rules to characterize the stable manifold in Chapter 3 would also approximate Uhlig's proposal to the method we have described in this chapter.

After applying the method to a standard growth model, we have shown that it performs well in situations where identification is weak, as is the case with physical capital and inventories as production inputs. We have also explained, in that same context, how the method will produce information on analytical restrictions among expectations in the model, which the researcher might not have perceived from the outset.

Finally, we have described how the method can easily be adapted to deal with endogenous growth models. In them, the steady state is not constant over time in the levels of the relevant variables, so that the standard linear approximation to the model cannot be obtained, and the method would not directly apply. However, extracting the deterministic trend from the variables and transforming the model in ratios of the relevant variables, allows for a stable solution to be obtained. The reason is that the stability conditions for the model in ratios, whose steady state is constant over time, can be used to solve for the variables in levels, once they have been normalized by their deterministic trend.

Part II

Nonlinear methods

5

DISCRETE STATE-SPACE METHODS FOR THE STUDY OF DYNAMIC ECONOMIES

Craig Burnside[1]

5.1 Introduction

In this chapter I discuss a number of numerical methods for solving dynamic stochastic general equilibrium models which fall within the common category of discrete state-space methods. These methods can be applied in situations where the state space of the model in question is given by a finite set of discrete points. In these cases, the methods provide an "exact" solution to the model in question.[2] On the other hand, these methods are frequently applied in situations where the model's state space is continuous, in which case the discrete state space can be viewed as an approximation to the continuous state space.[3]

I will discuss discrete state-space methods in the context of two well-known examples, a simple one-asset version of Lucas's (1978) consumption-based asset pricing model, and the one-sector neoclassical growth model. I will not exhaust the list of possible discrete state-space methods as they are very numerous. Rather, I will describe several examples which illustrate the basic principles involved.

Why use discrete state-space methods? In situations where log-linear approximations to the first-order necessary conditions of a model are close approximations to the exact conditions, there are many advantages to using these approximations. On the other hand, discrete state-space methods are useful when log-linear approximations are not accurate, or when we have no knowledge about their likely accuracy. They are justified on fairly intuitive grounds, but are also supported by a wealth of theoretical results.[4] They are

[1]The author's correspondence address is The World Bank, MC3-363, 1818 H Street NW, Washington DC 20433, USA.

[2]A simple example in the asset pricing literature is the paper by Mehra and Prescott (1985), in which the only state variable is the exogenous growth rate of the consumer's endowment income which is assumed to follow a simple two-state Markov chain. Many of the papers which have followed from this one have made similar assumptions, a notable exception being Cecchetti *et al.* (1993) who use a mixture distribution for the growth rate of the endowment. Because the distribution mixes a two-state Markov chain and an independently and identically distributed (i.i.d.). Gaussian random variable, a simple exact solution obtained using discrete state-space methods is still available.

[3]Examples include Baxter *et al.* (1990), Christiano (1990), Coleman (1990), Tauchen (1990) and Taylor and Uhlig (1990).

[4]Bertsekas (1976) contains numerous results pertaining to value function iteration over discrete state spaces. The typical result is that the fixed point of some discretized dynamic programming problem converges pointwise to its continuous equivalent. Atkinson (1976) and Baker (1977) present a wealth of convergence results pertaining to the use of discrete state spaces to solve integral equations. Tauchen and Hussey (1991) and Burnside (1993) present results, respectively, concerning pointwise and absolute

applicable to a wide variety of problems, and are often a good way of making a first pass at solving an unfamiliar model, because they are usually reliable. The main drawback of discrete state-space methods is their computational expense. For simple problems they present no difficulty, but for problems with a large state space, the expense of computing solutions can be great in terms of both time and computer memory.

In Section 5.2 I describe the basic principles of numerical quadrature which underlie most discrete state-space methods. In Section 5.3 I show how they can be applied in a very straightforward way to problems in which the state space consists entirely of exogenous variables. In Section 5.4 I describe methods that can be used when there are endogenous state variables. Section 5.5 gives some concluding thoughts.

5.2 The basics of quadrature

5.2.1 *How quadrature works*

Since we are concerned mainly with solving discrete-time dynamic stochastic general equilibrium models, a common feature of all of these models will be that there is at least one first-order necessary condition governing the intertemporal decisions of some agent. Typically, this condition will express the relationship between some variable today and the expected value of some other variable in the future. For example, the marginal cost today, in terms of utility forgone, of any decision must be matched by the sum of all expected future marginal benefits. When the state space of the model is discrete, evaluating the relevant expected value amounts to taking a weighted sum across all the possible values of the state variables in the future, where the weights are the relevant probabilities given the state today. When the state space is continuous the sum is replaced by an integral taken with respect to the conditional density of the future state given the current state. As one might expect, discrete state-space approximations to continuous state spaces involve approximating integrals by sums.

The methods for approximating integrals by sums that I will focus on here are formally referred to as *quadrature* methods. Abstracting, for the moment, from the Euler equations of some dynamic model, suppose that one had to compute the integral $\int_Y \psi(y) f(y)\, dy$, where I will refer to ψ as the *kernel* function and f is some density function defined over the set Y.[5] This would be, of course, the expected value of $\psi(y)$. Quadrature methods are based on the notion that one can use the approximation

$$\sum_{i=1}^{N} \psi(y_{i,N}) w_{i,N} \approx \int_Y \psi(y) f(y)\, dy \tag{5.1}$$

where the points $y_{i,N} \in Y, i = 1, \ldots, N$, are chosen presumably according to some rule, while the weight given to each point, $w_{i,N}$ presumably relates to the density function f in the neighbourhood of those points. In general, a quadrature method requires a rule for choosing the points, $y_{i,N}$, and a rule for choosing the weights, $w_{i,N}$.

convergence of solutions to asset pricing models obtained using discrete state spaces.

[5]The reader may be familiar with a more basic problem in numerical quadrature, which is to compute the integral $\int g(y)\, dy$ over some interval. We use the form $\int \psi(y) f(y)\, dy$ to emphasize the stochastic nature of the variable y.

There is a large mathematical literature on numerical integration which describes numerous techniques for implementing the left-hand side of (5.1) on a computer to obtain an approximation to the right-hand side.[6] The simplest method, at least when the density f has compact support, is to use an equally spaced grid of points and simply take the average of the function $\psi(y)f(y)$ evaluated at these points. The method I will focus on here is *Gaussian quadrature*, as advocated by Tauchen and Hussey (1991). This method is defined by a specific set of rules for choosing the points and weights which are related to the density function f. It has many attractive properties, not least of which is the fact that the approximation in (5.1) is exact for ψ functions which are polynomials of degree $2N-1$ or less.

In the next two subsections I will outline the rules for choosing points and weights under Gaussian quadrature and some of the useful properties of Gaussian quadrature rules than enable us to interpret them. The reader who is less interested in the details of quadrature may wish to skip ahead to Section 5.3.

5.2.2 *Selection of points and weights under Gaussian quadrature*

Since arbitrary accuracy of a Gaussian quadrature rule will typically require us to let N be arbitrarily large, it is a somewhat restrictive method, because this implies that all non-negative integer moments of y must exist. Assuming that this is the case, the method provides straightforward rules for determining the points and weights for numerical integration. These rules are based on the properties of the *orthogonal polynomials* corresponding to the density function, f.[7] The existence of these polynomials is guaranteed by the assumption made above concerning the moments of y.[8] The set of orthogonal polynomials, $\{\phi_N(y)\}_{N=0}^{\infty}$, for the density $f(y)$ are determined according to the rules

$$\phi_N(y) = \lambda_{N0} + \lambda_{N1}y + \lambda_{N2}y^2 + \cdots + \lambda_{NN}y^N, \quad \lambda_{NN} > 0 \tag{5.2}$$

$$\int_Y \phi_N(y)\phi_M(y)f(y)\,dy = \delta_{NM} \tag{5.3}$$

where $\delta_{NM} = 1$ if $N = M$ and 0 otherwise.

Notice that for $N = 0$, (5.3) implies that

$$\int_Y \phi_0^2(y)f(y)\,dy = \int_Y \lambda_{N0}^2 f(y)\,dy = \lambda_{00}^2 = 1 \tag{5.4}$$

or, given the sign restriction on λ_{00} implied by (5.2), $\lambda_{00} = 1$. But, then (5.3) implies that $\int_Y \phi_N(y)f(y)\,dy = 0$ for $N \geq 1$. In other words, each of the non-trivial polynomials is a mean-zero function of y. Furthermore, this provides (5.3) with the following natural interpretation: it requires that the non-trivial polynomials be mutually uncorrelated, and that they have unit variance.

[6] A good starting point for someone with an interest in numerical integration in general is the chapter on this subject in Press *et al.* (1992). They provide further detailed references.

[7] A classic reference on the properties of orthogonal polynomials is Szegö (1939).

[8] Uniqueness of the sequence of orthogonal polynomials follows if and only if $|E\,(1\ y\ \cdots\ y^N)\,(1\ y\ \cdots\ y^N)'\,|$ is non-zero for all N.

To take a specific example, suppose, for the moment, that $f(y)$ is the standard normal density. We have seen that $\phi_0(y) = 1$ for any f. For $N = 1$, $\phi_1(y) = \lambda_{10} + \lambda_{11}y$, and (5.3) implies that

$$0 = \int_Y \phi_1(y)\phi_0(y)f(y)\,dy = \int_Y (\lambda_{10} + \lambda_{11}y)f(y)\,dy = \lambda_{10} \tag{5.5}$$

$$1 = \int_Y \phi_1^2(y)f(y)\,dy = \int_Y (\lambda_{10} + \lambda_{11}y)^2 f(y)\,dy = \lambda_{10}^2 + \lambda_{11}^2 \tag{5.6}$$

Thus $\lambda_{10} = 0$ while the sign restriction from (5.2) implies that $\lambda_{11} = 1$. Therefore $\phi_1(y) = y$. For $N = 2$, we have $\phi_2(y) = \lambda_{20} + \lambda_{21}y + \lambda_{22}y^2$. It follows from (5.3) that

$$\begin{aligned} 0 &= \int_Y \phi_2(y)\phi_0(y)f(y)\,dy \\ &= \int_Y (\lambda_{20} + \lambda_{21}y + \lambda_{22}y^2)f(y)\,dy = \lambda_{20} + \lambda_{22} \end{aligned} \tag{5.7}$$

$$\begin{aligned} 0 &= \int_Y \phi_2(y)\phi_1(y)f(y)\,dy \\ &= \int_Y (\lambda_{20} + \lambda_{21}y + \lambda_{22}y^2)yf(y)\,dy = \lambda_{21} \end{aligned} \tag{5.8}$$

$$\begin{aligned} 1 &= \int_Y \phi_2^2(y)f(y)\,dy \\ &= \int_Y (\lambda_{20} + \lambda_{21}y + \lambda_{22}y^2)^2 f(y)\,dy = \lambda_{20}^2 + 2\lambda_{20}\lambda_{22} + \lambda_{21}^2 + 3\lambda_{22}^2 \end{aligned} \tag{5.9}$$

Thus $\lambda_{20} = -1/\sqrt{2}$, $\lambda_{21} = 0$, and $\lambda_{22} = 1/\sqrt{2}$, so that $\phi_2(y) = (y^2 - 1)/\sqrt{2}$. Continuing this process iteratively, one obtains the Nth orthogonal polynomial for the standard normal from the recursive formula

$$\phi_N(y) = \sqrt{\frac{1}{N}}\phi_{N-1}(y)y - \sqrt{\frac{N-1}{N}}\phi_{N-2}(y) \tag{5.10}$$

Once we have the set of orthogonal polynomials corresponding to the density f, obtaining the points and weights for quadrature is straightforward. If we are using an N-point Gaussian quadrature rule,[9] the N points are located at the roots of the Nth orthogonal polynomial. For the standard normal example this would mean that for $N = 1$ there is one point, $y_{1,1} = 0$, for $N = 2$ there are points $y_{1,2} = -1$ and $y_{2,2} = 1$, for $N = 3$ the points are $y_{1,3} = -\sqrt{3}$, $y_{2,3} = 0$ and $y_{3,3} = \sqrt{3}$, and so on.

The next step is to choose the weights. The weights for an N-point Gaussian quadrature rule are chosen so that if the kernel is a polynomial of order $2N - 1$ or lower the quadrature approximation is exact. Formally, define the set

$$\mathbf{P}_j = \{P(y) = p_0 + p_1y + p_2y^2 + \cdots \,|\, p_i = 0 \text{ for } i > j,\ p_i \in \mathbb{R} \text{ otherwise}\} \tag{5.11}$$

[9] That is, the number of terms in the sum on the left-hand side of (5.1) is N.

Then the weights are chosen so that

$$\sum_{i=1}^{N} P(y_{i,N})w_{i,N} = \int_Y P(y)f(y)\,dy, \quad \forall P(y) \in \mathbf{P}_{2N-1} \tag{5.12}$$

That weights with this property exist is proved in Szegö (1939, Theorem 3.4.1). Although (5.12) represents $2N$ restrictions (because the rule must be exact for all polynomials of 0th to $(2N-1)$th orders) on the N values of the weights, only N of the restrictions are unique.

To return to the standard normal example, a one-point rule must be exact for all polynomials up to first-order. Therefore

$$p_0 w_{1,1} = \int_Y p_0 f(y)\,dy = p_0 \tag{5.13}$$

$$\left(p_0 + p_1 y_{1,1}\right) w_{1,1} = p_0 w_{1,1} = \int_Y (p_0 + p_1 y) f(y)\,dy = p_0 \tag{5.14}$$

which both imply that $w_{1,1} = 1$ (notice that the second equation is redundant). For a two-point rule, all third- or higher-order polynomials must be exactly integrated. The two unique conditions implied by (5.12) are $w_{1,2} = w_{2,2}$ and $w_{1,2} + w_{2,2} = 1$. Therefore, the weights are $w_{1,2} = w_{2,2} = 1/2$.

5.2.3 *Properties of Gaussian quadrature rules*

One important general feature of Gaussian quadrature is that the weights generated by (5.12) will sum to one for any N. That is, $\sum_{i=1}^{N} w_{i,N} = 1$ for all N (Szegö, 1939, Theorem 3.4.2). This provides an important interpretation of the quadrature approximation (5.12). While the right-hand side of the equation is the expected value of $\psi(y)$ given the continuous density f, the left-hand side is an approximation to this which can be interpreted as the expected value of $\psi(y)$ when y has a discrete distribution over the set $\{y_{1,N}, y_{2,N}, \ldots, y_{N,N}\}$ with associated probabilities $\{w_{1,N}, w_{2,N}, \ldots, w_{N,N}\}$.

Another interesting feature of Gaussian quadrature rules is that there exist points, $z_{i,N}, i = 0, \ldots, N$, which satisfy

$$z_{0,N} < y_{1,N} < z_{1,N} < y_{2,N} < \cdots < y_{N-1,N} < z_{N-1,N} < y_{N,N} < z_{N,N} \tag{5.15}$$

such that

$$w_{i,N} = \int_{z_{i-1,N}}^{z_{i,N}} f(y)\,dy \tag{5.16}$$

The end points $z_{0,N}$ and $z_{N,N}$ represent the lower and upper limits of the set Y and can be infinite as in the case of the normal distribution. This means that

$$\begin{aligned}\sum_{i=1}^{N} \psi(y_{i,N})w_{i,N} &= \sum_{i=1}^{N} \psi(y_{i,N}) \int_{z_{i-1,N}}^{z_{i,N}} f(y)\,dy \\ &= \int_Y \sum_{i=1}^{N} \psi(y_{i,N}) \mathbf{1}_{(z_{i-1,N},z_{i,N})}(y) f(y)\,dy \end{aligned} \tag{5.17}$$

where $\mathbf{1}_{(z_{i-1,N}, z_{i,N})}(y)$ is the indicator function which is 1 if $y \in (z_{i-1,N}, z_{i,N})$, and is zero otherwise. Notice that if we define $\psi_N(y) = \sum_{i=1}^{N} \psi(y_{i,N}) \mathbf{1}_{(z_{i-1,N}, z_{i,N})}(y)$, an equivalent expression for (5.1) is

$$\int_Y \psi_N(y) f(y)\, dy \approx \int_Y \psi(y) f(y)\, dy \tag{5.18}$$

where we are approximating the expectation on the right-hand side by replacing the kernel $\psi(y)$ by a function that approximates it, in this case a step function. This provides an alternative interpretation of quadrature rules as a numerical method in which arbitrary integrands are replaced by functions which lie in a narrower class of functions, in this case step functions. Thus, there is a natural relationship between quadrature and the weighted residual methods discussed by McGrattan (Chapter 6, this volume).

Finally, in cases where Y is a compact set $[a, b]$, $f(y)$ is an arbitrary density on Y and $\psi(y)$ is any function for which the Riemann–Stieltjes integral on the right-hand side of (5.1) exists, it follows that

$$\lim_{N \to \infty} \sum_{i=1}^{N} \psi(y_{i,N}) w_{i,N} = \int_Y \psi(y) f(y)\, dy \tag{5.19}$$

To conclude, we have seen that Gaussian quadrature is a very natural method for several reasons. The orthogonal polynomials on which quadrature is based form an orthonormal basis with respect to the density function for y. The points and weights are selected in such a way that finite-order polynomials can be exactly integrated using quadrature formulae. And, finally, the weights have a natural interpretation as the probabilities associated with intervals around the quadrature points.

5.3 Solving models with exogenous state variables

5.3.1 *An asset pricing example*

To illustrate the manner in which models with strictly exogenous state variables can be solved using discrete state-space methods, I will use an asset pricing example based on Lucas (1978). Suppose there is an economy populated by N identical agents, each with instantaneous utility function

$$U(C_t) = \frac{C_t^{1-\gamma} - 1}{1 - \gamma} \tag{5.20}$$

where C_t is the agent's consumption at time t and γ is the coefficient of relative risk aversion. Suppose that all output in this economy is obtained from K assets which produce stochastic endowments of a single perishable consumption good for each unit the agent owns at the beginning of time t. That is, if the agent owns S_{kt} units of asset k at the beginning of time t, he receives an endowment of $S_{kt} D_{kt}$ units of the consumption good, where D_{kt} is identical for each unit of the kth asset held by an agent and is an exogenous stochastic process. These consumption goods can be consumed or traded for shares of the assets. If the price at date t of the kth asset in units of consumption is P_{kt}, each agent's budget constraint is given by

$$C_t + \sum_{k=1}^{K} P_{kt} S_{kt+1} \le \sum_{k=1}^{K} (P_{kt} + D_{kt}) S_{kt} \tag{5.21}$$

Assuming that agents discount their expected streams of utility with the factor β, at time 0 the agent maximizes

$$E_0 \sum_{t=0}^{\infty} \beta^t U(C_t) \tag{5.22}$$

by choosing contingency plans for C_t and $\{S_{kt+1}\}_{k=1}^{K}$ subject to (10.4) for $t = 0, 1, \ldots$. Substituting the budget constraint into the objective function, we obtain

$$E_0 \sum_{t=0}^{\infty} \beta^t U \left[\sum_{k=1}^{K} (P_{kt} + D_{kt}) S_{kt} - \sum_{k=1}^{K} P_{kt} S_{kt+1} \right] \tag{5.23}$$

The first-order conditions for this problem are

$$P_{kt} U'(C_t) = \beta E_t U'(C_{t+1})(P_{kt+1} + D_{kt+1}), \quad k = 1, \ldots, K \tag{5.24}$$

Since the agents are identical they will make the same decisions given the state of the world. As a result it is convenient to assume that the total supply of each asset is N, so that $S_{kt} = 1$, for all k and t, for every agent, in equilibrium. Then, the budget constraint implies that $C_t = \sum_{k=1}^{K} D_{kt}$ for all t. So we have the Euler equations

$$P_{kt} U' \left(\sum_{k=1}^{K} D_{kt} \right) = \beta E_t U' \left(\sum_{k=1}^{K} D_{kt+1} \right) (P_{kt+1} + D_{kt+1}), \quad k = 1, \ldots, K \tag{5.25}$$

5.3.2 *The case of a single i.i.d. shock*

If $K = 1$, so that there is only one asset, then we have one Euler equation for that asset which, dropping the k subscript, is

$$P_t U'(D_t) = \beta E_t U'(D_{t+1})(P_{t+1} + D_{t+1})$$

With the assumption that utility is isoelastic, as in (5.20), this becomes

$$P_t D_t^{-\gamma} = \beta E_t D_{t+1}^{-\gamma} (P_{t+1} + D_{t+1}) \tag{5.26}$$

It is convenient to express this equation in terms of the price–dividend ratio $V_t = P_t / D_t$:

$$V_t D_t^{1-\gamma} = \beta E_t D_{t+1}^{1-\gamma} (V_{t+1} + 1) \tag{5.27}$$

or

$$V_t = \beta E_t X_{t+1}^{1-\gamma} (V_{t+1} + 1) \tag{5.28}$$

where $X_{t+1} = D_{t+1}/D_t$. Equation (5.28) implicitly defines a solution for the price–dividend ratio at time t, as a function of those variables known at time t which are useful in forecasting functions of future values of dividend growth.

The special case we will focus on for the moment is when the logarithm of X_t is an i.i.d. normal random variable with mean μ and variance σ^2. Altug and Labadie (1994, p. 83) show that the solution for V_t in this case is

$$V_t = \frac{\beta \exp\left(\alpha\mu + \frac{1}{2}\alpha^2\sigma^2\right)}{1 - \beta \exp\left(\alpha\mu + \frac{1}{2}\alpha^2\sigma^2\right)} \tag{5.29}$$

as long as

$$\beta \exp\left(\alpha\mu + \tfrac{1}{2}\alpha^2\sigma^2\right) < 1 \tag{5.30}$$

where $\alpha = 1 - \gamma$.

Suppose we were unaware of this solution and tried to determine an approximate solution for V_t, as a function of $x_t = \ln(X_t)$, using a discrete state-space method. In other words, suppose we tried to find some function V such that

$$\begin{aligned} V(x_t) &= \beta E_t \exp(\alpha x_{t+1})[V(x_{t+1}) + 1] \\ &= \int \beta \exp(\alpha x_{t+1})[V(x_{t+1}) + 1] f(x_{t+1})\, dx_{t+1} \end{aligned} \tag{5.31}$$

where f is the density function for x_{t+1}. Imagine that we tried to approximate the integral on the right-hand side using an N-point Gaussian quadrature rule. We would then have the equation

$$V(x_t) \approx \sum_{i=1}^{N} \beta \exp(\alpha y_{i,N})[V(y_{i,N}) + 1] w_{i,N} \tag{5.32}$$

where the $y_{i,N}$, and $w_{i,N}$ are the points and weights corresponding to an N-point rule for a normal random variable with mean μ and variance σ^2.[10] Suppose we consider (5.32) for all $x_t \in \{y_{1,N}, y_{2,N}, \ldots, y_{N,N}\}$. We then have N equations

$$V(y_{j,N}) \approx \sum_{i=1}^{N} \beta \exp(\alpha y_{i,N})[V(y_{i,N}) + 1] w_{i,N}, \quad j = 1, \ldots, N \tag{5.33}$$

Now suppose we convert (5.33) into N strict equalities in the N unknowns $V(y_{j,N})$. Then we have

$$V(y_{j,N}) = \sum_{i=1}^{N} \beta \exp(\alpha y_{i,N})[V(y_{i,N}) + 1] w_{i,N}, \quad j = 1, \ldots, N \tag{5.34}$$

Since this is simply N linear equations in the N unknowns, $V(y_{j,N})$, it has a trivial solution.

[10] Suppose that the points and weights for an N-point rule for the standard normal are denoted $\bar{y}_{i,N}$ and $\bar{w}_{i,N}$ respectively. It turns out that when we generate an N-point rule for a normal random variable with arbitrary mean μ and variance σ^2, the quadrature points are given by $y_{i,N} = \mu + \sigma \bar{y}_{i,N}$ and the weights are $w_{i,N} = \bar{w}_{i,N}$.

The discrete state-space approximation interpretation of (5.34) is straightforward. Suppose that x_t, rather than being normally distributed, had, in fact, an i.i.d. discrete distribution such that $x_t = y_{j,N}$ with probability $w_{j,N}$. Then (5.34) would provide the exact solution for V_t given that $x_t = y_{j,N}$.

In this example, since nothing inside the sum depends on j, it is clear that $V(y_{j,N}) = V$, a constant, for all j. This implies that the approximate solution for V_t is the constant

$$V = \frac{\sum_{i=1}^{N} \beta \exp(\alpha y_{i,N}) w_{i,N}}{1 - \sum_{i=1}^{N} \beta \exp(\alpha y_{i,N}) w_{i,N}} \tag{5.35}$$

The reader may verify numerically that even though both the true solution and the approximation to it are constants, they will not be equal, in general, for all N.

5.3.3 *The case of multiple i.i.d. shocks*

Now suppose that there are $K > 1$ assets. We can imagine that the law of motion of the endowments from the K assets is such that $x_{1t} = \ln(D_{1t}) - \ln(D_{1t-1})$ and $x_{2t} = \ln(C_t) - \ln(C_{t-1})$, where $C_t = \sum_{k=1}^{K} D_{kt}$, are jointly normal. So, if we were interested in solving for the price–dividend ratio of the first asset, we might assume that $x_t = (x_{1t}\ x_{2t})'$ is distributed as an i.i.d. normal random vector with mean μ and variance-covariance matrix Σ. Defining $V_{1t} = P_{1t}/D_{1t}$, and assuming isoelastic utility, we have

$$V_{1t} = \beta E_t \exp(\alpha' x_{t+1})(V_{1t+1} + 1) \tag{5.36}$$

where $\alpha = (1 - \gamma)'$.

It is, again, possible to show that the price–dividend ratio is a constant:

$$V_{1t} = \frac{\beta \exp\left(\alpha'\mu + \frac{1}{2}\alpha'\Sigma\alpha\right)}{1 - \beta \exp\left(\alpha'\mu + \frac{1}{2}\alpha'\Sigma\alpha\right)} \tag{5.37}$$

as long as

$$\beta \exp\left(\alpha'\mu + \tfrac{1}{2}\alpha'\Sigma\alpha\right) < 1 \tag{5.38}$$

If we were unaware of this solution and tried to determine an approximate solution for V_{1t}, as a function of x_t, using a discrete state-space method, we would try to find some function V_1 such that

$$\begin{aligned} V_1(x_t) &= \beta E_t \exp(\alpha' x_{t+1})[V_1(x_{t+1}) + 1] \\ &= \int \beta \exp(\alpha' x_{t+1})[V_1(x_{t+1}) + 1] f(x_{t+1})\, dx_{t+1} \end{aligned} \tag{5.39}$$

where f is the density function for the vector x_{t+1}.

The question, in this case, is how to set up the quadrature rule when the state vector x_t is multi-dimensional. If the elements of x_t were uncorrelated, we might guess that a natural way to set up the quadrature rule would be to use separate grids of points for each dimension and simply use all possible combinations of these points in computing the relevant sum. The weights would be the cross-products of the weights for the individual grids. Let the univariate N-point quadrature rule for the standard normal be given by the points $\{\bar{y}_{i,N}\}_{i=1}^{N}$ and the weights $\{\bar{w}_{i,N}\}_{i=1}^{N}$. Suppose we set up a quadrature rule for an $M \times 1$ vector x_t, distributed normally with mean 0 and variance-covariance matrix, I_M. This rule might use N_m points for the mth element of x_t, x_{mt}. The most likely choice would be to have $N_m = N$ for all m. In any case, it would be natural to set up a rule such that

$$y_{i,N} = (\bar{y}_{j_1,N_1}\ \bar{y}_{j_2,N_2}\ \cdots\ \bar{y}_{j_M,N_M})' \tag{5.40}$$

and

$$w_{i,N} = \bar{w}_{j_1,N_1}\bar{w}_{j_2,N_2}\cdots\bar{w}_{j_M,N_M} \tag{5.41}$$

where

$$j_m = 1, \ldots, N_m \tag{5.42}$$

$$\begin{aligned} i =& (j_1 - 1)\, N_2 \cdots N_M + (j_2 - 1)\, N_3 \cdots N_M \\ &+ \cdots + (j_{M-1} - 1)\, N_M + j_M \end{aligned} \tag{5.43}$$

$$N = N_1 N_2 \cdots N_M \tag{5.44}$$

The rule for i is just a way of indexing the possible states using a single integer.

Now suppose the mean of x_t is μ, while its covariance matrix is given by Σ. Notice that $\xi_t = C'^{-1}(x_t - \mu)$ is distributed as $N(0, I_M)$, when C is the Cholesky decomposition of Σ. That is, $C'C = \Sigma$. Since this means we can write $x_t = \mu + C'\xi_t$, it is natural to consider as a quadrature rule

$$y_{i,N} = \mu + C'(\bar{y}_{j_1,N_1}\ \bar{y}_{j_2,N_2}\ \cdots\ \bar{y}_{j_M,N_M})' \tag{5.45}$$

and

$$w_{i,N} = \bar{w}_{j_1,N_1}\bar{w}_{j_2,N_2}\cdots\bar{w}_{j_M,N_M} \tag{5.46}$$

This means that our approximate solution to (5.39) based on quadrature will be

$$V_1(y_{j,N}) = \sum_{i=1}^{N} \beta \exp(\alpha' y_{i,N})[V_1(y_{i,N}) + 1]w_{i,N}, \quad j = 1, \ldots, N \tag{5.47}$$

which is a system of N linear equations in N unknowns. Again, because nothing on the right-hand side is dependent on j we obtain a constant approximate solution for V_{1t} given by

$$V_1 = \frac{\sum_{i=1}^{N} \beta \exp(\alpha' y_{i,N}) w_{i,N}}{1 - \sum_{i=1}^{N} \beta \exp(\alpha' y_{i,N}) w_{i,N}} \tag{5.48}$$

What is interesting about the example with correlated shocks is that if we give it the discrete state-space interpretation, the state space for the variable x_{jt} will be different

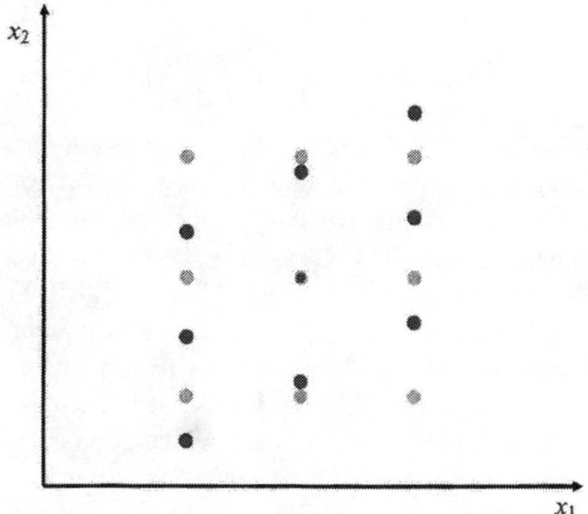

FIG. 5.1. Quadrature points for correlated normal random variables.
Note: The grey points are the 9 quadrature points that result from an example where $M = 2$, $N_1 = N_2 = 3$, and $x_t \sim N(\mu, I_2)$. The black points are for the case where $x_t \sim N(\mu, \Sigma)$ where $\Sigma_{11} = \Sigma_{22} = 1$, but $\Sigma_{12} = \Sigma_{21} = 0.5$.

depending on the values of x_{1t} through x_{j-1t}. This is best illustrated for the case of two shocks which are positively correlated, as in Fig. 5.1. The matrix C applies a trapezoidal transformation to the rectangular grid implied if the elements of x_t are uncorrelated.

5.3.4 *The case of serially correlated shocks*

More complexity is introduced if the growth rates of the endowments are serially correlated. To avoid burdensome notation I will return to the univariate example, and suppose that there is a single asset whose endowment behaves according to

$$x_t = \mu(1-\rho) + \rho x_{t-1} + \epsilon_t \tag{5.49}$$

where $|\rho| < 1$ and ϵ_t is an i.i.d. $N(0, \sigma^2)$ process.

The Euler equation in this case is

$$V_t = \beta E_t \exp(\alpha x_{t+1})(V_{t+1} + 1) \tag{5.50}$$

where $\alpha = 1 - \gamma$. It has a solution, derived in Burnside (1998), given by

$$\begin{aligned} V_t = \sum_{i=1}^{\infty} \beta^i \exp\Biggl\{\alpha\left(\mu\left[i - \frac{\rho(1-\rho^i)}{1-\rho}\right] + \frac{\rho(1-\rho^i)}{1-\rho} x_t\right) \\ + \frac{1}{2}\frac{\alpha^2}{(1-\rho)^2}\left[i - 2\frac{\rho(1-\rho^i)}{1-\rho} + \frac{\rho^2(1-\rho^{2i})}{1-\rho^2}\right]\sigma^2\Biggr\} \end{aligned} \tag{5.51}$$

as long as

$$\beta \exp\left(\alpha\mu + \frac{1}{2}\frac{\alpha^2}{(1-\rho)^2}\sigma^2\right) < 1 \tag{5.52}$$

While this is a solution, it is not a particularly useful one for at least two reasons. First, it is an infinite series of expressions rather than a single expression, so it must be recursively calculated for any specific value of x_t. Second, the series does not converge rapidly for some parameter values. This is easily verified for a trivial special case of log utility ($\gamma = 1$) in which case $\alpha = 0$. This yields $V_t = \sum_{i=1}^{\infty} \beta^i$. For a value of β close to 1, say $\beta = 0.99$, it takes many terms in the series before v_t approaches its true value of $\beta/(1-\beta) = 99$. For example, well over 600 terms must be added in order for the sum to be within 0.1 of 99, and over 900 terms to be within 0.01.

So, although the model has an exact solution which can be written in an analytical form, this form may not be useful in all circumstances, as it is an infinite series which will converge slowly for typical parameterizations. Furthermore, if the x_t process is something more general than a Gaussian process, there may not even be an analytical form for each term in the series.

We have seen, from equation (5.51), that the solution for V_t is of the form $V(x_t)$. If we tried to obtain an approximation to this using a discrete state-space method, we would start from the Euler equation written as an integral equation

$$V(x_t) = \int \beta \exp(\alpha x_{t+1})[V(x_{t+1}) + 1] f(x_{t+1}|x_t)\, dx_{t+1} \tag{5.53}$$

This equation differs significantly from the equation we had in the i.i.d. case because the density for x_{t+1} is conditional on the value for x_t. This implies that if we used quadrature to approximate the integral in (5.53), the quadrature rule would need to be different for each x_t. To get around this problem Tauchen and Hussey (1991) suggest the following transformation. Notice that (5.53) is equivalent to

$$V(x_t) = \int \beta \exp(\alpha x_{t+1})[V(x_{t+1}) + 1] \frac{f(x_{t+1}|x_t)}{f(x_{t+1}|\mu)} f(x_{t+1}|\mu)\, dx_{t+1} \tag{5.54}$$

Now, using an N-point rule based on the density function $f(x_{t+1}|\mu)$ we could approximate (5.54) by

$$V(x_t) \approx \sum_{i=1}^{N} \beta \exp(\alpha y_{i,N}) \left[V\left(y_{i,N}\right) + 1\right] \frac{f(y_{i,N}|x_t)}{f(y_{i,N}|\mu)} w_{i,N} \tag{5.55}$$

where the quadrature points are $y_{i,N} = \mu + \sigma \bar{y}_{i,N}$, and the weights are $w_{i,N} = \bar{w}_{i,N}$ with $\bar{y}_{i,N}$ and $\bar{w}_{i,N}$ defined as before.

If we imposed equality in (5.55) for $x_t \in \{y_{i,N}\}_{i=1}^{N}$ we would have N linear equations in N unknowns given by

$$V(y_{j,N}) = \sum_{i=1}^{N} \beta \exp(\alpha y_{i,N})[V(y_{i,N}) + 1] \frac{f(y_{i,N}|y_{j,N})}{f(y_{i,N}|\mu)} w_{i,N} \tag{5.56}$$

In this case the solution is not a constant, because the terms in the sum do depend on j.

Burnside (1993) derives a number of theoretical properties of the solution generated by (5.56). Primary among these is that, subject to a minor modification of the quadrature rule, if the solution in (5.56) is extended to the real line by using step functions over the intervals $(z_{i-1,N}, z_{i,N}) = (\mu + \sigma \bar{z}_{i-1,N}, \mu + \sigma \bar{z}_{i,N})$ then it can be shown to converge, as $N \to \infty$ in L^2 to the true solution to (5.53).

Unfortunately, the approximation in (5.56) does not have a direct interpretation as the exact representation of the Euler equation when x_t is a discrete state-space process. To see this, suppose that x_t was a simple first-order Markov process, with a discrete state space $\{y_{i,N}\}_{i=1}^N$. Suppose that the probability that $x_{t+1} = y_{i,N}$ given that $x_t = y_{j,N}$ was given by π_{ji}. The exact representation of the Euler equation for this model would be

$$V(y_{j,N}) = \sum_{i=1}^{N} \beta \exp(\alpha y_{i,N})[V(y_{i,N}) + 1]\pi_{ji} \tag{5.57}$$

This closely resembles (5.56) if we think of the terms $[f(y_{i,N}|y_{j,N})/f(y_{i,N}|\mu)]w_{i,N}$ as equivalent to π_{ji}. Since the π_{ji} terms are conditional probabilities, $\sum_i \pi_{ji} = 1$. However, in general, $\sum_i [f(y_{i,N}|y_{j,N})/f(y_{i,N}|\mu)]w_{i,N} \neq 1$. For this reason, Tauchen and Hussey (1991) suggest solving

$$V(y_{j,N}) = \sum_{i=1}^{N} \beta \exp(\alpha y_{i,N}) \left[V(y_{i,N}) + 1\right] \frac{f(y_{i,N}|y_{j,N})}{f(y_{i,N}|\mu)} \frac{w_{i,N}}{s_j} \tag{5.58}$$

where

$$s_j = \sum_{i=1}^{N} \frac{f(y_{i,N}|y_{j,N})}{f(y_{i,N}|\mu)} w_{i,N} \tag{5.59}$$

The approximate solution generated by (5.56) is the same as the exact solution for the price–dividend ratio in a model where x_t is a first-order Markov process with a discrete state space $\{y_{i,N}\}_{i=1}^N$ and transition probabilities given by

$$\pi_{ji} = \frac{f(y_{i,N}|y_{j,N})}{f(y_{i,N}|\mu)} \frac{w_{i,N}}{s_j} \tag{5.60}$$

It can be shown that $\lim_{N\to\infty} s_j = 1$ for all j so that the solutions to (5.56) and (5.58) converge to the same limit.

In the final section of this chapter I discuss extensions and limitations to the use of quadrature as the basis of a numerical solution method.

5.4 Solving models with endogenous state variables

5.4.1 *A one-sector neoclassical growth model*

To illustrate how discrete state-space methods may be applied to problems with endogenous state variables, I will take as an example a standard one-sector neoclassical growth model. Suppose that there is an economy populated by N identical agents who supply one unit of labour inelastically and have logarithmic preferences over the single consumption good. Output at date t, is given by $Y_t = A_t K_t^\theta$ where A_t is a stationary stochastic shock to the level of technology and K_t is the capital stock at the beginning of date t. The resource constraint for the economy is

$$C_t + K_{t+1} - (1 - \delta)K_t \leq Y_t \tag{5.61}$$

where δ is the depreciation rate of capital. A competitive equilibrium for a decentralized version of this economy is equivalent to the social planning problem in which the planner maximizes

$$E_0 \sum_{t=0}^{\infty} \beta^t \ln(C_t) \tag{5.62}$$

by choosing contingency plans for C_t and K_{t+1} subject to the resource constraint and K_0.

As in the asset pricing example, it is convenient to rewrite the problem by substituting the resource constraint into the planner's objective to obtain

$$E_0 \sum_{t=0}^{\infty} \beta^t \ln\left[A_t K_t^\theta + (1 - \delta)K_t - K_{t+1}\right] \tag{5.63}$$

The Euler equation for this problem is

$$\frac{1}{A_t K_t^\theta + (1-\delta)K_t - K_{t+1}} = \beta E_t \frac{\theta A_{t+1} K_{t+1}^{\theta-1} + (1-\delta)}{A_{t+1} K_{t+1}^\theta + (1-\delta)K_{t+1} - K_{t+2}} \tag{5.64}$$

Unlike the asset pricing example, this equation is not linear in the variable we wish to solve for, in this case K_{t+1}, as a function of the state variables at time t, A_t and K_t. Furthermore, one of the state variables, K_t, is endogenously determined over time. As a result of these two features of the model, for many assumptions about the distribution of the shocks to technology, A_t, there will be no analytic form for the optimal level of K_{t+1} in terms of the relevant state variables. One special case for which a closed form is well known, is the case where $\delta = 1$, so that capital depreciates completely from period to period. In this case the solution is $K_{t+1} = \beta\theta A_t K_t^\theta$ (see Sargent, 1987b).

In practice, we will assume that $a_t = \ln(A_t)$ is a Gaussian AR(1) process with the law of motion

$$a_t = \rho a_{t-1} + \epsilon_t, \tag{5.65}$$

where ϵ_t is i.i.d. $N(0, \sigma^2)$. The zero-mean assumption for a_t is for convenience and will play no important role in the solution of the model.

5.4.2 *Discrete state spaces and the growth model*

Tauchen's (1990) method for solving the growth model is perhaps the most straightforward given our discussion in the section on exogenous state variables. Rather than working with the Euler equation for the growth model, Tauchen works with the Bellman equation for the dynamic programming problem associated with it. This is given by

$$\begin{aligned} V(K,a) &= \max_{K' \in \mathcal{K}_C} \ln[\exp(a)\, K^\theta + (1-\delta)K - K'] + \beta E_t V(K',a') \\ &= \max_{K' \in \mathcal{K}_C} \ln[\exp(a)\, K^\theta + (1-\delta)K - K'] \\ &\quad + \beta \int V(K',a') f(a'|a)\, da' \end{aligned} \tag{5.66}$$

with $a' = \rho a + \epsilon$, where ϵ is orthogonal to a and any other predetermined variable.

The set $\mathcal{K}_C$ is the continuous state space for K. If we impose non-negativity of capital and consumption in each period then

$$0 \leq K' \leq \exp(a)\, K^\theta + (1-\delta)K \tag{5.67}$$

If we define

$$\bar{K} = \left[\frac{\exp(a)}{\delta}\right]^{1/(1-\theta)} \tag{5.68}$$

then because $\exp(a)\, K^\theta + (1-\delta)\, K$ is a monotonically increasing function of K, if $K \leq \bar{K}$ then $K' \leq \exp(a)\, \bar{K}^\theta + (1-\delta)\bar{K} = \bar{K}$. So it is convenient to define $\mathcal{K}_C = [0, \bar{K}]$.

To convert the dynamic programming problem in (5.66) to one involving discrete state spaces, Tauchen proposes the following procedure. First, approximate the law of motion of a using a discrete state-space process defined in exactly the same way as in Section 5.3.4. That is, redefine a to be a process which lies in a set $\mathcal{A} = \{a_{i,N}\}_{i=1}^N$ where $a_{i,N} = \sigma \bar{y}_{i,N}$, where $\{\bar{y}_{i,N}\}_{i=1}^N$, as before, is the set of quadrature points corresponding to an N-point rule for a standard normal. Let the probability that $a' = a_{i,N}$ given that $a = a_{j,N}$ be given by

$$\pi_{ji} = \frac{f(a_{i,N}|a_{j,N})}{f(a_{i,N}|0)} \frac{\bar{w}_{i,N}}{s_j} \tag{5.69}$$

where

$$s_j = \sum_{i=1}^N \frac{f(a_{i,N}|a_{j,N})}{f(a_{i,N}|0)} \bar{w}_{i,N} \tag{5.70}$$

and $\{\bar{w}_{i,N}\}_{i=1}^N$ are the quadrature weights for an N-point rule for the standard normal. After this first step in the approximation we might imagine a variation on the Bellman equation given by

$$\begin{aligned} \tilde{V}(K,a) &= \max_{K' \in \mathcal{K}_C} \ln\left[\exp(a_j) K^\theta + (1-\delta)K - K'\right] \\ &\quad + \beta \sum_{i=1}^N \tilde{V}(K', a_i)\pi_{ji}, \quad \text{given } a = a_j, \quad j = 1, \ldots, N. \end{aligned} \tag{5.71}$$

In the next step, which I will describe below, the set $\mathcal{K}_C$ will be replaced by a discrete set $\mathcal{K}_D \subset \mathcal{K}_C$. That is, we will define a set $\mathcal{K}_D = \{K_m\}_{m=1}^{M}$ from which the social planner must choose the optimal level of capital in the next period, K'. In other words, we will approximate the original dynamic programming problem with the Bellman equation

$$\hat{V}(K, a) = \max_{K' \in \mathcal{K}_D} \ln\left[\exp(a_j)K^{\theta} + (1-\delta)K - K'\right] + \beta \sum_{i=1}^{N} \hat{V}(K', a_i)\pi_{ji} \tag{5.72}$$

given $a = a_j$, $j = 1, \ldots, N$. Ideally, we would have a rule for constructing the discrete set K_D which would resemble the quadrature rule for constructing the set $\mathcal{A}$. Unfortunately, without knowledge of the solution to the model, our knowledge of the solution for K will be limited. We will, therefore, not have the information necessary to construct a Gaussian quadrature-based discrete state space for K.

A number of alternative rules for constructing $\mathcal{K}_D$ are available. One is to locate a grid of evenly spaced points, K_m, in the set $\mathcal{K}_C$. Another rule, proposed by Tauchen (1990), is to assume linear utility and compute the mean and standard deviation of the capital stock implied by the solution to that example. Then, he suggests using an equal spaced grid in a band of ± 4 standard deviations around the mean. Another possibility is to set up a grid in the logarithm of the capital stock based on the mean and standard deviation of the capital stock implied by the log-linear approximation to the model.

Results in Bertsekas (1976) imply that there will be unique bounded solutions to (5.71) and (5.72). In fact, there will be a well-defined sense in which the solution to (5.72) can be made arbitrarily close to the solution to (5.71), as long as in the limit, as $M \to \infty$, with $K_1 = 0$, $K_M = \bar{K}$, $K_m > K_{m-1}$, $\lim_{M\to\infty} \sup_m (K_m - K_{m-1}) = 0$.

In order to implement (5.72) on a computer, it is helpful to rely on standard results from dynamic programming. Suppose we guessed that the value function $\hat{V}$ which solves (5.72) takes some particular form $\hat{V}_0$. If we used this on the right-hand side of the Bellman equation and performed the necessary maximization over K' we would, unless our guess was correct, obtain a new function $\hat{V}_1$, on the left-hand side of the equation. This process could then proceed iteratively as

$$\hat{V}_S(K, a) = \max_{K' \in \mathcal{K}_D} \ln\left[\exp(a_j)K_i^{\theta} + (1-\delta)K_i - K'\right] + \beta \sum_{i=1}^{N} \hat{V}_{S-1}(K', a_i)\pi_{ji} \tag{5.73}$$

given $a = a_j$. Given a choice for $\hat{V}_0$ the process could continue until S became sufficiently large that $\sup_{m,j} |\hat{V}_S\left(K_m, a_j\right) - \hat{V}_{S-1}(K_m, a_j)|$ was less than some tiny convergence criterion. In fact, Tauchen suggests scaling this supremum relative to the minimum value of the value function $\inf_{m,j} |\hat{V}_S(K_m, a_j)|$.

That convergence will be obtained is a standard result in dynamic programming, discussed further in this volume by Díaz-Giménez (Chapter 2). Furthermore, as a by-product of iterating over the value function the optimal decision rule for capital is obtained. That is, we obtain a rule for setting the capital stock which defines $K' = \hat{h}(K, a)$.

Baxter *et al.* (1990) use a discrete state-space method which directly approximates the decision rules as opposed to the value function. In this respect, their method is symmetric to the methods we described for solving the Euler equations in asset pricing problems. The basis of their method is the observation that for the true model, the Euler equation for capital is given by

$$\frac{1}{\exp(a)K^{\theta} + (1-\delta)K - K'} = \beta \int \frac{\theta \exp(a')K'^{\theta-1} + (1-\delta)}{\exp(a')K'^{\theta} + (1-\delta)K' - h[K', \exp(a')]} f(a'|a)da' \tag{5.74}$$

where $h : \mathcal{K}_C \times \mathbb{R} \to \mathcal{K}_C$ is the true decision rule for capital.

As the first step in their algorithm, they set up discrete state spaces for the capital stock and the technology shock in the same way as we did for the dynamic programming problem. Assuming that one has a candidate decision rule $h_S : \mathcal{K}_D \times \mathcal{A} \to \mathcal{K}_D$ the next decision rule is obtained by finding the function $h_{S+1} : \mathcal{K}_D \times \mathcal{A} \to \mathcal{K}_D$ that best fits the Euler equation. That is, for each K and a that lie in the discrete state space (i.e. for each pair K_m and a_j) the method chooses K' to minimize the difference between

$$\frac{1}{\exp(a_j)K_m^{\theta} + (1-\delta)K_m - K'} \tag{5.75}$$

and

$$\beta \sum_{i=1}^{N} \frac{\theta \exp(a_i)K'^{\theta-1} + (1-\delta)}{\exp(a_i)K'^{\theta} + (1-\delta)K' - h_S[K', \exp(a_i)]} \pi_{ji} \tag{5.76}$$

This process implicitly defines a new decision rule $h_{S+1}(K, a)$.

The algorithm could be stopped if $h_{S+1}(K, a) = h_S(K, a)$, which frequently occurs in practice, or if the maximum change in the decision rule eventually satisfied some convergence criterion. Unfortunately, there is little known about the convergence properties of this algorithm. Although it is perfectly reasonable on intuitive grounds, it is not justified by the same fixed point arguments that justify the dynamic programming approach suggested by Tauchen (1990).

5.5 Extensions, limitations and concluding remarks

When we obtain a discrete state-space approximation to a model, we may be satisfied with examining the properties of the approximating model. However, in some cases our main interest is in the original continuous state-space model. In all cases there is a trivial extension of the discrete state-space solution to the continuous state-space that involves using step functions. This way of extending the solution is perhaps best illustrated using the univariate asset pricing example, where the discrete state-space method gave us a solution $V(y_{j,N})$ $j = 1, \ldots, N$, at N points on the real line. However, recall that the quadrature rule divided the real line into non-overlapping segments according to (5.15), $(z_{j-1,N}, z_{j,N})$ such that $y_{j,N} \in (z_{j-1,N}, z_{j,N})$. In this case we can extend the discrete state-space solution to the real line by letting

$$V(x) = \sum_{j=1}^{N} V(y_{j,N}) \mathbf{1}_{(z_{j-1,N}, z_{j,N})}(x) \tag{5.77}$$

where

$$\mathbf{1}_{(z_{j-1,N}, z_{j,N})}(x) = \begin{cases} 1 & \text{if } x \in (z_{j-1,N}, z_{j,N}) \\ 0 & \text{otherwise} \end{cases} \tag{5.78}$$

Similar trivial extensions are available for any of the approximate solutions we have examined in this paper.

To avoid the discontinuities implied by these sorts of extensions, another trivial form of extension involves using the step function in the outer limits of the state space, while using sloping functions to connect the inner quadrature points in a continuous way. For example, in the asset pricing example we could define

$$V(x) = \begin{cases} V(y_{1,N}) & \text{if } x \leq y_{1,N} \\ V(y_{j-1,N}) + \frac{(x - y_{j-1,N})}{(y_{j,N} - y_{j-1,N})}[V(y_{j,N}) - V(y_{j-1,N})] & \text{if } y_{j-1,N} < x \leq y_{j,N} \\ V(y_{N,N}) & \text{if } x > y_{N,N} \end{cases} \tag{5.79}$$

Finally, in the asset pricing context, there is the Nystrom extension. This involves substituting the solution to the discrete state-space model, $\{V(y_{i,N})\}_{i=1}^{N}$, into the approximate Euler equation (5.55), for any x,

$$V(x) \approx \sum_{i=1}^{N} \beta \exp(\alpha y_{i,N})[V(y_{i,N}) + 1] \frac{f(y_{i,N}|x)}{f(y_{i,N}|\mu)} w_{i,N} \tag{5.80}$$

Notice that this provides not only a continuous, but also a differentiable, function of x, as an approximate solution.

One of the major limitations of discrete state-space methods is their computational expense. In the section on asset pricing models with multivariate shocks, we illustrated an example in which, had the shocks been serially correlated, we would have had to obtain the solution to the model by solving N linear equations in N unknowns. But N was equal to $N_1 N_2 \cdots N_M$ where M was the number of variables in the state space, and N_m represented the number of points in the quadrature grid for each variable. Suppose, for illustration, that $N_m = n$ for all m, so that $N = n^M$. In solving the equations this means we need to store at least one matrix with dimension n^{2M}. In addition, and more importantly, computation time in standard methods for solving linear equations is approximately proportional to N^3, or in our case n^{3M}. So as either the number of state variables, M, or the number of quadrature points, n, increases, the computation involved rapidly becomes more difficult. This has been called the *curse of dimensionality*.

Related to this is the problem of choosing the grid of points for endogenous state variables, such as in our growth model. It turns out, from examples examined in the literature, that very fine grids of points appear to be needed to obtain any satisfactory level of accuracy from the discrete state-space solutions. This adds to the dimensionality problem by exaggerating the need for a large number of grid points. This also stands in contrast to examples based on the asset pricing model, where small numbers of points seem to be adequate for obtaining quite accurate approximations based on the Nystrom extension.

In conclusion, the main advantages of discrete state-space methods are threefold. First, they are easy to implement and are well grounded in intuition. Second, there are numerous theoretical results regarding convergence, described in more detail in references given here, which justify their use. And third, they tend to be rather reliable in providing plausible approximations to the solutions of a wide variety of dynamic models. The main disadvantages of these methods are twofold. First, they can be computationally expensive for relatively complicated problems with a large number of state variables. Second, they generally require the state variables to be stationary so that a process defined on a fixed discrete state space can adequately describe their laws of motion.

5.6 Software

There are several, .m files for use with MATLAB, associated with this chapter. The first of these is **apiid.m** which solves the asset pricing model for the single-shock i.i.d. case.

The second is **apsco.m** which solves the model for the serially correlated single-shock case, and plots the exact solution, the step function extension and the Nystrom extension.

The third file, **grtauch.m**, solves a version of the one-sector growth model using the method proposed by Tauchen. The fourth file, **grbcr.m**, solves the same model using the method proposed by Baxter *et al.* (1990).

A number of other files which contain procedures necessary to the functioning of the above, all of which are documented with extensive comment lines, are included as well. These include **condnorm.m**, a procedure for evaluating the conditional normal density function; **getprice.m**, a procedure for obtaining price–dividend ratios in the asset pricing example; **gettrans.m**, a procedure for obtaining a probability transition matrix that approximates the law of motion of a serially correlated normal random variable; and ghquad.dat, a table of quadrature points, weights and interval end points.

The example programs are implemented in what I would call a "naive" way, to make them as clear as possible. This means that they do not take advantage of many "tricks" for speeding up computation. However, they do serve as useful benchmarks for computation time.

6

APPLICATION OF WEIGHTED RESIDUAL METHODS TO DYNAMIC ECONOMIC MODELS

Ellen R. McGrattan[1]

Many problems in economics require the solution to a functional equation as an intermediate step. Typically, we seek decision functions that satisfy a set of Euler conditions or a value function that satisfies Bellman's equation. In many cases, we cannot derive analytical solutions for these functions and instead must rely on numerical methods. In this chapter, I will show how to apply weighted residual and finite-element methods to this type of problem.

In the case of weighted residual methods, the approximate solution to the functional equation is represented as a linear combination of known *basis functions*. In many cases, the basis functions are polynomials. The coefficients on each basis function are the objects to be computed to obtain an approximate solution. These coefficients are found by setting the residual of the equation to zero in an average sense. In other words, a weighted integral of the residual is set to zero.

The finite-element method can be viewed as a piecewise application of the weighted residual method. With the finite-element method, the first step in solving the functional equation is to subdivide the domain of the state space into non-intersecting subdomains called *elements*. The domain is subdivided because the method relies on fitting low-order polynomials on subdomains of the state space rather than high-order polynomials on the entire state space. The local approximations are then pieced together to give a global approximation. As the dimensionality of the problem increases, higher-order functions can be used where needed, with fewer elements.

My primary goal in this chapter is to illustrate the application of weighted residual and finite-element methods by way of examples. I start with a simple differential equation because the coefficients to be computed satisfy a linear system of equations. For this problem, I can work through examples without a computer. I then apply the methods to a deterministic growth model and a stochastic growth model – two standard models in economics.[2] In the growth model examples, the coefficients to be computed satisfy nonlinear systems of equations. Fortunately, these nonlinear equations are exploitably sparse if they are derived from a finite-element method.

[1] I thank Patrick Kehoe and an anonymous referee for comments on an earlier draft. The views expressed herein are those of the author and not necessarily those of the Federal Reserve Bank of Minneapolis or the Federal Reserve System.

[2] See Taylor and Uhlig (1990) for a summary of alternative algorithms used to solve the stochastic growth model.

6.1 The general procedure

The problem is to find $d : \mathbb{R}^m \longrightarrow \mathbb{R}^n$ that satisfies a functional equation $F(d) = 0$, where $F : C_1 \rightarrow C_2$ and C_1 and C_2 are function spaces. As an example, I can think of d as decision or policy variables and F as first-order conditions from some maximization problem. My goal here is to find an approximation $d^n(x; \theta)$ on $x \in \Omega$ which depends on a finite-dimensional vector of parameters $\theta = [\theta_1, \theta_2, \ldots, \theta_n]'$. Weighted residual methods assume that d^n is a finite linear combination of known functions, $\psi_i(x)$, $i = 0, \ldots, n$, called *basis functions*:

$$d^n(x; \theta) = \psi_0(x) + \sum_{i=1}^{n} \theta_i \psi_i(x) \tag{6.1}$$

The functions $\psi_i(x)$, $i = 0, \ldots, n$ are typically simple functions. Standard examples of basis functions include simple polynomials (for example, $\psi_0(x) = 1$, $\psi_i(x) = x^i$), orthogonal polynomials (for example, Chebyshev polynomials), and piecewise linear functions.

In Fig. 6.1, I display the first five polynomials in the class of Chebyshev polynomials, which is a popular choice for the basis functions. *Chebyshev polynomials* are defined on

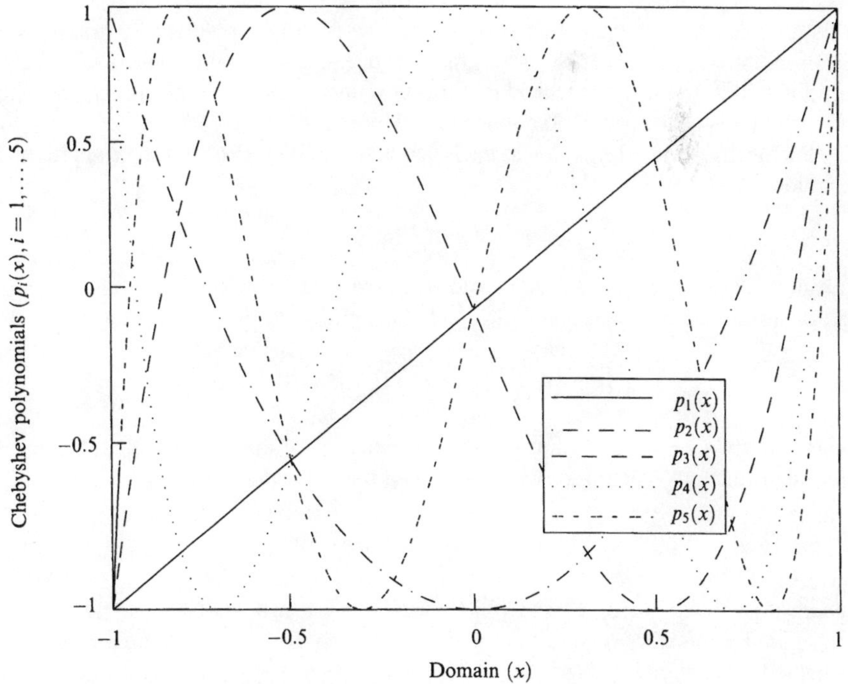

FIG. 6.1. The first five Chebyshev polynomial basis functions.

$[-1, 1]$ and are given recursively as follows: $p_0(x) = 1$, $p_1(x) = x$, and

$$p_i(x) = 2xp_{i-1}(x) - p_{i-2}(x), \quad i = 2, 3, 4, \ldots$$

(or, non-recursively, as $p_i(x) = \cos(i \arccos x)$). The domain Ω is not typically given by $[-1, 1]$. If the domain is instead $[a, b]$, then I can use $\psi_i(x) = p_{i-1}(2(x-a)/(b-a)-1)$ for $i = 1, 2, \ldots$ and $\psi_0(x) = 0$.

Chebyshev polynomials constitute a set of *orthogonal polynomials* with respect to the weight function $w(x) = 1/\sqrt{1-x^2}$, because $\int_{-1}^{1} p_i(x)p_j(x)w(x)\,dx = 0$ for all $i \neq j$. Using orthogonal polynomials in my representation d^n rather than the simple polynomials x^i may be preferable as n gets large. For large n, it is difficult to distinguish x^n from x^{n+1}. Thus, the approximation is hardly improved when I add x^{n+1}. With orthogonal polynomials, however, p_n is easily distinguished from p_{n+1} because they are orthogonal to each other.

In Fig. 6.2, I display basis functions that can be used to construct a piecewise linear representation for d^n. These basis functions are of the form

$$\psi_i(x) = \begin{cases} \dfrac{x - x_{i-1}}{x_i - x_{i-1}} & \text{if } x \in [x_{i-1}, x_i] \\ \dfrac{x_{i+1} - x}{x_{i+1} - x_i} & \text{if } x \in [x_i, x_{i+1}] \\ 0 & \text{elsewhere} \end{cases} \tag{6.2}$$

I do not need to have the points x_i, $i = 1, \ldots, n$ equally spaced. Therefore, if I want to represent a function that has large gradients or kinks in certain places – say, because inequality constraints bind – then I can cluster points in those regions. In regions where the function is near-linear, I do not need many points.

I define the *residual equation* as the functional equation evaluated at the approximate solution d^n:

$$R(x; \theta) = F(d^n(x; \theta))$$

I want to choose θ so that $R(x; \theta)$ is close to zero for all x. Weighted residual methods get the residual close to zero in the weighted integral sense. That is, I choose θ so that

$$\int_\Omega \phi_i(x)R(x; \theta)\,dx = 0, \quad i = 1, \ldots, n$$

where $\phi_i(x)$, $i = 1, \ldots, n$ are *weight functions*. Note that $\phi_i(x)$ and $\psi_i(x)$ can be different functions. Alternatively, the weighted integral can be written

$$\int_\Omega w(x)R(x; \theta)\,dx = 0 \tag{6.3}$$

where $w(x) = \sum_i \omega_i \phi_i(x)$ and (6.3) must hold for any non-zero weights ω_i, $i = 1, \ldots, n$. Therefore, instead of setting $R(x; \theta)$ to zero for all $x \in \Omega$, the method sets a weighted integral of R to zero.

I consider three specific sets of weight functions and, hence, three ways of determining the coefficients $\theta_1, \ldots, \theta_n$.

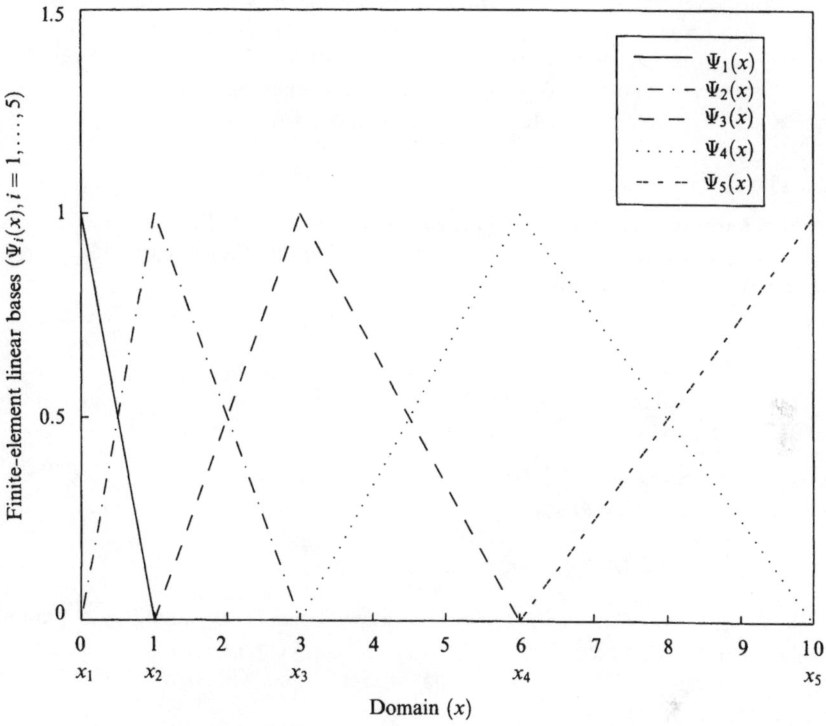

FIG. 6.2. Five piecewise linear basis functions.

1. **Least squares**: $\phi_i(x) = \partial R(x; \theta)/\partial\theta_i$. This set of weights can be derived by calculating the first-order derivatives for the following optimization problem:

$$\min_{\theta} \int_{\Omega} R(x; \theta)^2 \, dx$$

2. **Collocation**: $\phi_i(x) = \delta(x - x_i)$, where δ is the Dirac delta function. This set of weights implies that the residual is set to zero at n points $x_1, \ldots, x_n$ called the *collocation points*: $R(x_i; \theta) = 0$, $i = 1, \ldots, n$. If the basis functions are chosen from a set of orthogonal polynomials with collocation points given as the roots of the nth polynomial in the set, the method is called *orthogonal collocation*.
3. **Galerkin**: $\phi_i(x) = \psi_i(x)$. In this case, the set of weight functions is the same as the basis functions used to represent d. Thus, the Galerkin method forces the residual to be orthogonal to each of the basis functions. As long as the basis functions are chosen from a complete set of functions, then equation (6.1) represents the exact solution, given that enough terms are included. The Galerkin method is motivated by the fact that a continuous function is zero if it is orthogonal to every member of a complete set of functions.

To illustrate weighted residual methods, I start with a simple problem in which the coefficients θ_i, $i = 1, \ldots, n$, of (6.1) satisfy a linear system of equations (that is, $A\theta = b$, where A and b do not depend on θ). Once I have tackled the simple problem, I then apply the methods to standard growth models. (For other examples, see Aiyagari and McGrattan, 1998; Braun and McGrattan, 1993; and Chari *et al.*, 1997.)

6.2 The differential equation

Consider the following first-order problem: find d such that $d'(x) + d(x) = 0$, with $d(0) = 1$ and $x \in [0, \bar{x}]$. The solution to this problem is $d(x) = \exp(-x)$. Using the notation of Section 6.1, I have

$$F(d)(x) = d'(x) + d(x) = 0 \tag{6.4}$$

In this section, I consider various choices of basis functions (ψ_i) and weight functions (ϕ_i) to illustrate the weighted residual methods described in Section 6.1.

Example 6.1 Suppose that I start with simple polynomials x^i, $i = 1, \ldots, n$. Then the approximation to $d(x)$ is given by

$$d^n(x; \theta) = 1 + \theta_1 x + \theta_2 x^2 + \theta_3 x^3 + \cdots + \theta_n x^n \tag{6.5}$$

Note that I have chosen $\psi_0(x) = 1$ in order to satisfy the boundary condition at $x = 0$. I find the coefficients θ_i, $i = 1, \ldots, n$, by applying a weighted residual method with one of three possible sets of weights. In each case, I will solve a linear system of equations for θ, $A\theta = b$.

(a) **Least squares.** In this case, the problem is to find θ that minimizes the integral of the squared residual. The residual can be found by substituting equation (6.5) into equation (6.4). The first-order conditions of the minimization of the squared residual imply that $\theta_1, \ldots, \theta_n$ satisfy

$$\int_0^{\bar{x}} \frac{\partial R(x; \theta)}{\partial \theta_i} R(x; \theta)\, dx = 0, \quad i = 1, \ldots, n$$

where the residual and its derivative are given by

$$R(x; \theta) = 1 + \sum_{i=1}^{n} \theta_i \{ i x^{i-1} + x^i \}$$

$$\frac{\partial R(x; \theta)}{\partial \theta_i} = i x^{i-1} + x^i$$

Suppose that $n = 3$ and $\bar{x} = 6$. Then the following system of equations is solved for θ:

$$\left\{ \int_0^6 \begin{bmatrix} 1+x \\ 2x+x^2 \\ 3x^2+x^3 \end{bmatrix} \begin{bmatrix} 1+x & 2x+x^2 & 3x^2+x^3 \end{bmatrix} dx \right\} \begin{bmatrix} \theta_1 \\ \theta_2 \\ \theta_3 \end{bmatrix} = -\int_0^6 \begin{bmatrix} 1+x \\ 2x+x^2 \\ 3x^2+x^3 \end{bmatrix} dx$$

or, more simply,

$$\begin{bmatrix} 114.0 & 576.0 & 3067.2 \\ 576.0 & 3139.2 & 17496.0 \\ 3067.2 & 17496.0 & 100643.7 \end{bmatrix} \begin{bmatrix} \theta_1 \\ \theta_2 \\ \theta_3 \end{bmatrix} = \begin{bmatrix} -24 \\ -108 \\ -540 \end{bmatrix}$$

More generally, I can use the fact that

$$R(x;\theta) = (C\vec{x} + e)'\theta + 1$$

where $\vec{x} = [x, x^2, \dots, x^n]'$, $e = [1, 0, \dots, 0]'$, and

$$C = \begin{bmatrix} 1 & 0 & 0 & \dots & 0 & 0 \\ 2 & 1 & 0 & \dots & 0 & 0 \\ 0 & 3 & 1 & \dots & 0 & 0 \\ \vdots & \vdots & \vdots & \vdots & \vdots & \vdots \\ 0 & 0 & 0 & \dots & n & 1 \end{bmatrix}$$

Since the residual R is linear in θ, the derivatives with respect to θ are given by $C\vec{x} + e$. Thus, the system of equations to be solved to compute the coefficients θ for the least-squares method is given by

$$\left\{ \int_0^{\bar{x}} (C\vec{x} + e)(C\vec{x} + e)'\,dx \right\} \theta = -\int_0^{\bar{x}} (C\vec{x} + e)\,dx$$

or, more succinctly, $A\theta = b$ with

$$A = CMC' + ePC' + CP'e' + \bar{x}ee'$$
$$b = -CP' - \bar{x}e$$

and

$$M = \int_0^{\bar{x}} \vec{x}\vec{x}'\,dx = \begin{bmatrix} \bar{x}^3/3 & \bar{x}^4/4 & \cdots & \bar{x}^{n+1}/(n+1) \\ \bar{x}^4/4 & \bar{x}^5/5 & \cdots & \bar{x}^{n+2}/(n+2) \\ \vdots & \vdots & \vdots & \vdots \\ \bar{x}^{n+2}/(n+2) & \bar{x}^{n+3}/(n+3) & \cdots & \bar{x}^{2n+1}/(2n+1) \end{bmatrix}$$

$$P = \int_0^{\bar{x}} \vec{x}\,dx = \begin{bmatrix} \bar{x}^2/2 \\ \bar{x}^3/3 \\ \vdots \\ \bar{x}^{n+1}/(n+1) \end{bmatrix}$$

In Fig. 6.3, I plot the approximate function d^n for $n = 3$ and the exact solution $\exp(-x)$. If I had used $n = 5$, then the two lines would be visually indistinguishable.

(b) **Collocation**. In this case, the problem is to find θ so that the residual is equal to 0 at n points in $[0, \bar{x}]$: $x_1, \dots, x_n$. Suppose that the x_i are evenly spaced on $[0, 6]$ and that

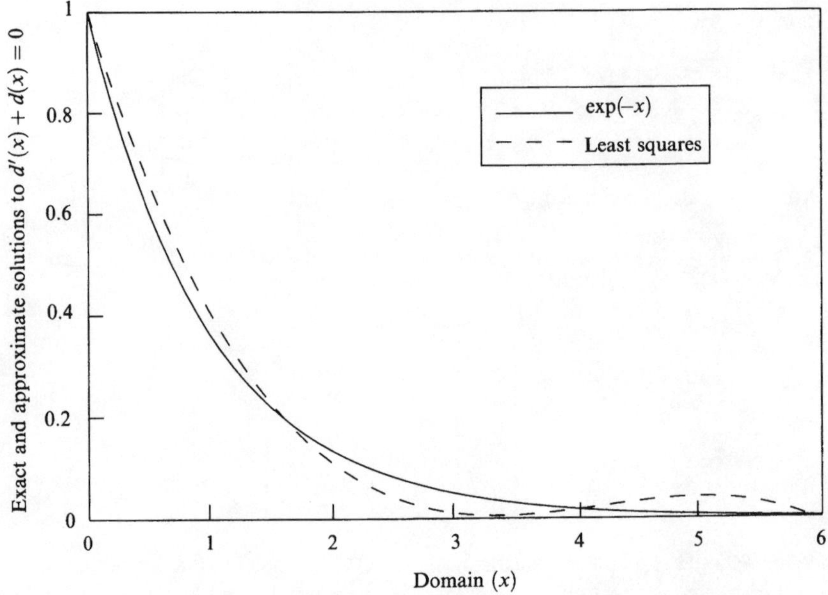

FIG. 6.3. Least-squares approximation to a first-order differential equation.

$n = 3$, so that $x_1 = 0$, $x_2 = 3$, and $x_3 = 6$. Then, θ must satisfy the following system of equations:

$$\begin{bmatrix} 1 & 0 & 0 \\ 4 & 15 & 54 \\ 7 & 48 & 324 \end{bmatrix} \begin{bmatrix} \theta_1 \\ \theta_2 \\ \theta_3 \end{bmatrix} = \begin{bmatrix} -1 \\ -1 \\ -1 \end{bmatrix}.$$

More generally, I can solve $A\theta = b$ with $(C\vec{x} + e)'$ defined above evaluated at x_i in the ith row of A and b set to a vector of -1s:

$$\begin{bmatrix} (C\vec{x} + e)'|_{x=x_1} \\ (C\vec{x} + e)'|_{x=x_2} \\ \vdots \\ (C\vec{x} + e)'|_{x=x_n} \end{bmatrix} \theta = \begin{bmatrix} -1 \\ -1 \\ \vdots \\ -1 \end{bmatrix}$$

In Fig. 6.4, I plot the approximate function d^n and the exact solution. If I choose $n = 5$, the two lines are nearly indistinguishable. However, for $n = 3$, the approximation is not as good as the least-squares approximation. I will show in a later example how to improve the fit for the collocation method.

(c) **Galerkin**. In this case, the problem is to find $\theta_1, \ldots, \theta_n$ that satisfy

$$\int_0^{\bar{x}} x^i R(x; \theta)\, dx = 0, \quad i = 1, \ldots, n \tag{6.6}$$

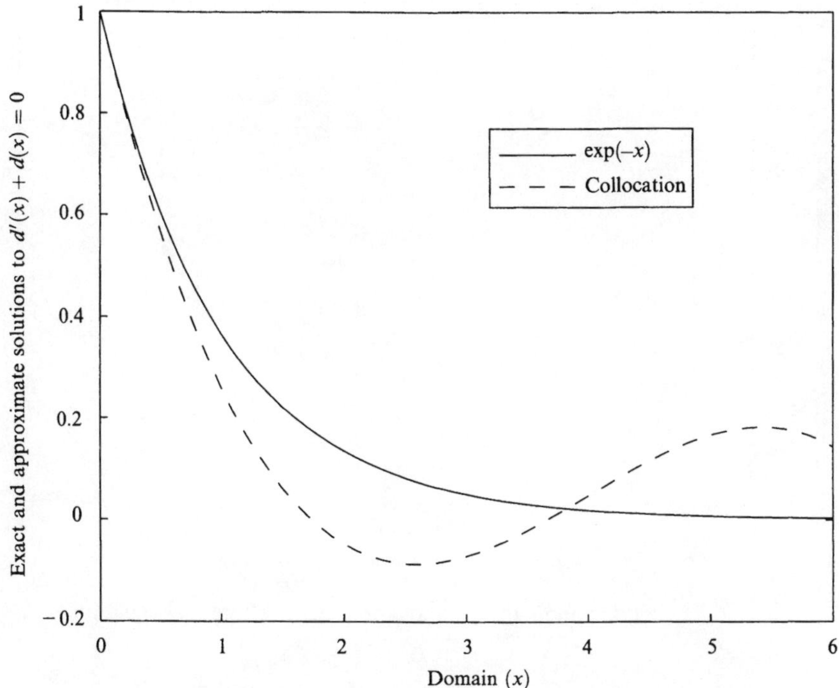

FIG. 6.4. Collocation approximation to a first-order differential equation.

Again, consider $n = 3$ and $\bar{x} = 6$. For these choices, the equations in (6.6) are given by

$$\left\{\int_0^6 \begin{bmatrix} x \\ x^2 \\ x^3 \end{bmatrix} \begin{bmatrix} 1+x & 2x+x^2 & 3x^2+x^3 \end{bmatrix} dx \right\} \begin{bmatrix} \theta_1 \\ \theta_2 \\ \theta_3 \end{bmatrix} = -\int_0^6 \begin{bmatrix} x \\ x^2 \\ x^3 \end{bmatrix} dx \tag{6.7}$$

Note that I have written these equations in the form $A\theta = b$. If I compute the integrals in equation (6.7), then the system of equations becomes

$$\begin{bmatrix} 90.0 & 468.0 & 2527.2 \\ 396.0 & 2203.2 & 12441.6 \\ 1879.2 & 10886.4 & 63318.9 \end{bmatrix} \begin{bmatrix} \theta_1 \\ \theta_2 \\ \theta_3 \end{bmatrix} = \begin{bmatrix} -18 \\ -72 \\ -324 \end{bmatrix}$$

For general n and $\bar{x}$, the coefficients solve $A\theta = b$, where A and b are the following functions:

$$A = MC' + P'e'$$
$$b = -P'$$

with M, C, P, and e as defined above. In Fig. 6.5, I plot the approximate function d^n and the exact solution. The results are similar to those obtained with the least-squares

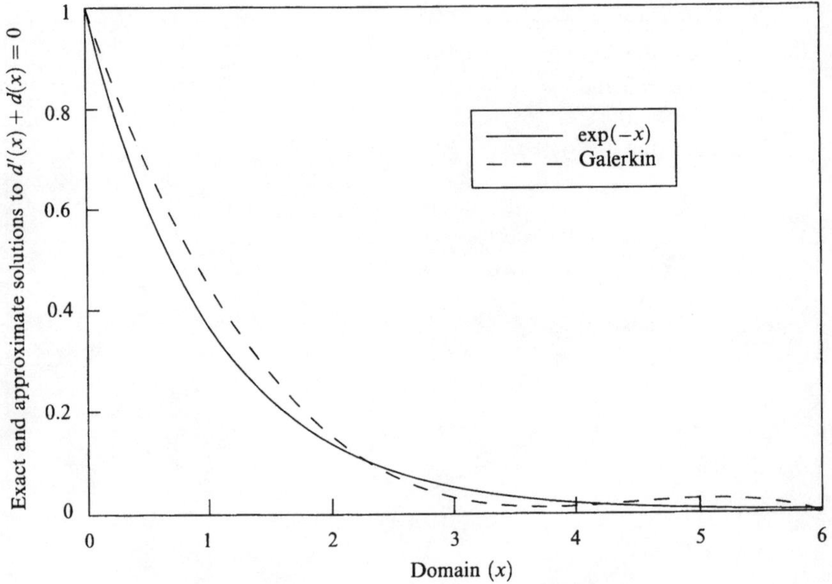

FIG. 6.5. Galerkin approximation to a first-order differential equation.

method. Again, if I choose $n = 5$, then the approximate and exact solutions are visually indistinguishable.

In Example 6.1, I assume that the basis functions are the set of simple polynomials, $\{1, x, \dots, x^n\}$. As I note in Section 6.1, numerical problems can arise with this set of bases when the order of the approximating function (that is, n) gets large. Suppose instead that I use a set of orthogonal polynomials. In particular, suppose I use the Chebyshev polynomials plotted in Fig. 6.1.

Example 6.2 Let the approximate solution to (6.4) be of the following form:

$$d^n(x; \theta) = 1 + x \sum_{i=1}^{n} \theta_i p_{i-1}(2x/\bar{x} - 1) \tag{6.8}$$

where p_i is the ith Chebyshev polynomial defined on $[-1, 1]$ and $\psi_i(x) = xp_{i-1}(2x/\bar{x} - 1)$ is the ith basis function defined on $[0, \bar{x}]$. Notice that because the polynomials are defined on $[-1, 1]$, I map points in $[0, \bar{x}]$ to points in $[-1, 1]$ by using the transformation $2x/\bar{x} - 1$.

If I apply the method of collocation, then I need to choose points x_i, $i = 1, \dots, n$, at which to evaluate the residual equation $R(x_i; \theta)$. A sensible choice of points is the n roots of the nth Chebyshev polynomial.[3] For smooth residual functions, mathematical

[3]The method of orthogonal collocation picks the points x_i, $i = 1, \dots, n$, to be the zeros of the nth basis function. This is not quite what I am doing here. Since the boundary condition needs to be satisfied

results indicate that choosing the points in this way forces the residual to be close to zero for all the points in the domain of interest (see Press *et al.*, 1986).

Suppose that $n = 3$ and $\bar{x} = 6$. In this case, I choose the collocation points to be the roots of the polynomial $p_3(2x/\bar{x} - 1) = 4(\frac{1}{3}x - 1)^3 - 3(\frac{1}{3}x - 1)$. The roots, therefore, are 0.4, 3, and 5.6, and the system of equations is

$$\begin{bmatrix} 1.4 & -1.1 & 0.2 \\ 4.0 & 1.0 & -4.0 \\ 6.6 & 7.6 & 9.8 \end{bmatrix} \begin{bmatrix} \theta_1 \\ \theta_2 \\ \theta_3 \end{bmatrix} = \begin{bmatrix} -1 \\ -1 \\ -1 \end{bmatrix} \tag{6.9}$$

The solution to (6.9) is substituted into (6.8). In Fig. 6.6, I plot this approximation along with the solution from Example 6.1(b) and the exact solution. Notice that the approximation using orthogonal polynomials is closer to the exact solution at all points in the domain.

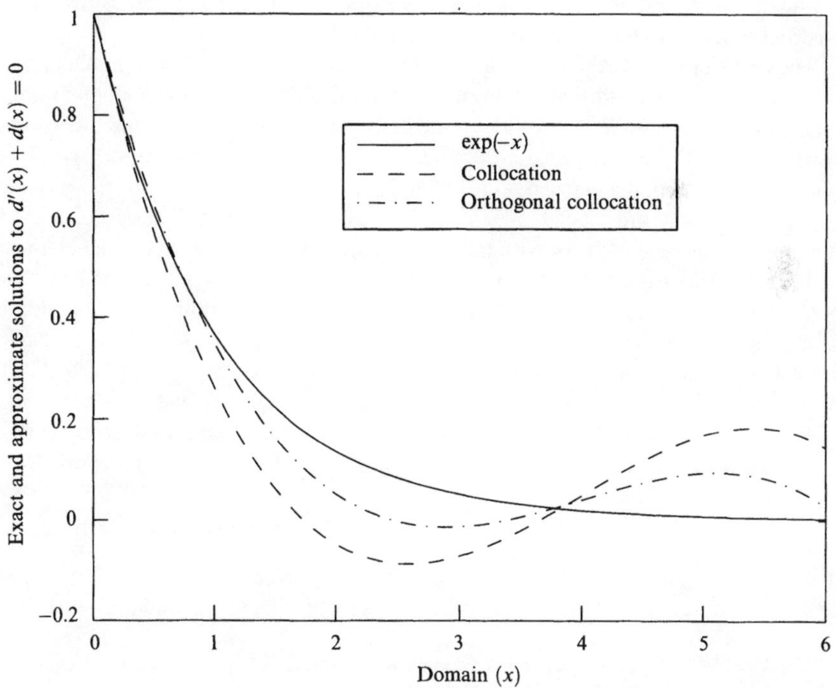

FIG. 6.6. Two collocation approximations to a first-order differential equation.

by my candidate solution, I have chosen $\psi_i(x) = xp_{i-1}(2x/\bar{x} - 1)$ rather than $\psi_i(x) = p_i(2x/\bar{x} - 1)$. But I choose the zeros of the nth Chebyshev polynomial as the points at which to evaluate the residual.

In Examples 6.1 and 6.2, I use polynomials in the representation of the approximate solution. These polynomials are non-zero on most of the domain of x. Next I will work with basis functions that are non-zero on only small regions of the domain of x. The resulting representations of d^n will be piecewise functions (for example, piecewise linear, piecewise quadratic). In the terminology of numerical analysts, I will be applying a *finite-element method*.[4]

The idea behind the finite-element method is to break up the domain of x into smaller pieces, use low-order polynomials to obtain good local approximations for the function d, and then piece the local approximations together to obtain a good global approximation. In effect, one can think of the finite-element method as a piecewise application of a weighted residual method. Thus, to apply a finite-element method, I first divide the domain into smaller non-overlapping subdomains. On each of the subdomains, I construct a local approximation to the function d. For the problem in (6.4), Ω is one-dimensional, and therefore, division of Ω means coming up with some partition, say, $[x_1, x_2, \ldots, x_n]$ on $\mathbb{R}$. Each subinterval $[x_i, x_{i+1}]$ is called an *element*.[5]

Suppose, for example, that I want to represent d as a piecewise linear function; that is, over each element, I assume that the approximation is of the form $a + bx$. Suppose also that I want the function d to be continuous on the whole domain Ω. How would I construct basis functions $\psi_i(x)$ so that I can write d^n as in (6.1)?

The first step is to assign *nodes* on the element. For the finite-element method, nodes are points on an element that are used to define the geometry of the element and to uniquely define the order of the polynomial being used to approximate the true solution over the element. Since I am assuming that an element is some interval $[x_i, x_{i+1}]$, two nodes – in particular, the two end points x_i and x_{i+1} – are needed to define the geometry. And only two points are needed to uniquely define a linear function. Therefore, the nodes on a one-dimensional element with linear bases are the two end points of the element.

The second step in constructing the basis functions is to assume that the undetermined coefficients are equal to the approximate solution at the nodal points. Assume that the numbering of elements and nodes is such that element i is the interval $[x_i, x_{i+1}]$: the first element is $[x_1, x_2]$, the second element is $[x_2, x_3]$, and so on. Assume also that the approximate solution on element i, $d_i^n(x; \theta)$, satisfies $d_i^n(x_i) = \theta_i$ and $d_i^n(x_{i+1}) = \theta_{i+1}$. In other words, assume that the undetermined coefficients represent the solution at the nodes. The approximation of d on element i, d_i^n, is therefore uniquely given by

$$d_i^n(x; \theta) = \theta_i \psi_i(x) + \theta_{i+1}\psi_{i+1}(x), \quad x \in [x_i, x_{i+1}]$$

where the basis functions are given by equation (6.2) and drawn in Fig. 6.2. Since elements are connected to each other at nodal points on the element boundaries, this choice

[4] Weighted residual methods can be divided into two categories: spectral methods and finite-element methods. Spectral methods use basis functions that are smooth (that is, C^∞) and non-zero on most of the domain of x (for example, sets of polynomials such as those drawn in Fig. 6.1). Finite-element methods use basis functions that are only non-zero on small regions of the domain of x (for example, the tent functions drawn in Fig. 6.2).

[5] In Section 6.4, I consider a two-dimensional problem. In such cases, the finite-element discretization consists of simple two-dimensional (non-overlapping) subdomains, such as triangles, rectangles, and quadrilaterals.

of basis functions guarantees that the approximation is continuous across elements. Notice also that any linear function (and, hence, any continuous piecewise linear d^n) can be represented with the basis functions given in (6.2).

In the examples below, I will focus on only the simplest finite-element approximations that are used in practice. For the one-dimensional examples, I will use linear and quadratic basis functions. For the two-dimensional examples, I will use rectangularly shaped elements with linear and quadratic basis functions. Extensions to higher dimensions and higher-order polynomials are relatively straightforward (see, for example, Hughes, 1987).

Example 6.3 Let the approximate solution to (6.4) be of the form

$$d^n(x;\theta) = \sum_{i=1}^{n} \theta_i \psi_i(x)$$

with $\psi_i(x), i = 1, \ldots, n$, given by (6.2). To impose the boundary condition $d^n(0;\theta) = 1$, I need to set θ_1 to one. Here I apply a Galerkin method. Therefore, the weight functions are given by the bases $\psi_i(x), i = 1, \ldots, n$.

(a) **Three elements**. Suppose that there are three elements with nodes at 0, 1, 3, and 6. Then the residual equation is given by

$$\begin{aligned} R(x;\theta) &= \sum_{i=1}^{4} \theta_i \left(\psi_i'(x) + \psi_i(x)\right) \\ &= \begin{cases} \theta_1(-x) + \theta_2(1+x) & \text{if } x \in [0,1] \\ \theta_2\left(1 - \frac{1}{2}x\right) + \theta_3\left(\frac{1}{2}x\right) & \text{if } x \in [1,3] \\ \theta_3\left(\frac{5}{3} - \frac{1}{3}x\right) + \theta_4\left(-\frac{2}{3} + \frac{1}{3}x\right) & \text{if } x \in [3,6] \end{cases} \end{aligned} \tag{6.10}$$

If I substitute the residual (6.10) into the weighted integral (6.3) with $\phi_i(x) = \psi_i(x)$, then I get the following system of equations:

$$\left\{ \int_0^1 \begin{bmatrix} 1-x \\ x \\ 0 \\ 0 \end{bmatrix} [-x \;\; 1+x \;\; 0 \;\; 0]\, dx + \int_1^3 \begin{bmatrix} 0 \\ \frac{3}{2} - \frac{1}{2}x \\ -\frac{1}{2} + \frac{1}{2}x \\ 0 \end{bmatrix} \left[0 \;\; 1 - \frac{1}{2}x \;\; \frac{1}{2}x \;\; 0\right] dx \right.$$

$$\left. + \int_3^6 \begin{bmatrix} 0 \\ 0 \\ 2 - \frac{1}{3}x \\ -1 + \frac{1}{3}x \end{bmatrix} \left[0 \;\; 0 \;\; \frac{5}{3} - \frac{1}{3}x \;\; -\frac{2}{3} + \frac{1}{3}x\right] dx \right\} \begin{bmatrix} 1 \\ \theta_2 \\ \theta_3 \\ \theta_4 \end{bmatrix} = \begin{bmatrix} 0 \\ 0 \\ 0 \\ 0 \end{bmatrix}$$

or if I compute the integrals,

$$\begin{bmatrix} -1/6 & 2/3 & 0 & 0 \\ -1/3 & 1 & 5/6 & 0 \\ 0 & -1/6 & 5/3 & 1 \\ 0 & 0 & 0 & 3/2 \end{bmatrix} \begin{bmatrix} 1 \\ \theta_2 \\ \theta_3 \\ \theta_4 \end{bmatrix} = \begin{bmatrix} 0 \\ 0 \\ 0 \\ 0 \end{bmatrix} \tag{6.11}$$

Note that I need to drop the first equation because I have to impose that $\theta_1 = 1$ for the boundary condition to be satisfied.[6] Therefore, the system of equations reduces to

$$\begin{bmatrix} 1 & 5/6 & 0 \\ -1/6 & 5/3 & 1 \\ 0 & 0 & 3/2 \end{bmatrix} \begin{bmatrix} \theta_2 \\ \theta_3 \\ \theta_4 \end{bmatrix} = \begin{bmatrix} 1/3 \\ 0 \\ 0 \end{bmatrix}$$

with three equations and three unknowns. In Fig. 6.7, I plot the finite-element approximation and the exact solution. By construction, the approximate function is piecewise linear. As in the case of Examples 6.1–2, with five degrees of freedom, it is difficult to distinguish the approximate from the exact solutions when they are plotted.

(b) ***m* elements, linear bases**. Because the same calculations are made for each element, derivation of the linear system of equations for θ can be simplified greatly.

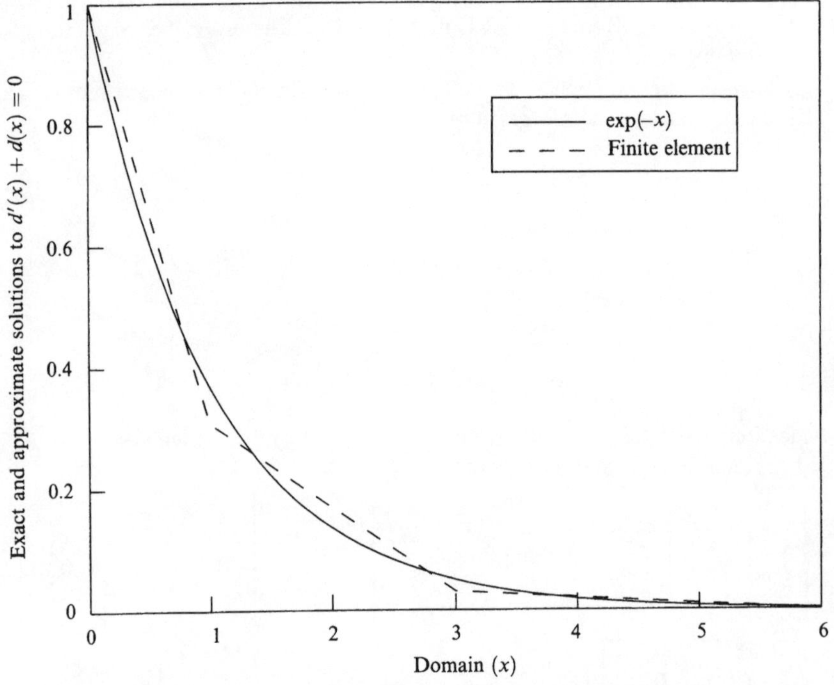

FIG. 6.7. Finite-element approximation to a first-order differential equation.

[6]Recall that the integral equation can be written as in (6.3), where in this case, $w(x) = \sum_i \omega_i \psi_i(x)$. The function $w(x)$ must satisfy the homogeneous counterpart of the boundary condition $d(0) = 1$, that is, $w(0) = 0$. For those familiar with the calculus of variations, w is like the variation of the solution and thus must satisfy the homogeneous counterparts of boundary conditions for d. Enforcing the condition $w(0) = 0$ is equivalent to dropping the first equation in (6.11).

The trick is to work with one *master element* and use the calculations for all elements. Consider the following master element. Assume that it has length ℓ_e, that node 1 is placed at 0, and that node 2 is placed at ℓ_e. To construct the approximation d^n on this master element, I use a linear combination of two functions,

$$\psi_1^e(\bar{x}) = 1 - \frac{\bar{x}}{\ell_e} \quad \text{and} \quad \psi_2^e(\bar{x}) = \frac{\bar{x}}{\ell_e}$$

where $\bar{x}$ lies in $[0, \ell_e]$. If I map element e given by $[x_e, x_{e+1}]$ to the master element, then the relationship between the *local coordinate* $\bar{x}$ and the *global coordinate* x (which lies somewhere between x_e and x_{e+1}) is given by $\bar{x} = x - x_e$.

Let

$$\Psi(\bar{x}) = \begin{bmatrix} 1 - \frac{\bar{x}}{\ell_e} & \frac{\bar{x}}{\ell_e} \end{bmatrix}$$

$$\frac{d\Psi(\bar{x})}{d\bar{x}} = \begin{bmatrix} -\frac{1}{\ell_e} & \frac{1}{\ell_e} \end{bmatrix}$$

Define K^e to be the integral

$$K^e = \int_0^{\ell_e} \left\{ \Psi(\bar{x})' \left(\Psi(\bar{x}) + \frac{d\Psi(\bar{x})}{d\bar{x}} \right) \right\} d\bar{x} \tag{6.12}$$

$$= \int_0^{\ell_e} \left\{ \begin{bmatrix} 1 - \frac{\bar{x}}{\ell_e} \\ \frac{\bar{x}}{\ell_e} \end{bmatrix} \left(\begin{bmatrix} 1 - \frac{\bar{x}}{\ell_e} & \frac{\bar{x}}{\ell_e} \end{bmatrix} + \begin{bmatrix} -\frac{1}{\ell_e} & \frac{1}{\ell_e} \end{bmatrix} \right) \right\} d\bar{x}$$

$$= \begin{bmatrix} \frac{\ell_e}{3} - \frac{1}{2} & \frac{\ell_e}{6} + \frac{1}{2} \\ \frac{\ell_e}{6} - \frac{1}{2} & \frac{\ell_e}{3} + \frac{1}{2} \end{bmatrix}$$

Then I can show that the residual equation is given by

$$\begin{bmatrix} \begin{bmatrix} K^1 \end{bmatrix} & & & & 0 \\ & \begin{bmatrix} K^2 \end{bmatrix} & & & \\ & & \begin{bmatrix} K^3 \end{bmatrix} & & \\ & & & \ddots & \\ 0 & & & & \begin{bmatrix} K^m \end{bmatrix} \end{bmatrix} \begin{bmatrix} 1 \\ \theta_2 \\ \vdots \\ \theta_{m+1} \end{bmatrix} = 0. \tag{6.13}$$

With the exceptions of $(1, 1)$ and $(m + 1, m + 1)$, the diagonal elements of the matrix multiplying θ in (6.13) are the sum of two numbers. For example, diagonal element

(2, 2) is found by summing $K^1(2, 2)$ and $K^2(1, 1)$, (3, 3) is found by summing $K^2(2, 2)$ and $K^3(1, 1)$, and so on. Again, I drop the first equation and solve a linear system of $m = n - 1$ equations in $n - 1$ unknowns.

Consider again the case in which $m = 3$ (that is, Example 6.3(a)). The first element is [0, 1], which has length 1; the second element is [1, 3], which has length 2; and the third element is [3, 6], which has length 3. Using the formula in equation (6.12), I have

$$K^1 = \begin{bmatrix} -1/6 & 2/3 \\ -1/3 & 5/6 \end{bmatrix}, \quad K^2 = \begin{bmatrix} 1/6 & 5/6 \\ -1/6 & 7/6 \end{bmatrix}, \quad K^3 = \begin{bmatrix} 1/2 & 1 \\ 0 & 3/2 \end{bmatrix}$$

Substituting K^1, K^2, and K^3 into equation (6.13) with $K^1(2, 2)$ added to $K^2(1, 1)$ and $K^2(2, 2)$ added to $K^3(1, 1)$ yields the matrix in (6.11).

What is evident from (6.13) is that the system I am solving is sparse. The matrix that will be inverted is $m \times m$, but it has only $3m - 2$ non-zero values. If $m = 20$, then 15% of the matrix elements are non-zero. If $m = 100$, 3% of the matrix elements are non-zero. Typically, a sparse matrix is defined as a matrix with very few non-zero elements. However, what is most relevant is whether or not I can apply methods to take advantage of the number and positioning of the zero elements. In the example above, the A matrix in $A\theta = b$ is tridiagonal and, therefore, has a structure that lends itself well to numerical techniques designed for solving sparse linear systems.

Although the computed examples in this chapter have a small number of unknowns and, therefore, can be solved without resorting to sparse equation solvers, problems such as that described in Chari *et al.* (1997) require solving systems on the order of 25 000 equations. In such cases, the memory limitations make standard (non-sparse) matrix inversion routines infeasible to use. In their example, Chari *et al.* (1997) have to invert a $24\,800 \times 24\,800$ matrix in which 0.14% of the elements are non-zero. As in the example above, the positions of the non-zero elements in their example are such that the system of equations is exploitably sparse. Saad (1996) describes a variety of methods for solving large sparse systems of equations.

In Example 6.3, I assume that the approximate solution on each element is a linear function. There are two possible ways to improve the approximation: increase the number of elements or increase the order of the polynomial approximation on each element. I next consider an approximation with quadratic basis functions. In this case, a typical element has three nodes: one at each end point and one in the interior. The nodes at the end points are needed to define the geometry of the element (which is the same as in the case of linear bases). The interior point is needed to determine uniquely the order of the polynomial; that is, there are three degrees of freedom if the approximate solution is of the form $a + bx + cx^2$ on the element. To allow flexibility, I do not necessarily assume that the third nodal point is at the midpoint of the element. However, because I want to avoid repeating the same calculations, I should calculate the functions and residuals for a master quadratic element just as I did in the linear case in Example 6.3(b). Consider the following master element. Assume that it has length ℓ_e. Let $\bar{x}$ be the local coordinate of the element, which has node 1 located at x_1^e. Then $\bar{x} = x - x_1^e$, where x is the global coordinate. Locally, assume that the nodes are located at $\bar{x} = 0$, $\bar{x} = \alpha\ell_e$, and $\bar{x} = \ell_e$, with $0 < \alpha < 1$.

As in the linear case, I can write the approximation on element e as a linear combination of basis functions that have the property that they are equal to 1 at one node and 0 at the other nodes; that is,

$$d_e^n(\bar{x};\theta) = \theta_1^e \psi_1^e(\bar{x}) + \theta_2^e \psi_2^e(\bar{x}) + \theta_3^e \psi_3^e(\bar{x})$$

where the ψ_i^es are constructed to satisfy $d_e^n(0) = \theta_1^e$, $d_e^n(\alpha\ell_e) = \theta_2^e$, and $d_e^n(\ell_e) = \theta_3^e$. The only functions that satisfy these conditions are given by

$$\begin{aligned}
\psi_1^e(\bar{x}) &= \left(1 - \frac{\bar{x}}{\ell_e}\right)\left(1 - \frac{\bar{x}}{\alpha\ell_e}\right) \\
\psi_2^e(\bar{x}) &= \frac{\bar{x}}{\alpha(1-\alpha)\ell_e}\left(1 - \frac{\bar{x}}{\ell_e}\right) \\
\psi_3^e(\bar{x}) &= -\frac{\alpha\bar{x}}{(1-\alpha)\ell_e}\left(1 - \frac{\bar{x}}{\alpha\ell_e}\right)
\end{aligned} \tag{6.14}$$

Notice that there are only three elements of the vector θ used to approximate the function on any particular element. I use the superscript e to indicate the element. In the example below, I will relate the coefficients θ_i^e to the elements in the $n \times 1$ vector θ.

Example 6.4 Let the approximate solution be piecewise quadratic. Assume that the interior nodes on each element are at the midpoints of the elements (so that $\alpha = 1/2$). Let

$$\Psi(\bar{x}) = \left[\psi_1^e(\bar{x}) \quad \psi_2^e(\bar{x}) \quad \psi_3^e(\bar{x})\right]$$

where $\psi_i^e(\bar{x})$ is given in (6.14), and define K^e to be the following integral:

$$\begin{aligned}
K^e &= \int_0^{\ell_e} \left\{\Psi(\bar{x})'\left(\Psi(\bar{x}) + \frac{d\Psi(\bar{x})}{d\bar{x}}\right)\right\} d\bar{x} \\
&= \begin{bmatrix}
\frac{2}{15}\ell_e - \frac{1}{2} & \frac{1}{15}\ell_e + \frac{2}{3} & -\frac{1}{30}\ell_e - \frac{1}{6} \\
\frac{1}{15}\ell_e - \frac{2}{3} & \frac{8}{15}\ell_e & \frac{1}{15}\ell_e + \frac{2}{3} \\
-\frac{1}{30}\ell_e + \frac{1}{6} & \frac{1}{15}\ell_e - \frac{2}{3} & \frac{2}{15}\ell_e + \frac{1}{2}
\end{bmatrix}
\end{aligned}$$

Then I can show that if there are m elements, the residual equations are given by

$$\begin{bmatrix}
\begin{bmatrix} K^1 \end{bmatrix} & & & & 0 \\
& \begin{bmatrix} K^2 \end{bmatrix} & & & \\
& & \begin{bmatrix} K^3 \end{bmatrix} & & \\
& & & \ddots & \\
0 & & & & \begin{bmatrix} K^m \end{bmatrix}
\end{bmatrix}
\begin{bmatrix} 1 \\ \theta_2 \\ \vdots \\ \theta_{2m+1} \end{bmatrix} = 0 \tag{6.15}$$

Diagonal element $(3,3)$ is the sum of $K^1(3,3)$ and $K^2(1,1)$, diagonal element $(5,5)$ is the sum of $K^2(3,3)$ and $K^3(1,1)$, and so on. The system of equations to be solved for $\theta_2, \ldots, \theta_{2m+1}$ is $A\theta = b$, which is the second through $(2m+1)$th equation of the system in (6.15). (Recall that the first equation is dropped, because I impose that $\theta_1 = 1$.) Again, it is evident that the system of equations to be solved is sparse. In this example, the matrix to be inverted is $2m \times 2m$. The number of non-zero elements in A is $8m-4$. If $m = 20$, then 10% of the elements of A are non-zero. If $m = 100$, then 2% of the elements of A are non-zero.

Note that a relationship exists between the θ_is and the θ_i^es: θ_i^e denotes the ith unknown coefficient on element e, $i = 1, 2, 3$, whereas θ_i denotes the unknown coefficient for node i, $i = 1, \ldots, 2m+1$. If I label nodes consecutively, then $\theta_2 = \theta_2^1, \theta_3 = \theta_3^1 = \theta_1^2, \theta_4 = \theta_2^2, \theta_5 = \theta_3^2 = \theta_1^3$, and so on.

If $m = 3$ and the elements are the same as in Example 6.3, namely, $[0,1]$, $[1,3]$, and $[3,6]$, then the approximate solution satisfies

$$\begin{bmatrix} 16 & 22 & 0 & 0 & 0 & 0 \\ -18 & 12 & 24 & -7 & 0 & 0 \\ 0 & -16 & 32 & 24 & 0 & 0 \\ 0 & 3 & -16 & 20 & 26 & -8 \\ 0 & 0 & 0 & -14 & 48 & 26 \\ 0 & 0 & 0 & 2 & -14 & 27 \end{bmatrix} \begin{bmatrix} \theta_2 \\ \theta_3 \\ \theta_4 \\ \theta_5 \\ \theta_6 \\ \theta_7 \end{bmatrix} = \begin{bmatrix} 18 \\ -4 \\ 0 \\ 0 \\ 0 \\ 0 \end{bmatrix}$$

Note that I have multiplied all the elements in the system by 30 to avoid writing them as fractions. In Fig. 6.8, I plot the approximate solution (the line marked "quadratic bases") along with the exact solution and the approximate solution with linear basis functions found in Example 6.3. Notice that the fit is better with quadratic functions. However, in this example, the number of unknowns doubles.

In general, the finite-element approximations must satisfy certain conditions to guarantee convergence of the method as the number of elements is increased. The approximate solution should be continuous and differentiable over each element – with the order of differentiability such that all terms in the residual equation are non-zero. The polynomials used to represent the approximate solution on an element should be complete, and the approximation should be continuous across element boundaries.

Although the finite-element method – as I applied it in Examples 6.3 and 6.4 – can be viewed as a Galerkin weighted residual method, a lot of structure is put on the bases and the element geometries. In fact, one criticism of spectral methods is that, unlike with the finite-element method, the selection of basis and weight functions seems arbitrary. This is why the finite-element method and spectral weighted residual methods are typically treated separately in textbooks (see, for example, Reddy, 1993).

In the next two sections, I apply weighted residual and finite-element methods to standard problems in economics. Unfortunately, these problems do not have the feature that the residual equations are linear in the unknown vector θ. However, as I will show, most of the computation will again involve solving a potentially large linear system of equations.

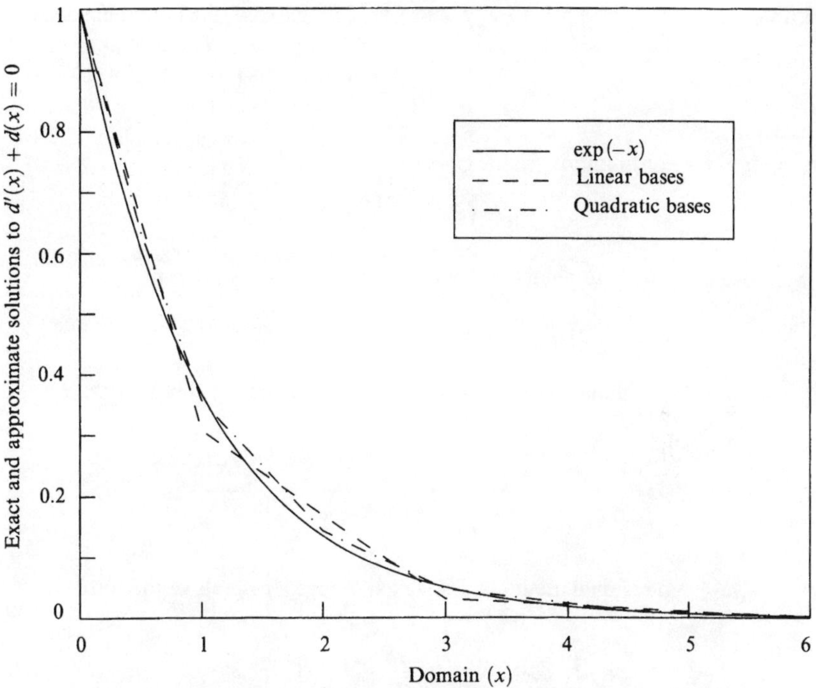

FIG. 6.8. Two finite-element approximations to a first-order differential equation.

6.3 The deterministic growth model

I now turn to the deterministic growth model:

$$\max_{\{c_t\}} \sum_{t=0}^{\infty} \beta^t u(c_t) \tag{6.16}$$

subject to

$$c_t + k_t = f(k_{t-1})$$

where c_t is consumption at date t, k_t is the capital stock at date t, $u(\cdot)$ is the utility function, $f(\cdot)$ is the production function, and $\beta < 1$ is a discount factor.[7] From the Euler equation, the functional equation is given by

$$F(c)(k) = \beta \frac{u'(c(f(k) - c(k)))}{u'(c(k))} f'(f(k) - c(k)) - 1 = 0$$

and the boundary condition is given by $c(0) = 0$. In this case, I want to compute an approximation $c^n(k; \theta)$ to the consumption function that sets $F(c)$ approximately equal to zero for all k.

[7] See Sargent (1987a) for a detailed discussion of the problems described here and in the next section.

Example 6.5 Let $u(c) = \ln(c)$ and $f(k) = \lambda k^\alpha$. In this case, the functional equation is

$$F(c)(k) = \frac{\beta\alpha\lambda\,(\lambda k^\alpha - c(k))^{\alpha-1}\, c(k)}{c\,(\lambda k^\alpha - c(k))} - 1$$

The solution for consumption in this case is

$$c(k) = (1 - \beta\alpha)\lambda k^\alpha$$

Suppose that I want to obtain an approximate solution of the form

$$c^n(k;\theta) = \theta_1 k + \theta_2 k^2 + \cdots + \theta_n k^n$$

which satisfies the boundary condition at $k = 0$. The residual equation is therefore

$$R(k;\theta) = \frac{\beta\alpha\lambda\left(\lambda k^\alpha - \sum_{j=1}^n \theta_j k^j\right)^{\alpha-1} \sum_{j=1}^n \theta_j k^j}{\sum_{i=1}^n \theta_i \left(\lambda k^\alpha - \sum_{j=1}^n \theta_j k^j\right)^i} - 1$$

To apply weighted residual methods, I have to compute integrals of the form

$$\int_0^{\bar{k}} \phi_i(k) R(k;\theta)\, dk, \quad i = 1, \ldots, n \tag{6.17}$$

where $\bar{k}$ is the upper bound of the domain for the capital stock. Since the residual R is a nonlinear function of θ, it makes sense to do numerical integration. If I apply Gaussian quadrature (which is typically done), then equation (6.17) is replaced by

$$\sum_l \omega_l \phi_i(k_l) R(k_l;\theta), \quad i = 1, \ldots, n \tag{6.18}$$

where ω_l are the *quadrature weights* and the grid points k_l are the *quadrature abscissae*. (See Press *et al.*, 1986, for the quadrature formulae and a description of how they are derived.) The values for ω_l and k_l do not depend on the function being integrated ($\phi_i(k)R(k;\theta)$ in this case). In other words, once I know the bounds of integration (for example, 0 and $\bar{k}$) and the number of quadrature points, I can look up the ω_ls and k_ls in a standard quadrature table.[8] Depending on the specific quadrature rule (for example, Legendre, Chebyshev, Hermite) used, the ω_ls and k_ls will differ, but the calculations of R and ϕ will look the same no matter what quadrature rule is used.

[8]The weights and abscissae are chosen so that the n-point quadrature rule is exact for integrals of all polynomials of order $2n - 1$ times some weight function, which depends on the specific rule. For example, Gauss–Legendre quadrature uses a weight function of 1 and Gauss–Chebyshev quadrature uses a weight function of $1/\sqrt{1 - x^2}$, where x is defined on $(-1, 1)$.

The final step is to solve the system of equations in (6.18). In this case, the system is nonlinear. The problem is to find θ such that $G(\theta) = 0$, where G has the same dimension as θ. Applying Newton's method to $G(\theta) = 0$ means iterating on

$$\theta^{j+1} = \theta^j - \left[\left. \frac{\partial G(\theta)}{\partial \theta} \right|_{\theta=\theta^j} \right]^{-1} G(\theta^j), \quad j = 1, 2, \ldots$$

with some initial guess θ^0, where θ^j is the vector of unknown coefficients at the jth iteration. Notice that as I iterate, I solve a sequence of problems of the following form: find θ such that $A\theta = b$, where A is the Jacobian matrix $\partial G/\partial\theta$ evaluated at θ^j and b is the function itself, $G(\theta^j)$.

For the three weighted residual applications below, assume that $\alpha = 0.25$, $\beta = 0.96$, $\lambda = 1/(\alpha\beta)$, and $\bar{k} = 2$. For this set of parameters, the steady-state capital stock is equal to one. Assume also that the quadrature rule is Legendre with 20 quadrature abscissae used to approximate the integral in (6.17). In this case, $\omega_l = \int_{-1}^{1} \prod_{i=1,i\neq l}^{20} (x - x_i)/(x_l - x_i)dx$, $l = 1, \ldots, 20$, and $x_1, \ldots, x_{20}$ are the roots of the 20th Legendre polynomial found recursively as follows: $p_0(x) = 1$, $p_1(x) = x$, $ip_i(x) = (2i-1)xp_{i-1}(x) - (i-1)p_{i-2}(x)$, $i = 2, \ldots, 20$. Since $\bar{k} = 2$, the points k_l are given by $k_l = x_l + 1$, $l = 1, \ldots, 20$.

(a) **Least squares**. To apply the method of least squares, I set $\phi_i(k) = \partial R(k;\theta)/\partial\theta_i$, where the derivative of the residual is given by

$$\frac{\partial R(k;\theta)}{\partial \theta_l} = -\frac{\beta\alpha\lambda\tilde{k}^{\alpha-1}k^{\ell}}{c^n(\tilde{k};\theta)} \left\{ 1 + \frac{(\alpha-1)c^n(k;\theta)}{\tilde{k}} - \frac{c^n(k;\theta)}{c^n(\tilde{k};\theta)} \left(\tilde{k}^{\ell} - k^{\ell} \sum_{i=1}^{n} i\theta_i \tilde{k}^{i-1} \right) \right\}$$

$l = 1, \ldots, n$, and $\tilde{k} = \lambda k^\alpha + \sum_j \theta_j k^j$. In Fig. 6.9, I plot the approximate solution c^n for $n = 5$ along with the exact solution. Since the derivative of the true function is infinite at $k = 0$ and relatively small for high values of k, I must add more polynomials to resolve the solution completely at all capital stocks. I also plot the result for a more restricted grid on the capital stocks, namely, $[\frac{1}{3}, \frac{5}{3}]$. This is the grid Judd (1992) uses when evaluating weighted residual methods for the deterministic growth model. For both approximations, I assume that $n = 5$. Notice that although the approximation on $[\frac{1}{3}, \frac{5}{3}]$ is very close to the true solution, the exact solution is very smooth – almost linear.

(b) **Collocation**. To apply the collocation method, I set $\phi_i(k) = \delta(k - k_i)$, where k_i, $i = 1, \ldots, n$, are collocation points in $[0, \bar{k}]$. In Fig. 6.10, I plot two approximations: one with five evenly spaced collocation points between 0.1 and 2 and one with five evenly spaced collocation points between $\frac{1}{3}$ and $\frac{5}{3}$. The problem of fitting functions with steep gradients becomes acute in this case, which is why I avoid the region of capital stocks below 0.1. Even so, the approximation on $[0.1, 2]$ is not very accurate. It is clear that I need better choices for basis functions and collocation points to make this method competitive with least squares. On $[\frac{1}{3}, \frac{5}{3}]$, I find that the approximation is not quite as good as that for least squares, but it is not too different from the exact solution. Here again, the fit is good because the exact solution is very smooth on $[\frac{1}{3}, \frac{5}{3}]$.

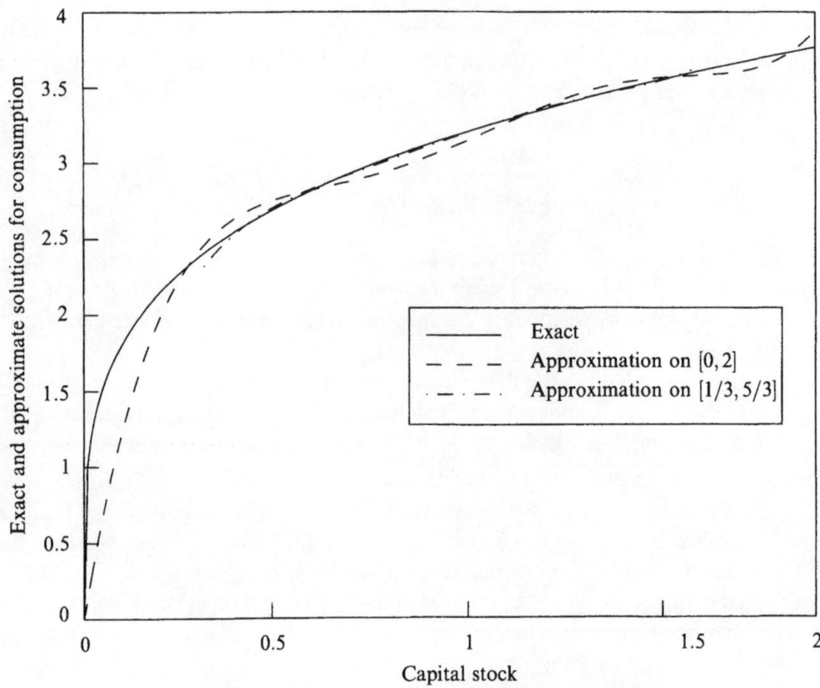

FIG. 6.9. Two least-squares approximations for the deterministic growth model.

(c) **Galerkin**. To apply the Galerkin method, I set $\phi_i(k) = k^i$, $i = 1, \ldots, n$. In Fig. 6.11, I plot approximate functions on $[0, 2]$ and $\left[\frac{1}{3}, \frac{5}{3}\right]$ along with the exact solution. The results here are similar to the results of the least-squares method.

Because I need to include more polynomials, which in the case of k^i, $i = 1, \ldots, n$, become similar to each other as n gets large, it makes sense to use a class of orthogonal polynomials. Judd (1992) uses a representation for consumption of the form

$$c^n(k; \theta) = \sum_{i=1}^{n} \theta_i \psi_i(k) \tag{6.19}$$

where $\psi_i(k) = p_{i-1}(2(k - \underline{k})/(\bar{k} - \underline{k}) - 1)$, $\underline{k}$ is a lower bound on the capital stocks, and $p_i(x)$ is the ith Chebyshev polynomial defined in equation (6.19).[9]

Example 6.6 In this case, assume that $u(c) = c^{1-\tau}/(1-\tau)$ and $f(k) = \lambda k^{\alpha} + (1-\delta)k$. Let $\tau = 5$, $\alpha = 0.25$, $\delta = 0.025$, $\beta = 0.99$, and $\lambda = (1 - \beta(1 - \delta))/(\alpha\beta)$ (so that the steady-state capital is equal to 1). Let c^n take the form of (6.19) with $n = 10$. In Fig. 6.12, I plot the approximate solutions for $\underline{k} = 0.03$, $\bar{k} = 2$ (marked with a square),

[9]Note that this approximation will not satisfy the boundary condition at $c(0) = 0$ if $\underline{k} = 0$ for any θ. However, if I make a slight modification, namely, $\psi_i(k) = kp_{i-1}(2k/\bar{k} - 1)$ defined on $[0, \bar{k}]$, then the boundary condition is satisfied for all possible choices of θ.

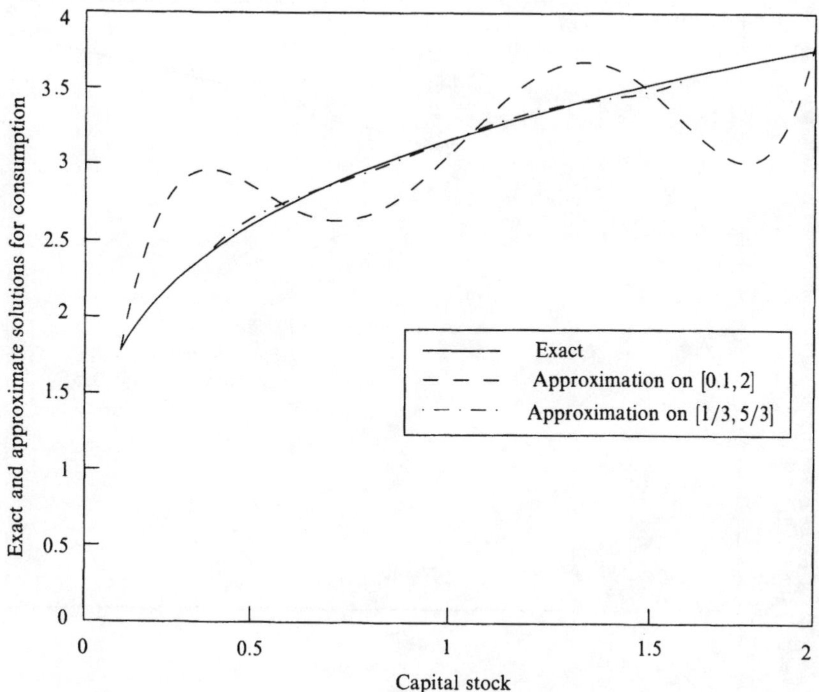

FIG. 6.10. Two collocation approximations for the deterministic growth model.

and $\underline{k} = 0.1$, $\bar{k} = 1.9$ (marked with a circle) along with the exact solution.[10] The locations of the points marked by squares or circles are the quadrature abscissae.

It is clear from Fig. 6.12 that more polynomials are needed for a good approximation on [0.03, 2]. This is because I am trying to approximate a very steep part of the function and a very flat part of the function using the same basis functions. When I restrict the domain to [0.1, 1.9], there is a significant improvement in the approximation over this region of the state space. The approximation is visually indistinguishable from the exact solution. In this restricted region of the domain, the function does not have any large gradients.

Suppose that, instead of using Chebyshev polynomials, I apply the Galerkin method with piecewise linear basis functions as is done for the finite-element method.

Example 6.7 Assume that $u(\cdot)$, $f(\cdot)$, and the parameterization are the same as in Example 6.6. Let $x_1 = 0$, $x_{11} = 2$, and $x_i = x_{i-1} + 0.005\exp(0.574(i-2))$. This partition implies that there are 10 elements with lengths that increase exponentially. Thus, there will be more points near the origin, where the function has a large (infinite

[10] What I call the *exact solution* here is actually a finite-element approximation with a large number of elements. Although this itself is an approximation, doubling the number of elements leaves Fig. 6.12 unchanged.

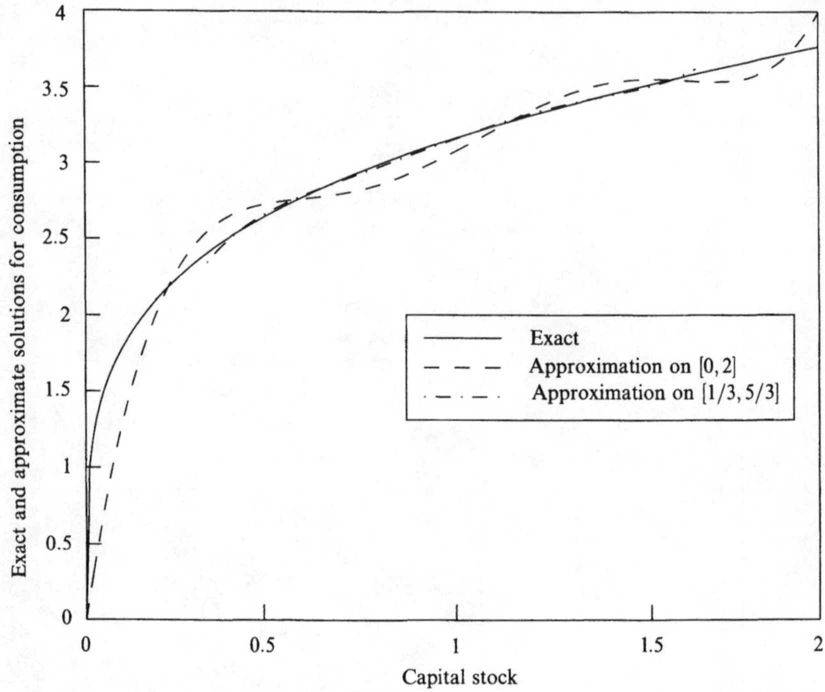

FIG. 6.11. Two Galerkin approximations for the deterministic growth model.

in this case) gradient. To compute the weighted integral, I use a Legendre quadrature rule with two quadrature points per element. On an element of length ℓ_e, the Legendre quadrature rule with two quadrature points implies the following weights and abscissae for (6.18): $\omega_l = \ell_e/2, l = 1, 2$, and $k_1 = k_e + 0.211\ell_e$, $k_2 = k_e + 0.789\ell_e$, where k_e is the first end point of the element.

In Fig. 6.13, I plot the finite-element approximation along with the exact solution. Because the finite-element method is a piecewise application of a weighted residual method, it is possible to get a more accurate approximation over the entire [0, 2] domain – I am not using the same basis functions in the very steep region and the very flat region of the consumption function.

To obtain the approximation in Fig. 6.13, the main computational task is the inversion of a 10×10 matrix. In this matrix, 68 of the 100 elements are zeros, and the structure of the matrix is band diagonal. As the number of unknowns becomes large, it becomes expensive and, in some cases, infeasible to invert the matrix without using inversion routines that exploit the fact that the matrix is band diagonal (see Saad, 1996).

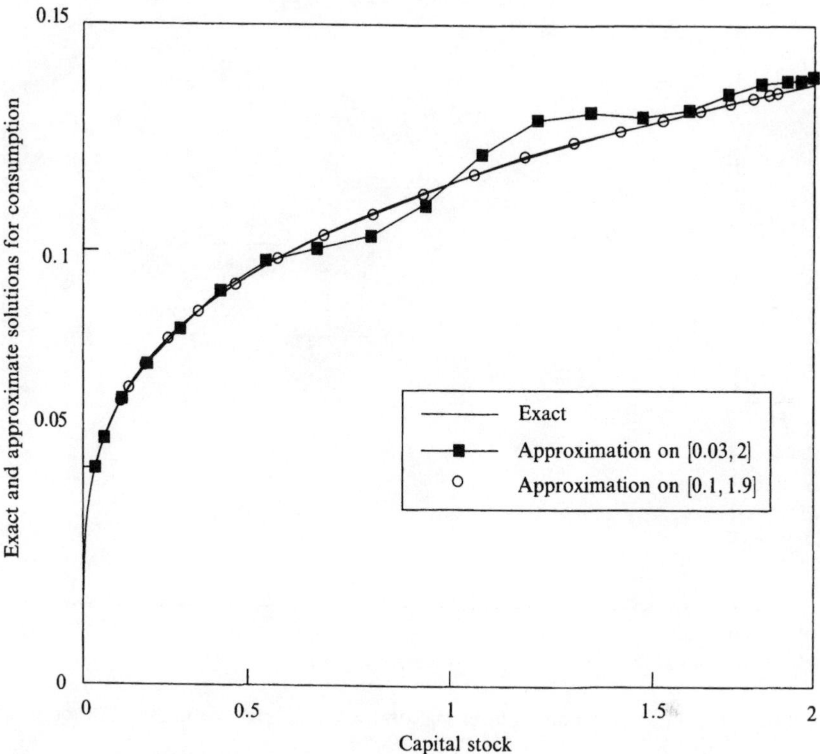

FIG. 6.12. Two Galerkin approximations with Chebyshev basis functions for the deterministic growth model.

6.4 The stochastic growth model[11]

Suppose that, instead of the deterministic growth model, I want to calculate the decision functions for the stochastic growth model in which decisions depend on the capital stock and a stochastic shock. The stochastic growth model assumes that output at date t can be allocated either to current consumption c_t or to current investment i_t. The consumption/savings decision is assumed to be optimal in that the preferences of households are maximized. The preferences are given by

$$E\left[\sum_{t=0}^{\infty} \beta^t u(c_t) \,|k_{-1}\right], \quad 0 < \beta < 1 \tag{6.20}$$

where k_t is the capital stock at t and k_{-1} is known. The maximization of equation (6.20) is done subject to the feasibility constraints

[11] See Judd (1992) for more details on spectral methods as applied to this problem and McGrattan (1996) for more details on the finite-element method as applied to this problem.

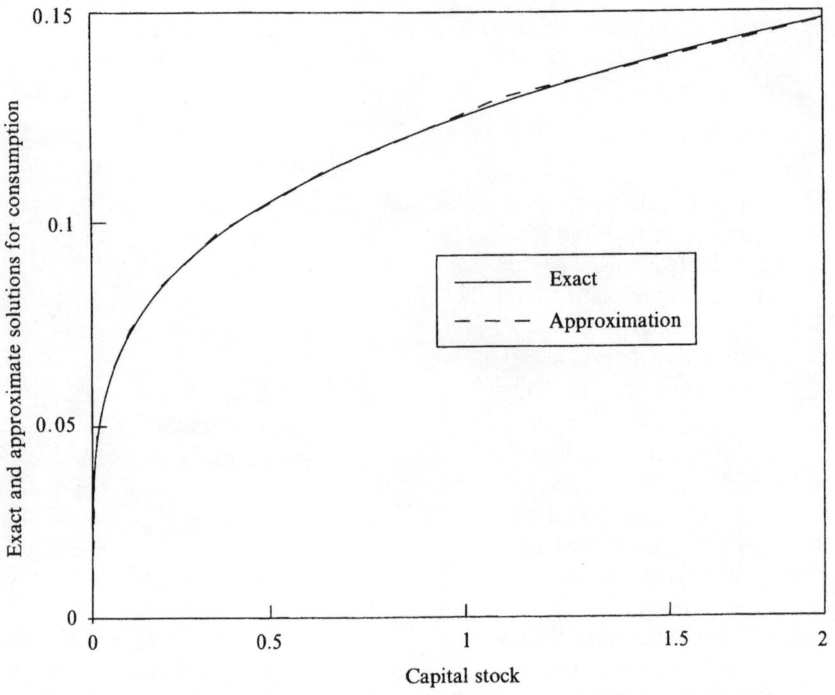

FIG. 6.13. Finite-element approximation for the deterministic growth model.

$$c_t + k_t - (1-\delta)k_{t-1} = \lambda_t k_{t-1}^{\alpha}, \quad 0 < \alpha < 1,\ 0 \leq \delta \leq 1 \tag{6.21}$$

the non-negativity constraints $c_t \geq 0$, $k_t \geq 0$ for all $t \geq 0$ and subject to the process for the technology shock,

$$\ln \lambda_t = \rho \ln \lambda_{t-1} + \varepsilon_t, \quad -1 < \rho < 1 \tag{6.22}$$

where ε_t is a serially uncorrelated, normally distributed random variable with mean zero and variance σ^2. Because ε is normally distributed, it does not have a compact support. The technology shock in this case takes on values between 0 and infinity. On the computer, I cannot specify an upper bound of infinity. Instead, I can either specify a large upper bound (in which the probability of observing a larger value is small) or make a transformation of variables and work with a bounded interval. Let $z = \tanh(\ln(\lambda))$, which is defined on $[-1, 1]$. Then I can rewrite equation (6.22) as

$$z_t = \tanh\left(\rho \tanh^{-1}(z_{t-1}) + \sqrt{2}\sigma \nu_t\right)$$

where $\nu_t = \varepsilon_t/(\sqrt{2}\sigma)$.

Because the stochastic shock takes on a continuum of values, I need to solve a two-dimensional problem. The representation of the approximate solution is then

$$c^n(k, z; \theta) = \sum_{i=1}^{n} \theta_i \psi_i(k, z)$$

A simple set of basis functions is all products of the elements of $\{1, k, k^2, \ldots, k^{n_k}\}$ and $\{1, z, z^2, \ldots, z^{n_z}\}$. Alternatively, I can use all products of the elements of two sets of orthogonal polynomials. In either case, however, the number of unknowns starts to add up quickly, especially if a large number of polynomials are needed to approximate consumption at both high and low values of the capital stock.

One way to keep the problem tractable is to use the set of complete polynomials rather than all products of terms in $\{k^i\}_{i=0}^{n_k}$ and $\{z^i\}_{i=0}^{n_z}$ (for example, bases $\{1, k, z, k^2, kz, z^2\}$ rather than $\{1, k, z, kz, k^2, z^2, k^2z, kz^2, k^2z^2\}$). Using the set of complete polynomials allows me to approximate higher-order functions but limits the number of unknown coefficients.[12] Another way to keep the problem tractable is to apply a finite-element method. As earlier examples show, the system of equations to be solved for the unknown coefficients θ is typically very sparse. Therefore, in big problems, I do not need as much storage as in a typical spectral method, and I can apply algorithms for solving sparse systems of equations.

Consider application of the finite-element method to the stochastic growth model. The first step is to write out the residual equation using the first-order condition for the problem in (6.20):

$$R(k, z; \theta) = \frac{\beta}{\sqrt{\pi}} \int_{-\infty}^{\infty} \frac{c^n(\tilde{k}, \tilde{z}; \theta)^{-\tau}}{c^n(k, z; \theta)^{-\tau}} \left(\alpha \tilde{k}^{\alpha-1} \sqrt{\frac{1+\tilde{z}}{1-\tilde{z}}} + 1 - \delta \right) e^{-\nu^2} d\nu - 1 = 0 \tag{6.23}$$

where

$$\tilde{k} = k^\alpha \sqrt{(1+z)/(1-z)} + (1-\delta)k - c^n(k, z; \theta)$$
$$\tilde{z} = \tanh\left(\rho \tanh^{-1}(z) + \sqrt{2}\sigma\nu\right)$$

$c^n(0, z; \theta) = 0$, ν is distributed normally with mean zero and variance 1/2, and the domain for the state space is $\Omega = [0, \bar{k}] \times [-1, 1]$. If I apply a Gauss–Hermite quadrature rule when computing the integral in equation (6.23), then the residual equation becomes

$$R(k, z; \theta) \simeq \frac{\beta}{\sqrt{\pi}} \sum_{l=1}^{m_\nu} \frac{c^n(\tilde{k}, \tilde{z}_l; \theta)^{-\tau}}{c^n(k, z; \theta)^{-\tau}} \left(\alpha \tilde{k}^{\alpha-1} \sqrt{\frac{1+\tilde{z}_l}{1-\tilde{z}_l}} + 1 - \delta \right) \omega_l - 1$$

where $\tilde{z}_l = \tanh(\rho \tanh^{-1}(z) + \sqrt{2}\sigma\nu_l)$ and $\nu_l, \omega_l, l = 1, \ldots, m_\nu$ are the abscissae and weights for an m_ν-point quadrature rule. (For the quadrature formulae, see Press *et al.*, 1986.)

[12] See Judd (1992) for a comparison of complete polynomials and tensor products in the stochastic growth model example.

The second step in applying the finite-element method is to divide up the domain into smaller non-overlapping subdomains called elements. In this problem, the domain is two-dimensional and rectangular: $\Omega = [0, \bar{k}] \times [-1, 1]$. A reasonable choice for the element shape, therefore, is a rectangle. Suppose that I divide the domain into smaller rectangular subdomains which do not overlap.[13] Each element will be a rectangle in Ω, say, $[k_i, k_{i+1}] \times [z_j, z_{j+1}]$, where k_i is the ith grid point for the the capital stock and z_j is the jth grid point for the technology shock.

I consider two types of approximations over the rectangular elements: linear and quadratic. Suppose the representation for consumption on some element e is linear,

$$c_e^n(k, z) = a + b\,k + c\,z + d\,kz \tag{6.24}$$

Because there are four unknowns, I require an element with four nodes. If I place the four nodes at the corners of the rectangle, then I can uniquely define the geometry of the element and use the values of the solution at the four nodes to pin down the constants in equation (6.24). That is, as in the one-dimensional case, I can rewrite the approximation in (6.24) so that $c_e^n(k, z; \theta) = \sum_i \theta_i^e \psi_i^e(k, z)$, $i = 1, \ldots, 4$, where the basis functions are such that ψ_i^e is 1 at node i and zero at the other three nodes on the element.

Before I give formulae for the basis functions, it is convenient to consider a mapping from global coordinates (k, z) to local coordinates (ξ, η) defined on a master element. This is done for convenience, since the master element has a fixed set of coordinates, while each element in Ω has a different set of coordinates. Thus, I can construct basis functions once but use them for each element. Consider functions $\xi(k)$ and $\eta(z)$ that map a typical element $[k_i, k_{i+1}] \times [z_j, z_{j+1}]$ to the square $[-1, 1] \times [-1, 1]$; that is, $\xi(k) = (2k - k_i - k_{i+1})/(k_{i+1} - k_i)$ and $\eta(z) = (2z - z_j - z_{j+1})/(z_{j+1} - z_j)$. Assume that the four nodes of the master element are $(-1, -1)$, $(1, -1)$, $(1, 1)$, and $(-1, 1)$ using the local coordinates. In this case, the basis functions are constructed so that $c_e^n(\xi, \eta; \theta) = \sum_i \theta_i^e \psi_i^e(\xi, \eta)$ with $\theta_1^e = c_e^n(-1, -1; \theta)$, $\theta_2^e = c_e^n(1, -1; \theta)$, $\theta_3^e = c_e^n(1, 1; \theta)$, and $\theta_4^e = c_e^n(-1, 1; \theta)$. These restrictions imply that

$$\begin{aligned} c_e^n(\xi, \eta; \theta) =& \tfrac{1}{4}(1 - \xi)(1 - \eta)\,\theta_1^e + \tfrac{1}{4}(1 + \xi)(1 - \eta)\,\theta_2^e \\ &+ \tfrac{1}{4}(1 + \xi)(1 + \eta)\,\theta_3^e + \tfrac{1}{4}(1 - \xi)(1 + \eta)\,\theta_4^e \end{aligned} \tag{6.25}$$

To attain a more accurate approximation, I can increase the number of elements while retaining linear basis functions or use higher-order polynomials. Consider, for example, quadratic functions in two dimensions. One simple way to construct these functions is to take the product of one-dimensional quadratic polynomials. A unique set of coefficients for the polynomial requires that there be nine nodes and, hence, nine interpolation functions. In this case, the approximation on the master element $[-1, 1] \times [-1, 1]$ is

[13]Extensions to non-rectangular element shapes require additional work but are not as useful in economic problems as in engineering problems, which sometimes involve irregularly shaped domains (see, for example, Hughes, 1987; Reddy, 1993).

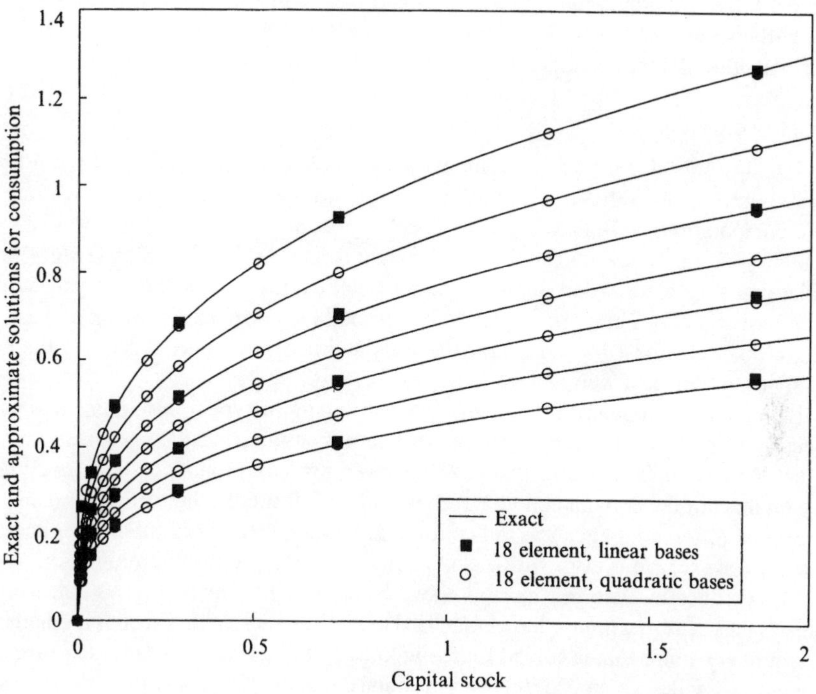

FIG. 6.14. Two finite-element approximations for the stochastic growth model.

given by

$$\begin{aligned} c_e^n(\xi,\eta;\theta) = & \tfrac{1}{4}\xi(\xi-1)\eta(\eta-1)\theta_1^e + \tfrac{1}{4}\xi(\xi+1)\eta(\eta-1)\theta_2^e + \tfrac{1}{4}\xi(\xi+1)\eta(\eta+1)\theta_3^e \\ & + \tfrac{1}{4}\xi(\xi-1)\eta(\eta+1)\,\theta_4^e + \tfrac{1}{2}(1-\xi^2)\eta(\eta-1)\,\theta_5^e + \tfrac{1}{2}\xi(\xi+1)(1-\eta^2)\,\theta_6^e \\ & + \tfrac{1}{2}(1-\xi^2)\eta(\eta+1)\,\theta_7^e + \tfrac{1}{2}\xi(\xi-1)(1-\eta^2)\,\theta_8^e + (1-\xi^2)(1-\eta^2)\,\theta_9^e \end{aligned} \tag{6.26}$$

Example 6.8 Let $\tau = 1$, $\delta = 0$, $\beta = 0.95$, $\alpha = 0.33$, $\rho = 0.95$, and $\sigma = 0.1$. Assume that the partition on z is given by $[-0.391, -0.123, 0.123, 0.391]$ and that the partition on k is given by $[0, 0.010, 0.036, 0.102, 0.273, 0.714, 1.85]$. I set the number of quadrature points on each element to nine, that is, three points for integration with respect to the capital stock and three points for integration with respect to the technology shock. For integration over ν, I set the number of quadrature points, m_ν, equal to 10.

In Fig. 6.14, I plot the approximate piecewise linear solution (marked with a square) along with the exact solution. Even though there are only 18 elements, it is hard to distinguish the two.

Example 6.9 Suppose that I use the same parameterization as in Example 6.8, but instead of linear basis functions, I use the quadratic functions in equation (6.26). In

Fig. 6.14, the solution is marked with a circle. Notice that the fit with quadratic bases is slightly better than that with linear bases – however, since the coarse piecewise linear approximation is very accurate, there is not much room for improvement.

6.5 Conclusions

My intent in this chapter was to demonstrate the potential power of weighted residual methods and to show that they are relatively easy to implement. I have shown that the main computational task is to solve a system of equations, $A\theta = b$, for θ – once if the problem is linear or several times if the problem is nonlinear. As with most algorithms, choices must be made when implementing a weighted residual method. In particular, a set of basis functions must be chosen to represent the approximate solution and a set of weight functions must be chosen for the weighted integral. I have discussed the most widely used basis and weight functions.

I have also distinguished the methods according to the type of basis functions used. Spectral methods use smooth functions, such as polynomials, that are non-zero on most of the domain. Finite-element methods, however, use basis functions that are equal to zero on most of the domain and non-zero on only a few subdivisions of the domain. For the simple differential equation in Section 6.2, both types of basis functions generated very accurate solutions even with a small number of bases in the approximation.

The distinction becomes more obvious in higher-order or highly nonlinear problems. In these cases, a finite-element method has advantages. With spectral methods, the system of equations that is solved for the unknown coefficients θ is dense because each element of θ will in general affect every residual equation. For problems with many state variables, there are typically many coefficients to compute. Inversion of a large, dense matrix may not be feasible. With the finite-element method, however, A is sparse and its structure can typically be exploited. With spectral methods, the same functions are used on all regions of the state space. For problems that are nonlinear, such as the growth examples in Sections 6.3 and 6.4, it is better to use different approximations in different regions of the state space. For this reason, I have concluded that a finite-element method may be better suited to problems in which the solution is nonlinear or kinked in regions where inequality constraints bind.

7

THE PARAMETERIZED EXPECTATIONS APPROACH: SOME PRACTICAL ISSUES

Albert Marcet[1] and Guido Lorenzoni

7.1 Introduction

We discuss some practical issues related to the use of the parameterized expectations approach (PEA) for solving nonlinear stochastic dynamic models with rational expectations. This approach is discussed formally in Marcet and Marshall (1994); and has been applied widely[2] as it turns out to be a convenient algorithm, especially when there are a large number of state variables and stochastic shocks in key conditional expectations terms. In this chapter we provide a detailed description of some practical issues and discuss in detail the application of the algorithm. We also discuss a FORTRAN program for implementing the algorithm. We discuss these issues in a battery of examples, each of which is described in three steps: first we show how each example fits into the general framework we consider (Section 7.2.1); then we show how the algorithm is adapted for each case; finally, we show how the program is adapted to each example (Section 7.4). The series of examples is as follows: Example 7.1 is the Lucas asset pricing model, which is offered for comparison with the other chapters of this book; Example 7.2 is the simple stochastic growth model, the simpiest model in which many of the computational issues related to solving nonlinear models arise. Examples 7.3–7.6 are variations of the simple stochastic growth model, each selected to demonstrate a different issue.

We hope that this chapter will help applied economists to solve nonlinear stochastic dynamic models, even if their knowledge of numerical analysis is almost non-existent; for this reason, we avoid discussing tools from numerical analysis as much as possible. The FORTRAN program is publicly available through the Internet[3] and contains some standardized subroutines that simplify enormously the task of applying PEA. However, the user will still have to do some programming in order to modify certain subroutines

[1]This research was partially supported by the Spanish Ministry of Education, the Catalan Conselleria of Education, and the European Commission. All errors are our own. This chapter owes much to conversations with previous coauthors, mainly Wouter den Haan, Ramon Marimon, David Marshall, Tom Sargent and Ken Singleton. We are indebted to the editors for their encouragement, their patience, and many helpful comments.

[2]An early description of the algorithm can be found in Marcet (1988). An early description of practical issues can be found in den Haan and Marcet (1990). Marcet and Marshall (1994) provide a long list of applications.

[3]`http://www.econ.upf.es/~marcet` and `http://web.mit.edu/glorenzo/www/home.html`.

that are model-dependent. To guide the user in this task, we provide versions of the model-dependent subroutines that solve each of the examples discussed in the text.

We discuss in detail how to solve models with Euler equations. Because Euler equations are easy to obtain in models with suboptimal equilibria, we can use the algorithm even in models where the equilibrium cannot be characterized as the solution to a maximization dynamic program. This is the case, for example, in models with distortionary taxes (see Example 7.3 below) or incomplete markets.

Having said what we do in the chapter, we should also specify what we do *not* do. The basic version of the algorithm that we present only works to approximate the solution at the stationary distribution. The algorithm can be modified to compute the transition towards the stationary distribution from an arbitrary initial condition. Also, we only study models characterized by Euler equations. This means we only scratch the surface of the possible applications of PEA. Variations of the algorithm have been used to solve models with incentive constraints, value functions, conditional expectations of discounted sums, models with a large number of heterogeneous agents, present value budget constraints, incomplete information, etc.[4] Many of these extensions are easy to implement, but we simply do not have enough space. Finally, we only address in passing issues related to the selection of the degree of approximation of the conditional expectation.

Technical issues are left out of the chapter. It is known that PEA can provide arbitrary accuracy if the approximation function is refined (e.g. if the degree of the polynomial approximation increases). Convergence to the correct solution is proved in Marcet and Marshall (1994). Also, we do not provide a detailed comparison with other approaches, but only offer some informal comments on such comparisons.

The layout of the chapter is as follows. In the next section we discuss the algorithm and how it can be applied to six examples; Section 7.3 discusses the FORTRAN program; Section 7.4 the application of the program to each example; Section 7.5 offers some concluding comments.

7.2 Parameterized expectations

We discuss the algorithm for models with a unique stationary and ergodic distribution,[5] and we will address the matter of approximating the solution at the support of this distribution. The current algorithm can be applied to non-stationary models if it is possible to transform all variables into a stationary representation. For example, if the model has balanced growth, all variables need to be divided by the appropriate growth rate until all normalized variables have a stationary distribution.

[4]For a more complete list of citations and different applications, see Marcet and Marshall (1994).

[5]The sufficient conditions for an equilibrium often include a set of transversality conditions. For most models, stationarity of the solution is a sufficient condition for satisfying the transversality condition; therefore, since we are imposing stationarity, we can ignore the transversality condition. Since we just deal with models that have a unique solution of the first-order conditions we do not address the issue that, due to non-convexities, the Euler equation might not be sufficient for the optimum. Similarly, we assume the existence of an equilibrium of a certain recursive form (this could be an issue in Example 7.3 below). These sins are committed by any Euler equation approach, and such approaches can be amended in several ways that we do not discuss here. So we provide an algorithm to find the equilibrium (or the optimum) where it exists and can be described uniquely by a certain system of first-order conditions.

The reason why many dynamic models are difficult to solve is that conditional expectations often appear in the equilibrium conditions, as we shall show in this chapter using a series of examples. We often know these expectations are a time-invariant function $\mathcal{E}$ of some state variables. We can almost never derive formulae for this function analytically, but we can almost always derive formulae for the Euler equations. We know a key property of $\mathcal{E}$: under rational expectations, if agents use $\mathcal{E}$ to form their decisions, the series generated is such that $\mathcal{E}$ is precisely the best predictor of the future variables inside the conditional expectation. So, if we knew $\mathcal{E}$, we could easily simulate the model and check that this is actually the conditional expectation; but, of course, we do not know $\mathcal{E}$ until we solve the model.

In order to break this circle the basic approach is to substitute the conditional expectations by parameterized functions of the state variables with arbitrary coefficients. Simulations of the model can then be easily obtained for a given set of coefficients and these simulations can be used to check if the parameterized expectation is close to the best predictor. If it is not, then we iterate on the coefficients until they deliver, approximately, the best possible prediction.

7.2.1 *A general framework*

We now discuss formally the general model to which we apply PEA. Consider an economy described by a vector of n variables z_t, and a vector of s exogenously given shocks u_t. The process $\{z_t, u_t\}$ is known to satisfy several Euler equations, feasibility constraints, equilibrium conditions, etc. which are summarized in a system

$$g(E_t[\phi(z_{t+1}, z_t)], z_t, z_{t-1}, u_t) = 0 \tag{7.1}$$

for all t, where $g : R^m \times R^n \times R^n \times R^s \to R^q$ and $\phi : R^{2n} \to R^m$. The vector z_t includes all endogenous variables, as well as those exogenous variables that appear inside the expectation. The process u_t is assumed to be Markov of order one. As usual, E_t denotes the conditional expectation given all information up to period t.

We consider solutions such that, in equilibrium, past information that is relevant for predicting $\phi(z_{t+1}, z_t)$ can be summarized in a finite-dimensional vector of state variables $x_t \in R^l$ satisfying

$$E_t[\phi(z_{t+1}, z_t)] = E[\phi(z_{t+1}, z_t)|x_t]$$

where x_t is a subset of (z_{t-1}, u_t). Furthermore, we compute solutions that satisfy a recursive framework in the sense that the conditional expectation is given by a time-invariant function $\mathcal{E}$ such that

$$\mathcal{E}(x_t) = E_t[\phi(z_{t+1}, z_t)] \tag{7.2}$$

It turns out that, in many economic models of interest, we can write down the functions g and ϕ that satisfy (7.1), and we know that (7.2) is satisfied for some function $\mathcal{E}$, but we do not know the form of this function.

Let us consider different examples that map into the framework (7.1) and (7.2). Since we are considering these models for simulation, we parameterize the functional form of all the fundamentals such as utility functions and production functions.

Example 7.1 (Lucas asset pricing model) A representative agent maximizes the utility function $E_0 \sum_{t=0}^{\infty} \delta^t\, c_t^{\gamma+1}/(\gamma+1)$. There are J assets in the economy (J stocks) each in net supply equal to 1. Each stock is traded in a competitive market at price $p_{j,t}$ and pays an exogenous dividend flow $\{d_{j,t}\}$ for ever. The exogenous process $\{d_t\}$ is Markov of order one, where d_t is the vector containing the dividends for all assets, and similarly for p_t. The Euler equation for the maximization problem of the consumer is

$$p_{j,t} = \delta\, E_t \left(\frac{c_{t+1}^{\gamma}}{c_t^{\gamma}} \, (p_{j,t+1} + d_{j,t+1}) \right) \tag{7.3}$$

Market clearing implies $c_t = \sum_j d_{j,t}$. Still, we need to solve for the stock prices using (7.3). To map this model into the above framework let $z_t = (p_t, d_t)$, and $u_t = d_t$; the system of equations corresponding to (7.1) is given by (7.3) and $\phi_j(z', z) \equiv c^{\gamma}\,(p_j + d_j)$. Lucas's original paper shows that a time-invariant solution for the asset price can be found for which (7.2) is satisfied if we take $x_t \equiv d_t$. Imposing these state variables ensures that we calculate a bubble-free solution, where the stock-price depends only on the discounted value of dividends.

This is a very simple model to solve. Notice that no endogenous variables appear in the state vector, which greatly simplifies finding the solution. The only endogenous variable is the stock price. The model is offered here for comparability with all the other chapters in the book. We also use the model to demonstrate how to use different classes of approximating functions and different driving processes u_t in the FORTRAN program.

Example 7.2 (Simple stochastic growth model) Consider the simple growth model where an agent maximizes the same utility as in the previous example, subject to

$$c_t + k_t - (1-d)k_{t-1} = k_{t-1}^{\alpha}\theta_t \tag{7.4}$$

for k_{-1} given, where c_t denotes consumption, k_t is the capital stock and θ_t is an exogenous stochastic productivity shock, Markov of order one. The first-order condition for optimality is

$$c_t^{\gamma} = \delta\, E_t\big[\, c_{t+1}^{\gamma}\, (k_t^{\alpha-1}\alpha\theta_{t+1} + 1 - d)\big] \tag{7.5}$$

To map this model into the above framework, set $z_t = (c_t, k_t, \theta_t)$, $u_t = \theta_t$, and $x_t = (k_{t-1}, \theta_t)$. The function g is given by the resource constraint (7.4) and the Euler equation (7.5). The function $\phi(z', z)$ is given by $c^{\gamma}(k^{\alpha-1}\alpha\theta + 1 - d)$. Standard results from dynamic programming guarantee that the conditional expectation is a time-invariant function of the state variables (k_{t-1}, θ_t), so (7.2) is also satisfied.

Example 7.3 (Stochastic growth model with flexible labour supply and proportional taxes) Assume that the representative agent's utility function is given by

$$E_0 \sum_{t=0}^{\infty} \delta^t \left(\frac{c_t^{\gamma+1}}{\gamma+1} + b\frac{(1-l_t)^{\gamma_l+1}}{\gamma_l+1} \right)$$

where l_t represents hours worked.

A representative firm has a production function $k_{t-1}^{\alpha} l_t^{\alpha_l} \theta_t$ and maximizes profits. Both the firm and the consumers are price takers. The consumer owns the capital stock, receives income from renting the capital stock to the firm at the rental price r_t and from selling his labour to the firm at the wage w_t. The consumer pays a tax proportional to its labour income at the fixed tax rate τ^l and at a rate τ^k for its capital income.

If we assume constant returns to scale and set $\alpha_l = 1 - \alpha$, the first-order conditions for the consumer are

$$c_t^{\gamma} = \delta\, E_t\big[\, c_{t+1}^{\gamma}\big(k_t^{\alpha-1} \alpha l_{t+1}^{1-\alpha} \theta_{t+1}(1-\tau^k) + 1 - d\big)\big] \tag{7.6}$$

$$c_t^{\gamma} = \frac{b(1-l_t)^{\gamma_l}}{\theta_t(1-\alpha)k_{t-1}^{\alpha}\, l_t^{-\alpha}(1-\tau^l)} \tag{7.7}$$

and the feasibility conditions are given by

$$c_t + k_t - (1-d)k_{t-1} = k_{t-1}^{\alpha} l_t^{1-\alpha} \theta_t \tag{7.8}$$

In the Euler equations we have introduced the fact that w and r are given by the marginal product of labour and capital.

Relative to Example 7.2, we have introduced taxes and endogenous labour supply; obviously, Example 7.2 is a special case of the current example if we set $b = 0$, $\alpha_l = 0$ and $\tau^l = \tau^k = 0$.[6] The interest of this example is two fold: first, it shows how to solve models with more decision variables than endogenous state variables (decision variables are c_t, l_t and the endogenous state variable is k_t). Second, the solution to this model is suboptimal (due to the distortionary tax) and it cannot be easily found with standard dynamic programming tools.

To map this model into the above framework, set $z_t = (c_t, l_t, k_t, \theta_t)$ and $u_t = \theta_t$. The function g is given by the resource constraint (7.8) and the first-order conditions (7.6), (7.7). The function $\phi(z', z) \equiv c^{\gamma}\ (k^{\alpha-1} \alpha l^{1-\alpha}(1-\tau^k)\theta + 1 - d)$. Results from Coleman (1991) guarantee that a time-invariant solution exists with $x_t = (k_{t-1}, \theta_t)$.

Example 7.4 (Simple growth model with non-negative gross investment) This example shows how inequality constraints can be easily handled by PEA, and it demonstrates the use of variables corresponding to Lagrange multipliers. Suppose we add to Example 7.2 a non-negativity constraint on gross investment:

$$k_t - (1-d)k_{t-1} \geq 0 \tag{7.9}$$

With this restriction, the first-order condition (7.5) is replaced by the Kuhn–Tucker conditions

$$c_t^{\gamma} - \lambda_t - \delta\, E_t\big[\, c_{t+1}^{\gamma}\big(k_t^{\alpha-1} \alpha \theta_{t+1} + (1-d)(1-\lambda_{t+1})\big)\big] = 0 \tag{7.10}$$

$$(k_t - (1-d)k_{t-1})\lambda_t = 0 \tag{7.11}$$

$$\lambda_t \geq 0, \qquad i_t \geq 0 \tag{7.12}$$

where λ_t denotes the Lagrange multiplier associated with constraint (7.9).

[6] For now, we ignore the budget constraint of the government; this is consistent with assuming a sufficiently high level of initial debt or with assuming that any surplus is returned as a lump-sum transfer to the agents.

To map this model into framework (7.1) we set $z_t = (c_t, k_t, \lambda_t, \theta_t)$, $u_t = \theta_t$. The system g is given by (7.4), and the Kuhn–Tucker conditions (7.9)–(7.12). Note that, in this case, $\phi(z', z) \equiv c^{\gamma}(k^{\alpha-1}\alpha\theta + (1-d)(1-\lambda))$. Again, using standard dynamic programming, the model can be shown to be recursive with the same x as in Example 7.2.

This example illustrates how to treat stochastically binding inequality constraints. Notice that the Lagrange multiplier is treated just like an additional variable by including it in z; we therefore have to solve for this multiplier jointly with all the other variables.

Example 7.5 (Habits in consumption) Modify Example 7.2 in order to introduce a per-period utility that depends on present and past consumption. More specifically, assume that utility at time t is given by $u(c_t, c_{t-1}) = (c_t + \eta c_{t-1})^{1+\gamma}/(1+\gamma)$. The Euler equation is

$$\begin{aligned}(c_t + \eta c_{t-1})^{\gamma} =& \delta E_t \left[-\eta(c_{t+1} + \eta c_t)^{\gamma} + \left((c_{t+1} + \eta c_t)^{\gamma} + \delta\eta(c_{t+2} + \eta c_{t+1})^{\gamma}\right) \right. \\ & \left. \left(\theta_{t+1}\alpha k_t^{\alpha-1} + 1 - d\right)\right] \end{aligned} \tag{7.13}$$

To map this model into framework (7.1) we take z and u as in Example 7.2. The system g is given by (7.13) and (7.4), and ϕ is given by

$$\begin{aligned}\phi(z_{t+2}, z_{t+1}, z_t) = & -\eta(c_{t+1} + \eta c_t)^{\gamma} + \left((c_{t+1} + \eta c_t)^{\gamma} + \delta\eta(c_{t+2} + \eta c_{t+1})^{\gamma}\right) \\ & \left(\theta_{t+1}\alpha k_t^{\alpha-1} + 1 - d\right)\end{aligned} \tag{7.14}$$

Notice that, in this case, ϕ depends on two leads of the endogenous variables[7]. Again, the model can be shown to be recursive with standard dynamic programming techniques but where we add one additional state variable to obtain the vector $x_t = (k_{t-1}, c_{t-1}, \theta_t)$ in order to have (7.2).

This example is used to illustrate three issues: first, the effects on computational costs of having an additional continuous state variable (namely c_{t-1}); second, the effects on computational costs of having two shocks (namely $\theta_{t+1}, \theta_{t+2}$) inside the conditional expectation.

We will also solve the model by rewriting the above Euler equation separating out two expectations. This is obviously an inefficient approximation since it will involve computing two functions, but it will be done for pedagogical reasons since it demonstrates the issues related with having more than one conditional expectation to solve for.

Example 7.6 (Two capital goods) This extends Example 7.2 to include two capital goods. More precisely, assume that the production function is Cobb–Douglas with two capital goods, so that the feasibility conditions are:

$$c_t + i_{1,t} + i_{2,t} = \theta_t k_{1,t-1}^{\alpha_1} k_{2,t-1}^{\alpha_2} \tag{7.15}$$

$$k_{j,t} = k_{j,t-1}(1 - d_j) + i_{j,t} \tag{7.16}$$

[7] Having two leads in ϕ means that it does not match exactly the framework of (7.1), but it is a trivial extension.

$k_{j,-1}$ given, for $j = 1, 2$. The Euler equations are:

$$c_t^{\gamma} = \delta E_t\big[c_{t+1}^{\gamma}\left(\theta_{t+1}\alpha_1 k_{1,t}^{\alpha_1-1}k_{2,t}^{\alpha_2} + 1 - d_1\right)\big] \tag{7.17}$$

$$c_t^{\gamma} = \delta E_t\big[c_{t+1}^{\gamma}\left(\theta_{t+1}\alpha_2 k_{2,t}^{\alpha_2-1}k_{1,t}^{\alpha_1} + 1 - d_2\right)\big]. \tag{7.18}$$

Relative to Example 7.2, we have to include the second capital stock both in z and in x and, by now, it is clear how we could set up the functions g and ϕ given the expressions above.

This example will serve to show how to deal with several potential pitfalls with PEA. First of all, the example demonstrates the issue that, sometimes, the natural way to write system g does not allow the researcher to invert the system; this issue is quite delicate, as it does not arise in other algorithms. Also, the example will serve to discuss some problems that arise because of the addition of another state variable; we will see that, unless we are careful, the second state variable tends to generate non-stationary simulations, and the algorithm breaks down. Finally, the simulations of this model will be of interest in themselves.

Given the assumptions of the model, if the depreciation rate is the same for the two types of capital goods the model can easily be transformed into a model with just one capital good, since the ratio of the two capital stocks will be constant over time.[8] We could therefore solve the case $d_1 = d_2$ directly from the solution of Example 7.2. In order to depart from the trivial solution, we will consider different depreciation rates. We will, however, study the case of equal depreciation rates by solving it ignoring this theoretical knowledge. This will serve to demonstrate some problems that arise with PEA when the state variables are highly correlated and we will be able to perform an elementary consistency check on the functioning of the algorithm, just checking if it reproduces this known property of the exact solution.

A key assumption that we will make concerning the system g is that it is invertible with respect to its second argument. Therefore, we will insist on writing the system of difference equations in such a way that, given a function $\mathcal{E}$ and past values of the series, we can then generate the current value for z by solving the system g. In this chapter, the term 'solving the model' refers to generating a stochastic process $\{z_t, u_t\}$ on the computer that satisfies, approximately, equations (7.1) and (7.2). Under the above invertibility requirement on g, we can back out the series $\{z_t\}$ from a candidate $\mathcal{E}$ and simulated values of u_t, so we will use the term 'solving the model' interchangeably with the term 'finding $\mathcal{E}$'.[9]

7.2.2 *Definition and calculation of an approximate PEA solution*

The general idea of PEA is to substitute the conditional expectations in (7.1) by flexible functions that depend on the state variables and some coefficients. Then (7.1) is used to generate simulations for z consistent with the parameterized expectations; with these

[8] From the Euler equations it is clear that the ratio $k_{1,t}/k_{2,t}$ is determined by $f_{k_1}/f_{k_2} = 1$.

[9] As is always the case in numerical analysis, these 'solutions' are only approximate, so we often do not use the term 'approximate solution'. Note also that the usual restrictions apply to all the parameters in these examples, namely: $\gamma, \gamma_l < 0$; $0 < d, d_1, d_2, \alpha, \alpha_1, \alpha_2, \delta < 1$; and $b > 0$.

simulations we can iterate on the parameterized expectations until they are consistent with the solutions they generate.

By a 'flexible functional form' we mean a function $\psi(\beta; x)$ for some coefficients $\beta \in R^{\nu}$ such that, as we increase the number of coefficients to let $\nu \to \infty$, we can approximate any function $f(x)$ arbitrarily well (e.g. polynomials, splines, etc.). By 'simulations for z consistent with the parameterized expectations' we mean a process $\{z_t(\beta), u_t\}_{t=0}^{\infty}$ that, for all t, solves the system

$$g\left(\psi(\beta; x_t(\beta)), z_t(\beta), z_{t-1}(\beta), u_t\right) = 0 \tag{7.19}$$

Obviously, the function $\psi(\beta; \cdot)$ could be quite different from $\mathcal{E}(\cdot)$ for an arbitrary β. We will ensure that $\psi(\beta; \cdot)$ is a good approximation by fixing an order of approximation ν (e.g. ν-degree polynomials, splines with ν intervals, ...), and choosing β in such a way that, within the approximating class for a given ν, the function is as close as possible to the conditional expectation function $\mathcal{E}$. For this purpose, we have to discuss how to find a good approximating β.[10]

We now describe an algorithm to solve for such a β. Here, we describe the structure of the algorithm. Many details will be discussed later and in the context of the examples.

- *Step* 1. Write the system g in (7.1) so that it is invertible with respect to its second argument; in other words, the system g has to be such that, given the first, third and fourth arguments, the value for z_t can be uniquely determined from (7.1). Find a set of state variables x that satisfies (7.2). Replace the true conditional expectation by the parameterized function $\psi(\beta; \cdot)$ to obtain (7.19). Fix the initial conditions u_0 and z_0. Draw a series $\{u_t\}_{t=0}^{T}$ from a random number generator that obeys the distribution of u in the model, with T sufficiently large.
- *Step* 2. For a given $\beta \in R^{\nu}$ such that $\{z_t(\beta), u_t\}$ has a stationary distribution, recursively calculate $\{z_t(\beta), u_t\}_{t=0}^{T}$ using (7.19) and the realization for u drawn in the previous step.
- *Step* 3. Find $G(\beta)$ that satisfies

$$G(\beta) = \arg\min_{\xi \in R^{\nu}} \frac{1}{T} \sum_{t=0}^{T} \| \phi(z_{t+1}(\beta), z_t(\beta)) - \psi(\xi; x_t(\beta)) \|^2 \tag{7.20}$$

  This minimization is easy to perform by computing a nonlinear least-squares regression with the sample $\{z_t(\beta), u_t\}_{t=0}^{T}$, taking $\phi\left(z_{t+1}(\beta), z_t(\beta)\right)$ as the dependent variable, $\psi(\xi; \cdot)$ as the explanatory function, and ξ as the parameter vector to be estimated.
- *Step* 4. Find the fixed point

$$\beta_{\mathrm{f}} = G(\beta_{\mathrm{f}}) \tag{7.21}$$

Then $\{z_t(\beta_{\mathrm{f}}), u_t\}_{t=0}^{T}$ is our approximate solution. Or, equivalently, $\psi(\beta_{\mathrm{f}}; \cdot)$ is our approximation to the conditional expectation $\mathcal{E}$ or, again equivalently, the inverse of g in (7.19) with respect to its second argument (setting $\beta = \beta_{\mathrm{f}}$) is the approximate

[10]We do not discuss here the issues related to convergence with arbitrary accuracy as $\nu \to \infty$. See Marcet and Marshall (1994) for a convergence proof.

equilibrium law of motion of the model. Clearly, in order to find the fixed point β_f one needs to iterate on steps 2 to 4 (there is no need to redraw the us or to change initial conditions) until a fixed point is found.

The nonlinear regression of step 3 is meant to approximate the best predictor in the steady-state distribution of the model. This is why, in step 2, the values of β are restricted to generate a stationary distribution for $\{z_t(\beta), u_t\}_{t=0}^{\infty}$; otherwise, there is no reason why $G(\beta)$ should deliver a good predictor and the solution might be explosive and give numerical errors.

We now discuss how to set up each example to apply the above steps. The issues related to algorithms for finding the nonlinear regressions of step 3 and the fixed point of step 4 will be discussed later. Also, in the discussion of this section we use only a first-degree approximation.

Example 7.1 Consider now the simplest case where there is only one asset $J = 1$. In step 1 we have to choose the functional form of ψ. We use a polynomial of order one:

$$\psi(\beta; x_t) = \beta_1 + \beta_2\, d_t \tag{7.22}$$

In order to apply step 2, notice that (7.3) delivers the following equation for the stock price:

$$p_t(\beta) = \delta\, \psi(\beta; d_t)$$

which is used to generate simulations for $p_t(\beta)$.

In order to apply step 3, we just need to construct the 'dependent variable'

$$Y_t(\beta) \equiv \frac{c_{t+1}^{\gamma}}{c_t^{\gamma}}(p_{t+1}(\beta) + d_{t+1})$$

and run a regression on the equation:

$$Y_t(\beta) = \xi_1 + \xi_2 d_t + \eta_t$$

where η_t is the regression error. The vector of parameters ξ that minimizes the sum of squared residuals (in this case, simply the ordinary least-squares estimator) is precisely $G(\beta)$.

Notice that, because we use a regular polynomial in ψ, it is possible for the approximate solution to deliver negative prices. This will not cause any problem in the implementation of the algorithm. Furthermore, under the assumption of no default and several assests, the correct solution might actually involve negative prices. This is in contrast with the other examples, where non-negativity of the expectation needs to be imposed.

The cases for $J = 2$ and positive dividends will be discussed in greater detail in Section 7.4.

Example 7.2 For the functional form of ψ, using a regular polynomial as in the previous example might be problematic because, eventually, it might generate a negative value for ψ and, since this number is raised to a real power in step 2 (see equation (7.24) below), a numerical error would ensue. Furthermore, since the variable inside the expectation is positive, we know that the true $\mathcal{E}$ takes only positive values so, by imposing this feature on our approximating ψ, we are likely to get a better fit with fewer parameters.

For these reasons, we use an exponentiated polynomial of order one:

$$\psi(\beta; x_t) = \beta_1 \exp(\beta_2 \, \log k_{t-1} + \beta_3 \, \log \theta_t) \tag{7.23}$$

which is guaranteed to be positive and so generate a positive solution for consumption. By increasing the degree of the polynomial inside exp we can approximate the conditional expectation with arbitrary accuracy.

In order to apply step 2, notice that system (7.19) delivers the following equation for consumption:

$$c_t(\beta) = (\delta \, \psi(\beta; k_{t-1}(\beta), \theta_t))^{1/\gamma} \tag{7.24}$$

and capital can be found from

$$k_t(\beta) = k_{t-1}(\beta)^\alpha \theta_t - c_t(\beta) + (1-d)k_{t-1}(\beta)$$

These equations generate simulations for $(c_t(\beta), k_t(\beta))$.

For step 3, we construct the 'dependent variable'

$$Y_t(\beta) \equiv \; c_{t+1}(\beta)^\gamma \; (k_t(\beta)^{\alpha-1}\alpha\theta_{t+1} + 1 - d)$$

and run a nonlinear regression on the equation:

$$Y_t(\beta) = \xi_1 \exp(\xi_2 \log k_{t-1}(\beta) + \xi_3 \log \theta_t) + \eta_t$$

where η_t is the regression error. The vector of parameters ξ that minimizes the sum of squared residuals in this regression is precisely $G(\beta)$.

Notice that it would *not* be correct to take logs on both sides of the last equation and run a *linear* regression of $\log Y_t(\beta)$ on $(\log k_{t-1}(\beta), \log \theta_t)$; this would only give the correct answer if the error were multiplicative (which is the case under log-normality), but it is not the case in general for conditional expectation errors. This is a reflection of the fact that this model is, in fact, nonlinear, and linear functions are at best good approximations.

Example 7.3 We choose ψ as in the previous example. As for step 2, the corresponding system (7.19) delivers

$$\delta \, \psi(\beta; k_{t-1}(\beta), \theta_t) = \frac{b(1 - l_t(\beta))^{\gamma_l} l_t(\beta)^\alpha}{\theta_t \; (1-\alpha) \; k_{t-1}(\beta)^\alpha \; (1 - \tau^l)} \tag{7.25}$$

which, given the state variables, is a nonlinear equation in $l_t(\beta)$. This nonlinear equation has to be solved numerically for each t and β. Consumption is found as in the previous example. Finally, from the resource constraint (corresponding to market clearing) we obtain $k_t(\beta)$.

Clearly, the nonlinear regression to be run in step 3 is similar to Example 7.2, the only difference being that labour and taxes enter in the calculation of $Y_t(\beta)$.

Example 7.4 We show how to use the Kuhn–Tucker conditions to find $\{c_t(\beta), k_t(\beta)\}$ while imposing inequalities (7.9) and (7.12). The system (7.19) is given by:

$$c_t(\beta)^{\gamma} - \lambda_t(\beta) = \delta\ \psi(\beta; k_{t-1}(\beta), \theta_t) \tag{7.26}$$

$$\lambda_t(\beta)\left[k_t(\beta) - (1-d)k_{t-1}(\beta)\right] = 0 \tag{7.27}$$

$$\lambda_t(\beta) \geq 0, \qquad k_t(\beta) - (1-d)k_{t-1}(\beta) \geq 0 \tag{7.28}$$

We can then proceed as follows, for each t:

(a) Compute $(c_t(\beta), k_t(\beta))$ from (7.26) under the conjecture that $\lambda_t(\beta) = 0$. In this case, the mechanics for computing consumption and capital will be exactly as in Example 7.2. If investment is positive, go to $t+1$. If investment is negative go to step (b).

(b) Set $k_t(\beta) = (1-d)k_{t-1}(\beta)$, find $c_t(\beta)$ from the feasibility constraint, and then compute $\lambda_t(\beta)$ from (7.26).

In applying this procedure, we have to make sure that the Kuhn–Tucker conditions are satisfied. Notice that, for a fixed value of $\psi(\beta; k_{t-1}(\beta), \theta_t)$, the left-hand side of (7.26) is increasing in $k_t(\beta)$. Hence, if step (a) delivers a negative investment, consumption will be lower when we go to step (b), so $c_t(\beta)^{\gamma}$ will be higher (relative to (a)), and (7.26) delivers a positive λ in step (b), so (7.28) is satisfied. Clearly, (7.27) is satisfied, since the terms in either set of brackets will be automatically set to zero.

Notice that the Lagrange multiplier is treated just like an additional variable in our problem. Its value is derived from solving a system of equalities and inequalities corresponding to the g system. In the present model the Lagrange multiplier affecting investment appears also inside the expectation, and so its realized values are needed to compute the ϕ expression; this is how the possibility of having future binding constraints affects today's investment.

It must be noticed that there are some ways of writing the Kuhn–Tucker conditions that would be inappropriate. For example, by multiplying both sides of (7.10) by $c_t^{-2\gamma}$, the Kuhn–Tucker conditions can be correctly expressed as

$$c_t^{-\gamma} - \lambda_t c_t^{-2\gamma} = \delta\ E_t\left[c_{t+1}^{\gamma}\ c_t^{-2\gamma}\ \left(\left(k_t^{\alpha-1}\alpha\ \theta_{t+1} + 1 - d\right) - (1-d)(1-\lambda_{t+1})\right)\right] \tag{7.29}$$

However, (7.29) would be an inappropriate choice for g if PEA is used as a solution algorithm, because the function $c^{-\gamma}$ is decreasing in today's k. Then, step (b) would deliver a negative value for the multiplier λ. In terms of the step-by-step description of the algorithm, (7.29) violates step 1, since it implies a representation for g that is not invertible with respect to its second element.

To summarize, one can simply simulate by setting the Lagrange multiplier to zero, checking the inequality constraint, if it is not satisfied, impose the inequality constraint as an equality and obtain the multiplier from the Euler equation. Due to our previous derivations, the researcher can be confident that the relevant inequalities for the Kuhn–Tucker conditions are satisfied, but this should be checked for a different example, in order to avoid situations such as that discussed with regard to (7.29).

Clearly, the nonlinear regression to be run is as in Example 7.2, except that now λ enters into the calculation of $Y_t(\beta)$.

Example 7.5 We choose the same kind of ψ as in Example 7.2, but now we need to include an additional state variable:

$$\psi(\beta; x_t(\beta)) = \beta_1 \exp(\beta_2 \log k_{t-1}(\beta) + \beta_3 \log \theta_t + \beta_4 \log c_{t-1}(\beta)) \tag{7.30}$$

In order to apply step 2 we obtain consumption from

$$c_t(\beta) = (\delta\, \psi(\beta; k_{t-1}(\beta), \theta_t, c_{t-1}(\beta))^{1/\gamma} - \eta c_{t-1}(\beta)$$

then we solve for capital as in Example 7.2. As in all previous examples, we run the regression of step 3 with $Y_t(\beta)$ given by the right-hand side of (7.14). Notice that inside the conditional expectation of the Euler equation (7.13) we now have random variables affected by the two shocks, θ_{t+1} and θ_{t+2}. However, the number of computations required by the algorithm has barely increased because of this fact. This is in contrast to algorithms that use explicit integration of the conditional expectation (e.g. algorithms that use quadrature to evaluate the conditional expectation at each point) where adding stochastic shocks with continuous distributions leads to a large increase in the cost of computing the integral. Of course, the number of computations will certainly increase because of the fact that now we have to solve for a fixed point of a four-coefficient vector, but this is common to all algorithms that approach this model.

We use this example to discuss the issues that arise when there is more than one conditional expectation in the model. Notice that (7.13) could have been written as

$$\begin{aligned}(c_t + \eta c_{t-1})^\gamma =& \delta E_t\big[\big((c_{t+1} + \eta c_t)^\gamma + \delta\eta(c_{t+2} + \eta c_{t+1})^\gamma\big) \\ & \big(\theta_{t+1}\alpha k_t^{\alpha-1} + 1 - d\big)\big] - \delta\eta E_t(c_{t+1} + \eta c_t)^\gamma \end{aligned} \tag{7.31}$$

and we can approximate each of these expectations with two different functions $\psi(\beta^1; x)$ and $\psi(\beta^2; x)$ where each β^i has four elements, and ψ is as in (7.30). Clearly, this option is computationally inefficient, because we now have to compute a fixed point of eight coefficients $\beta \equiv (\beta^1, \beta^2) \in R^{4\times 2}$, but it should give a correct approximation to the true solution.[11] Clearly, now the simulation generated in step 2 is given by

$$\begin{aligned} c_t(\beta) =& \big(\delta\psi\big(\beta^1; k_{t-1}(\beta), \theta_t, c_{t-1}(\beta)\big) - \delta\eta\psi\big(\beta^2; k_{t-1}(\beta), \theta_t, c_{t-1}(\beta)\big)\big)^{1/\gamma} \\ & - \eta c_{t-1}(\beta) \end{aligned}$$

Notice that the variables depend on the whole vector β, but the coefficient that appears as an argument of each ψ depends on $i = 1, 2$.

Now, in order to apply step 3, we need to run *two* separate nonlinear regressions, with the same right-hand side but with the explanatory variables

$$\begin{aligned} Y_t^2(\beta) &= (c_{t+1}(\beta) + \eta c_t(\beta))^\gamma \\ Y_t^1(\beta) &= \big(Y_t^2(\beta) + \delta\eta Y_{t+1}^2(\beta)\big)\big(\theta_{t+1}\alpha k_t(\beta)^{\alpha-1} + 1 - d\big) \end{aligned}$$

Now, letting $G^i(\beta)$ be the result of regression $i = 1, 2$, we define $G(\beta) \equiv (G^1(\beta), G^2(\beta))$, so that $G : R^{4\times 2} \to R^{4\times 2}$, and the fixed point of step 4 involves eight coefficients.

[11] Assuming T and ν go to infinity.

Example 7.6 We have two endogenous state variables and, unavoidably, two parameterized expectations. Each parameterized expectation is of the form $\psi(\beta^i; k_{1,t-1}(\beta), k_{2,t-1}(\beta), \theta_t)$, and the same issues discussed at the end of the previous example apply.

Consider the Euler equations (7.17) and (7.18) with $\psi(\beta^i; \cdot)$ in the right-hand side. We can obtain a value for $c_t(\beta)$ from any one of the two Euler equations, but we have no way to compute $k_{1,t}$ and $k_{2,t}$. This system is underdetermined for the capital stocks. But if we want both Euler equations to be satisfied, the system is overdetermined for consumption. This is the sense in which the system g in this example is, in principle, not invertible. We simply cannot proceed to step 2 with the Euler equations as initially written.

In order to proceed, we have to rearrange the Euler equations so as to allow us to compute the simulated series. There are many alternatives; we should choose one where the series are easily solved and, of course, we have to be careful that the new system still delivers a sufficient condition for an equilibrium. We could proceed by premultiplying both sides of the Euler equation by $k_{2,t}$ to obtain

$$c_t^{\gamma}\, k_{2,t} = \delta E_t\left[c_{t+1}^{\gamma}\, \left(\theta_{t+1}\, \alpha_2\, k_{2,t}^{\alpha_2}\, k_{1,t}^{\alpha_1} + (1-d_2)k_{2,t}\right)\right] \tag{7.32}$$

Clearly, since $k_{2,t}$ is never zero in equilibrium, this equation is satisfied if and only if the original Euler equation is satisfied, and it can replace the sufficient condition for the optimum. We can determine $c_t(\beta)$ from the first Euler equation as in Example 7.2, and then obtain $k_{2,t}$ from the second one by setting

$$k_{2,t}(\beta) = \delta \frac{\psi\left(\beta^i; k_{1,t-1}(\beta), k_{2,t-1}(\beta), \theta_t\right)}{c_t(\beta)^{\gamma}} \tag{7.33}$$

7.2.3 *An algorithm to find β_f and the use of homotopy*

Having discussed how to find G for a given β, we now turn to the problem of finding the fixed point of step 4. Our comments here apply to all examples.

Although we could use a standard hill-climbing algorithm for solving nonlinear systems of equations this may not be the best alternative. First of all, hill-climbing algorithms are relatively complicated, often unstable, and they require a knowledge of some numerical analysis; second, these algorithms work by calculating the gradient of G, which can become very expensive in models with many coefficients.

Applications of PEA often use the following algorithm, based on successive modified approximations:

$$\beta(\tau+1) = (1-\mu)\beta(\tau) + \mu G(\beta(\tau)) \tag{7.34}$$

for some $\mu > 0$ and some fixed initial condition $\beta(0)$; here, $\beta(\tau)$ represents the τth iteration of the algorithm. The algorithm is extremely easy to program and each iteration is calculated very fast. The most obvious point at which to stop the algorithm is when all the elements of the matrix $\beta(\tau)$ are sufficiently close to the corresponding element of $G(\beta(\tau))$.

There are two possible shortcomings of the above algorithm. First of all, (7.34) will typically need more iterations to converge than a hill-climbing algorithm;[12] because of

[12] This is because hill-climbing algorithms converge in one step when they are in the neighbourhood of the fixed point, and this is not the case in (7.34).

that, it could happen that the gain in speed from avoiding computation of the gradient is lost in the additional iterations. Second, hill-climbing algorithms are (typically) locally stable, but the above algorithm could be locally unstable. Nevertheless, it can be shown that the above algorithm is locally unstable only in models where the rational expectations algorithm *cannot* be learnt by agents in the economy. More precisely, consider a model of learning where agents, instead of having rational expectations, form their forecasts with $\psi(\beta_t; x_t)$, where β_t is the parameter that agents use on the basis of today's information. Assume that agents incorporate the new information that arrives at every period and they update their beliefs on β by using least-squares estimators using all past observations. It can be shown that such a learning model converges to rational expectations (locally) if and only if iterations on (7.34) are locally stable for μ sufficiently small. Therefore, it is possible to use the above algorithm in all models where the rational expectations equilibrium can be justified as the limit of a learning model. As many economists believe that rational expectations equilibria are only interesting if they can be learnt by agents in the model, this works precisely for models that, in this sense, are of interest.[13] In any case, it turns out that least-squares learning is locally stable in most applications, and the above algorithm can be used to compute the fixed point of step 4 in most applications.

In order to use the above algorithm successfully, we need good initial conditions; formally, we need $\beta(0)$ to be not too far away from β_f. This is necessary for two reasons. First, iterations are more likely to get 'lost' and never converge if the initial condition is too far away from the limit.[14] Second, a good initial condition is needed because in step 2 we need to consider βs that generate $\{z_t(\beta)\}$ with a stationary distribution. One could ensure stationarity by writing a general test for existence of a stationary and ergodic distribution,[15] and then impose the restriction that only βs that satisfy such a condition are considered in the algorithm that looks for the fixed point of step 4. This is a valid but rather cumbersome alternative since solving nonlinear systems of equations subject to restrictions is a tricky business. An alternative solution that works in practice is to use the ideas of homotopy, which amounts to imposing good initial conditions in a systematic way.

The idea of homotopy is very simple – start with a version of the model that is easy to solve, then modify these parameters slowly to go to the desired solution. As long as the model goes from the known to the desired solution in a smooth way (formally, as long as the solutions are continuous with respect to the parameter that drives the model from the known to the desired solution), we are always solving models with good initial conditions. It is often possible to find such 'known' solutions and to build a bridge that goes to the desired solution. For example, den Haan and Marcet (1990) explained how to solve the simple growth model of Example 7.2 by starting the solution at the case of $d = 0$ and $\gamma = -1$, which happens to have an analytic solution. The 'bridge' to the desired model is obtained by slowly setting depreciation to the desired level of, say, $d = 0.9$. In this case,

[13] One caveat to this claim is that the model of learning we outline in the main text is not the only way that a learning model could be specified.

[14] This is also a common problem with hill-climbing algorithms and with most algorithms for solving nonlinear systems, where only local stability is guaranteed.

[15] Some tests are provided by Duffie and Singleton (1993) and Domowitz and el Gamal (1993). The chapter by Novales *et al.* in this book has an explicit discussion of how to impose stationarity.

d is the parameter that drives the model from the known solution to the desired solution. Also, one can go from Example 7.2 to Example 7.3 by starting at $b = 0$ and zero taxes. One can go from Example 7.2 to Example 7.4 by adding to Example 7.2 the constraint $k_t - (1-d)k_{t-1} \geq K$; for a very low (and negative) value of K, the solution is as in Example 7.2; by increasing K to zero we approach the solution to Example 7.3. This exercise can even be performed when we change the functional forms of the fundamentals. For example, if we wanted to solve the simple growth model with the CARA instantaneous utility function, $e^{-\kappa c_t}$, we could consider solving the growth model with a utility function

$$-e^{-\kappa c_t}\zeta + \frac{c_t^{\gamma+1}}{\gamma+1}(1-\zeta)$$

Clearly, we know the solution for $\zeta = 0$ (since this is just Example 7.2) and to get to the desired solution with CARA utility we need to increase until $\zeta = 1$.

In each case, we would start at the solution that is known and change the relevant parameter slightly. We would solve the model for this slightly different value of the parameter, using as initial condition the solution to the model under the previous parameter. For example, assume that we have already solved Example 7.2 and we would like to calculate the solution to Example 7.4. Let us say that gross investment in Example 7.2 is never less than -50. Let β_{f}^{K} be the solution for a given K; clearly, we know the solution for β_{f}^{-50} (this is just the solution of Example 7.2), and we want to have the solution for β_{f}^{0} (which is the solution to Example 7.4). To use a homotopy algorithm we could increase K by, for example, one unit at a time, using the previous fixed point as the initial condition in the algorithm to find the new fixed point. More precisely, letting G^K be the mapping of step 3, for each K between -50 and 0 we would use the algorithm

$$\beta^K(\tau+1) = (1-\mu)\beta^K(\tau) + \mu G^K(\beta^K(\tau)) \tag{7.35}$$

with initial condition $\beta^K(0) = \beta_f^{K-1}$.

In this way, we only need local stability of the algorithm that solves for the fixed point, since we always have a good initial condition. Also, since the algorithm is never too far from the fixed point, all the βs we consider generate $\{z_t(\beta)\}$ with a stationary distribution, so that there is no need to impose the stationarity requirement on β explicitly.

In our personal experience, we have found that many researchers try to avoid the use of homotopy. Perhaps this is because homotopy slows down the algorithm and because it looks like a unsophisticated way to make an unstable algorithm converge.[16] In fact, using homotopy often ends up saving time to the researcher: researchers often spend hours in front of the computer (even though this activity is never discussed in papers) watching their hill-climbing algorithms drift all over the place or even diverge for no apparent reason. Then they spend even more hours trying to guess what initial condition could possibly work. By contrast, homotopy finds the good initial condition in a systematic way. So, even if it consumes more computing time, it is likely to save time elsewhere.

[16] A very good expression of this sentiment was provided by a referee for a previous PEA paper, who referred to the homotopy discussion as 'making a big deal out of finding good initial conditions, which is something we all know how to do'.

Here we have just discussed homotopy informally and in its most trivial form although there is a large mathematics literature on it. This literature discusses many tricks that can be used to speed up the algorithm. For example, along the homotopy it is not necessary to require high accuracy of the fixed point, since the intermediate models are only accessory. Also, this literature studies some pitfalls of the procedure. For example, if the model has a region of parameters where the solution is undefined, it is likely that the homotopy may cross it sooner or later, so one has to be careful about the existence and the continuity of the homotopy path. For example, we will show in Section 7.4 that setting up a *continuous* homotopy path for Example 7.3 is possible, but not trivial. We do not discuss this literature in detail for lack of space, but we hope to arise some interest. In the program we have a (very simple) built-in homotopy, and in the examples below we show how this can be applied.

7.3 General description of the program

The FORTRAN program **open** can be used to compute the steady-state dynamics of nonlinear stochastic models fitting into the general framework discussed above. In the following we will discuss issues related to the practical implementation of the algorithm, making reference to this program, and describing how to apply it to our examples.

The source code **open.for** (and its variants used in some of the examples) includes all the subroutines needed to perform the algorithm (matrix inversion, random number generator, etc.). Some parts of the program have been written in separate short files, called **psis.for, der.for, ginvert.for.**[17] These are the parts of the programs that are specific to the economic model at hand and to the functional form used to approximate the expectation terms. In principle, the user will need only to write these program files, and to fill the files containing the parameters (**alpha.dat, par.dat** and **pini.dat**) in order to use the main program **open.for** for different economic applications. On the Web there is a directory for each example, each containing the file **open.for** (or some variant of it) and all the auxiliary and parameter files needed to solve that example.

In this section we refer to variables in the program in italics; most variables in the program are named as in the chapter. For example, $beta$ is the coded version of β, phi is the coded version of ϕ, and so on. The index t always refers to time period.

Let us illustrate the functioning of the program following steps 1 to 4.

- *Step* 1. The program reads the control parameters for the algorithm (in **par.dat**), the parameters of the model (in **alpha.dat**) and the initial parameters $beta$ for the functions psi (in **pini.dat**). The program generates a random sequence of shocks $theta(l, t)$ (l is the index for the exogenous shock) that will be used throughout the computations.[18] All the model parameters are stored in a vector $alpha$, the parameters controlling the disturbance process are stored in the arrays am, cm, and dm, and the series are stored in the vector Z. Then, the iterative process for computing the $beta$ is started.
- *Subroutine* **simul** (*step* 2). The program simulates a time series $Z(t, i)$.

[17] Common FORTRAN compilers will automatically include the text of these auxiliary files into the main program, during the compiling phase.

[18] The program includes a subroutine that generates independently and identically distributed standard normal disturbances, and a subroutine that can be adapted to generate processes with different autocovariance structure. The parameters controlling the process for the shocks are also set in **alpha.dat**.

(a) In order to compute $psi(t, j)$ it uses the initial values for the state variables set in **par.dat** and the parameterized expressions defined in **psis.for** with the initial $beta$ set in **pini.dat**.

(b) With these data available the program can solve, for every time period, the system corresponding to equation (7.19), in order to obtain the variables in the current period $Z(t, i)$. The algebraic steps corresponding to the inversion of (7.19) are defined in **ginvert.for** by the user, according to the model at hand. This part of the program makes use of the parameters of the model set in **alpha.dat**. If a numerical approximation is needed for this purpose (as in Example 7.3) a subroutine for this task can be easily appended to the main program **open.for**.

(c) The program computes the realized values of the expressions that appear inside the expectations – that is, the $phi(t - nfor, j)$ in the same loop that computes the values for the $Z(t, i)$ variables. $nfor$ is the maximum number of leads appearing inside the expectations, and period t is the first time at which we are able to compute all the expressions whose value we were trying to predict $t - nfor$ periods before using psi. If $nfor$ is greater than 1 you can start to compute phi only after $nfor - 1$ periods. This is not a problem in the examples discussed since we are computing the steady-state solution. In this case the program drops the first observations (150 in the programs described) in the nonlinear regression and then it is set to compute phi just from the 150th period on.

- *Subroutine* **Gbeta** (*step* 3). The parameters $Gbeta$ are estimated with a nonlinear regression of $phi(t, j)$ on the state variables appearing in psi. The nonlinear regression is performed following a common iterative procedure described, for example, in Pindyck and Rubinfeld (1981) in which, at every step, the residuals and the derivatives of the ψ function, using the parameters from the previous step, are used to perform a linear regression that gives the coefficients for next step. Here the program needs to use both the form of psi defined by the user in **psis.for** and the derivatives of psi defined in **der.for**. After convergence is achieved for $Gbeta$ we pass to step 4. The convergence criterion for the nonlinear regression $acclnr$ and the maximum number of iterations $maxitnl$ are both set in **par.dat**.
- *Convergence check and updating (step 4)*: The parameters $Gbeta$ of the regression in step 3 are compared with the $beta$ parameters which we used to performed step 2. If the distance between them is smaller than acc the algorithm stops. Clearly, this distance can be evaluated in many different ways. In most of the examples discussed below it is computed simply as a sum of absolute differences, while in the program we use to solve Example 7.6 it is evaluated computing the distance (sum of squared differences) between the simulated series obtained using $beta$ and the simulated series using $Gbeta$.

  The parameters are updated according to: $beta' = mu \cdot Gbeta + (1 - mu) \cdot beta$. The value for mu is set in **par.dat**. In general a mu closer to 1 makes the algorithm faster but is more likely to result in non-convergence. If the algorithm converges the updated values for the beta are stored in **pini.dat** and the old parameters are discarded. In this way, the next time the program is used, it automatically uses the fixed point of the last run (keep this is mind if you want to store a fixed point for future use, in which case you need to save the contents of **pini.dat** in a different file).

After the iterations on *beta* converge (hopefully to β_f), a simulation of the series $Z(t, i)$ is stored in the output file **openout.dat**, along with descriptive statistics of the series. It is very easy to adapt this part of the program so as to obtain additional aggregate information on the series. Moreover, in the program (in particular in **ginvert.for**) the user can compute whichever auxiliary variable is needed, and store it as an additional series $(Z(t, i))$, obtaining other useful information on the model.

It is advisable to set the initial conditions of the endogenous state variables at levels that are often visited in the stationary distribution. This is because, with the algorithm described in Section 7.2, there is no guarantee that our approximation is any good outside the support of the stationary distribution. The output file may also be useful to choose an appropriate initial value for the state variable (e.g. k_{-1} in Example 7.2) when the parameters have been modified and hence the stationary distribution of the state variables has changed.

Notice the convention that the time subscript for $phi(t, j)$ refers to the period in which the expected value of $phi(t, j)$ is needed to solve the system (7.19) (and the approximated value $psi(t, j)$ is used instead). In step 3 of the program this notation gives the natural result that $phi(t, j)$ is the dependent variable to be explained by the state variables at time t in the parameterized expression psi, but $phi(t, j)$ depends on random variables whose value is realized in the future. This is why, in **ginvert.for**, we compute the past value $phi(t - nfor, j)$ at period t. As observed above, it is impossible to compute the value of $phi(t, j)$ until $nfor$ periods later when we have all the needed realized values.[19] $nfor$ is another parameter to be set in **par.dat**.

7.3.1 *Parameter files*

The parameters controlling the algorithm are listed in the file **par.dat**. In particular, in this file the user will set neq, the number of parameterized expressions corresponding to so many psi functions; $np(j)$, for $j = 1, \ldots, neq$, the number of parameters in expression j (i.e. the number of $beta$ coefficients in each psi); nz, the number of Z variables used; and the control parameters for the various iterative procedures performed by the program. Another file **alpha.dat** contains the parameters of the model and also parameters controlling the automatic homotopy steps.[20]

7.3.2 *Program files*

Here we summarize the content of program files that are model-dependent and have to be written by the user. The parameterized forms (psi) have to be written in the file **psis.for** and the derivatives of psi in the file **der.for**. In this version there is no predefined functional form; the user has to provide it in **psis.for** and to provide analytical derivatives for psi in **der.for**. Clearly, as far as you are satisfied with an exponentiated polynomial, you can simply adjust the expressions in the **psis.for** and **der.for** used in Examples 7.2–7.6.

In **ginvert.for** there are the algebraic or numerical steps to solve equation (7.19) and the expressions to compute the *ex post* values for phi.[21]. Finally, to avoid repeated

[19]This is also the reason why we have to drop the last $nfor$ observations when performing the regression, simply because the last values of phi are not available.

[20]See the detailed description of the files in the program.

[21]Notice also that in **psis.for** and **der.for** the parameters are named $b(h, j)$ (hth parameter of the jth expression), so that the program can use the same definition – substituting $beta(h, j)$ or $Gbeta(h, j)$ for

computation of logarithms we have introduced the auxiliary variables $Zlog(t, i)$ that may (but need not) be used along the program to store the values of the log of $Z(t, i)$. Usually the logarithms are computed in **ginvert.for** immediately after the computation of the $Z(t, i)$. The format of the parameter files is described in the program, along with a list of all the variable names.

7.3.3 *Built-in homotopy*

As discussed above, in order to ensure convergence of PEA it is often a good idea to change the parameters in small steps along a homotopy path, from a model already solved to the target model. Since this procedure is indispensable in many models, the program has been set up to perform it automatically. The built-in homotopy steps are activated setting 1 in the third line of **alpha.dat** (after the list of the $alpha$ parameters), and adding a line with the following control parameters: the identifier i of the parameter $alpha(i)$ to be changed, the target value for $alpha(i)$, and the size of the step of adjustment. As initial value the program takes the $alpha(i)$ in the list at the beginning of **alpha**. Notice that at the end of the program the file **alpha.dat** is updated automatically. In this way, once the program has finished the computations, the files **alpha.dat** and **pini.dat** are always correct. The file **alpha.dat** is not changed if the homotopy is not activated. Also, if the program finds the same target value as $alpha(i)$ the homotopy steps are omitted. If you do not want to activate the homotopy procedure just leave a zero in the third line of **alpha.dat**.

7.4 Solutions to examples

In this section we illustrate by means of Examples 7.1–7.6 the use of the general program **open**. We also discuss some of the results that we can observe in the computations. Along with the examples, we will describe some common problems and will give some practical suggestions for the use and extension of the program. In the programs available online the modifications to the basic model **open.for** are highlighted with two rows of comments ('C') at the beginning and at the end of each insertion.

Example 7.1 See files in the directory `~\ex1luc`. We begin with the case of one asset, computing it first with a regular polynomial and later with an exponentiated polynomial. Then we compute the case for two stocks ($J = 2$). The program file **open.for** allows for a general vector AR(1) structure of the shocks u_t (each component of the shock is labeled $theta(t, j)$), and can be easily modified to use a different distribution for this process. The current example is the only one in which we will consider more than one series of random shocks; all the others will use a one-dimensional log AR(1) exogenous process. We will take advantage of this example to show that the algorithm deals very easily also with fairly rich stochastic structures.

The labeling of model variables is as follows:

i	1	2
$Z(t, i)$	$p_{1,t}$	$p_{2,t}$
j	1	2
$alpha(j)$	δ	γ

$b(h, j)$ – in different steps of the algorithm.

The shocks *thetalog* follow a normal AR(1) process

$$thetalog(t) = D + A \cdot thetalog(t-1) + C \cdot q(t) \tag{7.36}$$

where $q(t)$ is a vector of dimension *nthe* of standard normal independent shocks, A and C are matrices (with components $am(j,k)$, $cm(j,k)$) and D is a vector determining the means, covariances and autocovariances of the *thetas*. The values of these parameters are also set in the file **alpha.dat**.

Consider first the case of one asset, serially independent dividends and log-utility. We set $D = 1$, $A = 0$ and $C = 0.4$, and we take as the dividends $d_t = thetalog(t)$, truncating negative values (later on we allow for negative values inside the conditional expectation). In this case we have an analytical solution for the asset price corresponding to

$$p_{j,t} = \frac{\delta}{1-\delta} d_{j,t} \tag{7.37}$$

Clearly, for this case, a first-degree polynomial for ψ with $beta(1,1) = 0$ and $beta(2,1) = 20$ gives the precise solution. We introduce a first-degree polynomial in the files **psis.for** and the derivatives of *psi* defined in **der.for**. Then, we can move the autocorrelation parameter to some other level, say $A = 0.8$ and $\gamma = -2$, to find a solution that is not analytic.

Next, take as the dividend process $d_t = \exp(thetalog(t))$. Since the expectation is now positive, we can use an exponentiated polynomial and, reasoning as before, we see that a first-order exponentiated polynomial with $beta(1,1) = 20$ and $beta(2,1) = 1$ gives the precise solution for the logarithmic case. To move to the case of $A = 0.8$, $\gamma = -2$, start with the appropriate initial conditions, modify **psis.for** and **der.for**, and set up the homotopy.

Let us now consider a model with two stocks so that $J = 2$, and let us maintain strictly positive dividends $d_t = \exp(thetalog(t))$. We can start the homotopy from the case of logarithmic utility and perfectly correlated dividends (the latter feature makes the model identical to one with a single asset). We now set

$$D = \begin{bmatrix} 0 \\ 0 \end{bmatrix}, \quad A = \begin{bmatrix} 0 & 0 \\ 0 & 0 \end{bmatrix}, \quad C = \begin{bmatrix} 0.4 & 0 \\ 0.4 & 0 \end{bmatrix} \tag{7.38}$$

Thus, in this case, an exponentiated first-order polynomial in the current *thetalogs* gives the exact solution. Since $theta(t,1) = theta(t,2)$, letting the parameters *beta* be (20, 0.5, 0.5), we have parameters to start the homotopy. Clearly, if the two *thetas* are perfectly correlated the nonlinear regression will fail because of perfect collinearity; thus we should start the homotopy with a small departure from the C matrix above (say $c(2,2) = 0.0001$). We also have to set the number of expectations $neq = 2$.

Then, with a sequence of homotopy steps, we can change the parameters of the dividend process to compute a model with two different risky assets by changing D, A, B; and we can also change the risk aversion γ. Moreover, if we make the second row of C go to (0, 0) we approximate the case of a riskless console bond that pays one unit of consumption with certainty in all periods from now into the future. If we proceed like this, at a certain point we have to eliminate $theta(t, 2)$ from the psi, since it gets close to being a constant, and the nonlinear regression would fail. Notice that even when $theta(t, 2)$ is a constant still we will have two psi expressions, and perform two nonlinear regressions, because the riskless asset's price is still a non-degenerate random variable.

Example 7.2 See files in the directory `~\ex2grow`. The psi and its derivatives are defined in **psis.for** and **der.for**. The variables and parameters are labelled as follows:

i	1	2		
$Z(t,i)$	k_t	c_t		
j	1	2	3	4
$alpha(j)$	δ	γ	α	$1-d$

The program **ginvert.for** solves for c_t in the equation

$$c_t = (\delta\ psi(1,t))^{1/\gamma} \tag{7.39}$$

and then solves for k_t using the resource constraint. Then it computes

$$phi(t-1,1) = c_t^{\gamma} \cdot \left(\theta_t\ \alpha k_{t-1}^{\alpha-1} + 1 - d\right)$$

The homotopy is started with the Brock–Mirman solution that applies in the case of depreciation 1 and logarithmic utility. To do that we start with an economy with the following parameters:

j	1	2	3	4
$alpha(j)$	δ	γ	α	$1-d$
	0.95	−1.00	0.33	0.00

In this case an appropriate exponentiated polynomial corresponds exactly to the optimal policy. Using the formulae derived by Brock and Mirman, we see that the relation between the expression for the optimal policy function and those in the (exact) expression for the expectation can be easily derived substituting $c_t = (1-\alpha\delta)\theta_t k_{t-1}^{\alpha}$ in (7.39). In particular, given the parameters fixed above, we have an equilibrium characterized by:

$$beta(1,1) = 1/(\delta(1-\delta\alpha)) = 1.533$$
$$beta(2,1) = -\alpha = -0.330$$
$$beta(3,1) = -1.000$$

We can run the program with these parameters to check that this is indeed the solution, and then change the parameters *alpha* manually or using the built-in homotopy procedure to compute an approximate solution for other sets of parameters; recall that, when the program ends, the last fixed point calculated is stored in **pini.dat**, and the initial condition is scratched. It is quite common that when there is full depreciation ($d = 1$) the series for capital becomes easily non-stationary for small changes in *beta* away from the solution, so that the algorithm may fail to converge. In the case we are discussing a solution is to set a value for *mu* smaller than one (say 0.5) as long as $1 - d$ is close to 0. This simple correction is enough to prevent *beta* from exiting the stable region (i.e. the asymptotic unit circle). For example, using twice the automatic homotopy we can compute an approximate solution for a model with depreciation, $1 - d = 0.8$, and $\gamma = -2.0$, and with an AR(1) process for $\log\theta$ with parameters $\rho = 0.9$ and $\sigma = 0.03$.

In general, the order in which we change the variables should not affect the results obtained, but in models where there is a depreciation rate it seems that it is better to move the depreciation rate away from 1, after which we can safely set *mu* closer to 1 and achieve faster convergence.

Example 7.3 See files in the directory `~\ex3lab`. We now have to address the issue of the numerical solution of the system g at each period t. Also, it will turn out that setting up the homothopy in order to have a continuous path is a non-trivial exercise.

As we discussed before, to complete the inversion of the g system we use a simple numerical procedure to compute hours worked. Rewriting (7.7), we see that solving for $l_t(\beta)$ amounts to finding the zero of the function

$$f(l) \equiv (1-\tau^l)\,\delta\,\psi(\beta; x_t(\beta))\,\theta_t\,(1-\alpha)\,k_t^{\alpha}\,l_t^{-\alpha} - (1-l_t)^{\gamma_l} b \tag{7.40}$$

in the interval [0,1]. A numerical algorithm to solve (7.40) is appended to the main program as a subroutine named **federzero**. Also, at the end of the main program there are the definitions of the function f and of its derivative.[22]

To save computing time during the simulation we use as the starting point for the numerical procedure at a given time period the solution found at the preceding period. This solution is stored as *whold* at the end of **ginvert.for** and retrieved at its beginning. Clearly, during the very first period there is no *whold*, so at the beginning of the **simul** subroutine the value of the labour supply is initialized at the value $Z(1,2) = l_1$ written, for convenience, in **par.dat** as if l_t were a state variable (the number of 'state' variables *nxini* is accordingly set to 2).

The other interesting question here is how to set up the homotopy path to move from the model already solved (Example 7.2) down to the model we want to solve. We need a general model that encompasses both the initial model and the 'new' model, with some parameters controlling the movement from one model to the other. Also, we need a small change in these parameters to produce only a small change in the solution.

[22]Notice that in order to allow the subroutine and the program to share the parameters *alpha* we have redefined the **common** commands. Moreover the external functions f and $fder$ have been declared in the main program and in the subroutine `simul`.

It is useful, though, to realize that all intermediate steps along the homotopy can correspond to a mechanical model where the equations do not necessarily correspond to rational forward-looking behaviour. The starting and end point clearly will be fully fledged models and in some cases the intermediate models can be interesting too. However, from a computational standpoint it is often easier to just see them as dummy models connecting one model to the other.

This is clear if we consider only the case of endogenous labour supply and, for now, set tax rates to zero. Here we could try to specify an economic model in which if a parameter takes on a particular value the labour supply is identically equal to 1 in equilibrium, thus replicating the basic model of growth. For example, we could let b in the utility function move from 0 to 1.

Unfortunately this procedure may bring additional problems from a computational point of view, since $(1 - l)^{\gamma_l}$ will typically have a derivative that tends to either infinity or 0 as l_t approaches 1. The subroutine **federzero** largely makes use of this derivative, and will easily fail to converge under these conditions. Formally, what happens is that the homotopy path defined in this way is discontinuous precisely at $b = 0$.

We can bypass this complication in the following way. We can solve at any period a model where actual working hours are given by $l_t^* = sl_t + (1 - s)$ (with $0 \leq s \leq 1$), where l_t solves the first-order condition of the original optimization problem. We use l_t^* to compute the return on capital, total production, and so on. In this way when $s = 0$ (and zero tax rates) the problem will be identical to the basic growth problem. For $0 < s < 1$ we cannot give an economic interpretation to our simulations, but eventually, as we reach $s = 1$, we have a correct solution to the model with endogenous labour supply. This is the procedure we adopted when first running the homotopy. Once we have an approximate solution for $s = 1$, we can eliminate it from our program. From then on it is straightforward to modify the tax rates from 0 to any level of interest, and in the same way to modify all the other parameters. The order in which the parameter values are changed should not matter for the final result, but sometimes the homotopy converges faster depending upon which parameter is changed first. As noticed above, if we start from the Brock–Mirman parameters, it is usually better to start by moving the depreciation rate away from 1, and then modify the other parameters (including the s).

Here we summarize the variable and parameter labels used by the program for this example.[23]

i	1	2	3					
$Z(t,i)$	k_t	l_t	c_t					
j	1	2	3	4	5	6	7	8
$alpha(j)$	δ	γ	α	γ_l	d	τ^l	τ^k	s

[23]The program uses an additional variable $Z(4, t)$ corresponding to the number of steps needed for **federzero** to converge. This kind of auxiliary variable is useful for checking the performance of the numerical subroutine used. Also, an additional parameter used by the program is $alpha(9)$ which controls the speed of adjustment in the subroutine **federzero**.

Example 7.4 See files in the directory ~\ex4inv. The labelling of variables and parameters, and the baseline parameters values, are as follows:

i	1	2	3	4	5
$Z(t,1)$	k_t	c_t	λ_t	i_t	bind.ind.
j	1	2	3	4	
$alpha(j)$	δ	γ	α	$(1-d)$	
	0.95	−1.00	0.33	0.9	
ρ	0.9				
σ	0.05				

Notice that we introduced some auxiliary variables $Z(t,i)$ that are not necessary from the purely computational point of view. The first is the investment level, $Z(t,4)$, that may be useful in the simulated series stored in **openout.dat**. The second is an indicator variable $Z(t,5)$, assuming the value 1 whenever the non-negativity constraint is binding. The mean of the $Z(t,5)$ variable represents the fraction of periods in which the non-negativity constraint is binding.[24]

The program **opent.for** is a slight modification of **open.for**. The computation of the summary statistics is performed not only at the end of the algorithm but also at each of the homotopy steps, producing a table with the values obtained. This program illustrates how the homotopy steps can be used to perform a comparative dynamics exercise. That is, along the homotopy paths we can see how changes in parameters affect the summary statistic of some simulated variable. In all cases in which the models at each step of the homotopy have economic meaning we can immmediately store the values of some statistic of interest. In this way the table we obtain displays the relation between a parameter of the model and some statistical features of the equilibrium path obtained.

For example, a simple qualitative result that we can expect from the model with non-negative investment is that lower depreciation rates are associated with a higher probability of being up against the constraint, and thus with a multiplier λ_t which is more frequently positive.

With the appropriate modification of the homotopy steps we obtain a table displaying the relation between a parameter and a summary statistic of the simulated model. For example, Table 7.1 displays the relation between the depreciation rate and the percentage of times at which the constraint binds in the simulated economies, confirming our intuition.

We can also study the effect of the elasticity of the instantaneous marginal utility γ on investment and on the probability of having a binding contraint. Again just performing the homotopy we obtain Table 7.2 ($1-d$ is now kept fixed at 0.975).

The relation we found between risk aversion (absolute value of γ) and average investment is increasing, while the relation with the frequency of the binding constraint

[24] To increase computational efficiency all the variables that are not strictly needed for the iterations, such as $Z(t,4)$ and $Z(t,5)$ in this case, would be computed after the fixed point has been found. In the current model, however, the gain in efficiency would be minimal.

Table 7.1 Frequency of binding constraint and $1 - d$

$(1-d)$	Binding fraction	$E(i_t)$	$E(\mu_t)$
0.9000	0.0000	0.3273	0.00000
0.9100	0.0000	0.3260	0.00000
0.9200	0.0000	0.3232	0.00000
0.9300	0.0000	0.3181	0.00000
0.9400	0.0000	0.3098	0.00000
0.9500	0.0010	0.2969	0.00000
0.9600	0.0032	0.2770	0.00004
0.9700	0.0203	0.2455	0.00032
0.9800	0.0998	0.1915	0.00208
0.9900	0.3677	0.0952	0.01216

Table 7.2 Binding constraint and γ

γ	Binding fraction	$E(i_t)$	$E(\lambda_t)$
−0.7	0.056	0.219	0.0009
−1.1	0.048	0.221	0.0009
−1.5	0.047	0.223	0.0009
−1.9	0.047	0.225	0.0009
−2.3	0.048	0.228	0.0009
−2.7	0.049	0.231	0.0009
−3.1	0.049	0.235	0.0009
−3.5	0.049	0.239	0.0008
−3.9	0.049	0.243	0.0008
−4.2	0.049	0.246	0.0007
−4.4	0.048	0.249	0.0007
−4.6	0.048	0.251	0.0006
−4.8	0.047	0.254	0.0006
−5.0	0.047	0.256	0.0005

is non-monotonic. A possible intuition for this result is the following. If the constraint binds often, this introduces higher volatility in consumption, since agents cannot smooth consumption by consuming their capital; the way to avoid this unpleasantly volatile consumption is to keep, on average, a larger investment and capital stock, so that hitting the constraint is less likely. With higher risk aversion $-\gamma$, agents are more willing to settle, in steady state, at a high level of the capital stock in order to reduce the probability of being up against the constraint. This, in turn, has ambiguous implications for the observed frequency of the binding constraint. When risk aversion is higher there is more need to buffer against bad shocks consuming the capital stock, but at the same time the capital stock is endogenously kept higher making this event less likely, as a consequence the frequency with which the lower bound is hit may be larger or smaller. Computation helps us to see these two opposite effects are balancing each other in our specific case, so that the binding frequency oscillates around 5 per cent.

Example 7.5 See the directory `~\ex5hco`. We only discuss here the case with two expectations.

The routine **Gbeta** now is performing two nonlinear regressions with four parameters each. The program lines in **ginvert.for** substitute the ψs for the corresponding expectations in the Euler equation and use the transition for k to solve for c_t and k_t, given the shock process and the past values of capital and consumption. Since c_{t-1} is now a state variable the number of x to be initialized ($nxini$) is 2, and there is a starting value c_1 for consumption in the file **par.dat**. The labelling of variables and parameters is exactly as in Example 7.2 with the addition of $alpha(5) = \eta$.

Notice that when $\eta = 0$ the model coincides with that in Example 7.2. Hence, the homotopy steps are taken in a natural way starting with the $beta$s computed for that case and $beta(i, 4) = 0$. Let $\eta = 0$ in **alpha.dat**, and set to 0 the β corresponding to $\log c_{t-1}$ in **pini.dat**. All the βs for the second expression ($psi(t, 2)$) can be set freely at the first stage of the homotopy, because when $\eta = 0$ they do not affect the simulated path and so they cannot cause non-stationarity (at this stage the problem for the series $phi(t, 2)$ is just a problem of estimation, which does not feed back into the simulation part). After estimating the βs for the two parameterized expressions in the case $\eta = 0$, we can safely proceed with the homotopy and move η towards the range we are interested in.

Example 7.6 Before discussing the use of the algorithm it is useful to describe the closed-form solution that can be obtained in the simple case in which $d_1 = d_2 = 1$ and utility is logarithmic. Using the result stated above of a constant ratio of $k_{2,t}$ to $k_{1,t}$ on the optimal path, this case can be made to fit into the Brock–Mirman framework if $\alpha_1 = \alpha_2 = \alpha$. In this case, the form of the optimal policy for consumption and investment can be shown to be

$$c_t = (1 - 2\delta\alpha)\theta_t k_{1,t-1}^{\alpha} k_{2,t-1}^{\alpha} \tag{7.41}$$

$$k_{1,t} = k_{2,t} = \delta\alpha\theta_t k_{1,t-1}^{\alpha} k_{2,t-1}^{\alpha} \tag{7.42}$$

In turn, the first of these equations implies the following (exact) form for the expectation in (7.17) and (7.18):

$$\delta E_t \cdots = (1 - 2\delta\alpha)^{-1} \exp(\log\theta_t + \alpha \log k_{1,t-1} + \alpha \log k_{2,t-1}) \tag{7.43}$$

This solution will be useful both as a starting point for the homotopy steps and as a reference in order to discuss the convergence of the algorithm.

As we try to implement the algorithm using equations (7.16), (7.17) and (7.32), the first problem we face is the choice of the state variables to be included in the parameterized expressions psi. The two capital stocks are natural candidates. But if we try, for example, to specify the function ψ as an exponentiated first-order polynomial in $k_{1,t-1}$, $k_{2,t-1}$ and θ_t, we will be in trouble with the nonlinear regression. The obvious reason is that the two capital stocks are highly collinear. Actually in the case already mentioned of $d_1 = d_2$, the two capital stocks are perfectly collinear, since $k_{2,t}/k_{1,t} = \alpha_2/\alpha_1$ on the optimal path.

On the other hand, if we use only one capital level as a state variable we incur in a different type of problem. For example, if we try simply to drop one of the capital stocks from the specification of psi, it turns out that the simulated series for consumption and capital stocks either diverge or take negative values, and the algorithm often fails to converge.

Now consider the two capital goods model and in particular consider the case $d = 1$, in which the Brock–Mirman solution applies and consumption and investment are proportional to current production. Suppose we omit the first capital good from the state variables and we use only $k_{2,t-1}$ to compute the psis. At the simulation stage every small numerical error in the ratio of the capital stocks is amplified during the simulation; for example, if $k_{2,t-1}/k_{1,t-1} = 1 + \epsilon$ the production will be overstated, c_t and $k_{2,t}$ will be larger, while $k_{1,t}$ is computed as a residual, the implied difference equation is explosive, and so the ratio will tend to increase. A similar problem of non-stationary behaviour of the simulated series arises also with different specification of the psis.

It seems that a source of this problem was the fact that one of the two capital stocks was computed as a residual, so we have chosen a different transformation of the second Euler equations, namely

$$c_t^{\gamma} \frac{k_{2,t}}{k_{1,t}} = \delta E_t c_{t+1}^{\gamma} \left[\theta_{t+1} \alpha_2 k_{1,t}^{\alpha_1 - 1} k_{2,t}^{\alpha_2} + (1 - d_2) \frac{k_{2,t}}{k_{1,t}} \right] \tag{7.44}$$

Then we have set the **ginvert.for** file to invert the system given by (7.16), (7.17), and (7.44), recovering the $k_{2,t}/k_{1,t}$ ratio from (7.44), and computing investment in the two capital goods according to this ratio and the total production available for capital (i.e. $y_t + (1 - d_1)k_{1,t-1} + (1 - d_2)k_{2,t-1} - c_t$).

Setting up the system (7.19) in this way, we are able to overcome the problems of non-convergence mentioned above. Thus, we can compute an approximate solution of the model for different sets of parameter values, using the built-in homotopy steps. Moreover as we move away from the case of identical depreciation we can add to the explanatory variables in the exponentiated polynomial the log of $k_{2,t-1}$, without having problems with the regression subroutine. Clearly the two variables are still highly correlated, but this is not a problem given that we are not interested in the values of the coefficients $beta$ but only in the predictions. Nevertheless the high correlation between two explanatory variables may be a practical problem if it generates spurious movements in the computed $beta$ while the algorithm is running (movements that the program interprets as non-convergent behaviour). For this reason, it is safer in these cases to use the convergence criterion based on the distance of the implied series. The program **opens.for** is designed for this purpose.

As noted above, this model differs in an interesting way from the growth model in Example 7.2 only in so far as the depreciation rates are different. A qualitative question we may ask is how investment is distributed between the two capital stocks with different depreciation rates over the cycle.

Table 7.3 Risk aversion and the co-movement of consumption with capital composition

γ	corr(c,ratio)	std.dev(c)	std.dev(ratio)
−1.0000000	0.1481591	0.0538640	0.0652414
−1.1000000	0.1683820	0.0537597	0.0676530
−1.2000000	0.1882749	0.0536681	0.0700300
−1.3000000	0.2081062	0.0535875	0.0723799
−1.4000000	0.2279308	0.0535159	0.0747565
−1.5000000	0.2470898	0.0534498	0.0770776
−1.6000000	0.2657092	0.0533886	0.0793931
−1.7000000	0.2837222	0.0533309	0.0817056
−1.8000000	0.3013010	0.0532761	0.0840440
−1.9000000	0.3177685	0.0532227	0.0863246
−2.0000000	0.3335457	0.0531707	0.0886010

We have computed a solution for the parameter values reported as follows, together with the labels of the variables.

i	1	2	3	4		
$Z(t,i)$	$k_{1,t}$	$k_{2,t}$	c_t	$k_{2,t}/k_{1,t}$		
j	1	2	3	4	5	6
$alpha(j)$	δ	γ	α_1	α_2	$(1-d_1)$	$(1-d_2)$
	0.96	−1.00	0.4	0.2	0.3	0.8

For the two *psi* forms we have specified exponentiated polynomials in θ, $\log k_1$ and $\log k_2$ (the last *beta* was set equal to zero in the region close to the identical depreciation case). The program output shows a correlation between $Z(t,3)$ and $Z(t,4)$ of 0.148, indicating a positive relation between consumption and the proportion of capital good $k_{2,t}$ to the total stock. This economy displays booms when accumulation is concentrated on capital goods with low depreciation rates, while during recessions the capital stock composition is costlessy modified in favour of $k_{1,t}$, in order to increase productivity in the short term (as $\alpha_1 > \alpha_2$).

Table 7.3 (obtained in the same way as Tables 7.1 and 7.2) displays the relation between the risk-aversion parameter and some statistics on the simulated series. As γ increases the co-movement of capital composition with the cycle is enhanced. That is, during booms more capital is shifted towards low-depreciation/low-return capital stocks. As a consequence of this policy consumption variability is slightly decreased for larger risk aversion.

If we let the homotopy steps go back to a case of identical depreciation rate (e.g. move d_1 to 0.8) we obtain the comforting result that the simulated ratio $k_{2,t}/k_{1,t}$ is on average 0.5056 with standard deviation of 0.0086, which is pretty close to the theoretical result of a ratio constant over time and equal to 0.5 ($= \alpha_2/\alpha_1$).

7.5 Conclusion

In this chapter we discuss some very practical aspects of solving nonlinear stochastic dynamic models with PEA. As we mentioned in Section 7.1, our purpose is not to describe the full scope of all the applications that can be performed with PEA, and we have limited our discussion to solving Euler equations at the stationary distribution. Restricted to this case, we have discussed many practical issues and the use of a publicly available FORTRAN program. We hope the reader will see that the ideas here are easy to apply. We have shown how the computational costs do not increase exponentially if more state variables or stochastic shocks are introduced, how one can refine the solution by introducing more flexible functional forms, and how the algorithm can be used to calculate suboptimal equilibria. More details on how to do the computations and some tricks are described in a text available at the internet addresses given in footnote 3.

The chapter makes no comparison with other methods, either at the theoretical or practical level. The reader will probably realize that this is an important issue, as each method has advantages and disadvantages, there is no algorithm that is the best one for all models, and there is no general framework that encompasses a large number of algorithms. Here, we can offer some informal comments on how PEA compares to other algorithms. It should be clear to the reader that a grid was never introduced in the state space and that an integral was never explicitly calculated (although step 3 does calculate an integral implicitly). This means that all the problems with grids and integration in multi-dimensional spaces are avoided here. There is no 'curse of dimensionality' as we introduce more state variables, and models with three or four state variables can be easily solved taking into account of the nonlinearities in the solution. Furthermore, the algorithm endogenously selects the values of the state variables at which to fit the solution, by performing the simulation of step 2. This is important because the user does not have to specify a range of relevant values for the state variables, we need a lower degree of the polynomial to achieve a reasonable fit, and the number of computations does not increase exponentially as the state space increases. For these reasons, this approach to solving nonlinear models is relatively more efficient when there are several state variables and stochastic shocks with continuous distributions.

The simple numerical analysis approach that we have taken here is overly simplistic and could be improved upon. There are better ways of computing integrals in step 3 than just running the long-run simulation of step 2. Certain forms of hill-climbing to find the fixed point might be a good idea. As to the possibilities for homotopy, we have only scratched the surface. But before we complicate our lives by introducing these techniques, it seems interesting to see just how far we can go in solving models by computing a few simulations and running a few regressions.

8

FINITE-DIFFERENCE METHODS FOR CONTINUOUS-TIME DYNAMIC PROGRAMMING

Graham V. Candler[1]

8.1 Introduction

Up until about 15 years ago, aircraft were designed very differently than they are today. An initial design was developed based on approximate theoretical methods, and a scale model was tested in a wind tunnel. Then, an experienced aerodynamicist would climb into the tunnel and use Plasticine and a file to alter the shape of the aircraft until better performance was obtained. A new model would be built and the process repeated until either the money ran out or the design was considered to be good enough. Typically, at least a dozen very expensive models were built and many thousands of hours of expensive wind-tunnel time were used.

Nowadays, aircraft are designed using computational fluid dynamics (CFD). A computational model of the aircraft is entered into the computer using computer-aided design programs, and the appropriate governing partial differential equations are solved for the computational aircraft model. The computer then alters the shape of the aircraft until an optimal design is obtained. This optimization process can be highly complex, even including the cost of manufacture of specific elements of the wing and fuselage. Thus, the cruise configuration of the aircraft is designed entirely with computational methods. Wind tunnels are only used to simulate the flow over the aircraft during take-off and landing because the landing gear and high-lift devices are too difficult to model accurately. Only about two wind-tunnel models must be built, and wind-tunnel time is very dramatically reduced. Thus, computational methods produce more efficient aircraft designs in less time and with a much reduced cost.

Not only has CFD revolutionized aircraft design, but it has become a new academic discipline in the study of fluid motion. It has largely replaced pencil-and-paper theory because much more interesting and complicated problems can be solved using numerical methods. Careful numerical simulations have become "theory" in fluid mechanics and are regularly used as a database to test traditional theoretical results.

The reader is probably wondering what this discussion has to do with economics. It has a great deal to do with economics, because the same revolution that occurred in fluid dynamics is going to occur in economics. Admittedly, the study of dynamic economies results in more complicated governing equations than traditional aerodynamics, and that is perhaps why computational methods have not yet taken over from theory. However,

[1]Correspondence address: Aerospace Engineering and Mechanics, University of Minnesota, Minneapolis, Minnesota 55455, U.S.A.

with the rapid increase in computing power and improvements in numerical methods, it is bound to take place.

Therefore, it is the purpose of this chapter to introduce some of the methods and underlying ideas behind computational fluid dynamics. Of course it is not possible to summarize 30 years of work in this field, so the chapter only provides a narrow view of this large field. In particular, we discuss the use of finite-difference methods for the simulation of dynamic economies. We consider a standard stochastic dynamic programming model of a macroeconomy and apply the finite-difference methods to this problem. This model results in a second-order nonlinear partial differential equation that has some features in common with the governing equations of fluid dynamics. We will introduce the idea of "upwind" or solution-dependent differencing methods and discuss the stability of the methods through the analysis of model problems. Then, an implicit solution to the problem is discussed with the motivation of reducing the computer time required to solve the problem. Finally, we consider a two-state dynamic programming problem.

8.2 Stochastic dynamic programming

For most of this chapter, we will analyse a simple continuous-time stochastic growth model. Assume that there is an infinitely-lived household that chooses consumption c to maximize expected lifetime utility

$$\max_c E \int_0^\infty e^{-\rho t} u(c)\, dt \tag{8.1}$$

subject to

$$dk = (f(k) - c)\, dt + \sigma(k)\, dz \tag{8.2}$$

for $k(0)$ given, where k is the capital stock, and z is a Wiener process. Let $V(t, k)$ be the value function at date t and capital stock $k(t)$. Then we can derive a partial differential equation, known as Bellman's equation, as follows:

$$\begin{aligned}
V(t,k) &= \max_c E \int_t^\infty e^{-\rho(s-t)} u(c)\, ds \\
&= \max_{\substack{c \\ t \le s \le t+\Delta t}} E\left\{ \int_t^{t+\Delta t} e^{-\rho(s-t)} u(c)\, ds \right. \\
&\qquad \left. + e^{-\rho\Delta t} \max_{\substack{c \\ t+\Delta t \le s}} \int_{t+\Delta t}^\infty e^{-\rho(s-t-\Delta t)} u(c)\, ds \right\} \\
&= \max_{\substack{c \\ t \le s \le t+\Delta t}} E\left\{ \int_t^{t+\Delta t} e^{-\rho(s-t)} u(c)\, ds + e^{-\rho\Delta t} V(t+\Delta t, k+\Delta k) \right\} \\
&= \max_c \left\{ u(c)\Delta t + V(t,k) - \rho V(t,k)\Delta t + V_t(t,k)\Delta t \right. \\
&\qquad \left. + V_k(t,k)(f(k)-c)\Delta t + \tfrac{1}{2} V_{kk}(t,k)\sigma(k)^2 \Delta t + \cdots \right\}
\end{aligned} \tag{8.3}$$

where V_t and V_k are first derivatives of V with respect to time and capital stock, and V_{kk} is the second derivative of V with respect to capital stock. The last equality uses a Taylor expansion of $V(t + \Delta t, k + \Delta k)$ around the point (t, k). This equality also uses (8.2) and the fact that if z is a Wiener process, then $z(t_1) - z(t_0)$ and $z(t_2) - z(t_1)$ are independently normally distributed with mean zero and variances $t_1 - t_0$ and $t_2 - t_1$, respectively. Thus, when expectations are taken, the term $(\Delta z)^2$ is replaced by Δt and terms multiplying Δz are dropped.

Subtracting $V(t, k)$ from both sides of (8.3) and rearranging terms yields the general dynamic programming equation for the value function[2]

$$-V_t(t,k) + \rho V(t,k) = \max_c \left\{ u(c) + (f(k) - c)V_k(t,k) + \tfrac{1}{2}\sigma(k)^2 V_{kk}(t,k) \right\} \quad (8.4)$$

Let the utility function have the form $u(c) = c^{\omega}/\omega$ with $\omega < 1$. Assume the production function is given by $f(k) = \lambda k^{\theta} - \delta k$, and choose $\sigma(k) = \sigma k$. Then, using the first-order condition, $u'(c) = V_k$, we obtain the second-order, time-dependent partial differential equation

$$V_t(t,k) + \rho V(t,k) = \frac{1-\omega}{\omega} V_k(t,k)^{\omega/(\omega-1)} + V_k(t,k)(\lambda k^{\theta} - \delta k) + \tfrac{1}{2}\sigma^2 k^2 V_{kk}(t,k) \quad (8.5)$$

In going from (8.4) to (8.5), we have changed the sign on V_t for the following reason. In time-dependent problems, a terminal condition at some final date is given and the solution of $V(t, k)$ is found by solving the problem backwards in time. To avoid cumbersome notation, we simply change the sign on V_t and integrate (8.5) with a positive time step; this is equivalent to integrating the original equation backwards in time.

In the next section we describe a method for constructing approximate numerical solutions to the value function V that satisfies the partial differential equation in (8.5). In the special case where $\theta = \omega = \frac{1}{2}$ we can compare our approximate solution to the exact solution given by

$$V(t,k) = \frac{2}{\sqrt{2\rho + \delta}}\sqrt{k} + \frac{\lambda}{\rho\sqrt{2\rho + \delta}} \quad (8.6)$$

Note that consumption is a linear function of the capital stock ($c = (2\rho + \delta)k$). For arbitrary values of the parameters, we cannot find analytical solutions. But for the nonstochastic versions, we can check to see if the derivative of the value function at the steady state is close to its exact value, given by $c_s^{\omega-1}$, where

$$c_s = \lambda k_s^{\theta} - \delta k_s, \quad k_s = \left(\frac{\rho + \delta}{\lambda\theta}\right)^{1/(\theta-1)} \quad (8.7)$$

are the steady-state values for consumption and capital.

[2]The derivation of this type of continuous-time dynamic programming problem is discussed in detail in Kamien and Schwartz (1981).

8.3 Finite-difference solution of $V(t, k)$

We would like to find the function $V(k)$ that satisfies (8.5) when the time derivative, V_t, is zero. We can find this time-independent solution in two ways. The most obvious thing to do is to set $V_t = 0$, and solve the functional equation

$$\rho V = \frac{1-\omega}{\omega} V_k^{\omega/\omega-1} + V_k(\lambda k^\theta - \delta k) + \tfrac{1}{2}\sigma^2 k^2 V_{kk} \tag{8.8}$$

subject to boundary conditions at $k = 0$ and $k = k_{\max}$ (a boundary value problem).

Alternatively, we can solve the time-dependent partial differential for the time-independent solution, subject to an initial condition and to the boundary conditions (an initial boundary value problem). In this case, we start with an arbitrary initial condition and integrate in time until the solution is no longer a function of the initial condition.

In computational fluid dynamics, the time-dependent approach is preferred because we are able to compute a solution that is physically consistent at each time step. If we attempt to solve the steady-state problem directly (with the time derivative of the solution set equal to zero), we must linearize the problem and solve it with a Newton–Raphson method. This requires a very good guess at the solution, otherwise the method does not converge and a new guess is needed. When the solution is well understood and the problem is uni-dimensional, perhaps this is acceptable, otherwise it is tedious at best and impossible at worst.

8.3.1 *Finite-difference methods*

There are several different approaches to the numerical solution of partial differential equations. In this paper, we focus on finite-difference methods because this approach is the most straightforward to develop and implement.[3] Finite-difference methods use Taylor series expansions to represent the partial derivatives that appear in the dynamic programming problem.

Let us approximate the function $V(t, k)$ on an equispaced time and capital-stock grid. In this case, we use the following notation for the function evaluated at a point on the grid:

$$V_i^n = V(t_n, k_i) = V(n\Delta t, i\Delta k) \tag{8.9}$$

where $n = 0, 1, 2, \ldots$ and $i = 0, 1, 2, \ldots, i_{\max}$. Using the definition of the partial derivative, we can represent the derivative of the value function with respect to the capital stock as

$$V_k(t, k) = \frac{\partial V}{\partial k} = \lim_{\Delta k \to 0} \frac{V(t, k + \Delta k) - V(t, k)}{\Delta k}$$

A Taylor series approximation for $V(t, k + \Delta k)$ is given by

$$V(t, k + \Delta k) = V(t, k) + \Delta k\, V_k(t, k) + \tfrac{1}{2}\Delta k^2\, V_{kk}(t, k) + \cdots$$

[3] Other approaches include finite-volume methods (see Hirsch, 1988) and finite-element methods (see McGrattan, Chapter 6, this volume). These methods differ in the way in which the derivatives are represented. However, in all of the methods the main computational task involves solving a sparse linear system of equations.

Therefore, we can show that the partial derivative at $t = n\Delta t$ and $k = i\Delta k$ is given by

$$\begin{aligned} V_k(t,k) &= \frac{V(t,k+\Delta k) - V(t,k)}{\Delta k} - \tfrac{1}{2}\Delta k\, V_{kk}(t,k) + \cdots \\ &= \frac{V_{i+1}^n - V_i^n}{\Delta k} + O(\Delta k) \\ &= (V_k)_i^n + O(\Delta k) \end{aligned}$$

where the last equality uses the notation of (8.9) for the partial derivative of the value function with respect to k. The first non-zero term in the approximation, $-\frac{1}{2}\Delta k\, V_{kk}(t,k)$, is the truncation error of the scheme, and the variation of the error term with the grid spacing gives the order of accuracy. Thus, this is a first-order accurate forward-difference approximation to $V_k(t,k)$.

Similarly, we can derive the first-order accurate backward-difference and second-order accurate central-difference approximations

$$\begin{aligned} (V_k)_i^n &= \frac{V_i^n - V_{i-1}^n}{\Delta k} + O(\Delta k) \\ (V_k)_i^n &= \frac{V_{i+1}^n - V_{i-1}^n}{2\Delta k} + O(\Delta k^2) \end{aligned}$$

respectively. We can derive approximations of arbitrary order of accuracy by taking linear combinations of Taylor series expansions of $V_{i\pm m}$. Generally, the more grid points used in the difference operator, the higher the accuracy of the approximation. Also, central differences are more accurate than difference approximations that are biased to the left or right. We can also derive higher-order derivatives using the same approach. For example, a second-order accurate central-difference approximation to the second derivative is

$$(V_{kk})_i^n = \frac{V_{i+1}^n - 2V_i^n + V_{i-1}^n}{\Delta k^2} + O(\Delta k^2)$$

Figure 8.1 gives a graphical representation of the three first derivative approximations discussed above. For this smoothly varying function, we can see that the central difference method gives a more accurate approximation than the first-order, one-sided differences. Thus in principle, the higher the order of accuracy, the fewer grid points are required to obtain a solution of a given accuracy. Or, for a given grid the solution will be more accurate. However, we will see that this is an overly simplified view of the quality of the solution.

8.3.2 *Finite-difference approximation of* $V(t,k)$

We next consider the derivation of a finite-difference approximation to the time-dependent differential equation in (8.5). For ease of solution, let us use a backward-difference approximation for V_t. This is an explicit time integration scheme, because we can solve explicitly for the future solution (at $n+1$), given the present solution (at n). We will discuss other implicit time integration approaches later. Thus, we have

$$(V_t)_i^n = \frac{V_i^{n+1} - V_i^n}{\Delta t} + O(\Delta t)$$

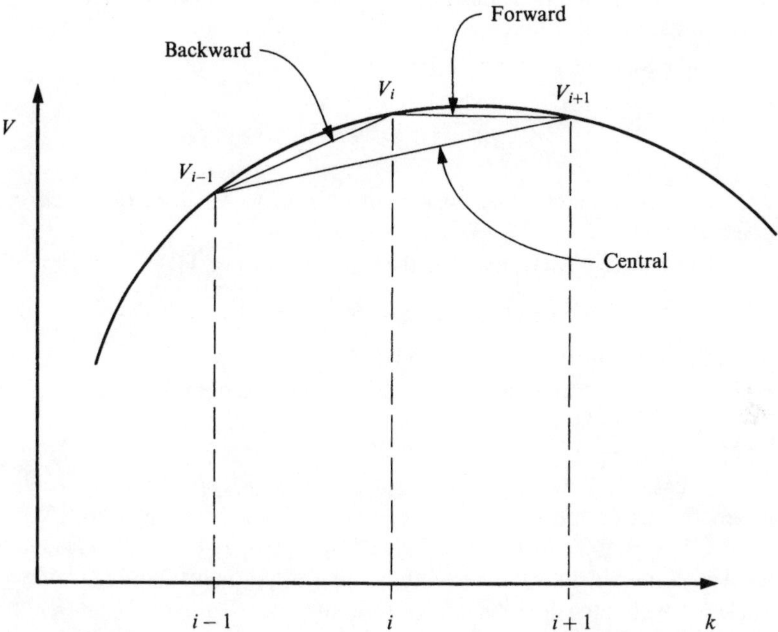

FIG. 8.1. Finite-difference approximations to the first derivative of a smoothly varying function.

From the preceding analysis, we know that the central-difference approximations to the derivatives with respect to the capital stock are more accurate than the one-sided difference approximations given the same grid spacing. Therefore, let us use the central-difference approximations for V_k and V_{kk}. We then obtain the difference equation

$$\frac{V_i^{n+1} - V_i^n}{\Delta t} + \rho V_i^n = \frac{1-\omega}{\omega}\left(\frac{V_{i+1}^n - V_{i-1}^n}{2\Delta k}\right)^{\omega/(\omega-1)} + \left(\frac{V_{i+1}^n - V_{i-1}^n}{2\Delta k}\right)(\lambda k_i^\theta - \delta k_i)$$
$$+ \tfrac{1}{2}\sigma^2 k_i^2\left(\frac{V_{i+1}^n - 2V_i^n + V_{i-1}^n}{\Delta k^2}\right) + O(\Delta t) + O(\Delta k^2) \tag{8.10}$$

Note that we can solve explicitly for V_i^{n+1}, $i = 0, 1, 2, \ldots, i_{\max}$, given V_i^n. We also need to specify some boundary conditions at the locations $i = 0$ and $i = i_{\max}$, corresponding to $k = k_{\min}$ and $k = k_{\max}$, respectively. This will be discussed later.

Therefore, the solution of the differential equation is now straightforward. We define a grid over the relevant region of the capital stock ($k_{\min} \le k \le k_{\max}$) by choosing a maximum number of grid points, $i_{\max}$. For the case considered here, let $k_{\min} = 0$, $k_{\max} = 2k_s$. Then $\Delta k = k_{\max}/i_{\max}$, $k_i = i\Delta k$. Next, we specify an initial condition, V_i^0; for this example, we know that the value function is concave, and therefore we choose $V_i^0 = \sqrt{k_i}$. Then, the solution of the difference equation proceeds with the following steps:

- Compute the time step:

$$\Delta t = CFL \frac{\Delta k}{a}$$

  (CFL is a constant and a is a characteristic rate of change of the solution, to be discussed later).
- Use (8.10) to compute the change in the solution: $\Delta V_i^n = V_i^{n+1} - V_i^n$, for all i.
- Compute the residual (L_2 error norm): $\varepsilon^n = \frac{1}{i_{\max} \Delta t} \sqrt{\sum_i (\Delta V_i^n)^2}$.
- Update the solution: $V_i^{n+1} = V_i^n + \Delta V_i^n$.
- Continue until ε^n is small (the solution is no longer changing).

8.3.3 *Results using central difference method*

Consider the case where we use (8.10) to solve the dynamic programming problem with parameters chosen such that we know the exact solution (given by (8.6)). We choose $\omega = \theta = 0.5$, $\rho = 0.05$, $\lambda = 1.0$, $\delta = 0.025$, $\sigma = 0.0$, and use the exact solution as the initial condition. In this case, the finite-difference approximation should preserve the exact solution within the differencing error, $O(\Delta k^2)$.

Figure 8.2 plots the results of this calculation after 40 time steps. We see that the numerical approximation is completely corrupted, with huge oscillations in the solution near $k = 0$. Clearly, this is not a good method.

8.3.4 *Model equation*

Let us consider a model equation that has the essential characteristics of the differential equation (8.10), without the nonlinearity. Note that with $\sigma = 0$, there are only first derivatives in the expression for V_t. Therefore, it is useful to consider the wave equation given by

$$V_t + a V_k = 0 \tag{8.11}$$

with a constant. This equation is linear and has an exact solution. For the case where $a > 0$, the initial data are simply propagated in the direction of increasing k, as illustrated in Fig. 8.3. That is, the solution is $V(t, k) = V(0, k - at)$ with $V(0, k)$ given.

Let us try solving this problem with the central-, backward-, and forward-difference approximations. For example, the central-difference approximation is

$$\frac{V_i^{n+1} - V_i^n}{\Delta t} = -a \frac{V_{i+1}^n - V_{i-1}^n}{2\Delta k} \tag{8.12}$$

If we start with a step function ($V = 1$ for $k < 0$, and $V = 0$ for $k > 0$), and use a time step given by $\Delta t = \Delta k / a$, we obtain the results plotted in Fig. 8.4 after five time steps. In this case, the backward difference gives the exact solution and the central- and forward-difference methods produce spurious oscillations similar to those obtained in Fig. 8.3. These oscillations continue to grow with more time steps.

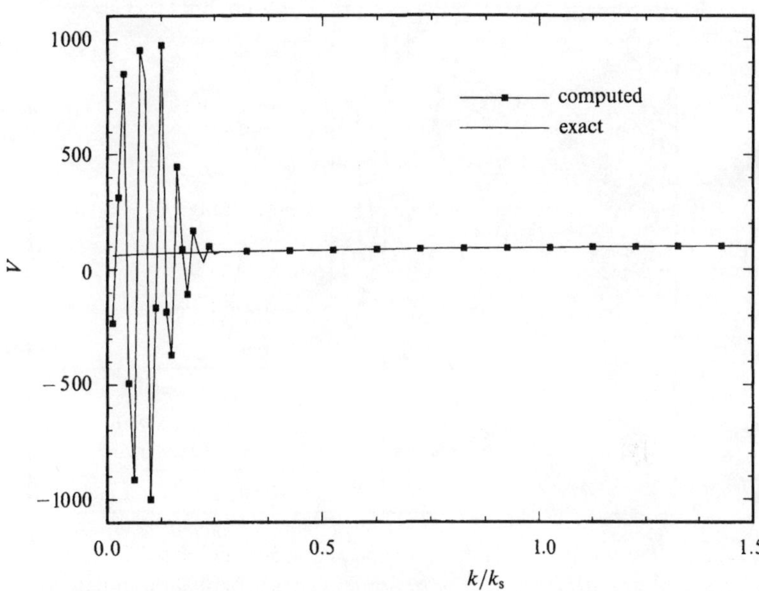

FIG. 8.2. Numerical solution of the dynamic programming problem using a central-difference method after 40 time steps, starting from the exact solution.

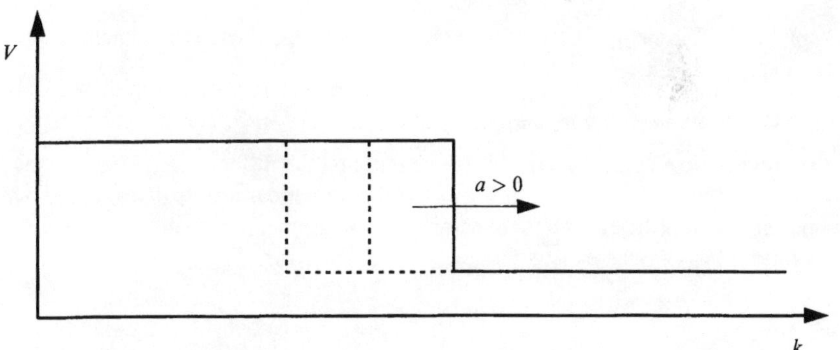

FIG. 8.3. Solution of the wave equation (8.11) for $a < 0$.

If a is negative, the solution propagates in the direction of negative capital stock; in this case, the forward-difference method gives the exact solution and the other two methods produce spurious oscillations. Clearly, the direction of propagation of the solution determines which differencing scheme should be used. We will see that, in general, the differencing stencil should use data that reflects the direction of information propagation. That is, if the solution is moving to the right in capital-stock time, the differencing stencil should be biased to the left, and vice versa. In CFD terminology, this biasing is known

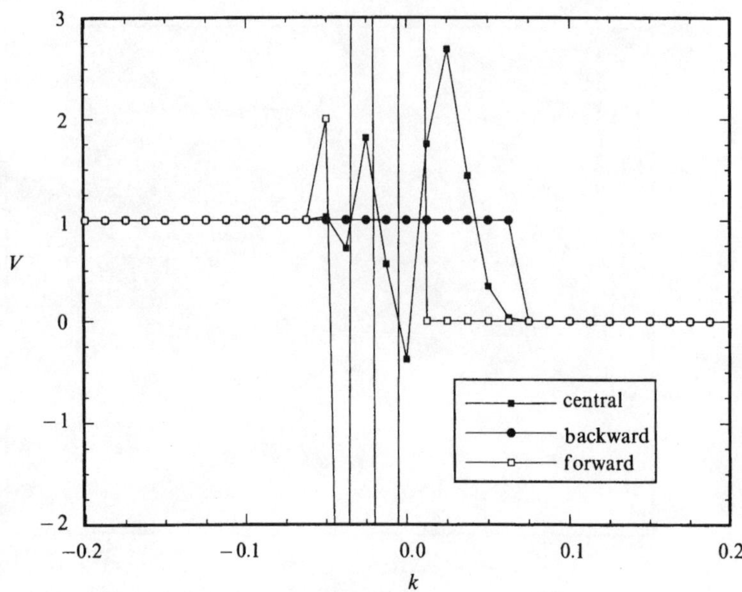

FIG. 8.4. Numerical solution of the wave equation (8.11) for $a > 0$ for three different finite-difference approximations after five time steps.

as "upwind" differencing. In the next section, we show that there is a mathematical basis for this approach.

8.3.5 *Von Neumann stability analysis*

In the previous examples we saw that, depending on the differencing scheme, the error may be amplified. It is possible to formalize the numerical results discussed above by computing the amplification factor of a finite-difference method. To do so, we decompose the solution, V_i^n, into the exact solution, $\bar{V}_i^n$, and the error, ϵ_i^n:

$$V_i^n = \bar{V}_i^n + \epsilon_i^n$$

Then, we substitute this expression into the differencing method and solve for the time evolution of the error.

Let us consider the central-difference method applied to the wave equation; the finite-difference approximation is given by (8.12). Since $\bar{V}_i^n$ satisfies the equation exactly, we obtain the equation for the errors

$$\frac{\epsilon_i^{n+1} - \epsilon_i^n}{\Delta t} = -\frac{a}{2\Delta k}\left(\epsilon_{i+1}^n - \epsilon_{i-1}^n\right)$$

Because the equation is linear, we can decompose the error into its Fourier components. If every Fourier component of the error is not amplified by the differencing method, then the error as a whole is not amplified. Thus, we represent the error as a Fourier series

$$\epsilon_i^n = \sum_{j=-N}^{N} E_j^n e^{\mathrm{i}\,i\phi(j)}$$

where $\mathrm{i} = \sqrt{-1}$ and E_j^n is the amplitude of the jth harmonic. $\phi = j\pi/N$ is the phase angle, where $-\pi \leq \phi \leq \pi$. A complete description of this analysis is given in Richtmyer and Morton (1967) and Hirsch (1988). If we substitute this expression for the error into the difference equation, we can determine how each harmonic is amplified by the scheme. For an arbitrary Fourier component of the error, we have

$$\frac{E^{n+1} - E^n}{\Delta t} e^{\mathrm{i}\,i\phi} = -\frac{a}{2\Delta k}\left(E^n e^{\mathrm{i}\,(i+1)\phi} - E^n e^{\mathrm{i}\,(i-1)\phi}\right)$$

$$E^{n+1} - E^n = -\frac{a\Delta t}{2\Delta k} E^n \left(e^{\mathrm{i}\phi} - e^{-\mathrm{i}\phi}\right)$$

If we define the amplification factor, G, as

$$G = \frac{E^{n+1}}{E_n}$$

the error will not grow over time if

$$|G| = \left|\frac{E^{n+1}}{E_n}\right| \leq 1, \quad \text{for all } \phi$$

For the case of the central-difference method, we have

$$G = 1 - \mathrm{i}\,\frac{a\Delta t}{\Delta k} \sin\phi$$

$$|G|^2 = 1 + \left(\frac{a\Delta t}{\Delta k}\right)^2 \sin^2\phi$$

Therefore, $|G| > 1$ for non-zero time steps, and the error is always amplified. Thus, the solution is always unstable, and the scheme is *unconditionally unstable.*

For the backward-difference scheme applied to the wave equation with positive a, the amplification factor is

$$G = 1 - 2\frac{a\Delta t}{\Delta k} \sin^2\frac{\phi}{2} - \mathrm{i}\,\frac{a\Delta t}{\Delta k} \sin\phi$$

and the scheme is stable if

$$0 < \frac{a\Delta t}{\Delta k} \leq 1$$

This result is commonly known as the Courant–Friedrichs–Lewy (CFL) condition. The quantity, $a\Delta t/\Delta k$, is known as the *CFL* number or the Courant number, and represents a non-dimensional time step. The backward-difference method is said to be *conditionally stable.*

The decomposition of the error into its Fourier components is the basis of von Neumann stability analysis. It should be noted that it relies on the linearity of the governing equations; for nonlinear problems, it is not possible to isolate the individual Fourier components. Thus, von Neumann stability analysis only serves as a guide to the solution of nonlinear equations. However, one can be assured that if the differencing scheme is not suitable for a linear problem, it will not be suitable for an analogous (non-constant coefficient) nonlinear problem. In practice, nonlinear problems usually have a more restrictive time step limit than that implied by the CFL condition.

Note that for the conditionally stable schemes, the maximum stable time step is proportional to the grid spacing, Δk. Thus, as the grid is refined to reduce the error in the solution, the maximum stable time step is also reduced. This typically results in more time steps to produce a converged steady-state solution. To counter this, we can derive an implicit time integration method that, at least for the linear wave equation, does not have this stringent time step limit. Consider the differencing scheme

$$\frac{V_i^{n+1} - V_i^n}{\Delta t} = -\frac{a}{2\Delta k}\left(V_{i+1}^{n+1} - V_{i-1}^{n+1}\right) + O(\Delta k^2) + O(\Delta t)$$

This method uses a central-difference approximation for the k derivative, but the derivative is evaluated at the future time level, $n + 1$. This is an implicit scheme because the solution at the new time level cannot be obtained explicitly from the solution at the present time level. Rather, it must be computed implicitly; in this case, we must solve a tridiagonal system of equations.

The amplification factor of this implicit method is given by

$$G = \frac{1}{1 + \mathrm{i}a\Delta t/\Delta k \sin\phi},$$

which always satisfies the stability condition. Therefore, the scheme is *unconditionally stable* for the linear wave equation. In principle, we can take infinite time steps and obtain a stable solution. This solution will not be time accurate because the differencing scheme is first-order in time. However, this is not a concern because we are only interested in the steady-state solution which is not a function of time. Therefore, any stable time step may be used to obtain the converged solution. For nonlinear problems, the method will be stable up to a limiting time step, but this time step cannot be predicted from von Neumann stability analysis.

8.3.6 *Upwind differencing method for $V(t, k)$*

The foregoing analysis can be used to develop methods that sense the appropriate direction of differencing and locally adjust the differencing scheme. For the linear wave equation, we saw that when $a > 0$ we use a backward difference, and when $a < 0$ we use a forward difference. We can develop a scheme that automatically switches the differencing method depending on the local coefficient on V_k. For example if $a = a(k)$

$$\frac{V_i^{n+1} - V_i^n}{\Delta t} = -\frac{a_i^+}{\Delta k}\left(V_i^n - V_{i-1}^n\right) - \frac{a_i^-}{\Delta k}\left(V_{i+1}^n - V_i^n\right) + O(\Delta k) + O(\Delta t),$$

where a_i^+ and a_i^- are determined by the sign of a:

$$a_i^+ = \tfrac{1}{2}(a_i + |a_i|)$$
$$a_i^- = \tfrac{1}{2}(a_i - |a_i|)$$

Thus, $a^+ = a$ and $a^- = 0$ when $a > 0$, and vice versa, and we obtain the correct biasing of the difference approximation for all values of a. This is an "upwind" method because the differencing scheme uses data from the upwind direction (in the opposite direction to the solution's trajectory in capital-stock time).

We can now return to our dynamic programming problem, and derive an upwind finite-difference approximation to the differential equation. Let us group terms in (8.5) to get a single coefficient on V_k:

$$V_t + \rho V = \left(\frac{1-\omega}{\omega} V_k^{1/\omega - 1} + \lambda k^\theta - \delta k\right) V_k + \tfrac{1}{2}\sigma^2 k^2 V_{kk}$$

Then, the first-order upwind difference method is

$$\frac{V_i^{n+1} - V_i^n}{\Delta t} + \rho V_i^n = -\frac{a_i^+}{\Delta k}\left(V_i^n - V_{i-1}^n\right) - \frac{a_i^-}{\Delta k}\left(V_{i+1}^n - V_i^n\right) + \tfrac{1}{2}\sigma^2 k_i^2 \left(\frac{V_{i+1}^n - 2V_i^n + V_{i-1}^n}{\Delta k^2}\right) + O(\Delta k) + O(\Delta t) \quad (8.13)$$

where

$$a_i = -\frac{1-\omega}{\omega}(V_k)_i^{1/\omega - 1} - \lambda k_i^\theta + \delta k_i$$

This is an extension of the upwind approach; in this case, the coefficients $a^\pm$ depend on k and V_k. Of course, since this is a nonlinear equation, there is no theory that dictates that this is a stable method. It is simply a matter of seeing if the method works in practice. However, we have a much better chance of getting the method to work because it is based on a method that is (conditionally) stable for a linear model equation. It is clear that the previous central-difference method, (8.10), did not have a chance of working.

The second derivative term in (8.5) has been represented with a central-difference approximation. This was chosen because a von Neumann stability analysis for the model equation,

$$V_t - \alpha V_{kk} = 0$$

shows that a central difference approximation is conditionally stable. The time step is governed by the Fourier number, $Fo = \alpha \Delta t / \Delta k^2$, and the scheme is stable for

$$0 \le Fo \le \tfrac{1}{2}$$

which implies that $\alpha \ge 0$, and $Fo \le \frac{1}{2}$. Generally, the second derivative terms are less difficult to approximate because they are diffusive in nature, and do not have a preferred direction.

8.3.7 *Numerical results*

Figure 8.5 plots the results of a calculation using the upwind method started from an initial guess for V_i^0, and run until the residual is small. The parameters used are: $\omega = \theta = 0.5$, $\rho = 0.05$, $\lambda = 1.0$, $\delta = 0.025$, $\sigma = 0.0$. We see that the solution is very close to the exact solution. Figure 8.6 plots the consumption function, $V_k^{1/\omega - 1}$, obtained from the numerical solution. Again, the numerical solution predicts the exact solution very well.

These calculations show that the finite-difference methods can indeed be used to solve the partial differential equations that govern the dynamic economies. However, the differencing methods must be chosen carefully, and the most obvious method is not always the best method.

At this point, it is useful to discuss the accuracy of the finite-difference solution of the dynamic programming problem. We know the exact value of the steady-state value of the capital stock, k_s, from (8.7). Thus, we can compare the computations to this result for various values of ω and different numbers of grid points. This is done in Fig. 8.7, and we see that the first-order accurate finite-difference approximation gives an accurate prediction of k_s for large values of ω. However, at $\omega = 0.1$, a large number of grid points has to be used to obtain a small error in k_s. This is because the solution, $V(k)$, increases in nonlinearity with decreasing ω. This is an illustration that this first-order accurate method has a truncation error that is proportional to $\frac{1}{2}\Delta k V_{kk}$. Note also from Fig. 8.7 that for a given value of ω, the error is reduced by a factor of 2 by doubling the grid size. That is, the error is linear in Δk as expected. This motivates the

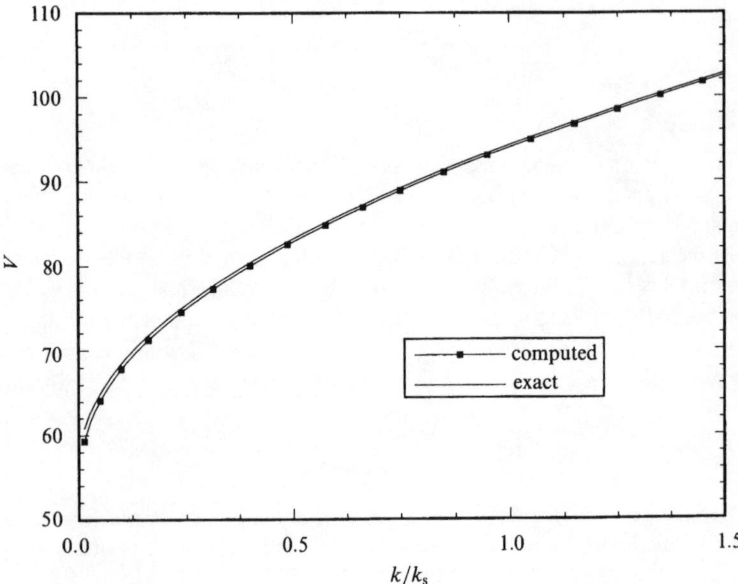

FIG. 8.5. Numerical solution of the dynamic programming problem (8.5) using an upwind differencing method; $\omega = \theta = 0.5$, $\rho = 0.05$, $\lambda = 1.0$, $\delta = 0.025$, $\sigma = 0.0$.

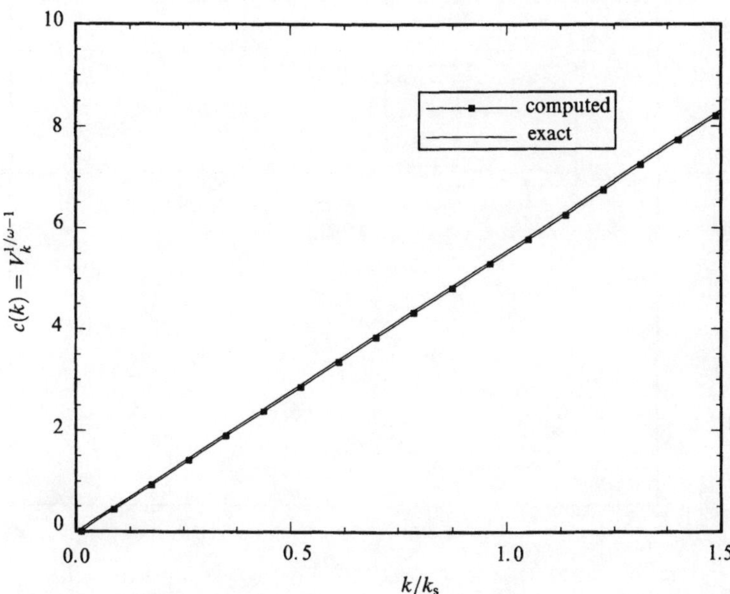

FIG. 8.6. Consumption function, $V_k^{1/\omega-1}$, computed from the numerical solution of the dynamic programming problem.

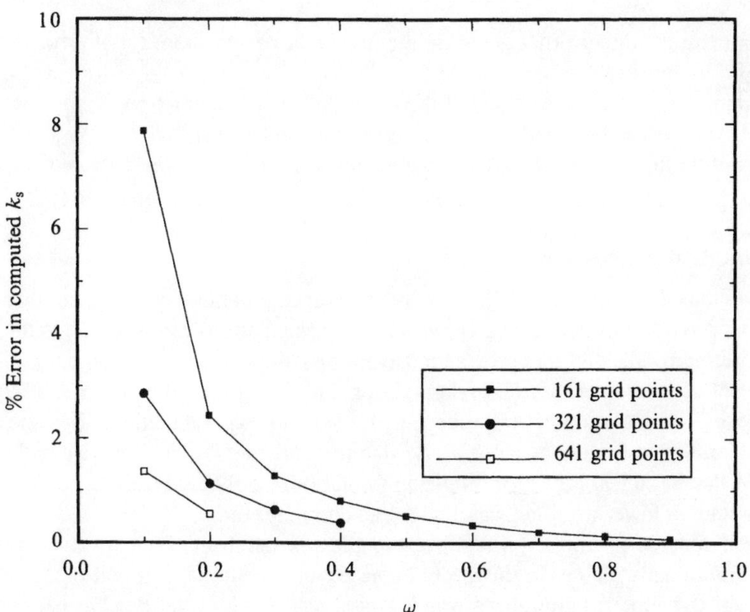

FIG. 8.7. Variation of error in the computed steady-state capital stock, k_s, as a function of ω; $\theta = 0.4$, $\rho = 0.05$, $\lambda = 1.0$, $\delta = 0.025$, $\sigma = 0.0$.

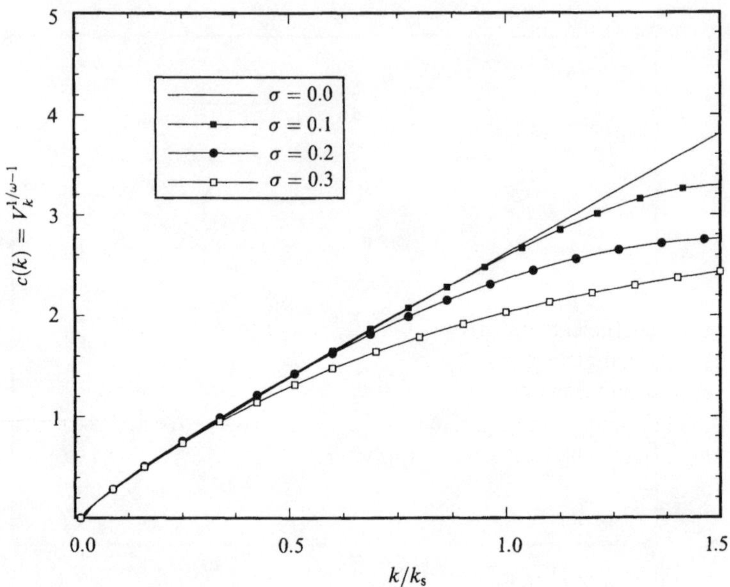

FIG. 8.8. Dependence of computed consumption function on σ, $\omega = 0.5$, $\theta = 0.4$, $\rho = 0.05$, $\lambda = 1.0$, $\delta = 0.025$.

development of higher-order accurate methods that have a more rapid error reduction with grid spacing.

Figure 8.8 presents the results of the finite-difference calculation for the case where $\sigma \neq 0$ with $\omega = 0.5$, and all of the other parameters unchanged. We see that the consumption function decreases at large values of capital stock, as expected.

8.4 Implicit method for $V(t, k)$

The previous results show that the upwind differencing method can be used to solve the dynamic programming problem. However, these calculations can be costly if the grid is highly refined or the problem is extended to multiple dimensions. The computational cost is a result of starting with an initial condition, and integrating the differential equation in time until the solution is time-independent. With an explicit method, the time step of this integration is limited because of the stability constraints. Thus, if we can develop a method that has a less stringent time-step limitation, we should be able to converge to a steady state in fewer time steps and with less computer time.

We discussed an implicit method above and saw that for the linear wave equation it is unconditionally stable. In this section, we develop a similar implicit method for the nonlinear dynamic programming problem and test its performance. We use the same upwind differencing method for derivatives with respect to the capital stock and evaluate those derivatives at the future $(n+1)$ time level. This results in the difference equation

$$\frac{V_i^{n+1} - V_i^n}{\Delta t} + \rho V_i^{n+1} = -\frac{a_i^+}{\Delta k}\left(V_i^{n+1} - V_{i-1}^{n+1}\right) - \frac{a_i^-}{\Delta k}\left(V_{i+1}^{n+1} - V_i^{n+1}\right)$$

$$+ \tfrac{1}{2}\sigma^2 k_i^2 \left(\frac{V_{i+1}^{n+1} - 2V_i^{n+1} + V_{i-1}^{n+1}}{\Delta k^2}\right) + O(\Delta t) + O(\Delta k)$$

Note that the coefficients on the first-derivative approximations, $a_i^\pm$, are functions of V also. To be completely consistent, we should evaluate those terms at the future time level as well. However, this is not required to obtain the correct answer, because at the time-independent solution $V_i^{n+1} = V_i^n$. Therefore, to simplify the derivation of the implicit method, let us evaluate these quantities at the present (n) time level.

If we let $\Delta V_i^n = V_i^{n+1} - V_i^n$, we can write the implicit problem as:

$$\left(\alpha_i^- - \beta_i\right)\Delta V_{i+1}^n + \left(1 + \alpha_i^+ - \alpha_i^- + 2\beta_i + \Delta t\,\rho\right)\Delta V_i^n + \left(-\alpha_i^+ - \beta_i\right)\Delta V_{i-1}^n$$

$$= -\alpha_i^+\left(V_i^n - V_{i-1}^n\right) - \alpha_i^-\left(V_{i+1}^n - V_i^n\right) + \beta_i\left(V_{i+1}^n - 2V_i^n + V_{i-1}\right) - \Delta t\,\rho V_i^n, \tag{8.14}$$

where $\alpha^\pm = \Delta t\, a^\pm/\Delta k$ and $\beta = \Delta t\,\sigma^2 k^2/2\Delta k^2$. We can see that this is a tridiagonal system of equations for ΔV_i^n. Symbolically, we have

$$\begin{pmatrix} B_0 & A_0 & C_0 & & & \\ & \ddots & \ddots & \ddots & & \\ & & B_i & A_i & C_i & \\ & & & \ddots & \ddots & \ddots \\ & & & B_{i_{\max}} & A_{i_{\max}} & C_{i_{\max}} \end{pmatrix}^n \begin{pmatrix} \vdots \\ \Delta V_{i-1} \\ \Delta V_i \\ \Delta V_{i+1} \\ \vdots \end{pmatrix}^n = \begin{pmatrix} \vdots \\ RHS_i \\ \vdots \end{pmatrix}^n$$

Again, the solution cannot be computed explicitly from the present solution; however, the tridiagonal system is easy and efficient to solve (see the Thomas algorithm in Hirsch, 1988; and Press *et al.*, 1992).

Note that because of the upwind differencing approach for the k derivatives, the system is diagonally dominant for any Δt. Thus, there are many approximate solution methods for the system of equations. For example, we could move the off-diagonal terms to the right-hand side, and iteratively include them in the solution using a series of relaxation steps. Because of the diagonal dominance of the system, this approach will converge. Also, we could completely neglect the off-diagonal terms, and again this method will converge. In any case, the time-dependent answer is independent of the implicit operator used.

The simplest approximate method is a "diagonal" method that may be derived by ignoring the off-diagonal terms

$$\begin{aligned}\left(1+\alpha_i^+ - \alpha_i^- + 2\beta_i + \Delta t\,\rho\right)\Delta V_i^n = &-\alpha_i^+\left(V_i^n - V_{i-1}^n\right) - \alpha_i^-\left(V_{i+1}^n - V_i^n\right)\\ &+ \beta_i\left(V_{i+1}^n - 2V_i^n + V_{i-1}\right) - \Delta t\,\rho V_i^n\end{aligned}$$

This set of equations is no more expensive to solve than the explicit method, and in some cases is considerably more effective. It also generalizes easily to multiple dimensions, unlike the full implicit method given by (8.14).

8.4.1 *Comparison of convergence rates*

Figure 8.9 compares the convergence rates of the explicit, implicit, and diagonal methods for the baseline parameters. We see that the implicit method converges to the final solution in the smallest number of iterations. Note that there is an optimal time step for the implicit method – in this case $CFL = 10$ gives the best convergence rate. At higher time steps, the method does not converge to machine zero. The diagonal method is not as effective as the more exact implicit method, but it is still at least twice as fast as the explicit method.

Even for the implicit method, about 2000 iterations are required to obtain a steady-state solution. It should be noted that a very poor initial guess for V was used and that the differential equation has a different form than those commonly solved in physics

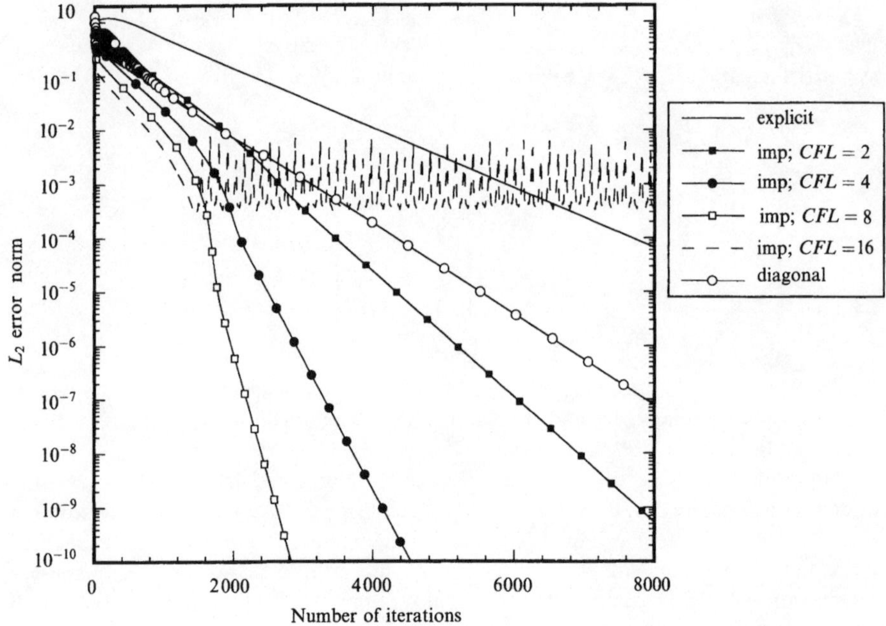

FIG. 8.9. Convergence history for different time integration methods.

and engineering. Thus, it is very likely that with more work the convergence properties could be improved significantly. For example, the coefficient on V_k could be linearized and included in the implicit solution. Also, to reduce the number of grid points, a non-uniform grid spacing could be used to cluster grid points near regions of strong nonlinearity.

8.5 Upwind method for $c(t, k)$

In this section, we discuss the solution of the differential equation for the consumption function, rather than the value function. To derive this equation, we consider the case where the stochastic term is zero, and obtain from (8.5) the time-dependent differential equation

$$c_t = (f(k) - c(k))c_k + \frac{u'(c)}{u''(c)}(f'(k) - \rho)$$

With $u(c) = c^\omega/\omega$ and $f(k) = \lambda k^\theta - \delta k$, we obtain

$$c_t = (\lambda k^\theta - \delta k - c)c_k + \frac{1}{\omega - 1}(\lambda\theta k^{\theta-1} - \delta - \rho)c$$

Using the same approach as above, an upwind finite-difference approximation to this equation is

$$\frac{c_i^{n+1} - c_i^n}{\Delta t} = -\frac{a_i^+}{\Delta k}\left(c_i^n - c_{i-1}^n\right) - \frac{a_i^-}{\Delta k}\left(c_{i+1}^n - c_i^n\right) + S_i^n$$

where

$$a_i = -\lambda k_i^\theta + \delta k_i + c_i$$
$$S_i = \frac{1}{\omega - 1}\left(\lambda\theta k_i^{\theta-1} - \delta - \rho\right)c_i$$

Figure 8.10 plots the computed and exact consumption functions. In this case, the numerical method gives the exact result for all of values of k. This is not surprising because the solution is linear in k, and therefore the first-order method has no truncation error.

8.5.1 *Implicit method for* $c(t, k)$

Now let us consider an implicit time integration method for the consumption function variation. Again, evaluate all of the quantities at the future time level

$$\frac{c_i^{n+1} - c_i^n}{\Delta t} = -\frac{a_i^+}{\Delta k}\left(c_i^{n+1} - c_{i-1}^{n+1}\right) - \frac{a_i^-}{\Delta k}\left(c_{i+1}^{n+1} - c_i^{n+1}\right) + S_i^{n+1}$$

To estimate the source term at the future time level, linearize using

$$S_i^{n+1} = S_i^n + \left.\frac{\partial S}{\partial c}\right|_i^n \left(c_i^{n+1} - c_i^n\right) + O(\Delta t)$$

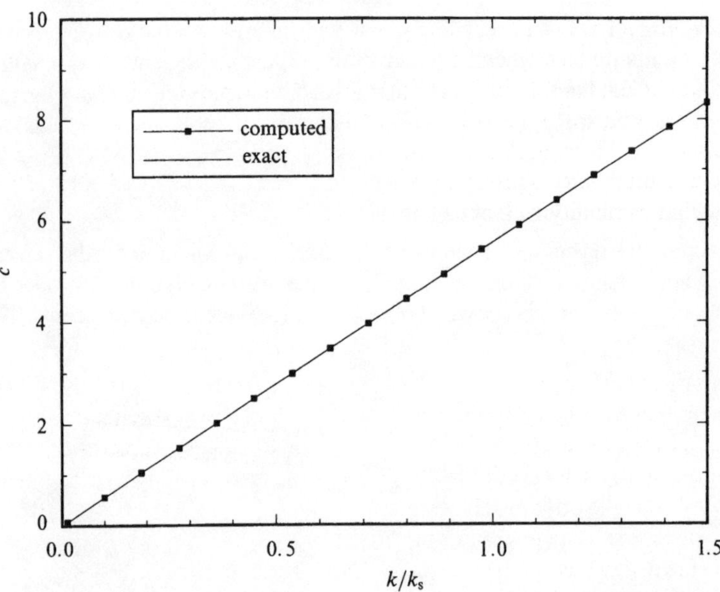

FIG. 8.10. Comparison of computed consumption function with exact solution; $\omega = \theta = 0.5$, $\rho = 0.05$, $\lambda = 1.0$, $\delta = 0.025$, $\sigma = 0.0$.

Thus, the implicit approximation is

$$\alpha_i^- \Delta c_{i+1}^n + \left(1 + \alpha_i^+ - \alpha_i^- - \Delta t \frac{\partial S}{\partial c}\right) \Delta c_i^n - \alpha_i^+ \Delta c_{i-1}^n$$
$$= -\alpha_i^+ \left(c_i^n - c_{i-1}^n\right) - \alpha_i^- \left(c_{i+1}^n - c_i^n\right) + \Delta t S_i^n \tag{8.15}$$

This method converges to the answer shown in Fig. 8.10, but the convergence rate is poor, and the maximum *CFL* number that can be used is about 2.

Let us consider a model equation for this problem to see if it is possible to determine the reason for this poor convergence and stringent time-step limitation. A useful model equation results from the situation where c_k is small. Then

$$c_t = \frac{1}{\omega - 1}(\lambda \theta k^{\theta - 1} - \delta - \rho)c = S$$

An implicit representation of the form used in (8.15) is

$$\frac{c^{n+1} - c^n}{\Delta t} = S^{n+1} \simeq S^n + \frac{\partial S}{\partial c}(c^{n+1} - c^n)$$
$$c^{n+1} = c^n + \frac{\Delta t \, S^n}{1 - s\Delta t}$$

where $s = \partial S/\partial c$. We can see that if $s > 0$ and Δt is large, the method will produce erroneous results. In fact, when $s\Delta t = 1$ the change in the solution is singular, and for larger values of Δt, the solution changes in the *wrong* direction.

Because $\omega < 1$, $s = 1/(\omega - 1)(\lambda\theta k^{\theta-1} - \delta - \rho)$ will be positive for large values of k. Therefore, there is an inherent time-step limitation given by $\Delta t < (1 - \omega)/(\delta + \rho)$. Note that this limitation is a result of the implicit time integration method. We can remove this limitation by modifying the linearization of S so that $\partial S/\partial c$ is always negative. For example, we can use

$$\frac{\partial S}{\partial c} = s \simeq \frac{1}{\omega - 1}\lambda\theta k^{\theta-1} \leq 0$$

It seems somewhat arbitrary to have removed these terms from the implicit operator. (Remember that by modifying the operator, we do not change the converged solution, we simply change the evolution towards the converged solution.) However, this change is motivated by the analysis of the model equation, but there is no guarantee that the method will actually work better.

In practice, this change in the method leads to a huge improvement in the convergence of the method, as can be seen in Fig. 8.11. Now there is no time-step limitation, and the implicit method converges in about 10 iterations with $CFL = 10^4$. With this modification, the diagonal method also works well, converging in about 130 iterations.

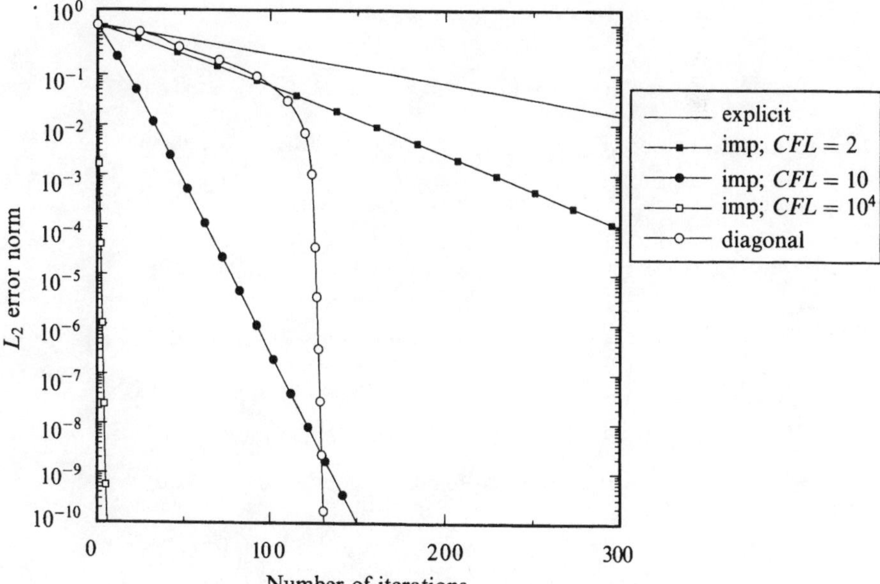

FIG. 8.11. Convergence history for modified implict methods for the consumption function.

Thus, the use of the model equation was instructive in showing how to improve the method.

8.6 Upwind method for a two-state problem

Now let us extend the finite-difference method to a problem with two states. Consider the agent's problem given by

$$\max_c E \int_0^\infty e^{-\rho t} u(c)\, dt$$

subject to

$$dk = ((1-\tau) r(K) k + w(K) - c + T(K))\, dt + \sigma(k, K)\, dz$$

$$dK = (F(K) - C(K) - G(K))\, dt + \sigma(K, K)\, dz$$

where c is the individual consumption level, k is individual capital stock, $C(K)$ is aggregate consumption, K is aggregate capital stock, $F(K)$ is aggregate output, $G(K)$ is government spending, and $T(K)$ is transfers. Let

$$u(c) = c^\omega/\omega, \quad F(k) = \lambda k^\theta - \delta k, \quad r = F_K, \quad w = F - F_K K, \quad G = \tau F_K K$$

The dynamic programming equation for the value function, $V(k, K)$, is

$$\begin{aligned} V_t + \rho V = \max_c \Big\{ & u(c) + V_k((1-\tau)(\theta \lambda K^{\theta-1} - \delta)k + \lambda K^\theta (1-\theta) - c) \\ & + V_K(\lambda K^\theta - C(K) - \tau(\theta \lambda K^\theta - \delta K)) \\ & + \tfrac{1}{2}(\sigma(k, K)^2 V_{kk} + 2\sigma(k, K)\sigma(K, K) V_{kK} + \sigma(K, K)^2 V_{KK}) \Big\} \end{aligned}$$

The first-order condition, $u'(c) = V_k(k, K)$, gives the differential equation

$$\begin{aligned} V_t + \rho V = & \frac{1-\omega}{\omega} V_k^{\omega/\omega - 1} + V_k \left((1-\tau)(\theta \lambda K^{\theta-1} - \delta)k + \lambda K^\theta (1-\theta) \right) \\ & + V_K \left(\lambda K^\theta - \delta K - V_k(K, K)^{1/\omega - 1} - \tau(\theta \lambda K^\theta - \delta K) \right) \\ & + \tfrac{1}{2} \left(\sigma(k, K)^2 V_{kk} + 2\sigma(k, K)\sigma(K, K) V_{kK} + \sigma(K, K)^2 V_{KK} \right) \end{aligned} \quad (8.16)$$

We define the value function on a two-dimensional, equispaced grid using

$$V(t, k, K) = V(t_n, k_i, K_j) = V(n\,\Delta t, i\,\Delta k, j\,\Delta K) = V_{i,j}^n$$

Now we can derive the upwind finite-difference approximation to (8.16):

$$\begin{aligned} \frac{V_{i,j}^{n+1} - V_{i,j}^n}{\Delta t} + \rho V_{i,j}^n = & -\frac{a_{i,j}^+}{\Delta k}\left(V_{i,j}^n - V_{i-1,j}^n\right) - \frac{a_{i,j}^-}{\Delta k}\left(V_{i+1,j}^n - V_{i,j}^n\right) \\ & - \frac{b_{i,j}^+}{\Delta K}\left(V_{i,j}^n - V_{i,j-1}^n\right) - \frac{b_{i,j}^-}{\Delta K}\left(V_{i,j+1}^n - V_{i,j}^n\right) \end{aligned}$$

where

$$a_{i,j} = -\frac{1-\omega}{\omega}(V_k)_{i,j}^{1/\omega-1} - (1-\tau)(\theta\lambda K_{i,j}^{\theta-1} - \delta)k_{i,j} - \lambda K_{i,j}^{\theta}(1-\theta)$$

$$b_{i,j} = -\lambda K^{\theta} + \delta K + V_k(K,K)^{1/\omega-1} + \tau(\theta\lambda K^{\theta} - \delta K)$$

Again, we choose $\omega = \theta = 0.5$, $\rho = 0.05$, $\lambda = 1.0$, $\delta = 0.025$. For $\sigma = \tau = 0$, we obtain the exact solution given by (8.6) along the line $k = K$; the numerical solution agrees with this result.

The extension of the method to implicit time integration is not completely straightforward because the resulting system of equations is expensive to solve. Instead, because the system of equations is diagonally dominant, it is customary to move the off-diagonal terms to the right-hand side and solve the system iteratively. One effective approach is to perform several relaxation steps where the off-diagonal terms are evaluated using the data from the previous relaxation step. For the first relaxation step, the off-diagonal terms are ignored. Usually about four of these relatively inexpensive relaxation steps is sufficient to solve the system of equations. This is far more efficient that directly inverting the system. (For more details, see Candler *et al.*, 1994.)

8.7 Boundary conditions

In the preceding discussion, we did not discuss the treatment of the boundary conditions at the edges of the computational domain. However, this is an important concern. In this section, we outline some of the approaches for determining the boundary conditions.

In the calculation of the single-state value function discussed above, boundary conditions had to be applied at $k = 0$ and $k = 2k_s$ for the grid chosen. We know that $c(t, 0) = 0$, and thus for the solution of the consumption function the first of these boundary conditions may be set easily. For the value function, $V_k(t, 0) \to \infty$; this is a very difficult boundary condition to set numerically. However, in this problem the boundary condition takes care of itself because for k near zero, $a^+ = 0$ in (8.13). Then, the differencing method uses data biased to the right of the origin, and the value of the solution at $k = 0$ is never used. Thus, in practice the boundary condition at $k = 0$ is not needed.

At the $k = k_{\max}$ boundary we know that $V_k(t, k \to \infty) = 0$, and thus it makes sense to set $V_k = 0$ at the edge of the domain. However, at $k = 2k_s$, the slope of the function is not close to zero and the boundary condition is not appropriate. In this case, we can do one of the following things:

- Use the boundary condition $V_k(t, k_{\max}) = 0$ and extend $k_{\max}$ far enough away from the region of interest that errors at the boundary are not important. This can be done efficiently by increasing the grid spacing for large values of k. (The differencing methods have to be modified slightly for the non-equispaced grid.)
- Assume a value for V_k at the boundary. This must be obtained from some other information.
- Extrapolate the value of $V(t, k_{\max})$ from the interior by assuming that the slope of the solution at the boundary is given by the slope at the last point in the interior. This approach may seem sensible, but it is prone to errors because extrapolations that do not contain any information about the solution are likely to cause large errors at the boundary.

- In some cases, $a^{-} = 0$ at $k_{\max}$ and the solution does not depend on the boundary condition. In this situation, any reasonable boundary condition (zeroth-order extrapolation, for example) will work effectively.

The first of these approaches is generally preferred (unless the latter condition holds). In the calculations presented above, this method is used and the solution for $k > 1.5k_s$ is affected by the boundary condition. The validity of this approach was tested by extending the domain and checking that the solution does not change.

8.8 Summary

Finite-difference methods have been used to solve the partial differential equations that result from a continuous-time representation of a dynamic economy. We have shown that with the appropriate choice of differencing methods we can obtain accurate solutions of these differential equations. The choice of the differencing method was motivated by the analysis of a simple linear model equation. This showed that the differencing method must be chosen depending on the trajectory of the solution. This idea was used to develop upwind or solution-dependent differencing methods that sense the appropriate direction of differencing.

Several implicit time integration methods were discussed. In principle, these methods are stable for any time step, and therefore it should be possible to reduce the cost of the calculation. We found that for the value function formulation we were able to increase the time step to about 10 times that of an explicit method; it is likely that this could be improved with some work. In the case of the consumption function formulation, we found that by analyzing a model problem we were able to stabilize the time integration for any time step, resulting in converged solutions in 10 time steps.

There are many books that may be consulted for more details concerning the development of these methods. Classical references that are useful concerning the analysis of model equations are those of Courant and Hilbert (1962) and Richtmyer and Morton (1967). More recent works that discuss the types of methods described in this chapter are by Yee (1989), LeVeque (1992), and Ferziger and Peric (1996); a less detailed but adequate description is also given in Hirsch (1988).

Part III

Solving some dynamic economies

9

OPTIMAL FISCAL POLICY IN A LINEAR STOCHASTIC ECONOMY

Thomas J. Sargent[1] and François R. Velde

9.1 Introduction

Computation of optimal fiscal policies for Lucas and Stokey's (1983) economy requires repeated evaluations of the present value of the government's surplus, an object formally equivalent to an asset price. The functional equation for an asset price is typically difficult to solve. In this chapter, we specify a linear quadratic version of Lucas and Stokey's economy, making both asset pricing computations and optimal fiscal policy calculations easy. The key steps are described in Section 9.7 for two basic kinds of stochastic process: a stochastic first-order linear difference equation and a Markov chain. We use the Lucas–Stokey economy to exhibit features of Lucas and Stokey's model, and how they compare to Barro's (1979) tax-smoothing model.[2]

9.2 Review of Barro's model

Barro (1979) formalized the idea that taxes should be smooth by saying that they should be a martingale, regardless of the stochastic process for government expenditures. Hansen *et al.* (1991) use the following linear quadratic model to formalize Barro's conclusions. The government chooses a rule for taxes to maximize the criterion

$$-E\sum_{t=0}^{\infty}\beta^t T_t^2 \tag{9.1}$$

subject to an initial condition B_0 and

$$\begin{aligned}\gamma(L)g_t &= \rho(L)w_t \\ B_{t+1} &= R(B_t + g_t - T_t)\end{aligned} \tag{9.2}$$

where T_t, g_t, B_t denote tax collections, government expenditures, and the stock of risk-free government debt inclusive of interest, respectively, and where R is a gross risk-free rate of return on government debt and $\beta \in (0, 1)$ is a discount factor. In (9.2), $\gamma(L)$ and $\rho(L)$ are stable one-sided polynomials in non-negative powers of the lag operator L, and w_t is a scalar martingale difference sequence adapted to its own history. Under the

[1] The views expressed herein do not necessarily represent those of the Federal Reserve Bank of Chicago or the Federal Reserve System.

[2] The asset pricing calculations emanate from Hansen (1987) and Hansen and Sargent (1999).

assumption that $R\beta = 1$, the solution of this problem that satisfies the side condition $E_0 \sum_{t=0}^{\infty} \beta^t T_t^2 < +\infty$ is a rule for taxes of the form

$$T_t - T_{t-1} = [(1-\beta)\rho(\beta)/\gamma(\beta)]w_t \tag{9.3}$$

Using (9.3) with (9.2) shows that B_{t+1} is cointegrated with T_t.[3]

Equation (9.3) asserts the striking property that the serial correlation properties of taxes are independent of the serial correlation properties of government expenditures. That a random walk with small innovation variance appears smooth is the sense of 'tax smoothing' that emerges from Barro's analysis. This outcome depends on the debt being risk-free.

The second equation of (9.2) can be written

$$\pi_{t+1} = B_{t+1} - R[B_t - (T_t - g_t)] \equiv 0 \tag{9.4}$$

where π_{t+1} is interpretable as the pay-off on government debt in excess of the risk-free rate. Barro's model has T_t adjust permanently by a small amount in response to a surprise in g_t, w_t, and has B_{t+1} make the rest of the adjustment to enforce (9.4) period by period. These adjustments make the cumulative excess pay-off to government creditors be

$$\Pi_t = \sum_{s=1}^{t} \pi_s \equiv 0 \tag{9.5}$$

The adjustments are very different in Lucas and Stokey's model.

Lucas and Stokey (1983) re-examined the optimal taxation problem in an equilibrium economy with complete markets, where the government issues state-contingent debt, not only the risk-free debt in (9.2). In their analysis, tax smoothing in the form emphasized by Barro does not emerge. Taxes are not a martingale but rather have serial correlation properties that mirror those of government expenditures. A martingale lurks in their analysis, but as a counterpart to (9.5) for the cumulated excess pay-off to the government's creditors, not taxes, and only after appropriate adjustments for risk and risk aversion.

9.3 Lucas and Stokey's model

We present a linear quadratic version of Lucas and Stokey's (1983) model of optimal taxation in an economy without capital and compute a variety of examples.

9.3.1 *Exogenous processes and information*

Let x_t be an exogenous information vector. We shall use x_t to drive exogenous stochastic processes $g_t, d_t, b_t, {}_0s_t$, representing, respectively, government expenditures, an endowment, a preference shock, and a stream of promised coupon payments owed by the government at the beginning of time 0:

$$g_t = S_g x_t \tag{9.6a}$$

$$d_t = S_d x_t \tag{9.6b}$$

$$b_t = S_b x_t \tag{9.6c}$$

$${}_0s_t = {}_0S_s x_t \tag{9.6d}$$

[3] See Hansen *et al.* (1991).

We make one of two alternative assumptions about the underlying stochastic process x_t.

ASSUMPTION 9.1 The process x_t is an $n \times 1$ vector with given initial condition x_0 and is governed by

$$x_{t+1} = Ax_t + Cw_{t+1} \tag{9.7}$$

Here $\{w_{t+1}\}$ is a martingale difference sequence adapted to its own past and to x_0, and A is a stable matrix.

ASSUMPTION 9.2 The process x_t is an n-state Markov chain with transition probabilities arranged in the $n \times n$ matrix P with $P_{ij} = \text{Prob}(x_{t+1} = \bar{x}_j | x_t = \bar{x}_i)$.

9.3.2 *Technology*

There is a technology for converting one unit of labour ℓ_t into one unit of a single non-storable consumption good. Feasible allocations satisfy

$$c_t + g_t = d_t + \ell_t \tag{9.8}$$

9.3.3 *Households*

Markets are complete. At time 0, a representative consumer faces a scaled Arrow–Debreu price system[4] $\{p_t^0\}$ and a flat rate tax on labour $\{\tau_t\}$, and chooses consumption and labour supply to maximize:

$$-0.5E_0 \sum_{t=0}^{\infty} \beta^t [(c_t - b_t)^2 + \ell_t^2] \tag{9.9}$$

subject to the time 0 budget constraint

$$E_0 \sum_{t=0}^{\infty} \beta^t p_t^0 [d_t + (1 - \tau_t)\ell_t + {}_0s_t - c_t] = 0 \tag{9.10}$$

This states that the present value of consumption equals the present value of the endowment plus coupon payments on the initial government debt plus after-tax labour earnings. The scaled Arrow–Debreu prices are ordinary state prices divided by discount factors and conditional probabilities. The scaled Arrow–Debreu price system is a stochastic process.

9.3.4 *Government*

The government's time 0 budget constraint is

$$E_0 \sum_{t=0}^{\infty} \beta^t p_t^0 [(g_t + {}_0s_t) - \tau_t \ell_t] = 0 \tag{9.11}$$

Given the government expenditure process and the present value $E_0 \sum_{t=0}^{\infty} \beta^t p_t^0 {}_0s_t$, a feasible tax process must satisfy (9.11).

[4]The scaled Arrow–Debreu prices are ordinary state prices divided by probabilities and the time-t power of the discount factor, transformations that permit representing values as conditional expectations of scaled prices times quantities. See Hansen (1987) and Hansen and Sargent (1999).

9.3.5 *Equilibrium*

Definition 9.1 *L_0^2 is the space of random variables y_t measurable with respect to x_t and such that $E_0 \sum_{t=0}^{\infty} \beta^t y_t^2 < +\infty$.*

Definition 9.2 A feasible allocation *is a stochastic process $\{c_t, \ell_t\}$ that satisfies* (9.8). A tax system *is a scalar stochastic process $\{\tau_t\}$. A price system is a stochastic process $\{p_t^0\}$. The time t elements of each of these processes are assumed to be measurable with respect to x_t, and to belong to L_0^2.*

Definition 9.3 *An* equilibrium *is a feasible allocation, a price system, and a tax system that have the following properties:*

1. *Given the tax and price systems, the allocation solves the household's problem.*
2. *Given the price system, the allocation and the tax system satisfy the government's budget constraint.*

9.3.6 *Properties*

The first-order conditions for the household's problem imply that the equilibrium price system satisfies $p_t^0 = \mu(b_t - c_t)$, where μ is a numeraire that we set at $b_0 - c_0$. The preference specification permits the scaled Arrow–Debreu price p_t^0 to be expressed in terms of ratios of linear functions of the state:

$$p_t^0 = M_p x_t / M_p x_0$$

The preference specification will make it possible to express government time t revenues as the ratio of a quadratic function of the state at t to a linear function of the state at 0. The forms of these prices and taxes, together with the other objects in (9.9), reduce the technical problem to evaluating geometric sums of a quadratic form in the state. For Assumptions 9.1 and 9.2, Section 9.7 shows how to compute such sums.

9.3.7 *Ramsey problem*

There are many equilibria, indexed by tax systems. The Ramsey problem is to choose the tax system that delivers the equilibrium preferred by the representative household. The Ramsey problem assumes that at time 0 the government commits itself to the tax system, once and for all.

Definition 9.4 *The Ramsey problem is to choose an equilibrium that maximizes the household's welfare* (9.9). *The allocation that solves this problem is called the Ramsey allocation, and the associated tax system is called the Ramsey plan.*

9.3.8 *Solution strategy*

In solving the Ramsey problem, the government chooses all of the objects in an equilibrium, subject to the constraint on the equilibrium imposed by its budget constraint. Following a long line of researchers starting with Frank Ramsey (1927), we shall solve this problem using a 'first-order' approach that involves the following steps. The steps incorporate the properties required by the definition of equilibrium.

1. Obtain the first-order conditions for the household's problem and use them to express the tax system and the price system in terms of the allocation alone.

2. Substitute the expressions for the tax system and the price system obtained in step 1 into the government's budget constraint to obtain a single isoperimetric restriction on allocations.
3. Use Lagrangian methods to find the feasible allocation that maximizes the utility of the representative household subject to the restriction derived in step 2. The maximizer is the Ramsey allocation.
4. Use the expressions from step 1 to find the associated Ramsey equilibrium price and tax systems by evaluating them at the Ramsey allocation.

9.3.9 *Computation*

We now execute these four steps. The problem is set so that the mathematics of linear systems can support a solution.

Step 1. The household's first-order conditions imply

$$p_t^0 = (b_t - c_t)/(b_0 - c_0) \tag{9.12}$$

$$\tau_t = 1 - \frac{\ell_t}{b_t - c_t} \tag{9.13}$$

Step 2. Using (9.12) and (9.13), express (9.11) as

$$E_0 \sum_{t=0}^{\infty} \beta^t [(b_t - c_t)(g_t + {}_0s_t) - (b_t - c_t)\ell_t + \ell_t^2] = 0 \tag{9.14}$$

Equation (9.14) is often called the implementability constraint on the allocation.
Step 3. Consider the maximization problem associated with the Lagrangian:

$$J = E_0 \sum_{t=0}^{\infty} \beta^t \Big\{ -0.5\big[(c_t - b_t)^2 + \ell_t^2\big] + \lambda_0\big[(b_t - c_t)\ell_t - \ell_t^2$$
$$-(b_t - c_t)(g_t + {}_0s_t)\big] + \mu_{0t}[d_t + \ell_t - c_t - g_t]\Big\}$$

where λ_0 is the multiplier associated with the government's budget constraint, and μ_{0t} is the multiplier associated with the time t feasibility condition. Obtain the first-order conditions:

$$c_t: \quad -(c_t - b_t) + \lambda_0[-\ell_t + (g_t + {}_0s_t)] = \mu_{0t} \tag{9.15a}$$

$$\ell_t: \quad \ell_t - \lambda_0[(b_t - c_t) - 2\ell_t] = \mu_{0t} \tag{9.15b}$$

$$d_t + \ell_t = c_t + g_t \tag{9.15c}$$

We want to solve equations (9.15a), (9.15b), (9.15c) and the government's budget constraint (9.14) for an *allocation*. Our strategy is to begin by taking λ_0 as given and to solve (9.15) for an allocation contingent on λ_0. Then we shall use (9.14) to solve for λ_0.

Using the feasibility constraint $c_t = d_t + \ell_t - g_t$, we can express (9.15a), (9.15b) as

$$\ell_t - \lambda_0[(b_t - d_t - \ell_t + g_t) - 2\ell_t] = -(d_t + \ell_t - g_t - b_t) + \lambda_0[-\ell_t + (g_t + {}_0s_t)]$$

or

$$\ell_t = \tfrac{1}{2}(b_t - d_t + g_t) - \frac{\lambda_0}{2 + 4\lambda_0}(b_t - d_t - {}_0s_t)$$

We also derive

$$c_t = \frac{1}{2}(b_t + d_t - g_t) - \frac{\lambda_0}{2 + 4\lambda_0}(b_t - d_t - {}_0s_t)$$

Define $\tilde{c}_t = (b_t + d_t - g_t)/2$, $\tilde{\ell}_t = (b_t - d_t + g_t)/2$ and $m_t = (b_t - d_t - {}_0s_t)/2$. We have:

$$\ell_t = \tilde{\ell}_t - \mu m_t \tag{9.16a}$$

$$c_t = \tilde{c}_t - \mu m_t \tag{9.16b}$$

where, for convenience, we define

$$\mu = \frac{\lambda_0}{1 + 2\lambda_0} \tag{9.17}$$

Using (9.16a)–(9.16b), the general term of (9.14) can be written as:

$$\begin{aligned}(b_t - \tilde{c}_t)(g_t + {}_0s_t) - (b_t - \tilde{c}_t)\tilde{\ell}_t + \tilde{\ell}_t^2 - \mu m_t[-(g_t + {}_0s_t) + \tilde{\ell}_t - (b_t - \tilde{c}_t)\\ + 2\tilde{\ell}_t] + \mu^2 a_t^2 = (b_t - \tilde{c}_t)(g_t + {}_0s_t) - 2m_t^2\mu + 2m_t^2\mu^2\end{aligned}$$

where we used the fact that $2\tilde{\ell}_t = b_t - d_t + g_t$ and the fact that $\tilde{\ell}_t = b_t - \tilde{c}_t$ to reduce the bracketed factor in the second line.

This allows us to write (9.14) as:

$$a_0(x_0)(\mu^2 - \mu) + b_0(x_0) = 0 \tag{9.18}$$

where

$$\begin{aligned}a_0(x_0) &= E_0 \sum_{t=0}^{\infty} \beta^t \tfrac{1}{2}(b_t - d_t - {}_0s_t)^2\\ &= E_0 \sum_{t=0}^{\infty} \beta^t x_t' \tfrac{1}{2}[S_b - S_d - {}_0S_s]'[S_b - S_d - {}_0S_s]x_t\end{aligned} \tag{9.19}$$

and

$$b_0(x_0) = E_0 \sum_{t=0}^{\infty} \beta^t [(b_t - \tilde{c}_t)(g_t + {}_0s_t) - (b_t - \tilde{c}_t)\tilde{\ell}_t + \tilde{\ell}_t^2] \tag{9.20}$$

$$= E_0 \sum_{t=0}^{\infty} \beta^t \tfrac{1}{2}(b_t - d_t + g_t)(g_t + {}_0s_t)$$

$$= E_0 \sum_{t=0}^{\infty} \beta^t \tfrac{1}{2} x_t' [S_b - S_d + S_g]'[S_g + {}_0S_s]x_t \tag{9.21}$$

where the fact that $b_t - \tilde{c}_t = \tilde{\ell}_t$ was used. The 0 subscripts on the forms a_0 and b_0 denote their dependence on ${}_0S_s$. The coefficients in the polynomial expression of (9.18) are only functions of x_0 alone because, given the law of motion for the exogenous state x_t, the infinite sums can be computed using the algorithms described in Section 9.7.

Notice that $b_0(x_0)$, when expressed by (9.20), is simply the infinite sum on the left-hand side of (9.14) evaluated for the specific allocation $\{\tilde{c}_t, \tilde{\ell}_t\}$. That allocation solves the problem:

$$\max_{c,\ell} -0.5[(c - b_t)^2 + \ell^2]$$

subject to $c + g_t = \ell + d_t$. In other words, $\{\tilde{c}_t, \tilde{\ell}_t\}$ is the allocation that would be chosen by a social planner, or the Ramsey allocation when the government can resort to lump-sum taxation. The term $b_0(x_0)$ is the present-value of the stream of government spending commitments $\{g_t + {}_0s_t\}$, evaluated at the prices corresponding to the $\{\tilde{c}_t, \tilde{\ell}_t\}$ allocation. If that present value is 0, distortionary taxation is not necessary, and $\mu = 0$ (that is, $\lambda_0 = 0$) solves (9.18): the government's budget constraint is not binding. One configuration for which $b_0(x_0) = 0$ is when $g_t = -{}_0s_t$ for all t, but there are many others. Because markets are complete, the timing of the government's claims on the household does not matter. If the government were able to acquire such claims on the private sector in a non-distortionary way, it would be able to implement a first-best allocation.

When the net present value of the government's commitments is positive, we must solve (9.18) for a μ in $\left(0, \tfrac{1}{2}\right)$, corresponding to $\lambda_0 > 0$. The polynomial $a_0(x_0)\mu(1-\mu)$ is bounded above by $a_0(x_0)/4$, which means that government commitments that are "too large" cannot be supported by a Ramsey plan. If $b_0(x_0) < a_0(x_0)/4$ there exists a unique solution μ in $\left(0, \tfrac{1}{2}\right)$ and a unique $\lambda_0 > 0$. The Ramsey allocation can then be computed as

$$c_t = \tilde{c}_t - \mu m_t$$

$$= \tfrac{1}{2}([S_b + S_d - S_g] - \mu[S_b - S_d - {}_0S_s])x_t \tag{9.22a}$$

$$\ell_t = \tilde{\ell}_t - \mu m_t$$

$$= \tfrac{1}{2}([S_b - S_d + S_g] - \mu[S_b - S_d - {}_0S_s])x_t \tag{9.22b}$$

Step 4. The Ramsey plan is

$$\begin{aligned}\tau_t &= 1 - \frac{\ell_t}{b_t - c_t} \\ &= 1 - \frac{\tilde{\ell}_t - \mu m_t}{b_t - \tilde{c}_t + \mu m_t} \\ &= \frac{2\mu m_t}{\tilde{\ell}_t + \mu m_t} \\ &= \frac{2\mu[S_b - S_d - {}_0S_s]x_t}{([S_b - S_d + S_g] + \mu[S_b - S_d - {}_0S_s])x_t}\end{aligned} \tag{9.23}$$

Expression (9.23) shows how the stochastic properties of the tax rate mirror those for government expenditures when the endowment and the preference shocks are constant.

9.4 Martingale returns on government debt

9.4.1 *Recursive formulation of the government budget*

The government's budget constraint can be written

$$B_0 = E_0 \sum_{t=0}^{\infty} \beta^t p_t^0 (\tau_t \ell_t - g_t) \tag{9.24}$$

where $B_0 \equiv E_0 \sum_{t=0}^{\infty} \beta^t p_t^0 {}_0s_t$ is the time 0 present value of initial government debt obligations. Define

$$B_t \equiv E_t \sum_{j=0}^{\infty} \beta^j p_{t+j}^t (\tau_{t+j} \ell_{t+j} - g_{t+j}) \tag{9.25}$$

Along the Ramsey allocation, B_t can be computed as

$$B_t = \frac{E_t \sum_{j=0}^{\infty} \beta^j \left[(b_{t+j} - c_{t+j})\ell_{t+j} - \ell_{t+j}^2 - (b_{t+j} - c_{t+j})g_{t+j}\right]}{(b_t - c_t)} \tag{9.26}$$

which can evidently be expressed as a function of the time t state x_t: in particular, a quadratic form in x_t plus a constant divided by a linear form in x_t. The quantity B_t can be regarded as the time t value of government state contingent debt issued at $t-1$ and priced at t.

The government budget constraint can be be implemented recursively by issuing one-period state contingent debt represented as a stochastic process B_t that is measurable with respect to time t information. In particular, we can replace the single budget constraint (9.11) with the sequence of budget constraints for $t \geq 0$:

$$B_t = [\tau_t \ell_t - g_t] + \beta E_t \left[p_{t+1}^t B_{t+1}\right] \tag{9.27}$$

where $p_{t+1}^t = (b_{t+1} - c_{t+1})/(b_t - c_t)$ is the scaled Arrow–Debreu state price for one-period ahead claims at time t. We can think of the optimal plan as being implemented as follows. The government comes into period t with state contingent debt worth B_t, all of which it buys back or 'redeems'. It pays for these redemptions and its time t net of interest deficit $g_t - \tau_t \ell_t$ by selling state contingent debt worth $E_t \beta p^t_{t+1} B_{t+1}$. The term structure of this debt is irrelevant (but see Section 9.8). We are free to think of it all as one-period state contingent debt promising to pay off B_{t+1} state-contingent units of consumption at $t+1$.

9.4.2 *The martingale equivalent measure*

Equation (9.27) looks like an asset pricing equation. The value of the asset at time t is B_t and the time t 'dividend' is the government surplus $\tau_t \ell_t - g_t$. Because we are working with complete markets, we can coax from (9.27) a martingale that forms a counterpart to (9.4) and (9.5); see Duffie (1996, Chapter 2). The argument proceeds as follows. We would like it if (9.25), the asset pricing equation, involved so-called risk-neutral pricing by collapsing to

$$B_t = E_t \sum_{j=0}^{\infty} R_{tj}^{-1} (\tau_{t+j} \ell_{t+j} - g_{t+j}) \tag{9.28}$$

where R_{tj} is the risk-free j-period gross rate of return from time t to time $t+j$. The j-period risk-free rate is $E_t \beta^j p^t_{t+j}$, but (9.25) does not imply (9.28), at least not under rational expectations (where E is taken with respect to the correct transition probabilities). But by computing the expectation in (9.28) with respect to another set of transition probabilities, we can make a version of (9.28) true.

Here is how to find transition probabilities that work. Note that the one-period risk-free interest rate R_t satisfies $R_t^{-1} = \beta E_t p^t_{t+1}$. Consider a portfolio formed by borrowing $(B_t - (\tau_t \ell_t - g_t))$, and using the proceeds to buy the vector of one-period claims B_{t+1}. The one-period profits from that portfolio will be

$$\pi_{t+1} = B_{t+1} - R_t [B_t - (\tau_t \ell_t - g_t)] \tag{9.29}$$

This investment costs no money, so that if risk-neutral investors' evaluations determined prices, the expected value of the pay-off should be zero. (Remember that in Barro's model, the corresponding object is *identically* zero, not just zero in conditional expectation.) But the representative household is risk-averse, and its preferences are reflected in state prices, making risk-neutral pricing fail, at least with the correct specification of probabilities. We can induce a risk-neutral pricing formula by suitably respecifying the probabilities. In particular, equations (9.27)–(9.29) state that

$$\tilde{E}_t \pi_{t+1} = 0 \tag{9.30}$$

where $\tilde{E}_t$ is the conditional expectation with respect to the *equivalent* transition measure defined as

$$\tilde{f}(x_{t+1}|x_t) = \frac{f(x_{t+1}|x_t) p^t_{t+1}}{E_t p^t_{t+1}} \tag{9.31}$$

in which $f(x_{t+1}|x_t)$ is the original Markov transition density for x. The transition measure $\tilde{f}$ is equivalent in the sense of putting positive probability on the same events as f.

Condition (9.30) states that π_{t+1} is a martingale difference sequence with respect to the equivalent transition measure.[5]

The martingale characterization of government debt encapsulates features of a variety of examples calculated by Lucas and Stokey (1983) in which surprise increases in government expenditures are associated with low realized returns on government debt, and low government expenditures are associated with high rates of return. We now turn to some examples of our own.

9.5 Three examples

All of the examples set $\beta = 1.05^{-1}$, $b = 2.135$, $d = 0$ and initial debt $B_0 = 0$. The first two examples let $w_{g,t+1}$ be a scalar martingale difference sequence, adapted to its own past, with unit variance. The first example uses the linear stochastic difference equation of Assumption 9.1 and sets

$$g_{t+1} - \mu_g = \rho(g_t - \mu_g) + C_g w_{g,t+1}$$

with $\rho = 0.7$, $\mu_g = 0.35$ and $C_g = 0.035\sqrt{1-\rho^2}$. The second example also uses Assumption 9.1 and sets

$$g_{t+1} - \mu_g = \rho(g_{t-3} - \mu_g) + C_g w_{g,t+1}$$

where $\rho = 0.95$ and $C_g = 0.7\sqrt{1-\rho^2}$. The third example uses Assumption 9.2 and sets the Markov chain

$$P = \begin{bmatrix} 0.8 & 0.8 & 0 \\ 0 & 0.5 & 0.5 \\ 0 & 0 & 1 \end{bmatrix}$$

with $g(x) = [\,0.5\ 0.5\ 0.25\,]'$. Here the first state of the Markov chain is war, the second armistice, the third peace. Government expenditures are identical in war and armistice, but the probabilities of transition to peace differ.

We calculated Ramsey plans for each of these three economies. We wrote a MATLAB program **lqramsey** for the Assumption 9.1 economies and **lqramsm** for the Assumption 9.2 economies. Figures 9.1, 9.2, and 9.3 display simulations of outcome paths.

Part (a) of each figure shows sample paths with tax smoothing, not in the sense of Barro, but in the sense of 'small variance'. As formula (9.23) shows, taxes inherit serial correlation properties from the government expenditure process. Parts (b) and (d) reveal important differences in the outcomes from Barro's model. Part (b) in each case shows how B_{t+1} falls when g_t is above average, and rises when g is below average. This behaviour is also reflected in part (d) where the pay-out on the public's portfolio of government debt, π_{t+1}, varies inversely with government expenditures. When government expenditures are high (low) relative to what had been expected, *ex post* government debt pays a low (high) return.

[5]The profit or gain $\Pi_t = \sum_{s=1}^{t} \pi_s$ is a martingale with respect to the measure over sequences of x_t induced by the equivalent transition density. We define $\tilde{\Pi}_t = \sum_{s=0}^{t} \pi_s$.

Figures 9.1 and 9.2 show linear time series versions of these patterns, Example 1 with first-order autoregressive government expenditures, Example 2 with seasonal government expenditures. The effects of the pattern of government expenditures on the pattern of tax collections are difficult to see from the pictures because the variance of tax collections is so small. The contemporaneous correlation of tax collections with government expenditures is 0.99 in both Examples 1 and 2.

Figure 9.3 shows the Markov example. The economy begins in war, and runs a deficit while war continues. During war, there is no building up of debt: each period of war the government pays zero gross return to its creditors (see Fig. 9.3(d)). When armistice arrives in period 5, it triggers a big positive pay-out π_{t+1}, even though government expenditures remain at their wartime level. Armistice lingers for another period, causing the pay-off on government debt to be negative again. Then peace arrives, causing a large pay-off during the first period of peace, to be followed by a permanent string of risk-free positive pay-outs equal to the permanent government surplus. Only during this period of permanent peace does formula (9.4) hold.

Figures 9.4, 9.5, and 9.6 display realizations of $p^t_{t+1}/E_t p^t_{t+1}$ and $\tilde{\Pi}_{t+1}$ for each of our three economies. The term $p^t_{t+1}/E_t p^t_{t+1}$ is the factor that π_t needs to be multipied

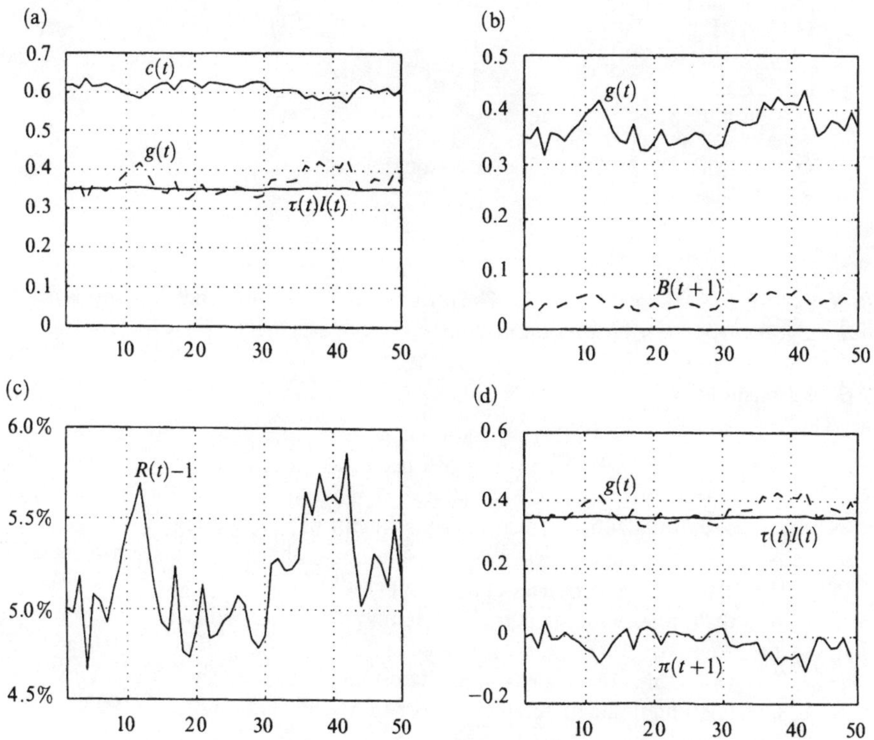

FIG. 9.1. The case of an AR(1) process for g_t.

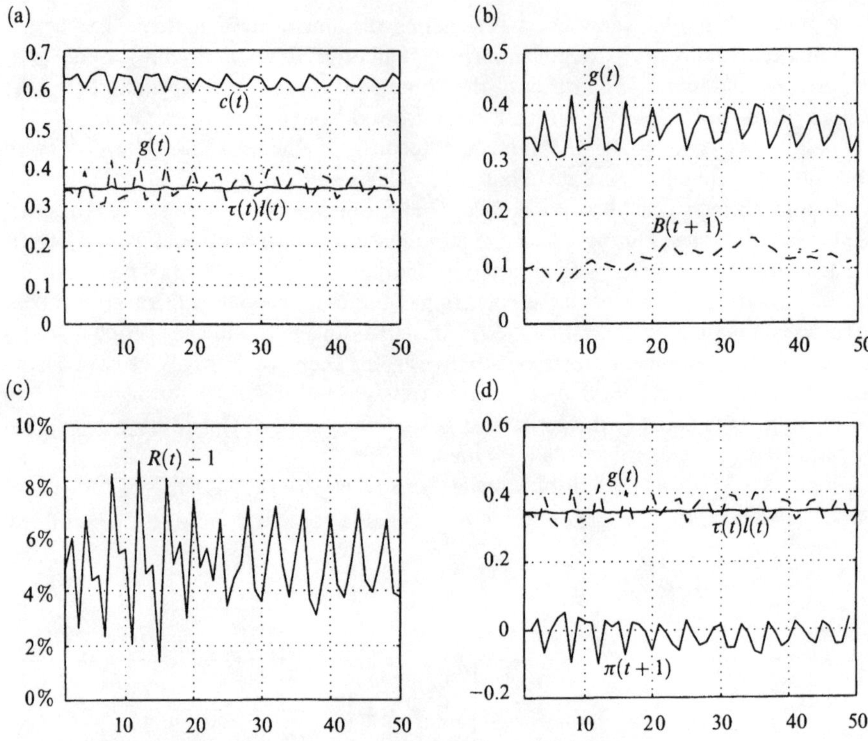

FIG. 9.2. The case of a seasonal AR(4) process for g_t.

to convert Π_t into the martingale $\tilde{\Pi}_t$. The factor is small, meaning that Π_t itself is nearly a martingale. Note how $\tilde{\Pi}_t$ becomes a constant once perpetual peace arrives in Fig. 9.6.

9.6 Extensions

Further calculations with linear quadratic economies appear in Hansen (1987) and Hansen and Sargent (1999). Extensions of Lucas and Stokey's analysis to economies with capital appear in Chari *et al.* (1994; 1996) and Jones *et al.* (1997). Chari *et al.* (1994) describe optimal policy in terms of a martingale of a return variable related to Π_t. For an analysis intermediate between Barro's and Lucas and Stokey's, see Marcet *et al.* (1996), who restrict the government in Lucas and Stokey's model to issue only risk-free debt. That limitation puts a large number of additional measurability restrictions on the Ramsey allocation, beyond those incorporated in (9.14). These restrictions deliver a version of (9.5) with a time-varying risk-free interest rate. The problem with only risk-free debt requires computational methods like those of Marcet and Marimon (1998).

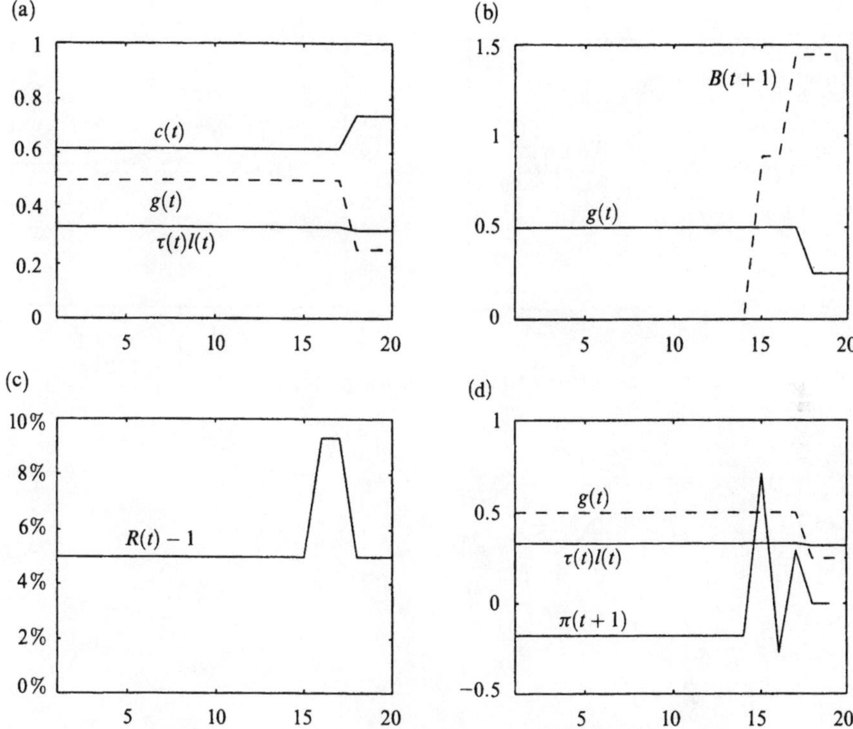

FIG. 9.3. Markov chain g with war, armistice, peace.

9.7 Appendix: Geometric sums of quadratic forms

The calculations in the text require repeated evaluations of discounted infinite sums of quadratic forms in future values of the state. This appendix gives formulae for these sums under two alternative specifications of stochastic process for the state: (1) the state is governed by a vector first-order linear stochastic difference equation; and (2) the state evolves according to an n-state Markov chain.

9.7.1 *Linear stochastic difference equation*

We want a formula for expected discounted sums of quadratic forms

$$q(x_0) = E_0 \sum_{t=0}^{\infty} \beta^t x_t' M x_t \tag{9.32}$$

where

$$x_{t+1} = Ax_t + Cw_{t+1}$$

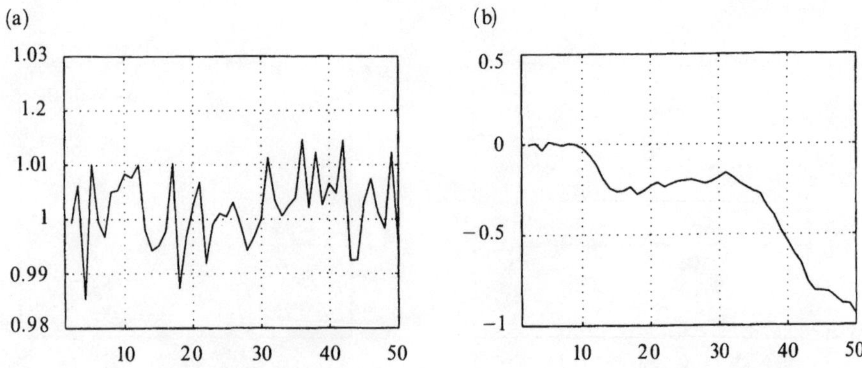

FIG. 9.4. The case of an AR(1) process for g_t: (a) $p^t_{t+1}/E_t p^t_{t+1}$; (b) $\tilde{\Pi}_t$.

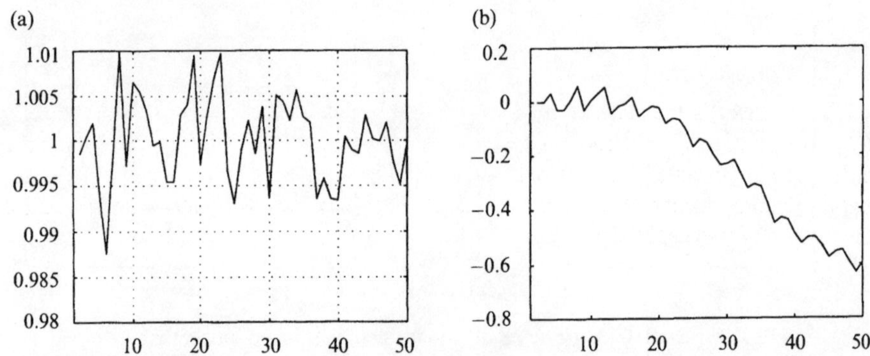

FIG. 9.5. The case of a seasonal AR(4) process for g_t: (a) $p^t_{t+1}/E_t p^t_{t+1}$; (b) $\tilde{\Pi}_t$.

and where w_{t+1} is a martingale difference sequence adapted to its own history and to x_0. The formula is

$$q(x_0) = x_0' Q x_0 + q_0$$

where

$$q_0 = \frac{\beta}{1-\beta} \mathrm{tr} C' Q C$$

$$Q = M + \beta A' Q A x \tag{9.33}$$

The second equation is a Sylvester equation in Q that can be solved by one of a variety of methods, including the doubling algorithm. See Anderson *et al.* (1996) for a review of methods for solving Sylvester equations. The standard MATLAB program **dlyap** can be used; so can a home-made one, **doubleo**, of Hansen and Sargent (1999).

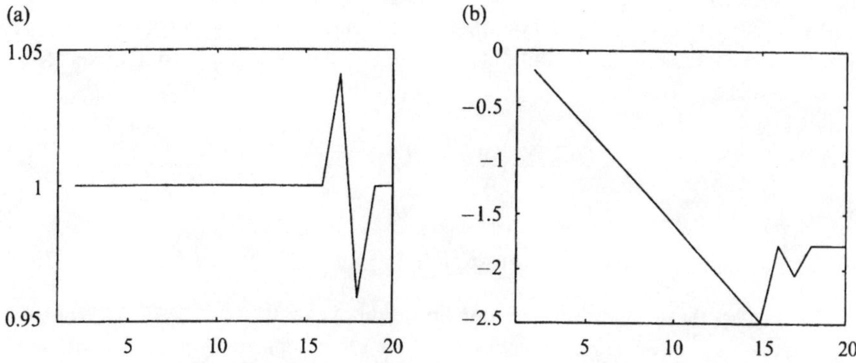

FIG. 9.6. Markov chain g with war, armistice, peace: (a) $p_{t+1}^t / E_t p_{t+1}^t$; (b) $\tilde{\Pi}_t$.

9.7.2 *Markov chain*

Assume that x_t is the state of an n-state Markov chain with transition matrix P with (i, j)th element $P_{i,j} = \text{Prob}(x_{t+1} = \bar{x}_j | x_t = \bar{x}_i)$. Here $\bar{x}_i$ is the value of x when the chain is in its ith state. Let $h(\bar{x})$ be a function of the state represented by an $n \times 1$ vector h; the ith component of h denotes the value of h when x is in its ith state. Then we have the following two useful formulae:

$$E[h(x_{t+k} | x_t = \bar{x})] = P^k h$$

$$E\left[\sum_{k=0}^{\infty} \beta^k h(x_{t+k} | x_t = \bar{x})\right] = (I - \beta P)^{-1} h(\bar{x})$$

where $\beta \in (0, 1)$ guarantees existence of $(I - \beta P)^{-1} = (I + \beta P + \beta^2 P^2 + \cdots)$.

9.8 Appendix: Time consistency and the structure of debt

Under complete markets, there are many government debt structures that have the same present value. One of the results of Lucas and Stokey (1983) is that a specific structure is required if the Ramsey plan is to be *time-consistent*; that is, if the Ramsey plan computed at $t = 1$ coincides with the continuation of the Ramsey plan computed at $t = 0$ for all realizations of x_1. We can compute the debt structure that will induce time consistency.

Assume that the government has solved for the Ramsey plan at $t = 0$, and restructured the debt, that is, chosen a new debt structure of the form ${}_1s_t = {}_1S_s x_t$. We want to find conditions on ${}_1S_s$ such that the Ramsey plan found at time $t = 0$ will be time-consistent. Suppose that, for $t = 1$, we compute the Ramsey plan. Following the same procedure as above, we will need to solve for μ_1 in the equation

$$a_1(x_1)(\mu_1^2 - \mu_1) + b_1(x_1) = 0 \tag{9.34}$$

where the subscript on a and b indicates the fact that these quadratic forms of x_1 depend on ${}_1S_s$ just as $a_0(x_0)$ and $b_0(x_0)$ depend on ${}_0S_s$ in (9.19) and (9.21). Once μ_1 is found, allocations can be computed using (9.22a)–(9.22b). Note that the $\tilde{\ell}_t$ and $\tilde{c}_t$ terms in (9.16a)–(9.16b) do not depend on the debt structure. Therefore, for the new Ramsey allocation to coincide with the continuation of the Ramsey allocation computed at $t = 0$, all we need is

$$\mu_0[S_b - S_d - {}_0S_s] = \mu_1[S_b - S_d - {}_1S_s]$$

or

$$\mu_1\,{}_1S_s = \mu_0\,{}_0S_s + (\mu_1 - \mu_0)(S_b - S_d) \tag{9.35}$$

To translate these conditions into conditions on ${}_1S_s$ alone, we use (9.35) to substitute ${}_1S_s$ in (9.34), solve for μ_1 as a function of x_1, and then replace μ_1 in (9.35).

Rewrite (9.35) as

$$S_b - S_d - {}_1S_s = \frac{\mu_0}{\mu_1}(S_b - S_d - {}_0S_s) \tag{9.36}$$

Using (9.36) in the definition of $a_1(x_1)$:

$$a_1(x_1) = E_1 \sum_{t=0}^{\infty} \beta^t x_{1+t}' \tfrac{1}{2}[S_b - S_d - {}_1S_s]'[S_b - S_d - {}_1S_s]x_{1+t}$$

we find that

$$a_1(x_1) = \left(\frac{\mu_0}{\mu_1}\right)^2 a_0(x_1)$$

For convenience, write $b_1(x_1) = c(x_1) + d_1(x_1)$, with

$$c(x_1) = E_1 \sum_{t=0}^{\infty} \beta^t \tfrac{1}{2} x_{1+t}'[S_b - S_d + S_g]'[S_b - S_d + S_g]x_{1+t} d_1(x_1)$$

$$= E_1 \sum_{t=0}^{\infty} \beta^t \tfrac{1}{2} x_{1+t}'[S_b - S_d + S_g]'[-S_b + S_d + {}_1S_s]x_{1+t}$$

The term $c(x_1)$ does not depend on ${}_1S_s$, and the term $d_1(x_1)$ can be rewritten, using (9.36), as:

$$d_1(x_1) = \frac{\mu_0}{\mu_1} d_0(x_1)$$

We now replace a_1 and d_1 in (9.34) and solve for μ_1:

$$\mu_1 = \mu_0 \frac{\mu_0 a_0(x_1) - d_0(x_1)}{\mu_0^2 a_0(x_1) + c(x_1)}$$

and substitute μ_1 in (9.35) to find:

$$
{}_1S_s = {}_0S_s \frac{\mu_0^2 a_0(x_1) + c(x_1)}{\mu_0 a_0(x_1) - d_0(x_1)} + (S_b - S_d) \frac{a_0(x_1)(\mu_0 - \mu_0^2) - c(x_1) - d_0(x_1)}{\mu_0 a_0(x_1) - d_0(x_1)} \tag{9.37}
$$

If we examine (9.37), we see that ${}_1S_s$ will not be independent of x_1 except when the forms a_1, c and d_1 are, in fact, constants with respect to x_1. A sufficient condition for this to hold is that b_t, d_t and ${}_0s_t$ be independent of t. When that obtains, the second term in (9.37) is zero (by (9.18)) and the time-consistent debt structure will be given by:

$$
{}_1S_s = {}_0S_s \frac{\mu_0^2 a + c}{\mu_0 a - d}
$$

9.9 Appendix: MATLAB program

9.9.1 *Stochastic difference equation*

```
% LQRAMSEY
%
% Compute Ramsey equilibria in an LQ economy with
distorting taxation:
% case of a stochastic difference equation
% The program computes allocation (consumption, leisure),
% tax rates,
% revenues and the net present value of the debt.
  % See also LQRAMSM.
% FRV Apr 10 1998
%%%%%%%%%%%%%%%%% customization required %%%%%%%%%%%%%%
% Gentle user:
% The only customization required is in part (1).
%%%%%%% (1) Define the parameters of the model
% Misc
T=50;       % length of simulation
beta=1/1.05;      % discount factor
% exogenous state
% specify a stochastic process for the state of the form
% x(t+1)= A * x(t) + C * w(t+1)
% where w is i.i.d. N(0,1)
% ex1: govt spending is AR(1), state = [g ; 1]
%mg=.35;
%rho=.7;
%A=[rho mg*(1-rho); 0 1];
%C=[mg/10*sqrt(1-rho^2);0];
%% These selector matrices are all 1*nx, where nx is the
% size of the state:
```

```
%Sg = [1 0]; % The selector matrix for the government
% expenditure
%Sd = [0 0]; % The selector matrix for the exogenous
% endowment
%Sb = [0 2.135]; % The selector matrix for the bliss point
%Ss = [0 0]; % The selector matrix for the promised coupon
% payments
% ex2: seasonal
rho=.95;
mg=.35;
A=[0 0 0 rho mg*(1-rho);
   1 0 0 0 0;
   0 1 0 0 0;
   0 0 1 0 0;
   0 0 0 0 1];
C=[mg/8*sqrt(1-rho^2);0;0;0;0];
Sg = [1 0 0 0 0];
Sd = [0 0 0 0 0];
Sb = [0 0 0 0 2.135];     % this is chosen so that
(Sc+Sg)*x0=1
Ss = [0 0 0 0 0];
%%%%%%%%%%%%%%%%%%% This concludes the customization.
% Let 'er rip! %%%%%%%%%%%%%%%
%%%%%%% (1) generate initial condition
[nx,nx]=size(A);
if ~exist('x0')
   x0=null(eye(nx)-A);
   if (x0(nx)<0)
   x0=-x0;
   end
   x0=x0./x0(nx);
end
%%%%%%% (2) solve for the Lagrange multiplier on the
% government BC
% we actually solve for mu=lambda/(1+2*lambda)
% mu is the solution to a quadratic equation
% a(mu^2-mu)+b=0
% where a and b are expected discounted sums of quadratic
% forms
% of the state; we use dlyap to compute those sums
% quickly.
Sm=Sb-Sd-Ss;      % a short-hand
Qa=dlyap(sqrt(beta)*A',-0.5*Sm'*Sm);
qa=trace(C'*Qa*C)*beta/(1-beta);
Qb=dlyap(sqrt(beta)*A',-0.5*(Sb-Sd+Sg)'*(Sg+Ss));
```

```
qb=trace(C'*Qb*C)*beta/(1-beta);
a0=x0'*Qa*x0+qa;
b0=x0'*Qb*x0+qb;
if a0<0     % normalize
  a0=-a0; b0=-b0;
end
disc=a0^2-4*a0*b0;
% there may be no solution:
if ( disc < 0 )
  disp('There is no Ramsey equilibrium.');
  disp('(Hint: you probably set government spending too
  high;');
  disp(' elect a Republican Congress and start over.)');
  return
end
mu=0.5*(a0-sqrt(disc))/a0;
% or it may be of the wrong sign:
if ( mu*(0.5-mu) < 0 )
  disp('negative multiplier on the government budget
  constraint!');
  disp('(Hint: you probably set government spending too
  low;');
  disp(' elect a Democratic Congress and start over.)');
  return
end
%%%%%%% (3a) solve for the allocation
Sc=0.5*(Sb+Sd-Sg-mu*Sm);
Sl=0.5*(Sb-Sd+Sg-mu*Sm);
Stau1=2*mu*Sm;
Stau2=Sb-Sd+Sg+mu*Sm;
%%%%%%% (4) run the simulation
[nx,nw]=size(C);
x=zeros(nx,T);
w=randn(nw,T);      % draw the shocks
x(:,1)=x0;     % initialize the state
for t=2:T     % compute x recursively
  x(:,t)=(A*x(:,t-1) + C*w(:,t));
end
% exogenous stuff:
g = Sg*x; % government spending
d = Sd*x; % endowment
b = Sb*x; % bliss point
s = Ss*x; % coupon payment on existing debt
% endogenous stuff:
c=Sc*x;          % consumption
```

```
l=Sl*x;          % labor
p=(Sb-Sc)*x;      % price
tau=(Stau1*x)./(Stau2*x);     % taxes
rev=tau.*l;      % revenues
QB=dlyap(sqrt(beta)*A',-((Sb-Sc)'*(Sl-Sg)-Sl'*Sl));
qB=trace(C'*QB*C)*beta/(1-beta);
B=(x'*QB*x+qB)/p; % debt
% 1-period risk-free interest rate
R=((beta*(Sb-Sc)*A*x)./p)'.^(-1);
pi=B(2:T)-R(1:T-1).*(B(1:T-1)-rev(1:T-1)'+g(1:T-1)');
% risk-adjusted martingale
adjfac=(((Sb-Sc)*x(:,2:T))./((Sb-Sc)*A*x(:,1:T-1)))';
Pitilde=cumsum(pi.*adjfac);
%%%%%%% (5) plot
set(0,'DefaultAxesColorOrder',[0 0 0],...
  'DefaultAxesLineStyleOrder','-|--|-|-.')
figure
subplot(2,2,1),
plot([c' g' rev']),grid %cons, g and rev
v=axis; axis([1 T 0 v(4)]);
set(gca,'FontName','Times New Roman');
subplot(2,2,2)
plot((1:T),g,(1:T-1),B(2:T)),grid %g(t) and B(t+1)
v=axis; axis([1 T v(3) v(4)]);
set(gca,'FontName','Times New Roman');
subplot(2,2,3)
plot((1:T),R-1),grid % interest rate
v=axis; axis([1 T v(3) v(4)]);
set(gca,'FontName','Times New Roman');
% format the vertical labels for the interest rate plot
yticks=get(gca,'YTick')';
set(gca,'YTickLabel',num2str(yticks*100,'%4.1f%%'));
subplot(2,2,4)
plot((1:T),[rev' g'],(1:T-1),pi), grid
v=axis; axis([1 T v(3) v(4)]);
set(gca,'FontName','Times New Roman');
figure
subplot(2,2,1),
plot((2:T),adjfac),grid
v=axis; axis([1 T v(3) v(4)]);
set(gca,'FontName','Times New Roman');
subplot(2,2,2),grid
plot((2:T),Pitilde)
v=axis; axis([1 T v(3) v(4)]);
set(gca,'FontName','Times New Roman');
```

```
% th-th-th-that's all, folks!
return
% labels to place on the graphs
gtext('\pi\it(t+1)');
gtext('\it g(t)');
gtext('\it g(t)');
gtext('\it g(t)');
gtext('\it c(t)');
gtext('\it\tau(t)l(t)');
gtext('\it\tau(t)l(t)');
h=gtext('\it B(t+1)');
h=gtext('\it R(t)-1');
```

9.9.2 *Markov chain*

```
% LQRAMSM
%
% Compute Ramsey equilibria in an LQ economy with
% distorting taxation:
%      case of a Markov chain
% The program computes allocation (consumption, leisure),
% tax rates,
% revenues, and the net present value of the debt.
%      See also LQRAMSEY.
% FRV Apr 10 1998
%%%%%%%%%%%%%%%% customization required %%%%%%%%%%%%%%
% Gentle user:
%      The only customization required is in part (1).
% (1) Define the parameters of the model
% model 1:
% 3 states
P = [0.8 0.2 0;... % The transition matrix
   0 0.5 0.5;
   0 0 1];
xbar = [ 0.5 0 2.2 0 1;...% Possible states of the world:
% each column
0.5 0 2.2 0 1;... % is a state of the world
 0.25 0 2.2 0 1]'; % is a state of the world
 % the rows are: [g d b s 1]
x0=1; % index of the initial state
% Sg = [1 0 0 0 0]; % The selector matrix for the government
% expenditure
Sd = [0 1 0 0 0]; % The selector matrix for the exogenous
% endowment
Sb = [0 0 1 0 0]; % The selector matrix for the bliss
% point
```

```
Ss = [0 0 0 1 0]; % The selector matrix for the promised
% coupon payments
% Misc
T=20; % length of simulation
beta=1/1.05; % discount factor
%%%%%%%%%%%%%%%%%%% This concludes the customization.
% Let 'er rip! %%%%%%%%%%%%%%%
% (2) solve for the Lagrange multiplier on the government
% BC
% we actually solve for mu=lambda/(1+2*lambda)
% mu is the solution to a quadratic equation
a(mu^2-mu)+b=0
% where a and b are expected discounted sums of quadratic
% forms
% of the state; we use dlyap to compute those sums
% quickly.
m = size(xbar,2);     % Number of possible states of
the world
Sm=Sb-Sd-Ss;          % a short-hand
invP=inv(eye(size(P))-beta*P);
a0=((1:m)==x0)*0.5*invP*((Sm*xbar)'.^2);
b0=((1:m)==x0)*0.5*invP*(((Sb-Sd+Sg)*xbar).
*((Sg+Ss)*xbar))';
if a0<0     % normalize
   a0=-a0; b0=-b0;
end
disc=a0^2-4*a0*b0;
% there may be no solution:
if ( disc < 0 )
   disp('There is no Ramsey equilibrium.');
   disp('(Hint: you probably set government spending too
   high;');
   disp(' elect a Republican Congress and start over.)');
   return
end
mu=0.5*(a0-sqrt(disc))/a0;
% or it may be of the wrong sign:
if ( mu*(0.5-mu) < 0 )
   disp('negative multiplier on the government budget
   constraint!');
   disp('(Hint: you probably set government spending
   too low;');
   disp(' elect a Democratic Congress and start over.)');
   return
end
```

```
% (3a) solve for the allocation
Sc=0.5*(Sb+Sd-Sg-mu*Sm);
Sl=0.5*(Sb-Sd+Sg-mu*Sm);
Stau1=2*mu*Sm;
Stau2=Sb-Sd+Sg+mu*Sm;
% (4) run the simulation
epsilon = rand(1,T);
cumP = cumsum(P')';      % The cumulative sum for each
row of P
x(:,1) = xbar(:,x0);
state=zeros(T,1);
state(1)=x0;
for t = 2:T
    state(t) = min(find(cumP(state(t-1),:) >=
    epsilon(t)));
    x(:,t) = xbar(:,state(t));
end
% exogenous stuff:
g = Sg*x; % government spending
d = Sd*x; % endowment
b = Sb*x; % bliss point
s = Ss*x; % coupon payment on existing debt
% endogenous stuff:
c=Sc*x; % consumption
l=Sl*x; % labor
p=(Sb-Sc)*x; % price
tau=(Stau1*x)./(Stau2*x); % taxes
rev=tau.*l; % revenues
% compute the debt
B=invP*(((Sb-Sc)*xbar).*((Sl-Sg)*xbar)-(Sl*xbar).^2)';
B=B(state,:)./p';
% 1-period risk-free interest rate
R=(beta*(P(state,:)*((Sb-Sc)*xbar)')./p').^(-1);
pi=B(2:T)-R(1:T-1).*(B(1:T-1)-rev(1:T-1)'+g(1:T-1)');
% risk-adjusted martingale
adjfac=p(2:T)'./(P(state(1:T-1),:)*((Sb-Sc)*xbar)');
Pitilde=cumsum(pi.*adjfac);
%%%%%%% (5) plot
set(0,'DefaultAxesColorOrder',[0 0 0],...
   'DefaultAxesLineStyleOrder','-|--|-|-.')
figure
subplot(2,2,1),%grid
plot([c' g' rev']) %cons, g and rev
v=axis; axis([1 T 0 v(4)]);
set(gca,'FontName','Times New Roman');
```

```
subplot(2,2,2),%grid
plot((1:T),g,(1:T-1),B(2:T)), %g(t) and B(t+1)
v=axis; axis([1 T v(3) v(4)]);
set(gca,'FontName','Times New Roman');
subplot(2,2,3),%grid
plot((1:T),R-1) % interest rate
v=axis; axis([1 T 0 v(4)]);
set(gca,'FontName','Times New Roman');
% format the vertical labels for the interest rate plot
set(gca,'YTickLabel',num2str(get(gca,'YTick')'*100,'
%3.0f%%'));
subplot(2,2,4),%grid
plot((1:T),[rev' g'],(1:T-1),pi),
v=axis; axis([1 T v(3) v(4)]);
set(gca,'FontName','Times New Roman');
figure
subplot(2,2,1),
plot((2:T),adjfac),grid
v=axis; axis([1 T v(3) v(4)]);
set(gca,'FontName','Times New Roman');
subplot(2,2,2),grid
plot((2:T),Pitilde)
v=axis; axis([1 T v(3) v(4)]);
set(gca,'FontName','Times New Roman');
% th-th-th-that's all, folks!
return
% labels to place on the graphs
gtext('\pi\it(t+1)');
gtext('\it g(t)');
gtext('\it g(t)');
gtext('\it g(t)');
gtext('\it c(t)');
gtext('\it\tau(t)l(t)');
gtext('\it\tau(t)l(t)');
h=gtext('\it B(t+1)');
h=gtext('\it R(t)-1');
```

10

COMPUTING MODELS OF SOCIAL SECURITY

Ayşe İmrohoroğlu, Selahattin İmrohoroğlu, and Douglas H. Joines[1]

10.1 Introduction

In the United States and most other developed countries, the public pension system and associated benefit payments to the retired and their families (including disability, medical, and survivor benefits) constitute the largest item in the government budget. Partly because of their scale, these payments have during the last quarter century become the object of intense study by economists.

Most of the issues concerning the effect of unfunded social security programmes on the economy have been analysed qualitatively using standard models such as the two- or three-period overlapping generations model, and some of the empirical predictions have been tested. More recently, some of these questions as well as other issues in fiscal policy have been analysed quantitatively using larger overlapping generations models. The starting point for this literature is Auerbach and Kotlikoff (1987) and a series of papers that preceded that book. Auerbach and Kotlikoff use a non-stochastic, 55-period overlapping generations model to analyse the effects of unfunded social security on both labour supply and the capital stock. Subsequent work modifies the Auerbach–Kotlikoff model by adding borrowing constraints, various sources of uncertainty, and other features. In particular, incorporating two sources of uncertainty into a model of social security seems to be important. First, an uncertain lifespan is essential for many interesting questions concerning social security, which provides partial insurance against this risk in the absence of private annuity markets. Second, introducing earnings uncertainty is desirable for at least two reasons: earnings uncertainty interacts with borrowing constraints and yields within-cohort heterogeneity which can address questions about the distribution of consumption and wealth; and an unfunded social security system with little or no linkage between benefits and contributions provides some insurance for earnings uncertainty.

10.2 A model of social security with heterogeneous agents

This section describes the İmrohoroğlu *et al.* (1995) set-up, which is related to several recent large-scale general equilibrium, overlapping generations models.[2]

[1]The authors' correspondence address is Department of Finance and Business Economics, Marshall School of Business, University of Southern California, Los Angeles, CA 90089-1421, USA.

[2]Among others, important quantitative work using overlapping generations models includes Hubbard and Judd (1987), Ríos-Rull (1996), Huggett and Ventura (1998), Cooley and Soares (1996; 1998), İmrohoroğlu *et al.* (1998a), Rust and Phelan (1997), Storesletten *et al.* (1997), İmrohoroğlu (1998) and Conesa and Krueger (1998).

10.2.1 *Demographics*

The economy is populated by overlapping generations of long but finite-lived individuals with total measure one. Individuals face random survival from age $j-1$ to j, as represented by the conditional survival probabilities $\psi_j \in (0,1)$. Some consumers may survive through the maximum possible lifespan, J. Each period the number of newborns grows relative to the last cohort by a constant proportion n. To obtain a stationary population, cohort shares $\{\mu_j\}_{j=1}^{J}$ are calculated by $\mu_j = \psi_j \mu_{j-1}/(1+n)$, $\sum_{j=1}^{J} \mu_j = 1$.[3] Aggregate quantities in the economy are weighted averages of individual quantities where individual measures as well as the cohort measures serve as weights.

10.2.2 *Budget constraints*

Each period individuals who are below a mandatory retirement age j_R face a stochastic employment opportunity. Let $s \in S = \{e, u\}$ denote the employment opportunities state and assume that it follows a first-order Markov process. The transition function for the individual earnings state is given by the 2×2 matrix $\Pi(s', s) = [\pi_{ij}]$, $i, j = e, u$, where $\pi_{ij} = \text{Prob}\{s_{t+1} = j \mid s_t = i\}$. If $s = e$, the individual is employed and earns $w\varepsilon_j$ where w is the wage rate per efficiency unit of labour, the labour supply is unity, and ε_j is an age-indexed efficiency of labour. If $s = u$, the agent is unemployed and receives unemployment insurance benefits in the amount $\phi w \varepsilon_j$, where ϕ is the replacement ratio. During retirement the individual receives a pension b and decumulates assets. The social security benefits are calculated to be a fraction, θ, of some base income, taken to be the average lifetime employed income. That is

$$b_j = \begin{cases} 0 & j = 1, 2, \ldots, j_R - 1 \\ \theta \dfrac{\sum_{i=1}^{j_R-1} w\varepsilon_i}{j_R - 1} & j = j_R, j_R + 1, \ldots, J \end{cases} \tag{10.1}$$

Note that an agent's social security benefit is independent of the agent's employment history. The after-tax income of an individual is given by

$$q_j = \begin{cases} (1 - \tau_s - \tau_u) w\varepsilon_j & j \in [1, j_R), s = e \\ \phi w \varepsilon_j & j \in [1, j_R), s = u \\ b & j \in [j_R, J] \end{cases} \tag{10.2}$$

where τ_s and τ_u are social security and unemployment insurance payroll tax rates, respectively.

The infinitely-lived government administers the unemployment insurance and social security schemes. Given unemployment insurance and social security benefits, the government chooses the unemployment insurance and the social security tax rates so that each of these schemes is self-financing.

In this economy, there are no private markets for insurance against the risk of unemployment or living longer than expected. Unfunded social security provides partial

[3]The cohort shares are assumed to be time-invariant in order to restrict the computations to steady states. In this class of general equilibrium, heterogeneous-agent, large-scale overlapping generations models, computing transitions is not a simple task.

insurance against the latter risk, but the former can only be partially insured against by private saving. We assume that agents may not have negative assets at any age. Hence, the restriction on the amount of assets carried over from age j to $j+1$, a_j, is that

$$a_j \geq 0 \tag{10.3}$$

Since there is no altruistic bequest motive and death is certain after age J, individuals who survive to age J liquidate all their assets at that age so that $a_J = 0$. However, uncertain survival until age J means that there are accidental bequests.

Consumption and asset accumulation at age j, denoted by c_j and $a_j - a_{j-1}$, respectively, follow

$$c_j + a_j = (1+r)a_{j-1} + q_j + \xi \tag{10.4}$$

where r is the return on physical capital net of depreciation and ξ is a lumpsum transfer of accidental bequests.[4]

10.2.3 *Preferences*

Each individual maximizes the expected, discounted lifetime utility

$$E_0 \sum_{j=1}^{J} \beta^{j-1} \left[\prod_{k=1}^{j} \psi_k \right] u(c_j) \tag{10.5}$$

where β is the subjective discount factor. The period utility function is assumed to take the form

$$u(c_j) = \frac{c_j^{1-\gamma}}{1-\gamma} \tag{10.6}$$

where γ is the coefficient of relative risk aversion.

10.2.4 *Technology*

The production technology of the economy is given by a constant returns to scale Cobb–Douglas function

$$Q = BK^{1-\alpha}N^{\alpha} \tag{10.7}$$

where $B > 0$, $\alpha \in (0,1)$ is labour's share of output, and K and N are aggregate capital and labour inputs, respectively. The aggregate capital stock is assumed to depreciate at the rate δ.

The profit-maximizing behaviour of the firm gives rise to first-order conditions which determine the net real return to capital and the real wage

$$r = (1-\alpha)B\left[\frac{K}{N}\right]^{-\alpha} - \delta \tag{10.8}$$

$$w = \alpha B\left[\frac{K}{N}\right]^{1-\alpha}$$

[4]The particular assumption for the redistribution of accidental bequests may have an impact on the quantitative results. See İmrohoroğlu *et al.* (1995) and İmrohoroğlu (1998).

10.2.5 *Decision rules*

Let $D = \{d_1, d_2, \ldots, d_m\}$ denote the discrete grid of points on which asset holdings will be required to fall. For any beginning-of-period asset holding and employment state $(a, s) \in D \times S$, define the constraint set of an age-j agent $\Omega_j(a, s) \in R_+^2$ as all pairs (c_j, a_j) such that equations (10.3) and (10.4) hold. Let $V_j(a, s)$ be the (maximized) value of the objective function of an age-j agent with beginning-of-period asset holdings and employment state (a, s). $V_j(a, s)$ is given as the solution to the dynamic program

$$V_j(a, s) = \max_{(c,a') \in \Omega_j(a,s)} \left\{u(c) + \beta\psi_{j+1} E_{s'} V_{j+1}(a', s')\right\}, \qquad j = 1, 2, \ldots, J \tag{10.9}$$

where a prime on a variable indicates its value for the next age and the notation $E_{s'}$ means that the expectation is over the distribution of s'.

The optimization problem faced by an individual in this economy is one of finite-state, finite-horizon dynamic programming.[5] The value functions and the decision rules for each age $j = 1, 2, \ldots, J$ can be found by a single recursion working backwards from the last period of life. Using the budget constraint (10.4) to substitute for c_j in Bellman's equation (10.9), the problem reduces to choosing the decision variable a_j. We assume that $a_j \in D \equiv \{d_1, d_2, \ldots, d_m\}$. For individuals at age j_R or older, namely the retired, the state space is an $m \times 1$ vector $X = \{x = a\colon\ a \in D\}$. For individuals who are subject to idiosyncratic employment risk, at age $j_R - 1$ or younger, the state space is an $m \times 2$ matrix $\tilde{X} = \{\tilde{x} = (a, s)\colon\ a \in D, s \in S\}$. The control space for individuals of all ages is the $m \times 1$ vector D. For $j = j_R, j_R + 1, \ldots, J$, the decision rules take the form of an $m \times 1$ vector of asset holdings that solves the above problem. For $j = 1, 2, \ldots, j_R - 1$, the decision rules are $m \times 2$ matrices, one such matrix for each j, showing the utility maximizing asset holding for each level of beginning-of-period assets and employment state realization.

Since death is certain beyond age J ($\psi_{J+1} = 0$) the value function at $J + 1$ is identically zero. Hence, the solution to

$$V_J(x_J) = \max_{\{c_J, a_J\}} u(c_J)$$

subject to

$$c_J = (1 + r)a_{J-1} + q_J + \xi$$

is an $m \times 1$ vector decision rule for age-J individuals, A_J. Note that this is a vector of zeros since there is no bequest motive and death is certain after J. The value function at age J, V_J, is an $m \times 1$ vector whose entries correspond to the value of the utility function at $(1 + r)a_{J-1} + b + \xi$ with a_{J-1} taking on the values $d_1, d_2, \ldots, d_m$. This value function V_J is passed on to the next step where the age-$(J - 1)$ decision rule and value function are calculated. The age-$(J - 1)$ decision rule is found by obtaining

$$V_{J-1}(x_{J-1}) = \max_{\{c_{J-1}, a_{J-1}\}} \{u(c_{J-1}) + \beta\psi_J V_J(x_J)\}$$

[5] See Sargent (1987) and Stokey *et al.* (1989) for a description of dynamic programming as a tool for solving a large class of general equilibrium models.

subject to

$$c_{J-1} + a_{J-1} = (1+r)a_{J-2} + b + \xi, \quad c_{J-1} \geq 0, \quad a_{J-1} \geq 0$$

The decision rule is found as follows.[6] For $a_{J-2} = d_1$, the value of $a_{J-1} \in D$ that solves the above problem is obtained by evaluating the objective function at each point on the grid D. This value is reported as the first element of the $m \times 1$ decision rule A_{J-1}. By repeating this procedure for all possible initial asset levels $a_{J-2} \in D$ the entire vector A_{J-1} is filled. Simultaneously, the age-$(J-1)$ value function V_{J-1} is found as an $m \times 1$ vector with entries corresponding to the right-hand side of the above objective function evaluated at the decision rule A_{J-1}.

Working the backward recursion, we come to age $j_R - 1$, the age immediately before the mandatory retirement age of j_R. The problem to solve is

$$V_{j_R-1}(\tilde{x}_{j_R-1}) = \max_{\{c_{j_R-1}, a_{j_R-1}\}} \{u(c_{j_R-1}) + \beta\psi_{j_R} V_{j_R}(\tilde{x}_{j_R})\}$$

subject to

$$c_{j_R-1} + a_{j_R-1} = (1+r)a_{j_R-2} + q_{j_R-1} + \xi, \quad c_{j_R-1} \geq 0, \quad a_{j_R-1} \geq 0$$

When the individual is at age $j_R - 1$ or younger, disposable income is no longer independent of the idiosyncratic employment risk. In fact, for $j = 1, 2, \ldots, j_R - 1$, disposable income can take one of two values, $(1 - \tau_r - \tau_u)w\varepsilon_j$ or $\phi w\varepsilon_j$, depending on the realization of s. The decision rule for age $j_R - 1$ (and also for younger individuals) is an $m \times 2$ matrix describing the utility maximizing levels of asset holdings for each point in the state space $\tilde{X} = D \times S$. Consequently, the value function V_{j_R-1} is also an $m \times 2$ matrix.

For $j = 1, 2, \ldots, j_R - 2$, the optimality equation is given by

$$V_j(\tilde{x}_j) = \max_{\{c_j, a_j\}} \left\{ u(c_j) + \beta\psi_{j+1} \sum_{s'} \Pi(s', s) V_{j+1}(\tilde{x}_{j+1}) \right\}$$

subject to

$$c_j + a_j = (1+r)a_{j-1} + q_j + \xi, \quad c_j \geq 0, \quad a_j \geq 0$$

For $a_{j-1} = d_1$ and $s = e$, we search over $a_j \in D$ that solves the above problem and report that value as the 1×1 element of the $m \times 2$ decision rule A_j. Then we search over $a_j \in D$ for given $a_{j-1} = d_1$ and $s = u$, and report the optimal value as the 1×2 element of the decision rule for age j. This process is repeated until all elements of the decision rule A_j are computed. This completes the computation of the decision rules A_j and value functions V_j for all ages; two $(j_R - 1)$ matrices each $m \times 2$ and two $(J - j_R + 1)$ vectors each $m \times 1$.

[6] Because of the concavity of the value function, it is not necessary to evaluate the second term on the right-hand side of equation (10.9) at every grid point. One useful approach is to start with a coarse grid over the entire decision space and then use successively finer grids in the neighbourhood of the optimum. An alternative approach is to compute the value function using a coarse grid on the state space and use linear interpolations to evaluate the value function for in-between grid points.

10.2.6 *Age-dependent distributions of agents*

To obtain the distribution of age-j agents, $\lambda_j(a, s)$, into beginning-of-period asset holding levels and employment categories, we start from a given initial wealth distribution λ_1. We assume that newborns have zero asset holdings, so λ_1 is taken to be an $m \times 2$ matrix with zeros everywhere except the first row, which is equal to (u_1, u_2), the expected employment and unemployment rates, respectively. The distribution of agents at the end of age 1, or equivalently, at the beginning of age 2, is found by

$$\lambda_2(a', s') = \sum_s \sum_{a:a' \in A_1(a,s)} \Pi(s', s)\lambda_1(a, s)$$

Starting from the initial wealth distribution λ_1, some individuals will be employed and some of them will be unemployed at age 1. Depending on the realization of the employment status, individuals will make asset holding decisions which are already calculated. Therefore, at the beginning of age 2, they will go to (possibly) different points in the state-space matrix (a, s). Each entry in the $m \times 2$ matrix λ_2 gives the fraction of 2-year-old agents at that particular combination of asset holdings (chosen at the end of the age-1 optimization problem) and period-2 employment status. Note that, for each j, each element of λ_j is non-negative, and the sum of all entries equals 1.

In general, given J decision rules A_j and an initial wealth distribution λ_1, the age-dependent distributions are computed from the forward recursion

$$\lambda_j(a', s') = \sum_s \sum_{a:a' \in A_j(a,s)} \Pi(s', s)\lambda_{j-1}(a, s) \tag{10.10}$$

Note that for $j = j_R, j_R + 1, \ldots, J$, λ_j is $m \times 1$ since the retired individuals are not subject to idiosyncratic employment risk.

Using these age-dependent distributions we can compute age profiles for consumption, assets, and income. We also compute aggregate values for these variables.

Alternatively, one could simulate the histories of a large number of agents using Monte Carlo methods and calculate the summary statistics from these simulations. This approach starts with an initial distribution of asset holdings and randomly draws the survival probabilities and the realization of the employment state for a single agent. Given these realizations, and the optimal decision rules, the next period's asset holdings are computed, which become the following period's state variables. This procedure is recursively followed forward until the agent dies, which is no later than age J. This procedure is repeated for a large number of agents, and averages are computed, until convergence of the calibrated cohort shares and the unemployment rate.[7]

10.2.7 *Stationary equilibrium*

A *stationary equilibrium* for a given set of policy arrangements $\{\theta, \phi, \tau_s, \tau_u\}$ is a collection of value functions $V_j(a, s)$, individual policy rules $A_j : D \times S \to R_+$, $A_j : D \times S \to D$, age-dependent (but time-invariant) measures of agent types $\lambda_j(a, s)$

[7] İmrohoroğlu *et al.* (1998b) replicate 220 000 agent histories to match the cohort shares to within 0.00001.

for each age $j = 1, 2, \ldots, J$, relative prices of labour and capital $\{w, r\}$, and a lump-sum transfer ξ such that the following hold:

1. Individual and aggregate behaviour are consistent:

$$K = \sum_j \sum_a \sum_s \mu_j \lambda_j(a, s) a_{j-1} \quad \text{and} \quad N = \sum_{j=1}^{j_R - 1} \sum_a \mu_j \lambda_j(a, s = e)\varepsilon_j \quad (10.11)$$

2. Relative prices $\{w, r\}$ solve the firm's profit maximization problem by satisfying equation (10.8).
3. Given relative prices $\{w, r\}$, government policy $\{\theta, \phi, \tau_s, \tau_u\}$, and a lump-sum transfer ξ, the individual policy rules $C_j(a, s)$, $A_j(a, s)$ solve the individuals' dynamic program (10.9).
4. The commodity market clears:

$$\sum_j \sum_a \sum_s \mu_j \lambda_j(a, s)\{C_j(a, s) + [A_j(a, s) - (1 - \delta)A_{j-1}(a, s)]\} = Q \quad (10.12)$$

   where the initial wealth distribution of agents, A_0, is taken as given.
5. The collection of age-dependent, time-invariant measures $\lambda_j(a, s)$ for $j = 2, 3, \ldots, J$, satisfies

$$\lambda_j(a', s') = \sum_s \sum_{a:a'=A_j(a,s)} \Pi(s', s)\lambda_{j-1}(a, s)$$

   where the initial measure of agents at birth, λ_1, is taken as given.
6. The social security system is self-financing:

$$\tau_s = \frac{\sum_{j=j_R}^{J} \sum_a \mu_j \lambda_j(a, s) b}{\sum_{j=1}^{j_R - 1} \sum_a \mu_j \lambda_j(a, s = e) w \varepsilon_j}$$

7. The unemployment insurance benefits scheme is self-financing:

$$\tau_u = \frac{\sum_{j=1}^{j_R - 1} \sum_a \mu_j \lambda_j(a, s = u) \phi w \varepsilon_j}{\sum_{j=1}^{j_R - 1} \sum_a \mu_j \lambda_j(a, s = e) w \varepsilon_j}$$

$$= \phi \frac{u_2}{u_1}$$

8. The lump-sum distribution of accidental bequests is determined by

$$\xi = \sum_j \sum_a \sum_s \mu_j \lambda_j(a, s)(1 - \psi_{j+1})A_j(a, s)$$

10.2.8 *Measures of utility and welfare benefits*

In order to compare alternative social security arrangements, we need a measure of "average steady-state utility". Given a policy arrangement $\Gamma = \{\theta, \phi, \tau_s, \tau_u\}$, we calculate

$$W(\Gamma) = \sum_{j=1}^{J} \sum_{y} \sum_{s} \beta^{j-1} \left\{ \prod_{k=1}^{j} \psi_k \lambda_j(a, s) u(C_j(a, s)) \right\} \tag{10.13}$$

as our measure of utility. $W(\Gamma)$ is the expected discounted utility a newborn individual derives from the consumption policy functions $\{C_j(a, s)\}$ under a given social security arrangement.

Second, we need a measure to quantify the welfare benefits (or costs) of alternative social security arrangements. As our reference economy, we take the benchmark equilibrium under a zero social security replacement rate. Our measure of welfare benefit (or cost) is calculated as the consumption supplement in each period of life required to make a newborn individual indifferent between being born into an economy with a given social security replacement rate and an economy with no social security. Let $W_0 = W(\Gamma_0)$ and $W_1 = W(\Gamma_1)$ denote the utility under policy arrangements $\Gamma_0 = \{\theta_0 = 0, \phi, \tau_{s0} = 0, \tau_u\}$ and $\Gamma_1 = \{\theta_1 > 0, \phi, \tau_{s1} > 0, \tau_u\}$, respectively. Our measure of welfare benefits is $\kappa = \ell / Q_0$ where ℓ is a lump-sum compensation required to make a newborn indifferent between policy arrangements Γ_0 with compensation ℓ in each period of life, and an alternative policy arrangement Γ_1 without compensation, and Q_0 is real gross national product under arrangement Γ_0.

Note that steady-state equilibria calculated in this class of models do not, in general, result in allocations that are Pareto optimal for a variety of reasons such as the presence of liquidity constraints and dynamic inefficiency associated with overlapping generations models. In order to quantify the extent to which these equilibria suffer from these problems, it might be desirable to characterize the following first-best solution. Consider the problem faced by a social planner whose task is to allocate the economy's output among investments in physical capital and consumption of the 65 generations alive in any period. The planner is restricted to choose among steady states, and the objective is to maximize the expected lifetime utility of an individual born into the chosen steady state. In a steady state, investment is equal to $(\delta + n)K$. The planner's problem is thus to choose a capital stock K and a consumption profile $\{c_j\}_{j=1}^{J}$ to maximize the objective function (10.13) subject to the constraint

$$f(K, N) = (\delta + n)K + \sum_{j=1}^{J} \mu_j c_j$$

The first-order condition associated with K is that the marginal product of capital equals $\delta + n$. This condition requires that the planner choose the golden rule capital stock, thus maximizing aggregate consumption. The remaining optimality conditions concern the allocation of aggregate consumption among the J living generations, or alternatively (because the planner is restricted to choose among steady states), over the J periods of an individual's life. Given the form of the utility function in equation (10.5), these conditions give rise to expressions of the form

$$\left(\frac{c_{j+1}}{c_j}\right)^{-\gamma} = \beta(1+n)$$

Note that the general shape of the consumption profile implied by these expressions does not depend on the level of aggregate consumption. If individuals were not subject to liquidity constraints, they would allocate consumption over the life cycle according to

$$E_0\left(\frac{c_{j+1}}{c_j}\right)^{-\gamma} = \beta(1+r)\psi_{j+1}$$

The consumption path implied by this condition differs from that chosen by the social planner for two reasons. First, the planner pools the mortality risks represented by ψ_js, whereas individuals in our model are unable to do so due to the absence of annuity markets. As a result, the age–consumption profile chosen by individuals tends to be less steep than that chosen by the planner. Second, the planner's optimality conditions involve the population growth rate (which equals the economy's growth rate in the absence of productivity growth), whereas the individual's involve the market interest rate. These rates will differ unless the economy is at the golden rule capital stock. In addition, an individual subject to binding liquidity constraints would not allocate consumption according to the above Euler equations, possibly causing a further divergence between the individual's consumption profile and that chosen by the planner. Social security can affect welfare by altering the steady-state capital stock, and thus aggregate consumption, and by influencing the shape of the age–consumption profile.

10.2.9 *Calibration*

In order to obtain numerical solutions to the model, it is necessary to choose particular values for the parameters. The general strategy is to choose parameter values so that the model economy reproduces certain long-run empirical characteristics of the economy being studied. This entails matching model quantities with empirical counterparts that should be constant along a balanced growth path. Examples of such quantities are the growth rates of population and total factor productivity and ratios such as the capital–output and investment–capital ratios. Although these empirical quantities are not literally constant, they generally appear to be mean stationary time series, and the means of these time series generally can be estimated fairly precisely. Cooley and Prescott (1995) provide a general discussion of this strategy for choosing model parameters. The specifics of calibration differ from model to model, and the reader is referred to individual papers for details. See, for example, İmrohoroğlu *et al.* (1998a; 1998c) for a detailed discussion of the calibration of a particular overlapping generations model as it is applied to social security.

10.2.10 *Computing a stationary equilibrium*

Let ϵ_1 and ϵ_2 denote the convergence criteria for the aggregate capital stock and unintended bequests, respectively. These criteria are usually obtained through experimentation. A smaller ϵ increases the number of iterations whereas a larger ϵ may change the results significantly. Also choose the step sizes $\hat{\alpha}_1$ and $\hat{\alpha}_2$ governing the adjustment to capital and bequests between iterations. Computing an equilibrium requires finding a fixed point in the capital stock, K, and the transfer of unintended bequests, ξ, and consists of the following steps:

1. Guess K_0 and ξ_0. Compute the aggregate labour input $N = u_1 \sum_{j=1}^{j_R-1} \mu_j \varepsilon_j$. Use the first-order conditions from the firm's profit maximization problem to obtain the implied values for the relative factor prices w and r, and substitute these in the individual's budget constraint.
2. Compute the decision rules for each cohort by completing a backward recursion, and the distribution of agent types for each cohort by completing a forward recursion.
3. Compute the new aggregate capital stock $K_1 = \sum_j \sum_a \sum_s \mu_j \lambda_j(a,s) A_j(a,s)$ and the new lump-sum transfer $\xi_1 = \sum_j \sum_a \sum_s \mu_j \lambda_j(a,s)(1-\psi_{j+1}) A_j(a,s)$, and check if $\frac{|K_1-K_0|}{K_0} < \epsilon_1$ and $\frac{|\xi_1-\xi_0|}{\xi_0} < \epsilon_2$. If not, compute $K_2 = \hat{\alpha}_1 K_0 + (1-\hat{\alpha}_1) K_1$ and $\xi_2 = \hat{\alpha}_2 \xi_0 + (1-\hat{\alpha}_2)\xi_1$. Set $K_0 = K_2$ and $\xi_0 = \xi_2$ and go to step 1. For each of the $j_R - 1$ working ages, computing the decision rules involves $d_m \times d_m \times 2$ function evaluations, and for each of $J - j_R + 1$ retired ages, obtaining decision rules requires $d_m \times d_m$ function evaluations.[8]
4. Compute aggregate consumption, investment, and output using the decision rules, distribution of agent types, and the population shares of cohorts, and check whether the commodity market clearing condition given by equation (10.12) is approximately satisfied.[9] If the problem is correctly specified and the code is accurate, *excess demand* is typically less than 0.01% of output when the capital stock converges. If *excess demand* is sufficiently small when the aggregate capital stock converges, then stop. If not, check the code for accuracy or the economic model for internal consistency and start again.

10.3 A linear quadratic model of social security

De Nardi *et al.* (1998) demonstrate how a demographic transition can be incorporated in a general equilibrium model with long-lived overlapping generations of individuals facing several sources of uncertainty. The emphasis is on the computation of an equilibrium transition path between steady states which is induced by a demographic transition and the government's fiscal response to it.

[8] The number of grid points varies from one paper to the next. For example, İmrohoroğlu *et al.* (1995) use 601 grid points, whereas İmrohoroğlu *et al.* (1998c) use 4097 grid points. In all cases, the computer code is written in FORTRAN. In the model with 4097 grid points, each iteration takes about 90 seconds on a 200 MHz Pentium Pro. Finding an equilibrium generally requires between five and eight iterations and rarely takes more than ten iterations.

[9] Note that this is merely a check on the internal consistency of the model and the accuracy of the code that performs the computations. When the model is well specified and the decision rules and the distribution of the agent types and the aggregate variables are calculated correctly, the market clearing condition should hold in equilibrium since it is a weighted average of the individuals' budget constraints.

10.3.1 *Demographics*

For any variable z, the subscript t denotes age and the index s in parentheses denotes calendar time. For example, $N_t(s)$ denotes the number of age-t people at time s.

Time is discrete and indexed by s. At each date s, a cohort of individuals of measure $N_0(s)$ arrives. These are "age 0" individuals who face random survival. The lucky ones live through $s, s+1, s+2, \ldots, s+T$, for a total of $T+1$ years. Let $\alpha_t(s)$ denote the conditional probability of surviving from age t to age $t+1$ at time s. The number age t people alive at time s moves according to

$$N_{t+1}(s+1) = \alpha_t(s)N_t(s) \tag{10.14}$$

Iterating on (10.14) gives $N_t(s) = \alpha_{t-1}(s-1)\,\alpha_{t-2}(s-2)\cdots\alpha_0(s-t)\,N_0(s-t)$. We compute the probability that a person born at $s-t$ survives to age t as

$$\lambda_t(s) \equiv \prod_{h=1}^{t} \alpha_{t-h}(s-h) \tag{10.15}$$

De Nardi *et al.* assume that at time s, the number of new individuals grows at the rate $n(s)-1$, so that $N_0(s) = n(s)N_0(s-1)$, which implies $N_0(s) = \prod_{h=1}^{s} n(h)N_0(0)$. Let $\nu(s) = \prod_{h=1}^{s} n(h)$. Then the fraction $f_t(s)$ of age-t people at time s is given by

$$f_t(s) = \frac{\lambda_t(s)\nu(s)}{\sum_{i=0}^{T} \lambda_i(s)\nu(s-i)} \tag{10.16}$$

which will be used as cohort weights to compute aggregate quantities. The entire population at time s is given by $N(s) = \sum_{t=0}^{T} N_t(s)$. The paths $n(s)$ and $\alpha_t(s)$ for $s = 1970, \ldots, 2060 + 3T$ are taken as given and calibrated using the projections of the Social Security Administration for the United States. Note that the people who enter the model at "age" 0 ($t = 0$) are 21 years old. The mandatory retirement age is 65 ($t = t_R + 2$) and old agents may live up to 90 years old ($t = T$).

During the first $t_R + 1$ periods of life, a consumer supplies labour in exchange for wages that he allocates among consumption, taxes, and asset accumulation. During the final $T - t_R$ periods of life, the consumer receives social security benefits. In addition to lifespan risk, agents face different income shocks that they cannot insure. They can smooth consumption by accumulating two risk-free assets: physical capital and government bonds. The government taxes consumption and income from capital and labour, issues and services debt, purchases goods, and pays retirement benefits. There is a constant returns-to-scale Cobb–Douglas aggregate production function and no aggregate uncertainty. As a consequence, factor prices will be time-varying but deterministic.

10.3.2 *Technology*

The aggregate technology is described by a constant returns to scale Cobb–Douglas production function. Prices of capital and labour at time s, denoted by $r(s-1)$ and $w(s)$, respectively, are determined from the firm's profit maximization problem in a competitive equilibrium:

$$r(s-1) = \tilde{\alpha} A \left[\frac{K(s-1)}{L(s)}\right]^{\tilde{\alpha}-1} \tag{10.17}$$

$$w(s) = (1-\tilde{\alpha}) A \left[\frac{K(s-1)}{L(s)}\right]^{\tilde{\alpha}} \tag{10.18}$$

where $L(s) = \sum_{t=0}^{t_R} \epsilon_t \, \ell_t(s) \, N_t(s)$ is the aggregate labour input in efficiency units, ϵ_t is a time-invariant and exogenous age-efficiency index, and $\ell_t(s)$ is the labour supply of an agent of age t at time s. The aggregate capital input is given by $K(s-1) = \sum_{t=0}^{t_R} k_t(s-1) \, N_t(s)$, where $k_t(s)$ is the physical capital holdings of an agent of age t at time s, $\tilde{\alpha} \in (0, 1)$ is the income share of capital, and A is total factor productivity.

10.3.3 *Government*

An age-t person divides his time-s asset holdings $a_t(s)$ between government bonds and private capital: $a_t(s) = b_t(s) + k_t(s)$, where $b_t(s)$ is government debt.[10] The government's budget constraint at s is:

$$\begin{aligned} g(s)N(s) &+ \sum_{t=t_R+1}^{T} S_t(s)N_t(s) + R(s-1)\sum_{t=0}^{T} b_t(s-1)N_t(s) \\ &= \tau_b R(s-1)Beq(s) + \sum_{t=0}^{T} b_t(s)N_t(s) + \sum_{t=0}^{T} N_t(s)\{\tau_a(s)[R(s-1)-1]a_{t-1}(s-1) \\ &\quad + \tau_\ell(s)w(s)\epsilon_t\ell_t(s) + \tau_c(s)c_t(s)\} \end{aligned} \tag{10.19}$$

where

$$Beq(s) = \sum_{t=0}^{T} [1-\alpha_t(s)] \, a_t(s-1)N_t(s-1) \tag{10.20}$$

and

$$a_{-1}(s-1) = \frac{Beq(s)(1-\tau_b)}{N_0(s)} \tag{10.21}$$

In equation (10.19), $g(s)$ is the amount of government purchases at time s, $S_t(s)$ is the social security benefits received by an age-t individual at time s, $R(s-1) = 1+r(s-1)-\delta$ is the rate of return on asset holdings net of depreciation, τ_b is the tax on inheritances, $\tau_a(s)$, $\tau_\ell(s)$ and $\tau_c(s)$ are taxes on asset income, labour income, and consumption, respectively. The amount of assets inherited at time s by each new worker is denoted by

[10] We assume that these two assets pay the same return, which implies that individual portfolios are indeterminate. We can compute the aggregate holdings of each asset since the economy's resource constraint yields the amount of aggregate physical capital, and government bond holdings are then computed as a residual after the total asset holdings are computed.

$a_{-1}(s-1)$, which is assumed to be divided between physical capital and government bonds in the same proportions that these are held in the aggregate portfolio:

$$k_{-1}(s-1) = \frac{\sum_{t=0}^{T}[1-\alpha_t(s)]\,k_t(s)N_t(s)}{N_0(s)} \qquad (10.22)$$

$$b_{-1}(s-1) = \frac{\sum_{t=0}^{T}[1-\alpha_t(s)]\,b_t(s)N_t(s)}{N_0(s)}$$

In the benefit formula, $fixben$, for people living in a steady state, is given by

$$fixben = fixrate \cdot AV$$

where AV records the average earnings of a worker who has survived to retirement age. For people living during the transition, $fixben$ is a linear combination of the contributions in the initial and final steady states.[11]

10.3.4 *Household's problem*

10.3.4.1 *Budget constraints* Individuals face the following budget constraints:

$$c_t(s) + a_t(s) = R(s-1)a_{t-1}(s-1) + w(s)\epsilon_t\ell_t(s) + S_t(s) - \Upsilon_t(s) + d_t \qquad (10.23a)$$

$$\Upsilon_t = \tau_0(s) + \tau_\ell(s)\,[w(s)\epsilon_t\ell_t(s) + d_t] + \tau_a(s)\,[R(s-1)-1]\,a_{t-1}(s-1) + \tau_c(s)c_t(s) \qquad (10.23b)$$

$$e_t(s) = e_{t-1}(s-1) + w(s)\epsilon_t\ell_t(s) \qquad (10.23c)$$

$$S_t(s) = \begin{cases} 0 & \text{for } t \le t_R + 1 \\ fixben_t(s) + rrate_t(s)e_{t-1}(s-1) & \text{for } t > t_R + 1 \end{cases} \qquad (10.23d)$$

$$z_{t+1} = A_{22}z_t + C_2\omega_{t+1} \qquad (10.23e)$$

$$\begin{bmatrix} d_t \\ \gamma_t \end{bmatrix} = \begin{bmatrix} U_{d,t} \\ U_\gamma \end{bmatrix} z_t \qquad (10.23f)$$

In equation (10.23a), $\tau_0(s)$ is a lump-sum tax, and $e_t(s)$ the cumulated earnings of an individual. The benefit formula (10.23d) allows for either a lump-sum retirement benefit or benefits that are related to past cumulated earnings. Equation (10.23e) describes the evolution of the information variable z_t, where ω_{t+1} is a martingale difference process. $U_{d,t}$ and U_γ are selector vectors that specify the income shock d_t and the stochastic bliss point γ_t. De Nardi *et al.* set the preference shock to a constant but specify d_t to be random process with mean zero: $d_t = \rho_1 d_{t-1} + \omega_{1t}$. The martingale difference sequence ω_{t+1} is adapted to $J_t = (\omega_0^t, x_0)$, with $E(\omega_{t+1}|J_t) = 0$, $E(\omega_{t+1}\omega_{t+1}'|J_t) = I$. We assume that the individual income shocks are independent across individuals. The law of large numbers then implies that all uncertainty at the individual level averages out and that the aggregate economy is deterministic.

[11] We distribute bequests as follows. Each agent born at time s begins life with assets $a_{-1}(s-1)$, which we set equal to a per-capita share of total bequests from people who died at the end of period $s-1$. This distribution scheme implies that within a steady state, per-capita initial assets equal per-capita bequests adjusted for population growth. However, during either policy or demographic transitions between steady states, this distribution scheme implies that what a generation receives in bequests no longer equals what it leaves behind.

10.3.4.2 *Preferences* The one-period utility function for an age-t person is given by

$$u\left(c_t(s), \ell_t(s)\right) = -\tfrac{1}{2}\left[(c_t(s) - \gamma_t(s))^2 + (\pi_2 \ell_t(s))^2\right] \tag{10.24}$$

where π_2 is a parameter and $\gamma_t(s)$ is a stochastic bliss point. There is a subjective discount factor β which is common across individuals and cohorts. The effective discount factor from age t to $t+1$ at time s is the product $\beta\alpha_t(s)$. Let $x_t(s) = \left[a_{t-1}(s-1), e_{t-1}(s-1), z_t'\right]'$ denote the *state* vector of an age t individual at the beginning of period s. If an individual dies at the end of age $t-1$, his value function is given by $V_t(x_t(s) \mid \text{dead at } t) = V_{T+1}(x_t(s)) = x_t(s)' P_{T+1} x_t(s)$, where P_{T+1} is a negative semi-definite matrix with parameters that determine the strength of the bequest motive. This formulation of bequest motive is termed "the joy of giving" in the literature.[12]

Our formulation gradually activates the bequest motive, intensifying it with age as the mortality table makes the household think more about the hereafter.

For $t = 0, \ldots, T$, let $V_t(x_t(s))$ be the optimal value function for an age-t person at time s. The household's Bellman equations are

$$\begin{aligned} V_t\left(a_{t-1}(s-1), e_{t-1}(s-1), z_t\right) = \max_{\{c_t(s), a_t(s), \ell_t(s)\}} & \{u(c_t(s), \ell_t(s)) \\ & + \beta\alpha_t(s) E_t V_{t+1}\left(a_t(s), e_t(s), z_{t+1}\right) \\ & + \beta[(1-\alpha_t(s)] E_t V_{T+1}\left(a_t(s), e_t(s), z_{t+1}\right)\} \end{aligned}$$

where the maximization is subject to the constraints (10.23).

Using standard linear quadratic control theory, the solution to the above finite-state, finite-horizon dynamic program is obtained as follows. Suppressing the time subscript for ease of exposition, we can express Bellman equations as

$$V_t(x_t) = \max_{u_t, x_{t+1}} \{u_t' Q_t u_t + x_t' R_t x_t + \beta E_t V_{t+1}(x_{t+1})\} \tag{10.25}$$

where

$$\begin{aligned} E_t V_{t+1}(x_{t+1}) &= \alpha_t(s) E_t[V_{t+1}(x_{t+1}) \mid \text{alive}] \\ &\quad + [1 - \alpha_t(s)] E_t[V_{t+1}(x_{t+1}) \mid \text{dead}] \\ V_t(x_t \mid \text{alive}) &= x_t' P_t x_t + \xi_t \\ V_t(x_t \mid \text{dead}) &= x_t' P_{T+1} x_t \\ x_t' P_{T+1} x_t &= -JG\left((1-\tau_b)a_{t-1} - JB\right)^2 \end{aligned} \tag{10.26}$$

The last equation describes the bequest motive. JG is a parameter governing the intensity of the bequest motive and JB is an inheritance bliss point. Since the individual's survival probability declines over the life cycle, equation (10.26) reveals the higher weight attached to death and hence bequests as the individual ages.

[12] An altruistic bequest motive helps the model to produce an empirically plausible capital–output ratio. Also, the presence of a bequest motive makes private saving and hence the aggregate capital stock more resilient to changes in the environment. Fuster (1997) emphasizes the importance of this feature of her model in yielding results that are different from those in Auerbach and Kotlikoff (1987).

The matrix Riccati equations for P_t, F_t and ξ_t are:

$$\begin{aligned}
F_t &= \left(Q_t + \beta\alpha_t(s)B_t'P_{t+1}B_t + \beta[1-\alpha_t(s)]B_t'P_{T+1}B_t\right)^{-1} \\
&\quad \times \left(\beta\alpha_t(s)B_t'P_{t+1}A_t + \beta[1-\alpha_t(s)]B_t'P_{T+1}A_t\right) \\
P_t &= R_t + F_t'Q_tF_t + \beta\alpha_t(s)[A_t - B_tF_t]'P_{t+1}[A_t - B_tF_t] \\
&\quad + \beta[1-\alpha_t(s)][A_t - B_tF_t]'P_{T+1}[A_t - B_tF_t] \\
\xi_t &= \beta\alpha_t(s)\left[\mathrm{tr}(P_{t+1}C'C) + \xi_{t+1}\right] + \beta[1-\alpha_t(s)]\left[\mathrm{tr}(P_{T+1}C'C)\right]
\end{aligned}$$

Reintroducing the time subscript, the above recursions produce the time- and age-dependent decision rules

$$u_t(s) = -F_t(s)x_t(s)$$

and the law of motion

$$x_{t+1}(s+1) = A_t(s)x_t + C_t(s)\omega_{t+1}$$

Note that the certainty equivalence specification of preferences makes the decision rules independent of the noise statistics, $\{C_t(s)\}$.[13]

Given a mean and covariance matrix for the initial state vector, $(\mu_0(s), \Sigma_0(s))$, the first two moments of the state vector follow the law of motion

$$\begin{aligned}
\mu_{t+1}(s+1) &= A_t(s)\mu_t(s) \\
\Sigma_{t+1}(s+1) &= A_t(s)\Sigma_t(s)A_t(s)' + C_t(s)C_t(s)'
\end{aligned}$$

The mean and standard deviation of aggregate quantities such as aggregate consumption, investment, output, and physical capital stock can then be easily computed as weighted averages of the above moments of the distribution of the state vector.

10.3.5 *Resource constraint*

The national income identity at time s in this economy is given by

$$g(s)N(s) + \sum_{t=0}^{T} c_t(s)N_t(s) + K(s) = R(s-1)K(s-1) + w(s)\sum_{t=0}^{t_R} \epsilon_t\ell_t(s)\,N_t(s)$$

10.3.6 *Time variation in demographics*

De Nardi *et al.* (1998) incorporate the ageing of the population in their model as a transition in the demographic structure of the model. An initial steady state, associated with constant pre-1975 values of the demographic parameters $\{\alpha_t, n\}$, is specified. Then, the

[13] Huang *et al.* (1997) depart from certainty equivalence by employing nonexpected utility. Following Hansen and Sargent (1995), the linearity of decision rules is preserved although the noise statistics influence the decision rules.

projected mortality tables from the Social Security Administration (SSA) are used for the years between 1975 and 2060, so that

$$\alpha_t(s) = \begin{cases} \alpha_t^0 & \text{for } s \leq 1974 \\ \hat{\alpha}_t(s) & \text{for } 1975 \leq s \leq 2060 \\ \alpha_t^1 & \text{for } s > 2060 \end{cases}$$

where $\alpha_t^0 = \alpha_t(1970)$ from the mortality table, $\alpha_t^1 = \alpha_t(2060 + t)$, and the SSA numbers for the cohort to be born in 2060; the $\hat{\alpha}_t(s)$ are taken from the SSA.[14] The path for the growth rate of newborns is calibrated in order to match the SSA's forecasts of the dependency ratio, which is projected to increase from 18% in 1974 to 50% in 2060.

De Nardi *et al.* assume that individuals in the economy suddenly realize in 1975 that the mortality tables have changed and that they start using the new tables. The mortality tables are assumed to reach a steady state in 2060 in line with the SSA projections. The demographic structure changes for another $T+1$ years, until it reaches a new steady state in 2060+$(T+1)$. The demographic transition requires the government to make fiscal adjustments and causes the individuals to recompute their decision rules in light of all the surprise changes in their environment. In steps, the government increases one tax rate (either τ_ℓ or τ_c) during a policy transition period, leaving all other tax rates constant. These tax changes are scheduled and announced as follows. In 1975 the government announces that, starting in year 2000, it will increase the tax on labour income (in experiments 1, 3, 5, and 6) or on consumption (in experiments 2 and 4) every 10 years in order to reach the terminal steady state with the desired ratio of debt to gross domestic product (GDP). Starting in 2060, that tax rate is held constant at its new steady-state level, but the wage rate and interest rate continue to vary for another $2(T+1)$ periods, after which time they are held fixed.

10.3.7 *Computing an equilibrium transition path*

1. Compute the initial steady-state equilibrium. Use a backward recursion to compute the agents' value functions and policy functions, taking as given government policy, bequests, and prices. Iterate until convergence on the following four-dimensional fixed-point problem with arguments given by:
   (a) the social security pension, in order to match the desired replacement rate;
   (b) bequests, so that planned bequests coincide with received ones;
   (c) the labour income or consumption tax to satisfy the government budget constraint;
   (d) factor prices, to match the firms' first-order conditions.[15]
2. Compute the final steady-state equilibrium. In addition to following the above procedure for the initial steady state, there is an additional do-loop layer in which iterations are performed on the government debt level to match the debt-to-GDP ratio to a prescribed value such as that in the initial steady state.

[14] The life tables are taken from Bell *et al.* (1992).

[15] In practice, the wage rate is a function of the real interest rate through the Cobb–Douglas production function. Therefore, the last component of the steady-state fixed point is just the real interest rate.

3. Compute the equilibrium transition path between the steady states. For a given time path of factor prices, bequests, and government policy parameters, compute the transition dynamics by solving backward the sequence of value functions and policy functions, and then:
   (a) iterate until convergence on a parameterized path for the tax rate to match the final debt-to-GDP ratio;
   (b) iterate until convergence on the time path of factor prices to match the firms' first-order conditions.

Although the model economy would converge to the final steady-state equilibrium only asymptotically (because prices are endogenous) De Nardi *et al.* follow Auerbach and Kotlikoff (1987) and assume that convergence obtains in $3T$ periods.[16]

10.4 Conclusions

This chapter presents two versions of an overlapping generations model with incomplete markets and describes how this model can be used to analyse issues related to public pension systems such as the unfunded social security system currently in place in the United States and many other developed countries. The first version of the model departs from the Arrow–Debreu world of complete contingent claims markets by assuming the presence of exogenously given borrowing constraints. Both versions of the model assume that private annuity markets are missing, thereby limiting the ability of agents to insure against uncertain lifespans.

The two versions of the model differ in their preference structures as well as in other respects. The first version assumes that labour is supplied inelastically, whereas the second version relaxes this assumption. The second version incorporates a form of bequest motive, whereas the first version is populated by pure life-cycle consumers. The first version allows for a richer set of within-cohort heterogeneity, whereas the second version (essentially) assumes that intra-cohort heterogeneity is normally distributed. Huggett and Ventura (1998) and Fuster (1997) have incorporated a variable labour supply into a model with preferences similar to those used in the first version of the model presented here. In addition, Fuster's model includes a bequest motive that is different from the one described here.

The chapter presents the numerical solution algorithms used to compute steady-state equilibria for each version of the model. For the second version of the model, the chapter also describes the solution algorithm for computing transition paths between steady states.

[16]To compute a steady-state equilibrium, De Nardi *et al.* (1998) use a secant algorithm which is a method to find the root of a system of nonlinear equations. In computing an equilibrium transition path between steady states, they use a relaxation algorithm which is a method for solving two-point boundary value problems. See Press *et al.* (1986) and references contained therein for a detailed description of the secant and relaxation algorithms.

11

COMPUTATION OF EQUILIBRIA IN HETEROGENEOUS-AGENT MODELS

José-Víctor Ríos-Rull[1]

11.1 Introduction

There are many questions in economics for which heterogeneous-agent dynamic models have to be used to provide answers. Examples of those questions where the desired answer is quantitative are as follows:

1. What changes in the distribution of wealth will occur if the tax system is changed from progressive to proportional?
2. What increases in taxation are needed to maintain the current level of US social security benefits under current population patterns?
3. What type of policy changes can be expected from changes in constitutions?

All these questions require models where the households that populate the economy are not identical. With respect to the first question, note that the key property of progressivity of the tax system is that different households face different tax rates. For the second question, the age distribution of the population determines the amounts collected and paid by the administrators of social security. Finally, the determinants of policy should be affected by the relations between different groups of households that do not have the same preferences over policies. In what follows, I describe the models that have been used to address these and related questions, and I pose the models in ways that are susceptible to computation.

I start with a model with infinitely-lived agents subject to uninsurable idiosyncratic shocks to earnings. I use a very simple version of such a model to address the distribution of wealth.[2] The steady state of such a model generates a well-defined distribution of wealth. Next, I look at non-steady-state allocations: the technical difficulties that they pose and different ways of avoiding such difficulties.

[1]This paper includes most of the material on computing equilibria in models with heterogeneous agents from lectures given at the European University Institute, the University of California at Los Angeles, and the University of Pennsylvania. The comments of many colleagues and students have been very useful, in particular, those of Tim Kehoe, Per Krusell and Ed Prescott. The author thanks the National Science Foundation for grant SBR–9309514. Correspondence to Department of Economics, University of Pennsylvania, 3718 Locust Walk, Philadelphia, Pennsylvania 19104-6297, USA.

[2]This model uses a specific theory of wealth differences. Other possible theories include a life-cycle theory where wealth differences are due to age differences and a preference-based theory where wealth differences are due to differences in the discount rate. In the theory proposed in this chapter, wealth differences are due to differences in past employment shocks.

Next, I move into overlapping generations models, or models where every year some agents die and new agents are born. These models are embodied in a neoclassical growth model structure with capital accumulation. The models are reviewed with the intention of being able to accommodate agents living a large number of periods. Again, I start reviewing steady-state allocations, and later move to non-steady-state situations. I end this section with a list of topics that have been studied with the aid of this type of model.

I finish this chapter with a section on dynamic voting models. These are models that endogenously generate government policies as part of a Markov equilibria, and that are starting to be used to study positive policy issues such as redistributional policies.

All these models have in common that they are populated by agents that are different from each other. Moreover, these differences are central in the sense that the question that these models are used to answer requires heterogeneity (how could we talk about distribution or redistribution of wealth if all agents were equal?). I have organized the exposition of these models to ease the computation of their equilibrium allocations.

11.2 A simple model of wealth distribution

Imagine a model economy populated with a large number (in fact a continuum) of households. The households care about streams of consumption in a standard way:

$$E_0 \left\{ \sum_{t=0}^{\infty} \beta^t u(c_t) \right\} \tag{11.1}$$

where, for each period t, c_t is restricted to belonging to C, the per-period consumption possibility set of the agent, which might specify non-negative consumption. Every period, households receive an endowment of the consumption good – let us call it coconuts – denoted $s \in S = \{s_1, \ldots, s_n, \ldots, s_N\}$ that follows a Markov process with transition matrix Γ. Note that s_t is then a random variable that is *independently distributed across individuals*. The fact that there are a large number of households guarantees that a law of large numbers holds (see Uhlig, 1996) and that the fraction of households with each shock depends only on the fraction of households that had each shock the previous period. I deal first with versions of this economy that are stationary in the sense that, besides this idiosyncratic shock, there are no other time-varying features which affect the problem the agent faces.

11.2.1 *Stationary economies: Steady states*

Households cannot borrow, but they can hold part of their endowment as inventory. Let $q > \beta$ denote the inventory technology, so that if one unit of the good is stored today, then $1/q$ units of the good are obtained tomorrow. The agent then maximizes equation (11.1) subject to

$$c_t = a_t + s_t - a_{t+1}\, q \tag{11.2}$$

with a_0 given.

At this point, it is useful to deal with this problem by looking at its associated recursive formulation via the value function:

$$v(s,a) = \max_{c,a'} u(c) + \beta E\{v(s',a')|s\} \tag{11.3}$$

subject to:

$$c = a + s - a'q \tag{11.4}$$

where I denote next period's variables by primes and where the solution is given by $a' = g(s,a)$, which describes how the household chooses asset holdings for the next period given the current state, the pair shock s and assets a.

Note that at any point in time, there are a number of households that differ in their current luck s and in their wealth a (that somehow summarizes all their past luck). To describe this economy, I need a mathematical object that is well suited to counting. This object is a measure. The key properties of measures are associated with the fact that they act as counting or weighting mechanisms. The main mathematical concepts are summarily reviewed in Section 11.6, although to understand the logic, the concepts are not really needed.

Next I describe some of the crucial properties of the solution to equation (11.3). These properties are stated without proof, and the reader is referred to Hugget (1993) for details.[3]

- Monotonicity and continuity are properties of the saving functions. Monotonicity only holds for certain types of Markov matrices Γ; in particular, it does hold for a two-state process.
- There are upper and lower bounds on the desired level of asset holdings, so that $a \in A = [\underline{a}, \bar{a}]$ when $q > \beta$. The lower bound can arise from borrowing constraints or, as in the preceding literal interpretation, from technological feasibility. Alternatively, in economies where borrowing is feasible, this lower bound on assets can arise endogenously from the fact that the agent has to pay its debts in every state of the economy, which prevents the possibility of bankruptcy. In this case, the lower bound on assets is that level which requires that the worst possible endowment is used entirely to pay interest. If I denote this lower bound by $\underline{a}$ and s_1 is the worst earnings shock, I have that $\underline{a} = -s_1/(1-q)$.
- With the agent decision rule $g(s,a)$ and the Markov matrix Γ that governs the law of motion of the idiosyncratic shock s, I can construct a transition function $Q(s,a,B)$ that describes the conditional probability of a type (s,a) household having a type in set $B \subset S \times A$ tomorrow.

I use this transition to obtain the dynamic equation of the model that gives tomorrow's distribution of households x' as a function of today's distribution x and the Markov

[3] The computation of the solution is relatively standard and many methods can be used. Linear quadratic methods, however, *cannot* be used since, as we will see, the assets that individuals hold are bounded both below and above, and this property does not hold when decision rules are linear. The chapters by Marcet and by McGrattan in this book describe methods to solve this type of problem. There are also other ways of solving this type of problem, for example with the use of splines as in Krusell and Smith (1998).

chain Γ by $x'(B) = \int_{S\times A} Q(s, a, B)\, dx$. Note that a theorem which states that x' is, in fact, a probability distribution (or probability measure) is needed. I denote the updating operator with $T(x)$; that is, $x' = T(x)$. I write

$$T(x) = x'(B) = \int_{S\times A} Q(s, a, B)\, dx \tag{11.5}$$

for all $B \in \mathcal{A}$.

This model is useful if there are not many possible distributions of wealth of interest. In other words, I would like the model to generate endogenously some unique distribution of wealth so that the model has some tight predictions. There is good news in this respect.

As long as a certain *monotone mixing condition* is satisfied, it can be proved that there is a unique fixed point x^* of equation (11.5). Furthermore, this point is the *weak** limit of successive applications of the operator associated with the above equation for any initial condition x_0. This mixing condition can be thought of, rather loosely, as the existence in this economy of both the *American dream* and the *American nightmare*. The condition requires that no matter how poor (rich) a household is, the probability that the household becomes one of the richest (poorest) is arbitrarily close to one, provided enough time passes.

Therefore, given a certain process $\{S, \Gamma\}$, there is a unique stationary distribution of wealth x^* associated with it. In this economy, the stationary distribution of wealth corresponds to a *steady state*. The issue is how to find x^*, given g. Two possibilities are outlined below.

1. As with probabilities, distribution functions can be used to describe the measures. For this type of economy, I can use distribution functions over assets, but densities over shocks. Let $\{\Gamma_n^*\}_{n=1}^N$ be the invariant distribution associated with Markov matrix Γ. If today's distribution of the shock is given by Γ^*, then so is tomorrow's. I approximate the distribution functions with, say, a piecewise linear function over some (very fine) grid of the asset space. To compute x^*, I use the following steps:
   (a) Place a grid on the set A, such as $\{a_1, \ldots, a_m, \ldots, a_M\}$, where $a_1 = \underline{a}$ and $a_M = \bar{a}$. Make sure that this grid is much finer than that used to compute g. The grid does not need to be equally spaced.
   (b) Initialize an arbitrary piecewise distribution function F^0 over that grid.[4] Note that F^0 is a matrix of dimension $N \times M$. For example, an initial distribution of wealth that is uniform can be represented by

$$F^0_{n,m} = \frac{a_m - a_1}{(a_M - a_1)}\Gamma_n^* \tag{11.6}$$

   Alternatively, an initial distribution of wealth where all households hold the minimum wealth $\underline{a}$ can be represented by

$$F^0_{n,m} = \frac{a_M - a_1}{(a_M - a_1)}\Gamma_n^* \tag{11.7}$$

[4]More precisely, F^0 is a distribution function over the assets, but a density over the shocks.

(c) Compute $g^{-1}(s_n, a_m) = \{a, a_m = g(s_n, a)\}$, the inverse of the decision rule (which is unique, given the established monotonicity of g). This process depends on how the decision rule g was obtained. Typically, the process involves some type of interpolation, since g is stored only on a finite set of points of the asset space.

$$F^1_{n,m} = \sum_{\hat{n}=1}^{N} F^0\big(\hat{n}_j, g^{-1}(s_{\hat{n}}, a_m)\big)\Gamma(s_n|s_{\hat{n}}) \tag{11.8}$$

Note that F^1 is written as a vector, while F^0 is written as a function. The reason is that F^1 is computed on a grid, while F^0 is evaluated in points that are not necessarily on the grid. To evaluate the value of F^0 outside the grid, interpolation is needed. Since the distribution function is approximated by a piecewise linear function, the interpolation is linear. Other interpolation techniques could also be used.

(d) Compare F^0 with F^1. If they are equal (up to the required precision), stop; if not, update so that $F^0 = F^1$, and repeat the process.

2. Alternatively, construct a sample of households and track them over time, as data collection agencies do. Let I be the size of that sample (tens of thousands is an appropriate sample size). Then do the following:
   (a) Initialize the sample by assigning a pair $\{s, a\}$ to each element i. This yields a sample distribution of wealth $\{\{s^1, a^1\}, \ldots, \{s^i, a^i\}, \ldots, \{s^I, a^I\}\}$.
   (b) Compute a set of statistics from this sample, such as the average, standard deviation, percentiles, and so on, and denote them $H(\{s^i, a^i\}_{i=1}^I)$.
   (c) Use the function g and a random number generator to obtain $\{(s')^i, (a')^i\}$ for all i, and compute its statistics H.
   (d) Continue this process until two consecutive sets of statistics are sufficiently close to each other. This means that consequent updates of the sample will not have distributional changes, and the sample is considered converged.

With the notation that I have used, s denotes shocks to labour earnings. However, it is clear that the same logic can be used to denote many other shocks as well, such as shocks to health, marital status, entrepreneurial success, and so on. This notation can also be used to determine household characteristics that evolve deterministically, such as genetic type or age.

So far, there are no equilibrium considerations: all households live in isolation and increase or decrease their stockpile of coconuts. However, I can actively introduce markets. Here are two simple examples:

1. Households borrow from and lend to each other, and there is no storage (Huggett, 1993). In this case, there is a market-clearing condition that did not exist before. Note that q is the inverse of the gross interest rate. The market-clearing condition can be written as

$$\int_{S\times A} a\, dx^*(q) = 0 \tag{11.9}$$

where I have made explicit the dependence of the invariant distribution on the rate q at which assets can be accumulated.

2. Assets take the form of real capital, and there is no borrowing and lending ($\underline{a} = 0$). Let $f(K, L)$ be an aggregate production function, where aggregate employment L is the total amount of efficiency units in the economy. The shock s should be interpreted as a shock on the endowment of efficiency units of labour. That is, $L = \sum_{n=1}^{N} s_n \Gamma_n^*$, which does not change over time. Note that in this case, the key variable to be determined is aggregate capital, since the rate of return that households face is given by aggregate productivity of capital. This can be summarized by the following condition:

$$f_1\left(\int_{S\times A} a\, dx^*(q), L\right) = \frac{1}{q} \tag{11.10}$$

The evaluation of the two market clearing conditions (11.9) and (11.10) involves the computation of an integral. These integrals can be readily computed once we have computed the stationary distribution x^* by either one of the two methods outlined above. If x^* is computed with the aid of a piecewise linear approximation to its distribution function $F_{n,m}$, then the market clearing condition (11.9) can be written as:

$$\int_{S\times A} a\, dx^*(q) = \sum_n \left(\sum_{m=2}^{M} (F_{n,m} - F_{n,m-1})\frac{a_m + a_{m-1}}{2} + F_{n,1}a_1\right) \tag{11.11}$$

Alternatively, if x^* is computed with a sample, then the computation of conditions (11.9) amounts to just the calculation of a sample mean.

An important thing to note about the market interpretation of economies of this type is that not all possible prices q are relevant: only those, if any, that clear markets. Therefore, those prices have to be found. The standard procedure for doing so is based on finding two prices – one at each side of the market clearing condition – and then iterating within those two bounds until market clearing occurs. A key property of those two prices is that $q > \beta$. Otherwise the household's problem does not have a bounded solution.

To be sure that a zero exists, a sufficient condition is that the moments of $x^*(q)$ are continuous. Such conditions are typically satisfied for economies like this one. Theorem 12.13 in Stokey and Lucas (1989) requires the state space $\{S \times A\}$ to be compact, the transition probabilities Q to be continuous in q, and each q to have a unique stationary distribution $x^*(q)$.

So far, the model encompasses only the choices of consumption and savings. Some applications might require the inclusion of other variables:

1. An hours-worked variable requires simply solving a slightly more complicated agent problem. Still, the same methods apply once the decision rules of the new problem are obtained. Unlike in methods designed to solve for the representative household of an economy, the possibility of corner solutions in hours worked might arise. That is, sometimes the members of the household choose to work zero hours. If that is the case and an Euler equation method is used to solve the agent's maximization problem, the typical procedure is to impose the restriction that hours worked are zero and then solve the intertemporal Euler equation under this restriction.

2. A discrete choice variable, such as to work a fixed number of hours or not to work, to become an entrepreneur or a worker, or to go college or not, is much more difficult to solve. Note that because of the discreteness, information on the value function has to be stored, because the Euler equation is not enough to characterize the optimal choice. Moreover, note that the iterations on the value function do not necessarily return concave functions, and the decision rules are not necessarily continuous in many points of the state space. To see this, imagine the discrete choice of whether to work a fixed number of hours or not to work at all. For each s, there is a level of wealth – denote it $\hat{a}_0$ – high enough that the members of the household will choose to enjoy their leisure, while for lower levels of wealth they will choose to work. Note that for values of wealth slightly lower than $\hat{a}_0$, income can be considerably higher than at $\hat{a}_0$, since the household has almost the same capital income but a lot more labour income. Therefore, the savings decisions are discontinuous at $\hat{a}_0$. Take the case of a good enough shock so that the household is accumulating assets for $a < \hat{a}_0$. In this case, there is another level of assets – denote it $\hat{a}_1$ – so that $\hat{a}_0 = g(s, \hat{a}_1)$. If $a \geq \hat{a}_1$ and if the shock does not change, the members of the household will choose not to work one period after, but if $a < \hat{a}_1$, the members of the household will choose to work the following period. Again, the same logic as before shows that there is another discontinuity in the savings function at $\hat{a}_1$. To deal with this type of problem, four approaches can be used:

   (a) Discretize the state space. This means that asset holdings can take only finitely many values. The optimal choice is just a finite maximization problem that can be solved with relative ease, typically taking advantage of the monotonicity, within the same discrete choice, of the decision rule. See, for example, Trick and Zin (1993).
   (b) Use lotteries. This means that households choose a probability of making the choice which makes the action space convex and allows the Euler equation approach to be used. However, this means that there is a contract between households, and a market clearing condition is necessary.
   (c) Use shocks with a continuous support. In this case, the discontinuity that shows up one period before the household achieves the critical level might disappear. The reason is that one period before, the households cannot be sure of how their savings will relate to the critical discontinuity point.
   (d) Use continuous-time models where the discontinuity problem is likely to disappear (at least the discontinuity that results from the rounding of the time periods). This method is still under development for this class of non-concave problems.

Unlike in the environment where there is a storage technology, the model economy cannot be thought of as having measures changing over time. This would imply that market clearing prices change every period, but that households solve their maximization problems under the assumption that prices are constant for ever.

I now turn to situations where there are prices, and where there are time-varying distributions.

11.2.2 *Non-steady-state allocations*

I am interested in economies with a large number of households that face uninsurable, idiosyncratic uncertainty, but not necessarily in steady-state situations. For example, I might want to know the business cycle properties of this type of economy. Or, perhaps, I want to know the implications of a policy change, say, a tax change. I will run into a big problem. To see the problem, consider a simple real business cycle version of the economy where the asset is real capital.[5] Households have s units of labour and own assets that can be used as real capital in an aggregate production function given by

$$Y_t = z_t f(K_{t-1}, L_t) \tag{11.12}$$

where Y_t is real output. Capital depreciates at rate δ. Productivity shock z_t follows a Markov process with transition Γ_z. Conditional on the aggregate shock z_t, the idiosyncratic shock s_t is Markov, too. The joint process for these shocks can be written as $\Gamma(z', s'|z, s)$. There are rental markets for labour and capital but, again, no insurance against bad realizations of the labour efficiency of each agent. Factor prices are marginal productivities. The problem of the agent in non-recursive form can be written as

$$\max_{c_t, a_{t+1}} E_0 \left\{ \sum_{t=0}^{\infty} \beta^t u(c_t) \right\} \tag{11.13}$$

subject to:

$$c_t = a_t(1 + r_t) + s_t w_t - a_{t+1} \tag{11.14}$$

with a_0 given and where w_t and r_t are the rental prices of factors. To solve this problem, the household has to know the process that determines those prices. Those prices are determined by marginal productivities, which in turn depend on the aggregate quantities of the inputs. In this simple case, only aggregate capital matters. I could be tempted to write (as in the representative agent case) the following problem:

$$v(z, K, s, a) = \max_{c, a'} \; u(c) + \beta E\{v(z', K', s', a')|z, s\} \tag{11.15}$$

subject to:

$$c = a\,(1 + r(z, K)) + sw(z, K) - a' \tag{11.16}$$

$$K' = G(z, K) \tag{11.17}$$

where $r(\cdot)$ and $w(\cdot)$ are functions that return the marginal productivity. This, however, is wrong. The problem is the function $G(\cdot)$. It is a problem because the pair $\{z, K\}$ is not, in general, a sufficient statistic for K': tomorrow's capital K' depends on the whole distribution of wealth x. Depending on how wealth is distributed, aggregate capital will be different tomorrow, except where individual decision rules are linear in a, which is not the usual case. The appropriate problem is then

$$v(z, x, s, a) = \max_{c, a'} u(c) + \beta E\{v(z', x', s', a')|z, s\} \tag{11.18}$$

[5]Many economists do not like real business cycle models because they are representative agent or *Robinson Crusoe* worlds. Perhaps they will like this version more.

subject to:

$$c = a\,(1 + r(z, K)) + sw(z, K) - a' \tag{11.19}$$

$$K = \int_{S\times A} a\,dx \tag{11.20}$$

$$x' = G(z, x) \tag{11.21}$$

where x' denotes next period's distribution. The problem is that, unlike a or the shocks z and s, the measures x and x' are not real numbers. On the contrary, they are infinite-dimensional objects, and keeping track of them requires a lot of storage. Moreover, computing the equilibrium requires not only solving the problem of the household, but also finding the function $G(z, x)$. Typically, the law of motion $G(z, x)$ of the economy is found by iterating on the space where this function belongs, but in this case the appropriate space is the set of functions from an infinite dimensional space into itself. The procedure involved is absolutely unmanageable.

There are three standard ways to get around this problem and still study economies with time-varying wealth distributions. I review them in order.

11.2.2.1 *The distribution is not a state variable* The most obvious way to get around the problem is to deal with economies for which there are prices that do not depend on x, but on some exogenous feature, such as a shock. This can be done by using simple technologies or by using the government to impose prices exogenously. See Díaz-Giménez*et al.* (1992), Ríos-Rull (1995), and Díaz-Giménez (1996). The latter procedure requires, of course, making sure that the government budget constraint is satisfied. In this approach, the distribution of wealth, x, is not a state variable of the household problem.

11.2.2.2 *Transition between steady states* The second way to get around the problem is to look at the transition between steady states. This method was pioneered in Auerbach and Kotlikoff (1987). It is very useful for deterministic economies that are in steady state and then undergo a completely unexpected change in, say, technology or government policy. This method also requires stability of the steady state under the new parameters. The procedure is to assume that the economy converges in finite time to the new steady state in, say, 200 periods. This approach can be illustrated with the economy in Huggett (1993) after a change in the Markov matrix from Γ to $\hat{\Gamma}$.

Given Γ and $\hat{\Gamma}$, the steady-state equilibrium interest rates, value functions and distributions for both Markov matrices, that is, $q(\Gamma)$, $v(s, a; \Gamma)$, $x(\Gamma)$ and $q(\hat{\Gamma})$, $v(s, a; \hat{\Gamma})$, $x(\hat{\Gamma})$, can be readily computed. Next, note that the Euler equations for the household problem can be written as

$$u'(a_t + s - a_{t+1}q_t) = \frac{\beta}{q_t}\sum_{s'} u'(a_{t+1} - a_{t+2}q_{t+1})\hat{\Gamma}(s'|s) \tag{11.22}$$

Given a sequence of prices $\{q_t\}$ for $t \in \{1, \ldots, 200\}$ and valuation given by $v(s, a; \hat{\Gamma})$ at $t = 200$, this problem can be readily solved and the assets held obtained.[6] Aggregation yields the aggregate demand for assets. This implies that given a sequence of prices $\{q_t\}$ we have a sequence of excess demand functions that we want to be zero.

There are different ways to solve this problem. One that is cheap to program and hard to compute is just to use a nonlinear equation solver. This is typically not very good as the system has too many equations. Another procedure is to think of the problem as that of a second-order difference equation in prices with two end conditions (at opposite ends). This procedure involves the following steps:

1. Guess q_1.
2. Given q_1 and $x(\Gamma)$, solve for the q_2 that clears the credit market.
3. Update $x(\Gamma)$ to get x_1 using the decisions implied by q_1 and q_2.
4. Continue this process until q_{200}. Check whether q_{200} and x_{200} equal $q(\hat{\Gamma})$ and $x(\hat{\Gamma})$. If they do not, update the guess for q_1.

Alternatively, rather than think of q_{200} as a function of q_1, think of q_1 as a function of q_{200} and proceed backwards. The backward procedure seems to be more efficient. The most used procedure is different, however. It uses a form of nonlinear Gauss–Seidel. (For a discussion of these points, see Kehoe and Levine, 1991; and Judd, 1998.) It reduces to the following steps:

1′ Guess a sequence of prices $\{q_t^0\}_{t=1}^{200}$.

2′ Given prices $\{q_t^0\}_{t=2}^{200}$, and valuation $v(s, a; \hat{\Gamma})$ at $t = 200$, and an arbitrary q_1, the problem of the agents can be solved. Find the first period price that clears the market in the first period given initial distribution $x(\Gamma)$. Denote it q_1^1, and update the distribution of assets to obtain x_1.

3′ Given q_1^1 and $\{q_t^0\}_{t=3}^{200}$, solve the problem of the agents for the price q_2^1 that clears the market in $t = 2$. Again, update the distribution of assets and to obtain x_2.

4′ Continue this procedure until a set of new prices $\{q_t^1\}_{t=1}^{200}$, has been obtained.

5′ Compare those new prices with the guessed ones. If they are equal, stop. If not, update and continue the process until convergence is achieved.

11.2.2.3 *Partial information* The third way to get around the problem, which was introduced in Krusell and Smith (1998) and also used in Castaneda *et al.* (1998), is based on the logic that perhaps by using a little bit of information about x, households do almost as well as by using all the information in the distribution x when predicting future prices. The type of information about x that the agents use can be described generically as *moments of the distribution*. These moments include average wealth, standard deviation of wealth, and so on. They can also include such things as the share

[6] This is a standard maximization problem with two end conditions, the initial assets a_1, and the valuation of assets at $t = 200$ given by $v(s, a; \hat{\Gamma})$. A good way to solve it is using nonlinear Gauss–Seidel techniques.

of the wealth held by the wealthiest 5% or even the Gini index. Mathematically, these moments are given by the integral of a certain function with respect to the measure x.

Under this approach, households are assumed to be *boundedly rational* in the sense that they do not use all the information available to them. In this case, current and lagged values of (z, x) are such information. They use only some bits and pieces of information of x, which I write as $\ell_j(x)$, where the index j denotes the amount of information in the simple sense that it is the number of statistics of x that is used. Function ℓ_j typically consists of integrals of functions of the state with respect to the measure x, such as the moments of x. For now, function ℓ_j must include sufficient statistics for factor prices, which are the reason the agent's problem is affected by the measure. Below I discuss the extension of this approach to the case when current prices depend on the current actions of the agents. Consider the following problem where, to simplify the notation, I define $y \equiv \ell_j(x)$:

$$v(z, y, s, a; h_j, \ell_j) = \max_{c \geq 0, a' \in [\underline{a}, \bar{a}]} u(c) + \beta E\left\{v(z', y', s', a'; h_j, \ell_j)|s, z\right\} \quad (11.23)$$

subject to:

$$y' = h_j(y, z) \quad (11.24)$$

$$c = a\,(1 + r(z, y)) + sw(z, y) - a' \quad (11.25)$$

where $r(z, y)$ and $w(z, y)$ are functions for the factor prices that now depend on y. It is important to note that in this economy, factor prices only depend on the aggregate shock z and on aggregate capital K. Note that I have indexed the value function both by function ℓ_j, which returns the functions that serve as a proxy for measure x as state variables, and by the forecasting function h_j, which returns the future values of those functions. The households that solve this problem are boundedly rational for two reasons. One is that when households predict the future values of prices, they do not use all the information at their disposal. They approximate the distribution by a finite set of its statistics, and they consider only the current-period values of those statistics to predict their future values. The other is that when households make forecasts of y', they act as if their forecasts were perfectly accurate, which they are not. Note that the forecasting errors are not random in the sense that if the distribution were used to forecast the value of y', there would be no prediction errors.

The solution to problem (11.23) is an optimal savings rule $g(z, y, s, a; h_j, \ell_j)$, which, together with the process on z, generates a law of motion for the economy, $G(z, x; h_j, \ell_j)$. Let $b_j(h_j, \ell_j)$ denote the best unbiased forecasting function of $y' = \ell_j(x')$ within a certain parametric class B; that is, $\hat{y}' = b_j(z, y; h_j, \ell_j)$. Note that $b_j(\cdot, \ell_j)$ maps the set of j-dimensional functions in parametric class B into itself and can be readily computed through long simulations. The procedure is simple: given $\{h_j, \ell_j\}$, solve the problem of the agent that obtains $g(z, y, s, a; h_j, \ell_j)$. Then initialize a large sample of agents of dimension I by giving agents a pair consisting of a shock s and assets a, which yields $\{s_i^0, a_i^0\}_{i=1}^I$. From this sample, compute $\ell_j(x^0)$, which obtains y^0, and initialize the aggregate shock z^0. Use Γ and g to update the sample $\{s_i^1, a_i^1\}_{i=1}^I$, and compute y^1. Continue this procedure for a large number of periods (at least thousands).

Drop the first half of the sample to avoid dependence on the initial conditions that were set arbitrarily. Use the values of the shocks z and of the statistics y in the second half of the sample to estimate a new forecasting function within parametric class B.[7] This will give the best predictor of y' within the parametric class B, the $b_j(h_j, \ell_j)$. Compare the values of $b_j(h_j, \ell_j)$ with h_j. If they are very similar, stop. If not, update h_j using the information provided by b_j, and repeat the process. Typically, successive approximations are used to obtain $h^*(\ell_j) = b_j(h_j^*, \ell_j)$. Note that this fixed point is an essential part of any equilibrium in a model economy with boundedly rational households: when the households use the linear predictor $h^*(\ell_j)$, their behaviour generates a law of motion in which the best linear predictor is also $h^*(\ell_j)$.

Because a given distribution x can be approximated by a large class of functions $\ell_j(x)$, and because forecasts can be made with different families of parametric forecasting functions B, I am not done yet. I have to single out an ℓ_j and a B.

Let $\{\ell_j(x)\}_{j=1}^{\infty}$ be a nested sequence of multivariate functions of dimension j. The larger the j, the more statistics it includes and, in the limit, all moments of x are used. My objective is to find a multivariate function ℓ_j of small dimension j with the property that economies in which the agents use functions of larger dimension to approximate the distribution display a similar equilibrium behaviour. To determine whether the equilibrium behaviours of two economies are similar, a metric has to be chosen to compare those behaviours. There are several candidates for this metric. The distance between the stochastic realizations of the economies is one, and the distance between the optimal decision rules a_j' is another. A specific example is as follows. Choose a function ℓ_j. Compute its associated equilibrium predictor $h^*(\ell_j)$. Compute a measure of its predictive accuracy, its R^2 or the variance of the one-period-ahead forecasting errors, for instance.[8] Then choose a multivariate function of dimension $j+1$ such that $\ell_j \subset \ell_{j+1}$, compute the accuracy of the best forecasts of $\ell_j(x')$ conditional on $\{\ell_{j+1}(x), z\}$, and compare them with those implied by $h^*(\ell_j(x), z)$. If the difference is small, then the approximation to the equilibrium with boundedly rational agents that use ℓ_j is satisfactory. Otherwise, a multivariate function of higher dimension must be used. One approach is to follow Krusell and Smith (1998) by choosing $j = 1$ and define $\ell_1(x)$ to be aggregate capital. This approximation turns out to work remarkably well in many environments.

To choose a family of forecasting functions, typically, the procedure is to start using linear forecasts and check whether those forecasts can be improved by using other types of forecasting functions, such as log-linear or simple polynomials. The choice of the type of forecasting function depends on the accuracy of the forecasts. Linear and log-linear forecasts turn out to work quite well.

Note that this procedure works only when the function ℓ_j that is chosen includes sufficient statistics for prices. Decision rules $g(\cdot; h_j, \ell_j)$ and the process for the shock z are the only objects required to generate large samples of the actions of agents and, hence, of the statistics of the distributions y^t that are needed to find the required fixed

[7] Note that an obvious parametric class of forecasting functions is the set of linear forecasting functions. In this case, the estimation step becomes a simple linear regression.

[8] Continuity of the decision rules with respect to predicted values of $\ell_j(x')$ guarantees that small improvements in prediction imply small changes in actions. This property relates the metric defined on the accuracy of the predictor to the metric defined on the decision-rule space.

point of the forecasting function h_j. However, if the prices are not *ex ante* known statistics of the distribution, those prices have to be found before the behaviour of agents can be simulated. Otherwise, the requirement that the simulated actions of agents clear the markets cannot be imposed. I turn now to modification of the use of partial information in order to overcome this difficulty.

11.2.2.4 *Unknown sufficient statistics for prices* When current prices are not given by *known* statistics of the distribution, a two-step process can be used. The extra step ensures that markets clear and allows households to observe current prices before they act.

To illustrate how to deal with environments where the prices have to be dealt with, I consider two examples: a growth model with leisure and a growth model with both real assets and bonds. These examples are drawn from Krusell and Smith (1997; 1998). The first example is slightly simpler because agents forecast aggregate employment which, together with aggregate capital, is a sufficient statistic for factor prices. Determining the realized value of aggregate employment is simple: it is given by the actual actions of the agents. The second example is slightly more complex, because of the need to compute the equilibrium risk-free interest rate.

A growth model with leisure Consider a version of the previous model in which households now care about leisure, so that the current utility function is given by $u(c, l)$. Aggregate factor prices now depend not only on aggregate capital, but also on the aggregate labour input N, which is not a known moment of the distribution because it depends on the current actions of all households. In the example without leisure, I looked for a set of moments ℓ_j and predictor h_j for the values of the moments. In this example with leisure, I add a function that helps to predict aggregate employment and denote it $\xi_j(y)$. To avoid useless repetition, I restrict the predicting functions h_j and $\xi_j(y)$ to be linear.

To illustrate how to adapt this procedure to the existence of prices that depend on the current actions of agents, it suffices to show the changes in the procedures to iterate on the value function and in the updating of the best linear predictors. Let $v^0(z, y, s, a; h_j, \xi_j, \ell_j)$ be a value function for agents that predict future moments with h_j and aggregate employment with ξ_j. Two problems have to be dealt with. One is how to obtain v^1, the value function for this period given that next period's value is determined by v^0. Iterations on these value functions yield upon convergence the time-invariant solution to the household's problem $v(z, y, s, a; h_j, \xi_j, \ell_j)$. The other problem is how to generate samples of the economy to obtain values for y^t and N^t when households use forecasting functions h_j and ξ_j. Recall that this is a necessary step in order to iterate on the forecasting functions themselves.

To deal with the iterations on the value function, consider the following problem

$$\Omega^0(z, y, s, a, N; h_j, \xi_j, \ell_j) = \max_{c,l,a'} u(c, l) + \beta E\{v^0(z', y', s', a'; h_j, \xi_j, \ell_j)|s, z\} \tag{11.26}$$

subject to:

$$y' = h_j(y, z) \tag{11.27}$$
$$c = a\,(1 + r(z, y, N)) + s\ w(z, y, N) - a' \tag{11.28}$$

where Ω^0 depends explicitly on aggregate employment N. It also depends on the forecasting function ξ_j, because v^0 depends on it too. The solution to this problem delivers decision rules for consumption $c^0_\Omega(z, y, s, a, N; h_j, \xi_j, \ell_j)$, leisure $l^0_\Omega(z, y, s, a, N; h_j, \xi_j, \ell_j)$, and savings $a'^0_\Omega(z, y, s, a, N; h_j, \xi_j, \ell_j)$. Now I can use the forecasting function ξ_j to update the value function and reduce its arguments to the state variables by getting rid of aggregate employment:

$$v^1(z, y, s, a; h_j, \xi_j, \ell_j) \equiv \Omega^0\left(z, y, s, a, \xi_j\,(z, y)\,; h_j, \xi_j, \ell_j\right) \tag{11.29}$$

Iterations on this procedure yield upon convergence the value function $v(\cdot; h_j, \xi_j, \ell_j)$. I also obtain the decision rules, which I index by Ω because they depend separately on aggregate employment N. The decision rules are $c_\Omega(\cdot; h_j, \xi_j, \ell_j)$, $l_\Omega(\cdot; h_j, \xi_j, \ell_j)$, and $a'_\Omega(\cdot; h_j, \xi_j, \ell_j)$.

The next step is to generate a large number of realizations of the economy to obtain values for y^t and N^t that will be used in the computation of the next best linear predictors and pricing function. To obtain a series for aggregate employment, I compute in each period the value for aggregate employment N^t that solves

$$N^t = \int_{S\times A} \left[1 - l_\Omega\left(z^t, y^t, s, a, N^t; h_j, \xi_j, \ell_j\right)\right] dx^t. \tag{11.30}$$

I use this value as the argument in the function $a'_\Omega(\cdot; h_j, \xi_j, \ell_j)$ to update the distribution x^{t+1}. Recall that a large sample of agents is typically used to keep track of the distribution x^t. The use of the decision rules indexed by Ω ensures that agents' labour choices are consistent with the value for aggregate employment that they respond to. In other words, this two-step procedure allows households to react to *actual* prices, and not just to forecast prices.

I use another illustration for the case in which households trade a riskless bond in addition to holding real capital. The approach is similar, provided the right transformation of the state variables at the individual level is used.

A growth model with two assets: Real capital and bonds Consider a stochastic growth model with two assets: real capital (stocks) and a one-period zero coupon bond that should be in zero net supply (bonds). The rate of return on stocks is the marginal productivity of capital. The rate of return on bonds is the inverse (minus one) of whatever bond price clears the market. The market clearing price for bonds needs to be found in order to generate large samples of the economy and then update the forecasting functions. Let d denote the total resources available to a household whose members do not work at all: that is, the sum of capital income, real capital, and bond holdings. Let a' denote the household's holdings of real capital between this period and the next, and let b denote the household's holdings of bonds between this period and the next. It is easy to see that I do not have to know the portfolio composition of the households; all relevant information is embodied in the variable d. Let q be the current price of the bond. The distribution of agents across $\{d, s\}$, again denoted x, is the state variable I want to avoid in the problem of the agents. Note that the current aggregate shock z affects the current distribution x. Let ℓ_j denote a set of statistics that the households use to summarize the distribution x, with $y = \ell_j(x)$. Let h_j be a forecasting function of those statistics. Finally, let $\xi_j(y)$ be a forecasting function for the price q. Again, let $v^0(z, y, s, a; h_j, \xi_j, \ell_j)$ be a value function of an agent that forecasts with h_j and ξ_j. Consider the following problem:

$$\Omega^0(z, y, s, d, q; h_j, \xi_j, \ell_j) = \max_{c,b,a'} u(c) + \beta E \left\{ v^0(z', y', s', d'; h_j, \xi_j, \ell_j) | s, z \right\} \tag{11.31}$$

subject to:

$$y' = h_j(y, z) \tag{11.32}$$

$$c = d + s\ w(z, y) - a' - b\ q \tag{11.33}$$

$$d' = a' \left(1 + r(z', y')\right) + b \tag{11.34}$$

where the associated procedure to update the value function is given by

$$v^1(z, y, s, a; h_j, \xi_j, \ell_j) \equiv \Omega^0 \left(z, y, s, a, \xi_j\left(z, y\right); h_j, \xi_j, \ell_j\right). \tag{11.35}$$

Iterations on this procedure yield upon convergence the time-independent value function $v(z, y, s, a; h_j, \xi_j, \ell_j)$ and decision rules $c_\Omega(\cdot; h_j, \xi_j, \ell_j)$, $b_\Omega(\cdot; h_j, \xi_j, \ell_j)$, and $a'_\Omega(\cdot; h_j, \xi_j, \ell_j)$.

The next step is to generate a large number of realizations of the economy to obtain values for y^t and q^t that will be used in the computation of the next best linear predictors. To obtain a series for the price of the bond, I compute in each period the bond price that clears the market: that is, the value of q^t that solves

$$0 = \int_{S \times D} b_\Omega(z^t, y^t, s, d, q^t; h_j, \xi_j, \ell_j)\ dx^t. \tag{11.36}$$

I use this value as the argument in the functions $a'_\Omega(\cdot; h_j, \xi_j, \ell_j)$ and $b_\Omega(\cdot; h_j, \xi_j, \ell_j)$ along with the law of motion of the aggregate shock z to update the distribution x^{t+1}, and, consequently, its moments y^{t+1}. With these elements, I am now in a position to upgrade the prediction functions, and I can proceed with the method described above to compute the equilibria of the economy with boundedly rational agents.

Krusell and Smith (1997; 1998), who developed this type of approach with models in which the distribution of wealth across agents is a state variable, found that typically the first moment of the wealth distribution suffices to produce an extremely high-quality approximation, with the forecasting functions being linear or log-linear.

This discussion concludes the consideration of economies in which the distribution of agents across individual states changes over time. I now turn to the study of overlapping generations economies.

11.3 Overlapping generations economies

These are economies in which the heterogeneity of households has the added dimension of age, and thus I will refer to them as agents. The term *overlapping generations* refers to the fact that agents are born in each period, and die after a certain number of years. There is another type of model, a sort of hybrid between infinitely-lived agent models and overlapping generations models, in which new agents are born in each period and then face a constant probability of death. In these models, ageing, or death, is stochastic, while in the overlapping generations models, ageing is deterministic and agents die with probability one once they reach a certain age. These hybrid models are sometimes referred to as models with *exponential population* and can be analysed with methods very similar to the ones described here.

I start by describing the environment for an overlapping generations economy embodied in a standard neoclassical growth model. The demographics is very simple: there is no population growth and no early death. Each period, a large number, a continuum that I normalize to unity, of agents are born. Agents live for I periods, and then they die. So at any point in time, there is a set of agents indexed by $i \in \mathcal{I} = \{1, \ldots, I\}$. Note that I do not keep track of ages in the same way as is done with people, since upon birth, agents have age 1. These agents have standard preferences over consumption at different ages, which can be represented by a time-separable utility function with age-specific weights β_i, given by $\sum_{i \in \mathcal{I}} \beta_i \, u(c_i)$. I assume that at each age, agents are endowed with ϵ_i efficient units of labour that they supply inelastically. The problem of an agent born in period t is given by

$$\max_{c_{it}, a_{i+1,t}} \sum_{i \in \mathcal{I}} \beta_i \, u(c_{it}) \tag{11.37}$$

subject to:

$$a_{1t}, a_{I+1,t} = 0 \tag{11.38}$$

$$c_{it} = a_{it}(1 + r_{t+i-1}) + \epsilon_i \, w_{t+i-1} - a_{i+1,t} \tag{11.39}$$

where a_{it} denotes the wealth of an age-i agent born in period t, and where r_τ and w_τ denote the rental prices of capital and labour in period τ. The first constraint states that the agent is born with zero wealth and that, upon death, the agent cannot have debts. The second constraint is the standard budget constraint. Note that in this specification of the model, agents are allowed to borrow, because there is no non-negativity constraint for the assets. Typically, equilibrium for this economy is defined as a sequence of factor prices and allocations such that, given factor prices, the allocations are utility-maximizing and the markets clear. However, this definition is generally not very useful for computational purposes. I turn now to the discussion of steady states, because it is the simplest context in which to study this class of economies.

11.3.1 *Steady states*

A *steady state* is an equilibrium that does not change over time. In this context, a steady state consists of a pair of rental prices for capital and labour and age profiles for assets and consumption. Computation of a steady state for this economy requires solving one equation with one unknown in the aggregate capital-to-labour ratio, but each evaluation of the equation requires a solution to a maximization problem that is effectively a two-boundary difference equation. The bounds are those implied by equation (11.38), and the equation is the first-order condition of problem (11.37). The standard reference for this problem is Auerbach and Kotlikoff (1987). The following steps are involved:

1. Compute the aggregate labour input $L = \sum_{i \in \mathcal{I}} \epsilon_i$.
2. Initialize aggregate wealth K^0. Recall that in this economy, aggregate wealth is the sum of the assets held by agents of all ages.
3. Given K^0 and L, use marginal conditions to obtain a pair of factor prices $\{r^0, w^0\}$.
4. Given $\{r^0, w^0\}$, solve the problem of the agent, thereby obtaining $\{a_i\}_{i \in \mathcal{I}}$. To do this, obtain a second-order difference equation in assets from the first-order conditions of (11.37). When utility is of the constant relative risk aversion (CRRA) class, $u(c) = c^{1-\sigma}/(1-\sigma)$. The difference equation is of the form

$$a_{i+2} = [a_{i+1}(1+r) + w\epsilon_{i+1}] - \left[\frac{\beta_{i+1}}{\beta_i}(1+r)\right]^{1/\sigma} [a_i(1+r) + w\epsilon_i - a_{i+1}] \tag{11.40}$$

   Solving this equation for $a_1 = a_{I+1} = 0$ is relatively easy. A simple, but perhaps not very efficient, way of doing so is to think of the difference equation (11.40) as a single equation that for each value of a_2 yields a value for a_{I+1}. Then solve such single equation. Perhaps a more efficient way of solving the difference equation is to go backwards. Rewrite (11.40) so that a_i is a function of a_{i+1} and of a_{i+2}. Think of successive applications of (11.40) as yielding a function that, given a_I, returns a_1, and solve for a zero of such a function. Again, see Judd (1998) for a discussion of why the backward procedure is more efficient.
5. Obtain a new value for aggregate wealth K^1 as the sum of the assets obtained from the previous step.
6. If $K^1 = K^0$, stop. If not, upgrade the guess for K^0. The most efficient way to upgrade K^0 is to do it in the context of a solution algorithm, to find the zero of one single equation. That equation is $K^0 - K^1(K^0)$.

I now review approaches to situations outside the steady state.

11.3.2 *Non-steady-state allocations*

Just as I am interested in the model with infinitely-lived agents with idiosyncratic shocks, I am also interested in the behaviour of the overlapping generations model outside a steady state. Also, as in the previous class of models, there are three ways of getting around the problem of having measures as state variables in the agent's problem: having constant prices, computing the transition between steady states, and looking at recursive equilibria. Computationally, under certain conditions, recursive equilibria with fully rational agents can be approximated. Otherwise, compute the equilibria of a similar economy with approximating, not fully rational, agents as was done in the model with infinitely-lived agents.

11.3.2.1 *Constant Factor Prices* Again, one simple mechanism that prevents the distribution of wealth from affecting the decision of the agents is to make the factor prices, which provide the channel through which the state of the economy affects individual decisions, independent of the distribution. The easiest way of doing this is to assume the factor prices constant. To be able to do this, the small-country assumption should be made. This assumption states that world interest rates cannot be affected by anything that happens in the small country, and it prevents the agents from having to perform complicated calculations to predict interest rates. Real wages in this context become just a matter of normalization of units, and their value is irrelevant. For stochastic environments, the small-country assumption can also be used as long as the structure of the shocks does not interact with the decision of the agents to determine prices. Whether this approach is justifiable or not depends, of course, on the question being asked.

11.3.2.2 *Transition between steady states* In exactly the same fashion as in economies with infinitely-lived agents subject to uninsurable idiosyncratic risk, overlapping generations economies can be studied by looking at the transition between steady states. In fact, it is in this type of economy that this method was pioneered in Auerbach and Kotlikoff (1987). The approach is identical to that described in the previous section.

11.3.2.3 *Recursive stochastic equilibria* In this section, I show how to define and compute equilibria recursively for stochastic versions of overlapping generations economies; see also Ríos-Rull (1992; 1994a; 1995; 1996).

To illustrate how to implement a stochastic version of the overlapping generations model, I look at a real business cycle version of the basic model. There is a neoclassical production function, $f(K, L)$, which is affected by a multiplicative shock $z \in Z = \{z_1, z_2, \dots, z_{N_z}\}$. This shock follows a Markov process with transition matrix $\Gamma(z'|z)$, and the shock is observed at the beginning of the period. Output can be used either for consumption in the same period as production takes place or for increasing the capital stock in the next period. Capital depreciates at rate δ, and for notational simplicity I assume that undepreciated capital can also be used for consumption. If I denote next period's variables by primes, all this can be written as

$$\sum_{i=1}^{I} c_i\, x_i + K' = z\, F(K, L) + (1 - \delta)K \tag{11.41}$$

where aggregate factors K and L are obtained as before by adding the assets and the endowment of efficiency units of labour across all cohorts.

Before I make the problem of the individual agent explicit, it is important to note that aggregate shocks to productivity present the possibility of state-contingent markets which allow for trades that pay only in the event of specific realizations of the shock. Ríos-Rull (1994a) studies the importance of the existence of these markets and concludes that they are quantitatively unimportant. For this reason, I am going to abstract from them.[9] Consequently, the allocations I obtain will not be Pareto optimal. Note also that in this model,

[9] See Ríos-Rull (1995) for a description of the recursive implementation of this type of economy with complete markets and leisure.

the economy-wide state is the pair $\{z, A\}$: the shock and the *distribution* of assets across age groups. Because all agents within the same cohort are identical, $A \in \mathbb{R}^{I-1}$. Recall that agents are born with zero wealth, which implies that I only have to keep track of the wealth of agents of ages 2 to I. Also note that as in the previous section, aggregate capital K is a sufficient statistic for prices in this period, but it is *not* a sufficient statistic for aggregate capital in the next period. The distribution of assets has been known to predict aggregate capital next period. Given these considerations, the individual state is $\{z, A, a\}$, where $a \in \mathbb{R}$ is the individual wealth. Denote by $v_i(z, A, a)$ the residual utility of an age-i agent with wealth a when the aggregate state is given by $\{z, A\}$. Then the agent's problem is

$$v_i(z, A, a) = \max_{c,a'} u(c) + \beta_{i+1} \sum_{z' \in Z} v_{i+1}(z', A', a')\ \Gamma(z'|z) \tag{11.42}$$

subject to:

$$c = a\,(1 + r(z, A)) + \epsilon_i w(z, A) - a' \tag{11.43}$$

$$A' = G(z, A) \tag{11.44}$$

with the solution given by $a_{i+1} = g_i(z, A, a)$, where $r(z, A)$ and where $w(z, A)$ are the marginal productivities of capital and labour that depend on aggregate capital, which is obtained by adding the assets of all the households, and where $G(z, A)$ is the evolution of the distribution of assets over time. Note that $G : Z \times \mathbb{R}^{I-1} \to \mathbb{R}^{I-1}$. Also note that G is unknown and is part of the equilibrium process, and it should be computed simultaneously with the solution to the agent's problem. The equilibrium condition of this model is that agents are representative of their cohort:

$$g_i(z, A, A_i) = G_{i+1}(z, A) \tag{11.45}$$

In this context, a feasible computational procedure to solve for the equilibrium of this economy is to use *linear quadratic approximations* to the current return as a function of the states and the decisions and to follow the standard practices in the real business cycle as described, for example, in Hansen and Prescott (1995). The following is a summary description of this process.

1. Compute the steady state of the model economy when the shock has been set to its unconditional mean. I have already described how to do this computation.
2. Compute a set of linear quadratic approximations to the current return around the steady state. This step yields a set of $I N_z$ symmetric matrices R_{iz} of dimension $I+3$, where the quadratic form $(1, A, a, a')R_{iz}(1, A, a, a')^T$ gives the current utility of an agent when the state is $\{z, A, a\}$ and the agent's choice is a'. These matrices can be obtained by numerical computation of the Hessian. Again, see Hansen and Prescott (1995) for details.
3. Initialize v^0_{iz} for $i = \{1, \ldots, I\}$, $z = \{z_1, \ldots, z_{N_z}\}$.
4. Solve the following problem:

$$\max_{a'} R_{iz}(A, a, a') + \beta_{i+1} \sum_{z' \in Z} v^0_{i+1,z'}(z', A', a')\ \Gamma(z'|z) \tag{11.46}$$

   with $v^0_{I+1} = 0$.

Note that to avoid very cumbersome notation, I have written the current and future returns as if they were functions when they are quadratic forms. Also note that the solution is a set of linear functions $a_i' = \varphi_{iz}(A, a, A')$. Finally, note that the φs are not the decision rules, since these functions depend on the next-period distribution of wealth.

5. Solve for the fixed point of the asset accumulation equation: when agents are equal to those representative of their age, they make the same choice as the other members of their cohort. This implies the system (which I write compactly by piling up the i individual terms in each row)

$$A' = \varphi_z^{01} A + \varphi_z^{02} A' \tag{11.47}$$

where φ_z^{01} are those terms of φ_{iz}^0 that affect current variables with the term that depends on a added to the corresponding term that multiplies A_i.

6. Now obtain the economy-wide law of motion of asset holdings from the φ by

$$A' = G_z^1 A = (I - \varphi_z^2)^{-1} \varphi_z^1 A \tag{11.48}$$

7. Update the value functions by substituting the law of motion of the asset distribution G^1 and the individual decisions φ in equation (11.42) to obtain v_{iz}^1.
8. Compare v_{iz}^0 with v_{iz}^1. If they are equal, stop. Otherwise, update v_{iz}^0 (perhaps by letting $v_{iz}^0 = v_{iz}^1$), and go again to step 4.

The procedure just outlined has the advantage that it lets the agents use all the relevant information to predict the future distribution of wealth. The procedure has, however, the disadvantage that it is very time-consuming when the number of periods is large. It has the property that the quality of the approximations is not necessarily very good when the economy is not too close to the steady state. Recall that the current objective is a linear quadratic approximation around the steady state.

11.3.2.4 *Other approaches to approximating recursive equilibria* An alternative procedure for computing recursive equilibria is to do exactly as in the previous section: let the agents approximate the distribution with some of its moments and use sample realizations to update the predicting rule. This alternative procedure avoids the problem of the previous procedure when the economy is not close to the steady state. Another advantage is that it can be applied to economies in which not all agents within the same age group are identical. I use the same notation as in Section 11.2 and allow for both idiosyncratic and aggregate shocks. Let x denote a measure over the individual states, which in this case can be written as $\{I \times S \times A\}$. In this context, $x(i, S, A)$ is the measure of agents with age i. The demographic evolution of the population can be easily implemented into the law of motion of x. Let ℓ_j be a set of statistics of x. The set must include aggregate capital and whatever is needed to compute current prices, but it may also include other features, such as the dependency ratio, the variance of wealth, and so on.[10] Again, I define

[10]See above for the case in which there is no moment of the wealth distribution that is a sufficient statistic for current prices.

$y \equiv \ell_j(x)$. Now I can write the problem of the age-i agent as

$$v_i(z, y, s, a; h_j, \ell_j) = \max_{c \geq 0, a' \in [\underline{a}, \bar{a}]} u(c) + \beta E\left\{v(z', y', s', a'; h_j, \ell_j)|s, z\right\} \quad (11.49)$$

subject to:

$$y' = h_j(y, z). \quad (11.50)$$

$$c = a(1 + r(z, y)) + s\ w(z, y) - a' \quad (11.51)$$

where, again, h_j is the predictor function the agents use. Let the solution to this problem be $g_i(z, y, s, a; h_j, \ell_j)$, and let the associated law of motion of the economy be $x' = G(z, x; h_j, \ell_j)$. Let $b_j(h_j; \ell_j)$ denote the best linear unbiased forecasting function of $y' = \ell_j(x')$; that is, $\hat{y}' = b_j(h_j, \ell_j)y$. Note that $b_j(\cdot, \ell_j)$ maps the set of linear j-dimensional functions into itself and can be readily computed through long simulations. Successive approximations can be used to obtain a fixed point in the space of predictor functions, $h^*(\ell_j) = b_j(h_j^*, \ell_j)$. Note that this fixed point is an essential part of any equilibrium in a model economy with boundedly rational agents: when agents use the linear predictor $h^*(\ell_j)$, their behaviour generates a law of motion in which the best linear predictor is also $h^*(\ell_j)$. Now I can use the same logic as in Section 11.2 to choose an appropriate set of statistics ℓ_j.

Among the possible advantages of this procedure is the fact that I can look at economies with a very large number of periods and, therefore, ages of agents. Then rather than compute I different decision rules with the associated large computational costs, I can make the decision rule depend parsimoniously on the age i of the agent. This will avoid the linear quadratic approach, which will make this procedure more useful.

11.3.3 *Other issues in overlapping generations models*

To conclude the section on overlapping generations models, let me describe some issues that have been addressed with the aid of these models. Auerbach *et al.* (1989), Ríos-Rull (1994b), Storesletten (1994) and Cubeddu and Ríos-Rull (1996) look at how demographic changes (for example, population ageing, drops in fertility, changes in immigration policy, and increased incidence of divorce and out-of-wedlock births) affect the long-term behaviour of savings. İmrohoroğlu *et al.* (1994) and Huang *et al.* (1997) look at properties of the US social security system.

11.4 Dynamic voting models

Next I study economies where, in equilibrium, the policies are determined jointly with the allocations through a political mechanism. Rather than look at a very general model, I will look at an example where the policy is a proportional income tax where the proceeds are redistributed in lump-sum form to all agents. The issue is the level of taxation and the associated values for the economic variables. In this world, poor households want high income taxes, while rich households want low (actually negative) income taxes. The question of interest is how much redistribution occurs, and how economic and institutional variables shape the amount of redistribution. Note that because taxation is distortionary, complete confiscation cannot be optimal. Finally, a constitution has to be in place that determines the set of feasible policies, how often they are reassessed, and how individual preferences over policies translate into a policy for the economy. In the example that I give, in every period the tax rate for the following period is chosen by majority rule. The ideas that I develop have a much wider applicability: for example, they can be applied to study the behaviour of a government (altruistic or not) that cannot commit itself to future actions. By construction, the equilibrium policies that I obtain are time-consistent. The main references are Krusell and Ríos-Rull (1994) and Krusell *et al.* (1996; 1997).

I define equilibrium recursively, which means I am interested in Markov perfect equilibria. I define economic equilibrium given that policy follows a certain arbitrary function Ψ. Then I turn to the fixed-point problem that generates a Ψ.

11.4.1 *The environment*

The environment is once again the standard growth model. There are a finite number of infinitely-lived agents of type $i \in \mathcal{I} = \{1, \dots, I\}$, where x_i is the fraction of each type. Types differ in the amount of initial assets a_i and in their (constant) endowment of efficiency units of labour ϵ_i. In this environment, agents care about consumption and leisure. Preferences are standard and are given by $\sum_i \beta^t u(c_t, l_t)$. There is also a standard neoclassical production function $f(K, L)$, and capital depreciates at rate δ. Agents' assets are in the form of capital that they rent to competitive firms.

There is a government that taxes income proportionally and distributes the proceeds in a lump-sum fashion to all agents. For now, I assume that the tax rate of the current period was determined in the past and that the tax rate for the following period is determined this period through a function Ψ of the aggregate state of the economy. Note that there is no uncertainty in this environment; therefore, all households of the same type will always be identical. This lack of uncertainty guarantees that the distribution of wealth can be represented by $A \in I\!R^I$. The aggregate state is thus the pair $\{A, \tau\}$, where τ is the tax rate inherited from the previous period.

11.4.2 *Economic equilibrium*

I start by considering the equilibrium of an economy in which policy is set by an arbitrary policy function Ψ. I refer to this as the *economic equilibrium.*

I can write the maximization problem of household i in its dynamic programming formulation as follows:

$$v_i(A, \tau, a; \Psi) = \max_{c,l,a'} u(c, l) + \beta v_i(A', \tau', a'; \Psi) \tag{11.52}$$

subject to:

$$\begin{aligned} a' &= a + [ar(K/L) + w(K/L)\,(1-l)\,\epsilon_i]\,(1-\tau) + T - c \\ T &= \tau\,(f(K, L) - \delta K) \\ \tau' &= \Psi(A, \tau) \end{aligned}$$

$$A' = G^A(A, \tau; \Psi)$$
$$K = \sum_i x_i A_i$$
$$L = G^L(A, \tau; \Psi)$$

where K and L are aggregate capital and aggregate labour, T is the per-capita transfer, r and w are the factor pricing functions that depend only on the capital-to-labour ratio, G^A is the economy-wide law of motion for asset holdings, and G^L is the aggregate labour input function. Note that these functions are indexed by Ψ, since the behaviour of the economy depends on the policy rule that determines the evolution of taxation. The solution to this problem is a pair of functions for the next period's asset holdings $a' = g_i(A, \tau, a; \Psi)$ and leisure $l = \ell_i(A, \tau, a; \Psi)$ of the type i households.

A recursive competitive equilibrium, given the function Ψ, is a standard concept. It is a set of functions $\{G^A, G^L, \{g_i, \ell_i\}_{i \in \mathcal{I}}\}$ such that

$$G_i^A(A, \tau; \Psi) = g_i(A, \tau, A_i; \Psi) \tag{11.53}$$

$$G^L(A, \tau; \Psi) = \sum_i x_i \left(1 - \ell_i\left(A, \tau, A_i; \Psi\right)\right) \epsilon_i \tag{11.54}$$

for all τ, A, and i. These conditions represent the fixed-point problem of the recursive equilibrium formulation; that is, they require that the optimal laws of motion of the individual households reproduce the aggregate laws of motion the households perceive when solving their decision problems. The economic equilibrium can be easily computed by standard methods. In particular, it can be solved by linear quadratic approximations. Later, I will discuss where I should do the approximation, what a steady state is, and how to find it.

A steady state here is a pair $\{A, \tau\}$ such that

$$A = G_i^A(A, \tau; \Psi) \tag{11.55}$$

$$\tau = \Psi(A, \tau) \tag{11.56}$$

Note that, in general, there will be more than one unique steady state. It is more like an $(I-1)$-dimension set of steady states. To see why, imagine a Ψ that delivers a constant tax rate and a version of the economy in which all households have the same efficiency and in which leisure is not valued. It is immediately evident that in such a version, any $\{A_i\}_{i=1}^I$ with the property that $f'(\sum_i x_i A_i)(1-\tau) = \beta^{-1}$ is a steady state. Such a set of A_is is an $(I-1)$-dimensional subspace of the state space.

In the above economic equilibrium, taxes are given by Ψ at every point in time. In order to define the political equilibrium, I need also to consider economic equilibria where taxes are set slightly differently: that is, one-period deviations in tax policies. I need to be able to assess the utility that alternative policies yield. Consider that τ' is set arbitrarily but that all tax rates at later dates are determined by the function Ψ. These are the situations that the household needs to think through when contemplating a current vote. Let $\tilde{G}^A$ and $\tilde{G}^L$ denote the law of motion of assets and the total labour supply function, respectively, for these deviations; these functions have τ' as an argument. Therefore, consider the following problem for a given agent of type i who has wealth a:

$$\tilde{v}_i(A, \tau, \tau', a; \Psi) = \max_{c,l,a'} u(c, l) + \beta v_i(A', \tau', a'; \Psi) \tag{11.57}$$

subject to:

$$\begin{aligned} a' &= a + [ar(K/N) + w(K/N)(1 - l)\epsilon_i](1 - \tau) + T - c \\ T &= \tau(F(K, N) - \delta K) \\ A' &= \tilde{G}^A(A, \tau, \tau'; \Psi) \\ K &= \sum_i x_i A_i \\ N &= \tilde{G}^L(A, \tau, \tau'; \Psi) \end{aligned}$$

In this problem – where the next period's tax rate is given, as opposed to determined by Ψ – it is important to note that the next period's value function is given by the solution to problem (11.52). The decision rules for problem (11.57) are given by $a' = \tilde{g}_i(A, \tau, \tau', a; \Psi)$ and $l = \tilde{\ell}_i(A, \tau, \tau', a; \Psi)$. The equilibrium conditions for the deviation problem are $\tilde{G}_i^A(A, \tau, \tau'; \Psi) = \tilde{g}_i(A, \tau, \tau', A_i; \Psi)$ and $\tilde{G}^L(A, \tau, \tau') = \sum_i x_i\big(1 - \tilde{\ell}_i(A, \tau, A_i; \Psi)\big)\epsilon_i$ for all τ, τ', A, and i. These functions can be readily computed by standard methods. Note that the computation does not involve iterations, because once the function v_i is known, calculation of functions $\tilde{v}_i$ and $\tilde{G}$ is a one-step procedure.

11.4.3 *Politico-economic equilibrium*

The objects I have computed so far are the economy's law of motion for the distribution of wealth $G^A(\cdot, \cdot; \Psi)$, household i's utility when policy is given by Ψ, $v_i(\cdot, \cdot, \cdot; \Psi)$, the economy's law of motion for the distribution of wealth when the tax rate of the next period is given by τ' and the economy reverts to using Ψ to set the policies, $\tilde{G}^A(\cdot, \cdot, \cdot; \Psi)$, and agent i's utility when the tax rate of the next period is τ' and the economy reverts to Ψ, $\tilde{v}_i(\cdot, \cdot, \cdot; \Psi)$. I am now ready to determine the policy rule, the Ψ that arises in equilibrium.

The highest utility achievable for a household of type i is the tax rate that solves

$$\psi_i(A, \tau, A_i; \Psi) = \operatorname*{argmax}_{\tau'} \tilde{v}_i(A, \tau, \tau', A_i; \Psi) \tag{11.58}$$

This function returns the most preferred value for the next period's tax rate of agent i, given that at all later dates the tax policy is given by the function Ψ.

Now I need a procedure to go from individual most preferred policies to society's policy choice. Such a procedure in this example is majority rule. In this case, if preferences are single-peaked in τ' for all i and there is only one dimension of heterogeneity (either wealth a or efficiency ϵ), a median voter theorem applies. This means that once I label groups so that group 1 is the poorest and group I the richest, the median household will be in the group that has the property that the accumulated share of the population includes the 50% mark. I refer to the type that includes the median household with an m.

The fixed-point condition determining Ψ is thus

$$\Psi(A,\tau) = \psi_m(A,\tau,A_m:\ \Psi) \tag{11.59}$$

for all A, τ.

11.4.4 *Computation*

The procedure involves linear quadratic approximations that solve for recursive equilibria for given policies (Ψ functions). The problem of the median household is then solved given these equilibrium functions, again by using linear quadratic approximations. If the choice of the median voter coincides with the original Ψ function, an equilibrium is found; if not, I update and continue until convergence occurs.

To do this, note that if all households have the same efficiency, then the pair $\{A,\tau\} = \{K,\ldots,0\}$ of equal distribution and zero taxes where K satisfies $f'(K/L)(1-\tau) = \beta^{-1}$ is a steady state.

11.4.4.1 *Algorithms for finding steady states* I am searching for an $(I-1)$-dimensional subspace of steady states. This means that for every relative distribution of wealth, I want to find its associated steady state. I fix such a relative distribution. Then I search for the tax rate associated with that relative wealth distribution. The procedure for computing such a tax rate can be described as follows.

1. Make a guess τ_0 as a value for the tax rate, and compute the implied steady-state values of the other variables. This involves computing a value for aggregate capital with the property that the after-tax rate of return is the inverse of the discount rate.
2. Let $R_i^0(A,\tau,\tau',a,a')$ be a quadratic function that approximates the utility function in a neighbourhood of the point where the distribution of wealth has the relative shares for all types that I fixed, where the total wealth is the one determined in the previous step and where both today's and tomorrow's taxes are set at τ_0. Note that the budget constraint has been used here to substitute out consumption.
3. Fix an initial affine tax policy Ψ^0.
4. Given Ψ_0, use standard methods to solve for the equilibrium elements h_i^0, G^{L0}, g_i^0, and G^{A0} as linear functions and v_i^0 as a quadratic function.
5. Solve for the one-period deviation equilibrium elements. Note that this is a simple static problem, since I already have obtained functions v_i^0. The key difference is that in this case, I do not use Ψ^0 as an update for the next period's tax rate. Instead, I leave the dependence on τ' explicit. The application of a representative-type assumption on $\tilde{g}_i^0$, the summing up of the $\tilde{\ell}_i^0$s, and the matrix inversion then deliver the equilibrium elements $\tilde{G}^{A0}$ and $\tilde{G}^{L0}$.
6. Substitute the decision rules and the obtained equilibrium functions into the maximand in (11.57) to obtain the function $\tilde{v}_i^0$.
7. Maximize $\tilde{v}_i^0$ with respect to τ' to obtain a function ψ_i^0 of the distribution of wealth and the wealth of the agent. Check for the concavity of the function $\tilde{v}_i^0$ with respect to τ', ensuring that the first-order conditions deliver a maximum.
8. Use the representative-type condition on the median household to obtain the function Ψ^1 by letting $\Psi^1(A,\tau) \equiv \psi_m^0(A,\tau,A_m)$.

9. Compare Ψ^1 with Ψ^0. If these functions are close enough, continue to step 10. If not, redefine Ψ^0 to be a linear combination of its old value and Ψ^1, and go back to step 4. This updating procedure has been used before, and it is necessary in our case for avoiding "overshooting" problems. I have found that quite a large step (about 0.9 in the direction of Ψ^1) works well.
10. Verify that the policy function Ψ reproduces the conjectured tax rate. In other words, the following condition has to be verified:

$$\tau^0 = \tau^1 \equiv \Psi(A, \tau^0) \tag{11.60}$$

If it is not, go back to step 1 and update the guess for τ. Update using $\tau_0 = (\tau_0 + \tau_1)/2$.

In these experiments, I use two procedures to characterize the set of steady states. One consists of steps 1 through 9 above. The other procedure, which is much simpler and less time-consuming, has been mentioned in the description of the mechanics of the model. It is based on the knowledge that a zero tax and an equal distribution constitute a steady state. By using the law of motion for the economy approximated around this point, I can compute the set of steady states by simply finding the set of values for A_1 and A_2 that are reproduced by this law of motion. Clearly, this procedure is strictly valid only locally, and it is likely to give lower accuracy further away from the point of perfect equality. Finally, note that this procedure can also be applied to extend locally the set of steady states around any steady-state point found with the first procedure.

11.4.4.2 *Algorithms for computing transitional dynamics* As for computing steady states, two alternative procedures to compute transitional dynamics can be applied. One uses the linear law of motion for the zero-tax steady state to generate a path for wealth and taxes after a small initial perturbation in asset holdings. The other essentially follows steps 1–8 above; that is, it also involves a separate linearization around each new point the economy passes through. The slight complication needed is an additional round of iterations within step 2: it is necessary to make sure that, at each point on the dynamic path, the point (A, A') around which the linearization is made coincides with the equilibrium outcome. Note that the equilibrium elements take on different forms for each point on the path, and the accuracy of this procedure is, hence, better the more slowly, or the more linearly, the exact equilibrium evolves.

11.5 Conclusion

We have reviewed in this chapter three main classes of models with heterogeneous agents: infinitely-lived models, overlapping generations models, and dynamic voting models. The first family is a heterogeneous-agent version of the basic neoclassical growth model that is so widely used in macroeconomics. Models with overlapping generations are the other main class of models in macroeconomics and they have different characteristics that justify their independent treatment. Dynamic voting models are an interesting example of how to use differences in agents' characteristics to generate government policies endogenously. All these models have been reviewed in a way that makes possible the computation of their equilibrium allocations.

We have come a long way in terms of the features that these models can incorporate and still be suitable for the computation. Still, there is a long way to go in terms of what features we can include. As more economists use these types of models to address quantitative issues, and as the software and hardware keeps improving there is no doubt that our ability to incorporate more features will improve dramatically and this will enhance the class of issues that we can satisfactorily study in a quantitative way.

11.6 Appendix

- A σ-algebra is a family of subsets $\mathcal{A}$ of a certain set A, so that $\emptyset, A \in \mathcal{A}$ and $\mathcal{A}$ is closed under complementarity and under countable intersection.
- Borel σ-algebras are the σ-algebras generated by a family of open sets.
- A measure x is a function $x : \mathcal{A} \to \mathbb{R}_+$ such that $x(\emptyset) = 0$, and if $B = \cup_{n=1}^{N} B_N$, $B_n \in \mathcal{A}$ with $B_n \cap B_{\hat{n}} = \emptyset$ for any pair $n, \hat{n} \in \{1, \cdot, N\}$, then $x(B) = \sum_{n=1}^{N} x(B_n)$. That is, the measure of disjoint sets should be the sum of the measure of each, they should be non-negative, and that is it. Note that when $x(A) = 1$, the measures are probabilities.
- A function g is measurable with respect to $\{A, \mathcal{A}\}$ if the set $\{a\colon\ g(a) \leq c\}$ belongs to $\mathcal{A}$ for all $c \in \mathbb{R}$.
- A function $Q\colon A \times \mathcal{A} \to \mathbb{R}$ is a transition function if given $a \in A$, $Q(a, \cdot)$ is a probability measure and if given $B \in \mathcal{A}$, $Q(\cdot, B)$ is a measurable function.
- A measure x^* is an invariant distribution with respect to the transition function Q if for all $B \in \mathcal{A}$, $x^*(B) = \int_A Q(a, B)\, dx^*$.

REFERENCES

Aiyagari, S. R. and McGrattan, E. R. (1998). The optimum quantity of debt. *Journal of Monetary Economics*. Forthcoming.

Altug, S. and Labadie, P. (1994). *Dynamic Choice and Asset Markets*. Academic Press, San Diego, CA.

Amman, H. M., Kendrick, D. A., and Rust, J. (1996). *Handbook of Computational Economics*, **1**. Elsevier, Amsterdam.

Anderson, E. van W., Hansen, L. P., McGratten, E. R., and Sargent, T. J. (1996). Mechanics of forming and estimating dynamic linear economies. In H. M. Amman, D. Kendrick, and J. Rust (eds) *Handbook of Computational Economics*, Vol. 1. North Holland, Amsterdam.

Atkeson, A. (1997). A modification of Harald's program (class notes). University of Pennsylvania.

Atkinson, K. E. (1976). *A Survey of Numerical Methods for the Solution of Fredholm Integral Equations of the Second Kind*. Society for Industrial and Applied Mathematics, Philadelphia.

Auerbach, A. J. and Kotlikoff, L. J. (1987). *Dynamic Fiscal Policy*. Cambridge University Press, New York.

Auerbach, A. J., Kotlikoff, L. J., Hagemann, R. P., and Nicoletti, G. (1989). The economic dynamics of an ageing population: The case of four OECD countries. *OECD Economic Studies*, **12**, 97–130.

Baker, Christopher T. H. (1977). *The Numerical Treatment of Integral Equations*. Clarendon Press, Oxford.

Barro, R. J. (1979). On the determination of the public debt. *Journal of Political Economy*, **87**(5), 940–971.

Baxter M., Crucini, M., and Rouwenhorst, K. G. (1990). Solving the stochastic growth model by a discrete-state-space, Euler equation approach. *Journal of Business and Economic Statistics*, **8**, 19–22.

Bell, F. C., Goss, S. C., and Wade, A. (1992). Life tables for the United States Social Security area: 1900–2080. Actuarial Study No. 107, Social Security Administration, Washington, DC.

Bellman, R. (1957). *Dynamic Programming*. Princeton University Press, Princeton, NJ.

Benhabib, J. and Perli, R. (1994). Uniqueness and indeterminacy: On the dynamics of endogenous growth. *Journal of Economic Theory*, **63**, 113–142.

Bertsekas, D. (1976). *Dynamic Programming and Stochastic Control*. Academic Press, New York.

Binder, M. and Pesaran, H. M. (1995). Multivariate rational expectations models and macroeconomic modeling: A review and some new results. In M. H. Pesaran and M. Wickens (eds) *Handbook of Applied Econometrics: Macroeconomics*. Basil Blackwell, Oxford.

Blanchard, O. J. and Fisher S. (1989). *Lectures on Macroeconomics*. MIT Press, Cambridge, MA.

Blanchard, O. J. and Kahn, C. M. (1980). The solution of linear difference models under rational expectations. *Econometrica*, **48**(5), 1305–1311.

Brock, W. A. and Mirman L. J. (1972). Optimal economic growth and uncertainty: The discounted case. *Journal of Economic Theory*, **4**(3), 497–513.

Braun, R. A. and McGrattan, E. R. (1993). The macroeconomics of war and peace. In *NBER Macroeconomics Annual 1993*. MIT Press, Cambridge, MA.

Burnside, C. (1993). Consistency of a method of moments estimator based on numerical solutions to asset pricing models. *Econometric Theory*, **9**, 602–632.

Burnside, C. (1998). Solving asset pricing models with Gaussian shocks. *Journal of Economic Dynamics and Control*, **22**, 329–340.

Caballé, J. and Santos, M. (1993). On endogenous growth with physical and human capital. *Journal of Political Economy*, **101**, 1042–1067.

Calvo, G. A. (1978). On the time consistency of optimal policy in a monetary economy. *Econometrica*, **46**, 1411–1428.

Campbell, J. (1994). Inspecting the mechanism: An analytical approach to the stochastic growth model. *Journal of Monetary Economics*, **33**(3), 463–506.

Candler, G. V., Wright, M. J., and McDonald, J. D. (1994). A data parallel LU relaxation method for reacting flows. *AIAA Journal*, **32**(12), 2380–2386.

Castañeda, A., Díaz-Giménez, J., and Ríos-Rull, J.-V. (1998). Exploring the income distribution business cycle dynamics. *Journal of Monetary Economics*, **42**(1), 93–130.

Cecchetti, S. G., Lam, P.-S., and Mark, N. C. (1993). The equity premium and the risk-free rate: Matching the moments. *Journal of Monetary Economics*, **31**, 21–45.

Ceria, S. and Ríos-Rull, J.-V. (1992). On the existence, uniqueness, and computability of nonoptimal recursive equilibria in linear quadratic economies. Draft paper, Carnegie Mellon University.

Chari, V. V., Christiano, L. J., and Kehoe, P. J. (1994). Optimal fiscal policy in a business cycle model. *Journal of Political Economy*, **102**(4), 617–652.

Chari, V. V., Christiano, L. J., and Kehoe P. (1996). Optimality of the Friedman rule in economies with distorting taxes. *Journal of Monetary Economics*, **37**(1), 203–223.

Chari, V.V., Kehoe, P., and McGrattan, E. R. (1997). The poverty of nations: A quantitative investigation. Staff Report No. 204, Federal Reserve Bank of Minneapolis.

Cho, J. O. and Rogerson, R. (1988). Family labor supply and aggregate fluctuations. *Journal of Monetary Economics*, **21**, 233–246.

Christiano, L. J. (1988). Why does inventory investment fluctuate so much? *Journal of Monetary Economics*, **21**, 247–280.

Christiano, L. J. (1990). Solving the stochastic growth model by linear-quadratic approximation and by value-function iteration. *Journal of Business and Economic Statistics*, **8**, 23–26.

Christiano, L. J. and Fisher, J. D. M. (1998). Algortihms for solving dynamic models with occasionally binding constraints. *Journal of Economic Dynamics and Control*. Forthcoming.

Christiano, L. J. and Valdivia, V. H. (1994). Notes on solving models using a linearization method. Working paper, Northwestern University.

Coleman, W. J. (1990). Solving the stochastic growth model by policy-function iteration. *Journal of Business and Economic Statistics*, **8**, 27–29.

Coleman, W. J. (1991). Equilibrium in a production economy with an income tax. *Econometrica*, **59**, 1091–1104.

Conesa, J. C. and Krueger, D. (1998). Voting on social security reform with heterogeneous agents. Working paper, University of Minnesota.

Cooley. T. F. (ed.) (1995). *Frontiers of Business Cycle Research*. Princeton University Press, Princeton, NJ.

Cooley, T. F. and Prescott, E. C. (1995). Economic growth and business cycles. In T. F. Cooley (ed.) *Frontiers of Business Cycle Research*. Princeton University Press, Princeton, NJ.

Cooley, T. F. and Soares, J. (1996). Will social security survive the baby boom? *Carnegie-Rochester Conference Series on Public Policy*, **45**, 89–121.

Cooley, T. F. and Soares, J. (1998). A positive theory of social security based on reputation. *Journal of Political Economy*. Forthcoming.

Correia, I., Neves, J. C., and Rebelo, S. (1995). Business cycles in a small open economy. *European Economic Review*, **39**, 1089–1113.

Courant, R. and Hilbert, D. (1962). *Methods of Mathematical Physics*, Vols I and II. Interscience, New York.

Cubeddu, L. M. and Ríos-Rull, J.-V. (1996). Marital risk and capital accumulation. Unpublished manuscript, University of Pennsylvania.

Danthine, J. P. and Donaldson, J. (1995). Computing equilibria of non-optimal economies. In T. F. Cooley (ed.) *Frontiers of Business Cycle Research*, Princeton University Press, Princeton, NJ.

De Nardi, M., İmrohoroğlu, S., and Sargent, T. J. (1998). Projected U.S. demographics and social security. *Review of Economic Dynamics*. Forthcoming.

Debreu, G. (1959). *The Theory of Value*. Yale University Press, New Haven, CT.

Den Haan, W. J. and Marcet, A. (1990). Solving the stochastic growth model by parameterizing expectations. *Journal of Business and Economic Statistics*, **8**, 31–34.

Den Haan, W. J. and Marcet, A. (1994). Accuracy in simulations. *Review of Economic Studies*, **61**, 3–17.

Díaz-Giménez, J. (1996). Uninsured idiosyncratic risk, liquidity constraints and aggregate fluctuations. Working Paper, Universidad Carlos III de Madrid.

Díaz-Giménez, J., Prescott, E. C., Fitzgerald, T., and Alvarez, F. (1992). Banking in computable general equilibrium. *Journal of Economic Dynamics and Control*, **16**, 533–559.

Domowitz, I. and el Gamal, M. A. (1993). A consistent test of stationarity-ergodicity. *Econometric Theory*, **9**(4), 589–601.

Duffie, D. (1996). *Dynamic Asset Pricing Theory* (2nd edn). Princeton University Press, Princeton, NJ.

Duffie, D. and Singleton, K. J. (1993). Simulated moments estimation of Markov models of asset prices. *Econometrica*, **61**, 929–952.

Farmer, R. E. A. (1993). *The Macroeconomics of Self-fulfilling Prophecies.* MIT Press, Cambridge, MA.

Farmer, R. E. A. and Guo, J.-T. (1994). Real business cycles and the animal spirits hypothesis. *Journal of Economic Theory*, **63**, 42–72.

Ferziger, J. H. and Peric, M. (1996). *Computational Methods for Fluid Dynamics.* Springer-Verlag, Berlin.

Fuster, L. (1997). Is altruism important for understanding the long-run effects of social security? Working paper, Universitat Pompeu Fabra.

Greenwood, J., Hercowitz, Z., and Huffman, G. W. (1988). Investment, capacity utilization and the real business cycle. *American Economic Review*, **78**, 402–417.

Hamilton, J. D. (1994). *Time Series Analysis.* Princeton University Press, Princeton, NJ.

Hansen, G. D. (1985). Indivisible labor and the business cycle. *Journal of Monetary Economics*, **16**, 309–327.

Hansen, G. D. (1997). Technical progress and aggregate fluctuations, *Journal of Economic Dynamics and Control*, **21**, 1005–1023.

Hansen, G. D. and Prescott, E. C. (1995). Recursive methods for computing equilibria of business cycle models. In T. F. Cooley (ed.) *Frontiers of Business Cycle Research*, Princeton University, Princeton, NJ, 39–64.

Hansen, G. and Sargent, T. J. (1988). Straight time and overtime in equilibrium. *Journal of Monetary Economics*, **21**, 281–308.

Hansen, L. P. (1987). Calculating asset prices in three example economies. In T. F. Bewley (ed.) *Advances in Econometrics*, **1**(4). Cambridge University Press, Cambridge.

Hansen, L. P. and Sargent, T. J. (1995). Discounted linear exponential quadratic Gaussian control. *IEEE Transactions on Automatic Control*, **40**, 968–971.

Hansen, L. P. and Sargent, T. J. (1999). *Recursive Models of Dynamic Linear Economies.* Princeton University Press, Princeton, NJ. Forthcoming.

Hansen, L. P., Sargent, T. J., and Roberds, W. (1991). Time series implications of present value budget balance and of martingale models of consumption and taxes. In L. Hansen and T. J. Sargent (eds) *Rational Expectations Econometrics.* Westview Press, Boulder, CO.

Hansen, L., McGrattan, E. R., and Sargent, T. J. (1994). Mechanics of forming and estimating linear economies. Federal Reserve Bank of Minneapolis Staff Report 182.

Hirsch, C. (1988). *Numerical Computation of Internal and External Flows*, Vols I and II. Wiley, New York.

Huang, H., İmrohoroğlu, S., and Sargent, T. J. (1997). Two computations to fund social security. *Macroeconomic Dynamics*, **1**(1), 7–44.

Hubbard, R. G. and Judd, K. L. (1987). Social security and individual welfare. *American Economic Review*, **77**(4), 630–646.

Huggett, M. (1993). The risk-free rate in heterogeneous-agent incomplete-insurance economies. *Journal of Economic Dynamics and Control*, **17**(5/6), 953–970.

Huggett, M. and Ventura, G. (1998). On the distributional effects of social security reform. *Review of Economic Dynamics.* Forthcoming.

Hughes, T. J. R. (1987). *The Finite Element Method: Linear Static and Dynamic Finite Element Analysis.* Prentice-Hall, Englewood Cliffs, NJ.

İmrohoroğlu, A., Imrohoroğlu, S., and Joines, D. H. (1994). Effect of tax-favored retirement accounts on capital accumulation and welfare. Unpublished manuscript, University of Southern California.

İmrohoroğlu, A., İmrohoroğlu, S., and Joines, D. H. (1995). A life cycle analysis of social security. *Economic Theory*, **6**(1), 83–114.

İmrohoroğlu, A., İmrohoroğlu, S., and Joines, D. H. (1998a). A dynamic stochastic general equilibrium analysis of social security. In T. J. Kehoe and E. C. Prescott (eds) *The Discipline of Applied General Equilibrium*. Springer-Verlag, Berlin.

İmrohoroğlu, A., İmrohoroğlu, S., and Joines, D. H. (1998b). The effect of tax-favored retirement accounts on capital accumulation. *American Economic Review*, **88** (4).

İmrohoroğlu, A., İmrohoroğlu, S., and Joines, D. H. (1998c). Social security in an overlapping generations economy with land. *Review of Economic Dynamics*. Forthcoming.

İmrohoroğlu, S. (1998). A quantitative analysis of capital income taxation. *International Economic Review*, **39**(2), 307–328.

Jones, L. E., Manuelli, R. E., and Rossi, P. E. (1997). On the optimal taxation of capital income. *Journal of Economic Theory*, **73**(1), 93–117.

Judd, K. L. (1991). Minimum weighted residual methods for solving dynamic economic models. Federal Reserve Bank of Minneapolis Discussion Paper No. 99.

Judd, K. L. (1992). Projection methods for solving aggregate growth models. *Journal of Economic Theory*, **58**(2), 410–452.

Judd, K. L. (1998). *Numerical Methods in Economics*. MIT Press, Cambridge, MA. Forthcoming.

Kamien, M. I. and Schwartz, N. L. (1981). *Dynamic Optimization: The Calculus of Variations and Optimal Control in Economics and Management*. North Holland, New York.

Kehoe, T. and Levine, D. (1991). Computing equilibria of deterministic, dynamic economies. Unpublished manuscript, University of Minnesota.

King, R. G. and Rebelo, S. T. (1993). Low frequency filtering and real business cycles. *Journal of Economic Dynamics and Control*, **17**(1–2), 207–231.

King, R. G. and Watson, M. W. (1995). The solution of singular linear difference systems under rational expectations. University of Virginia working paper.

King, R. G. and Watson, M. W. (1997). System reduction and solution algorithms for singular linear difference systems under rational expectations. University of Virginia, Computational Economics working paper.

King, R. G., Plosser, C. I., and Rebelo, S. T. (1987). Production, growth and business cycles: technical appendix. University of Rochester, Computational Economics working paper.

King, R. G., Plosser, C. I., and Rebelo, S. T. (1988). Production, growth and business cycles. I. The basic neoclassical model. *Journal of Monetary Economics*, **21**, 195–232.

Klein, P. (1998). Using the generalized Schur form to solve a system of linear expectational difference equations. Stockholm University (IIES) working paper.

Kollintzas, T. (1985). The symmetric linear rational expectations model. *Econometrica*, **53**(4), 963–976.

Krusell, P. and Ríos-Rull, J. V. (1994). What constitutions promote capital accumulation? A political economy approach. Unpublished manuscript, University of Pennsylvania.

Krusell, P. and Smith, A. (1997). Income and wealth heterogeneity, portfolio choice, and equilibrium asset returns. *Macroeconomic Dynamics*, **1**(2), 387–422.

Krusell, P. and Smith, A. (1998). Income and wealth heterogeneity in the macroeconomy. *Journal of Political Economy*, **106**(5), 867–896.

Krusell, P., Quadrini, V., and Ríos-Rull, J. V. (1996). Are consumption taxes really better than income taxes? *Journal of Monetary Economics*, **37**(3), 475–504.

Krusell, P., Quadrini, V., and Ríos-Rull, J. V. (1997). Politico-economic equilibrium and economic growth. *Journal of Economic Dynamics and Control*, **21**(1), 243–272.

Kydland, F. E. (1984). Labor force heterogeneity and the business cycle. *Carnegie-Rochester Conference Series on Public Policy*, **21**, 173–208.

Kydland, F. E. and Prescott, E. C. (1977). Rules rather than discretion: The inconsistency of optimal plans. *Journal of Political Economy*, **85**, 473–491.

Kydland, F. E. and Prescott, E. C. (1982). Time to build and aggregate fluctuations. *Econometrica*, **6**, 1345–1370.

Kydland, F. E. and Prescott, E. C. (1988). The workweek of capital and its cyclical implications. *Journal of Monetary Economics*, **21**, 343–360.

Kydland, F. E. and Prescott, E. C. (1991). The econometrics of the general equilibrium approach to business cycles. *Scandinavian Journal of Economics*, **93**, 161–178.

LeVeque, R. L. (1992). *Numerical Methods for Conservation Laws* (2nd edn). Birkhäuser, Basel.

Lucas, R. E. (1978). Asset prices in an exchange economy. *Econometrica*, **46**, 1429–1445.

Lucas, R. E. (1987). *Models of Business Cycles*. Basil Blackwell, New York.

Lucas, R. E., Jr and Stokey, N. (1983). Optimal fiscal and monetary policy in an economy without capital. *Journal of Monetary Economics*, **12**(3), 55–59.

Marcet, A. (1988). Solving nonlinear stochastic models by parameterizing expectations. Working paper, Carnegie Mellon University.

Marcet, A. (1993). Simulation analysis of dynamic stochastic models. In C. A. Sims (ed.) *Advances in Econometrics*. Cambridge University Press, Cambridge.

Marcet, A. and Marimon, R. (1992). Communication, commitment and growth. *Journal of Economic Theory*, December, 219–250.

Marcet, A. and Marimon, R. (1998). Recursive contracts. Mimeo, European University Institute, Florence, Italy.

Marcet, A. and Marshall, D.A. (1994). Convergence of approximate model solutions to rational expectations equilibria using the method of parameterized expectations.

Working Paper No. 73, Department of Finance, Kellogg Graduate School of Management, Northwestern University.

Marcet, A., Sargent, T. J., and Seppala, J. (1996). Optimal taxation without state-contingent debt. Working paper, University of Chicago.

McCallum, B. T. (1983). On non-uniqueness in rational expectations models. *Journal of Monetary Economics*, **11**, 139–168.

McCallum, B. T. (1998). Solutions to linear rational expectations models: A compact exposition. Mimeo, Carnegie Mellon University, Pittsburgh.

McGratten, E. R. (1994). A note on computing competitive equilibria in linear models. *Journal of Economic Dynamics and Control*, **18**, 149–160.

McGrattan, E. R. (1996). Solving the stochastic growth model with a finite element method. *Journal of Economic Dynamics and Control*, **20**, 19–42.

Mehra, R. and Prescott, E. C. (1985). The equity premium: A puzzle, *Journal of Monetary Economics*, **15**, 145–161.

Mendoza, E. (1991). Real business cycles in a small open economy. *American Economic Review*, **81**, 797–818.

Muth, J. F. (1961). Rational expectations and the theory of price movements. *Econometrica*, **29**, 315–335.

Obstfeld, M. and Rogoff, K. (1996). *Foundations of International Macroeconomics*. MIT Press, Cambridge, MA.

Phillips, A. W. (1958). The relationship between unemployment and the rates of change of money wages in the United Kingdom, 1861–1957. *Economica*, **25**(November), 283–299.

Pindyck, R. S. and Rubinfeld, D. L. (1981). *Econometric Models and Economic Forecasts* (2nd edn). New York, McGraw-Hill.

Prescott, E. C. (1986). Theory ahead of business cycle measurement. *Federal Reserve Bank of Minneapolis Quarterly Review*, Fall, 9–22.

Press, W. H., Flannery, B. P., Teukolsky, S. A., and Vetterling, W. T. (1986). *Numerical Recipes: The Art of Scientific Computing*. Cambridge University Press, Cambridge.

Press, W. H., Flannery, B. P., Teukolsky, S.A., and Vetterling, W. T. (1992). *Numerical Recipes in Fortran: The Art of Scientific Computing* (2nd edn). Cambridge University Press, Cambridge.

Ramsey, F. P. (1927). A contribution to the theory of taxation. *Economic Journal*, **37**, 47–61.

Reddy, J. N. (1993). *An Introduction to the Finite Element Method*. McGraw-Hill, New York.

Richtmyer, R. D. and Morton, K. W. (1967). *Difference Methods for Initial Value Problems* (2nd edn). Wiley/Interscience, Chichester.

Ríos-Rull, J.-V. (1992). Business cycle behavior of life-cycle economies with incomplete markets. *Cuadernos Económicos de ICE*, **51**(2), 173–196.

Ríos-Rull, J.-V. (1994a). On the quantitative importance of market completeness. *Journal of Monetary Economics*, **34**, 463–496.

Ríos-Rull, J.-V. (1994b). Population changes and capital accumulation: The aging of the baby boom. Unpublished manuscript, University of Pennsylvania.

Ríos-Rull, J.-V. (1995). Models with heterogenous agents. In T. F. Cooley (ed.) *Frontiers of Business Cycle Research*. Princeton University Press, Princeton, NJ.

Ríos-Rull, J.-V. (1996). Life cycle economies and aggregate fluctuations. *Review of Economic Studies*, **63**, 465–490.

Rust, J. and Phelan, C. (1997). How social security and medicare affect retirement behavior in a world of incomplete markets. *Econometrica*, **65**(4), 781–831.

Saad, Y. (1996). *Iterative Methods for Sparse Linear Systems*. PWS, Boston.

Sargent, T. J. (1987a). *Dynamic Macroeconomic Theory*. Harvard University Press, Cambridge, MA.

Sargent, T. J. (1987b). *Macroeconomic Theory* (2nd edn). Academic Press, Boston, MA.

Sargent, T. J. (1998). *The Conquest of American Inflation*. Mimeographed book, Stanford University.

Sargent, T. J. and Ljungqvist, L. (1998). *Recursive Macroeconomic Theory*. Mimeographed book, Stanford University.

Sims, C. A. (1994). A simple model for study of the determination of the price level and the interaction of monetary and fiscal policy. *Economic Theory*, **4**, 381–399.

Sims, C. A. (1999). Solving linear rational expectations models. *Journal of Computational Economics*. Forthcoming.

Stokey, N. L. and Lucas, R. E. with Prescott, E. C. (1989). *Recursive Methods in Economic Dynamics*. Harvard University Press, Cambridge, MA.

Storesletten, K. (1994). Sustaining fiscal policy through immigration. Unpublished manuscript, Carnegie Mellon University.

Storesletten, K., Telmer, C., and Yaron, A. (1997). Consumption and risk sharing over the life cycle. Graduate School of Industrial Administration, Carnegie Mellon University, November.

Strang, G. (1980). *Linear Algebra and Its Applications* (2nd edn). Academic Press, Orlando, FL.

Szegö, G. (1939). *Orthogonal Polynomials*. American Mathematical Society, Providence, RI.

Tauchen, G. (1990). Solving the stochastic growth model by using quadrature methods and value-function iterations. *Journal of Business and Economic Statistics*, **8**, 49–52.

Tauchen, G. and Hussey, R. (1991). Quadrature-based methods for obtaining approximate solutions to nonlinear asset pricing models. *Econometrica*, **59**, 371–396.

Taylor, J. B. and Uhlig, H. (1990). Solving nonlinear stochastic growth models: A comparison of alternative solution methods. *Journal of Business and Economic Statistics*, **8**, 1–17.

Trick, M. A. and Zin, S. E. (1993). A linear programming approach to solving stochastic dynamic programs. Unpublished manuscript, Carnegie Mellon University.

Uhlig, H. (1996). A law of large numbers for large economies. *Economic Theory*, **8**(1), 41–50.

Uhlig, H. and Xu, Y. (1996). Effort and the cycle: Cyclical implications of efficiency wages. CentER Discussion Paper No. 9649, Tilburg University.

Uzawa, H. (1965). Optimum technical change in an aggregative model of economic growth. *International Economic Review*, **6**, 18–31.

Whiteman, C. H. (1983). *Linear Rational Expectations Models: A User's Guide*. University of Minnesota Press, Minneapolis.

Wright, B. D. and Williams, J. C. (1984). The welfare effects of the introduction of storage. *Quaterly Journal of Economics*, **99**, 169–182.

Xie, D. (1994). Divergence in economic performance: Transitional dynamics with multiple equilibria. *Journal of Economic Theory*, **63**, 67–112.

Yee, H. C. (1989). A class of high-resolution explicit and implicit shock-capturing methods. NASA TM-101088.

SUBJECT INDEX

AUTHOR INDEX

Made in the USA
Lexington, KY
18 August 2012